Fighting Back

Fighting Back

What governments can do about terrorism

Edited by
Paul Shemella

Stanford Security Studies
An Imprint of Stanford University Press
Stanford, California

FOUNDATION® BOOKS

Delhi • Bangalore • Mumbai • Kolkata • Chennai • Hyderabad • Pune

Published by
Cambridge University Press India Pvt. Ltd.
under the imprint of Foundation Books
Cambridge House, 4381/4 Ansari Road, Daryaganj, **New Delhi** 110 002

Cambridge University Press India Pvt. Ltd.
C-22, C-Block, Brigade M.M., K.R. Road, Jayanagar, **Bengaluru** 560 070
Plot No. 80, Service Industries, Shirvane, Sector-1, Nerul, **Navi Mumbai** 400 706
10 Raja Subodh Mullick Square, 2nd Floor, **Kolkata** 700 013
21/1 (New No. 49), 1st Floor, Model School Road, Thousand Lights, **Chennai** 600 006
House No. 3-5-874/6/4, (Near Apollo Hospital), Hyderguda, **Hyderabad** 500 029
Agarwal Pride, 'A' Wing, 1308 Kasba Peth, Near Surya Hospital, **Pune** 411 011
T.C. 25/ 2731 Lukes Lane, Ambujavilasam Road, **Thiruvananthapuram** 695 001

This edition has been published by Cambridge University Press India Pvt. Ltd. by arrangement with Stanford University Press.

First South Asia Edition 2014

ISBN 978-93-82993-07-0

Published by Manas Saikia for Cambridge University Press India Pvt. Ltd. and printed at Akash Press, New Delhi 110 020

To the growing network of professionals around the world,
working hard every day to keep us all safe.

Acknowledgments

I WOULD LIKE TO THANK MY WIFE, EVA, FOR HER ADVICE AND support throughout this project. Special thanks go to Elizabeth Skinner for her skilled and careful editing. It would have been very much more difficult to write this book without the strong support of Dennis Walters at the Defense Security Cooperation Agency. I also owe a debt of gratitude to my director, Richard Hoffman, for believing in the power of self-organization.

Paul Shemella
Editor/Author

Contents

PART II: Comprehensive Government Responses

PART III: Selected Case Studies

Preface: A Different Approach

ALMOST TEN YEARS AFTER THE TERRORIST ATTACKS OF 11 September 2001, a decade in which terrorism has become the focal point of national-security studies all over the world, it is difficult to find fresh approaches that can yield new insights on the subject. The faculty of the Center for Civil–Military Relations (CCMR), who have been conducting seminars for colleagues and military professionals from more than 130 countries that are dealing with terrorist threats, have developed a new analytical approach that we believe is important to share with a wider audience. We titled this series of seminars "Civil–Military Responses to Terrorism," a rubric that emphasizes the common ground necessary to stimulate meaningful, collaborative thought. Each nation faces the difficulty of mixing civilian and military instruments in a series of effective strategies aimed at preventing terrorism or managing the consequences of terrorist attacks that cannot be prevented. Working from this premise, we have, since 2002, helped our international colleagues develop insights into what will constitute the most effective approaches to the complex problem of terrorism in their home countries.

The teaching portion of a seminar is only the beginning of the learning process; discussion is the key to developing notions into useful ideas. In order to stimulate fruitful discussion among our diverse participants, we needed to develop content devoid of U.S.-centric explanations and prescriptions. While the U.S. point of view is important to an understanding of global strategy, what our colleagues really needed was a spectrum of concepts and principles that appear to work in the general case and might be applied successfully in their *specific* cases. Each government confronts the same basic challenges, but every government manages those challenges according to its own historical, cultural, and political circumstances. Even within the growing family of democratic nations, governments diverge quite a bit in their approaches to similar problems. Indeed, the ability to reform and adapt to ever-changing conditions is the major strength of democracy as a system. Democratic governments do this by tapping into a steady stream of new ideas from both domestic and international sources.

CCMR has positioned itself to be one of the international sources of new ideas that democratic governments can turn to as they confront issues of national security. Fresh, creative, primary-source content; Socratic methods of lively interaction to elicit personal views; case studies of selected government responses and lessons learned; scenario-driven tabletop exercises; and working groups to analyze specific problems are all thrown into the mix. We conduct our seminars and workshops in Monterey, California, but we mostly travel to where *they* live. We have been pleased to see our participants leave CCMR programs ready to share a wealth of new intellectual capital with colleagues in their own governments and regions.

Manichean-minded Americans tend to search for "school solutions" to ambiguous problems, apply those solutions, and move on to another problem. The complex and enduring problem of terrorism does not lend itself to such linear thinking. The development of effective strategy against terrorism is a continuous exercise in thinking out of the box, measuring effectiveness, and adjusting our approaches. This need for iterative strategizing has inspired policy makers within the U.S. government with the notion that we should help *educate* members of the global coalition against terrorism, in addition to training them. Whereas training focuses the mind on a specific task, education opens the mind to a more complete understanding of when, where, and how to apply that training. As faculty members of the U.S. Naval Postgraduate School, we have embraced this role.

There are two broad areas on which to target such education: national strategy and collective regional planning. Governments cannot contain or defeat the near-universal threat of terrorism alone. They must first learn to make the decisions needed to mobilize the tools available to them; then they must learn how to work together against a threat that places whole regions at risk. One without the other will not work. Because the core competency of CCMR since its inception has been to assist partner governments to make better security decisions, combating terrorism fell naturally within our set of responsibilities. Our mandate has been to help friendly nations build their own capacities and to enable them to assist one another within regional coalitions against terrorism. To achieve these goals, we began working with three distinct types of audience: global, regional, and national.

It soon became clear that we were learning even more than our international colleagues about how governments can respond to terrorism. We kept searching for a textbook to guide the seminars but quickly discovered that there was no book available that presented this kind of dynamic, acquired knowledge. As they say, if you don't find the book you need, write it. We wrote the book for two purposes. The first is to serve as a textbook in our seminars; the second is to help U.S. government officials develop the best means to help other governments develop the capacity to fight terrorism successfully. It is easy for governments to make terrorism worse through poorly considered or repressive policies; we wanted to give them the strategic tools they need to remove the threat from the minds of their frightened citizens.

It may not be possible to rid the world of terrorism as a tactic for extremists, but democratic governments are obliged to do whatever they can to protect their citizens. The chapters that follow are intended to illuminate the ways in which national governments, sometimes working together and sometimes not, have tackled the challenges of terrorism in all its variations. We have attempted to draw lessons learned and best practices from these efforts, analyze and distill all the information thus gathered, and present it to the reader in a manner that is both engaging and enlightening. We are all students in this ever-changing field of study; wrestling terrorism off the world stage will require us to share our best ideas.

1 Introduction

Paul Shemella

THERE IS NO BETTER EXAMPLE OF CIVIL–MILITARY DECISION making than a government's response to the complex problem of terrorism. Preparing for the *threat* requires a mix of intelligence, investigative, and emergency-services capacity; the *response* may well involve the application of coercive force. Governments have a wide range of civilian and military tools with which to manage both.[1] In this volume we will attempt to explain how governments can design more effective responses to terrorism, including ways to undermine the strength, appeal, and effectiveness of terrorist groups themselves.

Terrorism has been a problem for governments for a long time. In the modern context, David Rapoport has described four waves of terrorism, beginning with the anarchists of the late nineteenth century and manifesting in our time with the rise of militant Islam after 1979.[2] In a real sense the anarchists are back, fueled by a far less discriminating ideology.[3] There are currently two species of terrorists confronting governments, and distinguishing one from the other is a crucial factor in crafting wise responses. The first kind of terrorist uses violence as a means to a political end, usually overthrowing a government; the second kind uses violence as an end in itself, driven by overwhelming ideological zeal. Stated another way, the former wants to change the political system, and the latter wishes to destroy it, along with many of its citizens.[4]

Both categories of terrorists use terror as a weapon, but, as Thomas Mockaitis explains in Chapter 2, so do threatened states, insurgents, and criminal gangs. How do we distinguish "terror" the weapon from "terror*ism*" the phenomenon? A universal definition of *terrorism* is elusive because most governments, influenced by local context, define it differently.[5] Despite wide recognition of the value of a common definition, they have so far been unable to agree on one.[6] However, there is a large body of international law proscribing activities related to terrorism that individual states frequently use as a basis for diplomacy and justice.[7]

Terrorists live and metastasize where governments are least likely to find them, such as remote border areas and "ungoverned spaces" where state sovereignty is weak or nonexistent. This also includes those theaters of human activity that do not belong to any single government, the so-called "global commons." Scott Jasper and colleagues have described in detail the challenges of securing the global commons, which comprise the high seas beyond territorial control, aerospace, outer space, and cyberspace.[8]

But the fight against terrorism must extend the battlefield even farther than that. We now live in a world where what is happening in the sovereign space of one country can pose a direct threat to all other countries. Terrorists have taken the global commons global. Unaffiliated with any nation, they ignore borders and often force governments to ignore them as well. How do we fight terrorists within the ungoverned spaces of other countries?

One way we do it is to cooperate much more than ever before. Terrorists have organized themselves horizontally, testing the vertical structure of individual governments with faster decision cycles and greater mobility. They have formed international networks, aided by cyberspace, that confound established institutions. Phil Williams discusses these networks in Chapter 3: why they are so powerful and how governments can attack them. In Chapter 4 Williams goes on to discuss terrorist financing as one application of networked operations, and one that has proved surprisingly difficult for governments to understand, much less shut down.

Tim Doorey takes on the special challenge of cyber terrorism in Chapter 5. This is an area of acute vulnerability where terrorists appear to be far ahead of most governments. As governments transfer more and more of their administrative and public services to online networks, they will become even more exposed to hacking and criminal activities.[9] Modern critical infrastructure depends increasingly on cyber control, a reality that sets societies up for disruptive cascading effects. Cyberspace is so new that laws, regulations, and security architecture are themselves embryonic, constantly playing catch-up with the next breakthrough technology. Terrorists are taking advantage of those capacity gaps.

Peter Chalk deals with maritime threats in Chapter 6, warning that political violence may become more deadly as well as more frequent. The original global commons is also ridden with piracy and smuggling that could aid the logistical designs of terrorists who wish to exploit the maritime domain. Ed Hoffer goes on to explain in Chapter 7 that weapons of mass destruction are linked to terrorism in ways that are often misleading, creating widespread fear of the most unlikely scenarios, and thereby wasting scarce security resources on the wrong responses. Hoffer's piece is a long-overdue counternarrative that serves to warn us that terrorists can win without having actually to deploy a weapon of mass destruction.

The first seven chapters complete our description of the problem of terrorism itself, but what can governments actually *do* about terrorism?[10] How can they devise national and regional approaches to *preventing* terrorism, at the same time that they prepare to manage the consequences of terrorist attacks that they cannot prevent? Nationally and regionally, governments must use a host of creative strategies to both increase the terrorists' expected costs of doing business and decrease their expected benefits.[11]

In Chapter 8 Jim Petroni introduces an all-hazards risk-assessment model that can help governments prioritize the distribution of scarce resources. No government has enough resources to protect everything; all need to distinguish what they *must* protect from what they cannot. From there, governments must understand the specific threats they have to defend against. The next step would be to perform "net assessments" that compare the strengths and weaknesses of their institutions and societies against the strengths and weaknesses of each terrorist threat.[12] Armed with an honest net assessment, governments can meet the very difficult challenge of how to develop effective strategies against individual terrorist threats.

Chapter 9 suggests a universal model for any government wishing to develop a comprehensive set of strategies. It argues that a government needs three different *kinds* of strategies—directed, in turn, at the root causes of terrorism, terrorist threats, and the government's vulnerabilities—if it is to manage terrorism effectively. Government institutions must be prepared to execute all three kinds of strategies at the same time; the neglect of one will degrade the effectiveness of the others.

Chapter 10 goes on to explain how governments can build more effective institutions for fighting terrorism. Strong institutions act as crucibles for the development of capabilities that can then be deepened to produce sustained capacity. But overreliance on a *single* institution, the army for instance, concentrates precious resources within a limited "capacity box" that cannot possibly deliver all the services that are needed.[13] The key to fighting terrorism successfully is to have a network of institutions, each focused on distinct roles, and all coordinating their operations with one another.

In Chapter 11, Lawrence Cline examines how government institutions can coordinate more effectively in making decisions and managing conflict. Simply sharing information is not enough; there must be persistent coordination—and often collaboration—among institutions despite their separate identities and cultures. The habit of coordination must also extend to other governments and to the regional security structures they share. Institutions must look inward and outward at the same time. No government is large enough to fight terrorism on its own, and none is so small that it cannot make a significant contribution to the collective effort.

Chapter 12 fits the challenge of countering extremist ideas into an analytical framework applicable to all dangerous ideologies. It concludes by observing that trying to counter extremist ideology from outside the ideological grouping is a dead end. Countering extremism may be a local effort, but the effects of *not* countering it are global. All governments must learn to inoculate their citizens against the ideology virus. This can be done first by offering good governance as a counterweight to extremist grievances, and then by supporting moderate elements within the broader ideological culture in their appeal to individuals who have not yet shifted from strongly held beliefs to extremism.[14]

Lawrence Cline explains in Chapter 13 how intelligence for fighting terrorism is different from traditional security intelligence and suggests avenues for reform. Good counterterrorist strategy is completely dependent on accurate and timely information. But what constitutes good intelligence when the threat is ambiguous, is covert, and does not conform to expected modes? In the absence of rules, patterns, and hardware, the intelligence analyst must rely on judgment more than ever. Put simply, intelligence in fighting terrorism is more art than science.[15]

Even with the best intelligence, societies will continue to be attacked by terrorists. Ed Hoffer examines in Chapter 14 how governments and their institutions can best manage the consequences of terrorism that they fail to prevent. Following Jim Petroni's lead, Hoffer takes an all-hazards approach to restoring order and services. Terrorism is, after all, a disaster that happens to be a consequence of deliberate human action. The management of disaster is a comprehensive undertaking that involves a wide variety of law enforcement, public safety agencies, medical personnel, and perhaps military forces.

No government can claim legitimacy without strict adherence to the ethical standards that are the very foundation of democracy. Robert Schoultz observes in Chapter 15 that fighting ethically can be a short-term constraint, but it is a long-term advantage. He considers the worst-case context of military combat, but the ethical guidelines for using coercive force go beyond the armed forces.[16] Terrorists understand, perhaps better than we do, that if we sacrifice our values, the most important distinction between us and them is lost. With a level moral playing field, terrorists can claim to be "freedom fighters" and make a case for violent change.[17]

But how will we know whether all these responses are leading us to the results we want? How do we know when we've won, and what does winning look like? Is it even *possible* to win against terrorism? If strategy development starts by posing the question "What strategic effects do we wish to create?" then we must develop ways to measure those effects. Chapter 16 discusses how we can measure our progress toward creating desired outcomes. It also introduces a methodology for quantifying government prevention efforts, extending that template to the assessment of a state's institutional capacity to fight terrorism.

The insights articulated in the first sixteen chapters were derived largely from case studies of governments in the process of confronting terrorist threats. We considered examples from all over the world, but six cases stand out as particularly useful. We have included them here for easy reference and to set the global context within which all governments now operate. This set of cases is meant to cover the most important teaching points regarding how any government can fight terrorism successfully. Sadly, most of the governments profiled have either failed catastrophically or have yet to succeed completely. There are simply not a lot of success stories out there (although the long British campaign in Northern Ireland is certainly one). However, failure can teach us a great deal.

Somalia shows us not what governments can do but what terrorists, pirates, and other criminals can do in the *absence* of government. The Tokyo subway attack of 1995 takes us back to what may be the future of terrorism: improvised weapons of mass destruction. The Madrid train bombings provide a lesson in terrorist financing and remind us that terrorist actions can determine the fate of elected officials. The Mumbai attack made devastatingly clear that the maritime domain, which includes seaports, presents another extremely vulnerable border region for most governments. The long history of the Irish Republican Army provides us with lessons useful for dealing with terrorists who want to *change* the system, whereas the group Al Qaeda in the Arabian Peninsula teaches us the difficulty of dealing with terrorists who want to *destroy* the system.

The concluding chapter draws from all the chapters to extract a number of strategic precepts that should guide any government's civil–military responses to terrorism. State responses to terrorism are situational, but there are certain prescriptions that seem to work in most cases. Governments can learn from the experiences of other governments, but they should not assume that what has worked for one will necessarily work for another. Terrorists are smart adversaries who learn fast. Those who are trying to stop them are on a collective learning curve to try and stay ahead of them. Acting together, governments, in tandem with private enterprise and civil society, have far more resources than do terrorists. Success can be achieved only by full cooperation and coordination among all the stakeholders.

Some of the work in this volume is biased toward the theoretical, while some of it is more practical.[18] Taken together, these pages constitute a comprehensive course in how governments can respond to terrorism without sacrificing the values that bind their societies together. Indeed, governments that apply these precepts successfully will generate greater social cohesion and a higher quality of life for all their citizens. These are worthy goals in themselves, but the benefits of fighting terrorism successfully go further, by strengthening the crucial mutual trust between governments and their societies.

Notes

1. Taking into account the organizational diversity of almost 200 countries, the term *military* in this volume will refer to any institution capable of wielding coercive

force on behalf of an elected government. The term *armed forces* will be used specifically to refer to traditional military services.

2. David C. Rapoport, "The Four Waves of Modern Terrorism," in *Attacking Terrorism: Elements of a Grand Strategy,* ed. Audrey Kirth Cronin and James M. Ludes (Washington, D.C.: Georgetown University Press, 2004).

3. Traditionally, anarchist targets were largely heads of state, with limited collateral damage. Al Qaeda and its affiliates recognize no such limitations.

4. Ralph Peters calls those who use violence as a means to an end "practical terrorists" and those who see violence as the end "apocalyptic terrorists." Peters, *Beyond Terror: Strategy in a Changing World* (Mechanicsburg: Stackpole, 2002).

5. Governments define *terrorism* as a threat to citizens and property by making laws against it. Every government exists within a unique context of political, social, and economic circumstances that will be reflected in its antiterrorism laws.

6. The principal obstacle to United Nations efforts to draft a definition of terrorism is the Organization of the Islamic Conference, which seeks to insert wording into the Convention: "The activities of the parties during an armed conflict, including situations of foreign occupation . . . are not governed by this convention." In "Eye on the UN," report of the Hudson Institute of New York and Touro College for Human Rights, 28 May 2010, http://www.eyeontheun.org/facts.

7. There are thirteen existing UN conventions that bind ratifying states to abide by their international provisions. However, not all states have ratified all the conventions.

8. Scott Jasper, ed., *Securing Freedom in the Global Commons* (Palo Alto: Stanford University Press, 2010).

9. Persistent cyber attacks on U.S. national security systems began in 2003 and are thought to be coming from China. The first "cyber war" in history was launched against the government of Estonia, organized by Russian hackers in 2007. See Joshua Davis, "Hackers Take Down the Most Wired Country in Europe," *Wired* 15, no. 9 (21 August 2007).

10. In this volume we will use the term *fighting terrorism* more often than not and avoid the poorly conceived *war on terror* so popular with the George W. Bush administration. Even the term *combating terrorism*—which has gained wide acceptance in our source documents—will be avoided whenever possible, lest we create the impression that governments should use the armed forces as a principal tool of statecraft.

11. Government is nothing more than a system of incentives and disincentives to encourage citizens to behave in certain ways. This system is applied to citizens who have already become terrorists, as well as those who are motivated to go that way.

12. Sun Tzu reminds us that it is more important to know ourselves than to know the enemy. Net assessment forces governments to examine themselves in ways they might otherwise overlook. See Sun Tzu, *The Art of War,* Lionel Giles, trans., 1910: III, 15. This version is available online: http://www.au.af.mil/au/awc/awcgate/artofwar.htm.

13. This is a particularly common situation in the developing world, where the army is often the only government institution that can get things done. In this

context, building a set of robust institutions becomes necessary for improving civil–military relations as well as governance.

14. Extremist ideology arises from three sources: political philosophy, ethnic nationalism, and mainstream religion. The line between belief and ideology is crossed when someone begins to believe that he or she is right and that everyone else is wrong. Terrorist ideologues then wield the threat of violence against those who deviate from their extremist views.

15. See Malcolm Gladwell, "Open Secrets," *New Yorker*, 8 January 2007. Gladwell, having consulted Gregory Treverton, a former vice-chair of the National Intelligence Council, discusses the difference between puzzles and mysteries. In the field of countering terrorism, intelligence analysis is about unraveling mysteries.

16. Given the emphasis that many decision makers place on armed forces, we thought an operational-level discussion of military-ethics issues should be included in these pages.

17. So-called "freedom fighters" have choices, only one of which is terrorism. Nonviolence has proven effective in many cases (Martin Luther King, Jr., and Mahatma Gandhi are the prime examples), as has the political process (used by indigenous-rights leader Evo Morales of Bolivia to win that nation's presidency).

18. The more practical pieces in this book have fewer notes, primarily because they are the result of field experience rather than academic research.

I THE COMPLEX PROBLEM OF TERRORISM

2 Terrorism, Insurgency, and Organized Crime

Thomas R. Mockaitis

Terrorism has become for the first decade of the twenty-first century what genocide was for the last decade of the twentieth: a popular term bandied about with such imprecision that it risks losing all meaning. In the years following the terrorist attacks of 11 September 2001, the U.S. government labeled all forms of nonstate violence terrorism. President George W. Bush furthered this simplistic view by proclaiming, "Either you are with us, or you are with the terrorists."[1] By dividing the world into them and us, he revived a most unhelpful Cold War mentality in which terrorism became the new anti-Western bogyman.

This chapter begins with an overview of terrorism as it has been used by states, criminals, insurgents, and religious extremists. It is a tactic that has been wielded throughout human history by those in power as well as those seeking power. Empires and revolutionary governments have used terror to destroy residual dissent to the new regime. However, terrorism also serves the purposes of resistance to the status quo. It is a tool that criminal enterprises use to quash both competition and recourse to the law, and that insurgents and revolutionaries, who wish to overthrow the status quo altogether, use to undermine official legitimacy. It has also been a favorite tool of religious fanatics who have no compunction about killing unbelievers or those who fail to believe in the "right way."

The chapter then looks at the problem of defining modern terrorism and the pitfalls of getting the definition wrong. It goes on to differentiate the types of extant terrorist organizations according to structure and ideology. Finally, the chapter examines Al Qaeda and details why this organization is different from its predecessors, both in structure and relative impact. Terrorists choose their audiences according to their goals. Criminals want neighborhoods to pay attention so that residents don't interfere with illegal activities. Al Qaeda wants the world to watch so that it can change the course of history.

Terror as a Weapon

The prominence of the term *terrorism* in emotionally charged political discourse demands that the term be clearly understood before it can be precisely discussed. The root, "terror," connotes a weapon or a tactic, not an organization or a movement. Once we grasp the nature of the weapon, we can discuss those who use it: states, criminal organizations, insurgent movements, and extremist (terrorist) groups. This discussion, based on historical examples, can yield relevant lessons on how to deal with contemporary threats.

Terror is a unique weapon. Like all weapons, those who wield it seek to destroy property and kill and maim people. However, this damage is an indirect means to a political end. Terror, as one analyst has noted, is a macabre form of theater: "Its real targets are not the innocent victims but the spectators."[2] The perpetrators intend this fear to motivate the "spectators" to react in a manner that furthers the perpetrators' goals. Gruesome public executions of criminals are aimed to deter crime. The 1983 suicide bombing of the U.S. Marine barracks in Beirut, Lebanon, sought to force the United States to withdraw from Lebanon, which it did. Sometimes perpetrators use terror to provoke a government backlash that ultimately strengthens support for their cause among the victimized population. Whatever group, movement, or organization it serves, terror has been used as a weapon since antiquity.

States and Terror

The oldest practitioners of terror are not clandestine organizations but states. From ancient empires to modern dictatorships, states have used what one analyst dubbed "enforcement terror" to frighten their own people into submission.[3] The Romans crucified thousands of slaves captured during the Spartacus revolt in the first century BCE, hanging them on crosses along both sides of the Appian Way from Rome to Ostia, a distance of 200 kilometers. The empire was sending a clear message that promised devastation to anyone else who even considered defying it. Even modern Western democracies carried out public executions until at least the middle of the nineteenth century, in the vain hope that such poignant examples would deter crime.

In the contemporary international system, the issue of state terrorism has become quite contentious. The five permanent members of the United Nations Security Council have blocked efforts to include state actions in any definition of terrorism. The Russian Federation does not want its operations in Chechnya scrutinized, nor does China wish its internal-security policy in Tibet to be examined. The United States would be hard pressed to defend Israeli actions in Gaza and might have to explain some of its own behavior in Iraq. Its enemies and even some human rights organizations claim that the use of standoff weapons such as predator drones and indiscriminate killers such as cluster munitions are acts of state terror.[4] Ultimately, these questions are as much moral as legal and political, and cannot be resolved here. However, any state or coalition engaged in combating terrorists must seriously consider how its own actions can make a bad situation worse by alienating populations—those who are being killed or its own, who may vote. If they wish to preserve their own legitimacy, states must resist the temptation to use methods similar to those of the extremists they fight. Even when deploying weapons long established as legitimate for use in conventional interstate war, states must consider how their use of such weapons in the far murkier environment of unconventional conflict appears to the rest of the world. In such conflicts, perception is reality.

Organized Crime

Criminal groups are as old as states. For centuries they have organized themselves along family and kinship lines. Although the Sicilian Mafia is probably the best-known organized criminal group in the United States, in the early twentieth century it coexisted with several other ethnic crime syndicates, all of which gained support from the immigrant communities they protected. In New York City, Jewish, Irish, and German criminal organizations battled the Sicilians for control of lucrative illicit activities (prostitution, gambling, and later bootlegging). The Mafia won out, largely because it had existed in Sicily for centuries and relied upon tight-knit kinship ties, ruthless discipline, and a strict code of silence, all of which gave it a competitive edge.[5]

The Mafia and other organized criminal groups also use terror, killing in a deliberately gruesome fashion to send a warning to rivals or their own foot soldiers. Like states, however, criminal groups use terror selectively. They have a similar vested interest in preserving the status quo, which generates the economic activity on which they exist. Keenly aware that all societies tolerate a certain amount of criminality, provided that it does not disrupt civil life or kill too many innocent people, criminal organizations usually remain just below the threshold of public tolerance. The Chicago Mafia learned from the Saint Valentine's Day Massacre what happens when they rise above this threshold. On 14 February 1929, Al Capone struck the archrival North Side organization of Bugs Moran, killing a dozen of his henchmen and narrowly missing the crime boss himself. Public outrage at the brazen public massacre led law enforcement to crack down on Capone's organization. Since then, the Mafia has avoided such bloodbaths, which are bad for business.

Contemporary Chicago street gangs offer a further example of this phenomenon. The police have traditionally contained gang violence within the affected neighborhoods, where gangs have long used terror tactics such as firebombings and drive-by shootings to keep rivals away or prevent neighbors from cooperating with the police. As long as gang members killed only one another and terrorized their own neighborhood, their deaths produced little public outcry. In the past decade, however, gentrification has displaced ethnic communities and disrupted gang turf, which has brought rival gangs into violent conflict over control of the city's drug trade. As more and more innocent children have been killed in the crossfire, their deaths have produced a growing demand for more vigorous law enforcement.

Insurgency

According to the U.S. Department of Defense, *insurgency* is "an organized movement aimed at the overthrow of a constituted government through use of subversion and armed conflict."[6] Though technically correct, this definition is far too broad to be useful, and it leaves out the important element of terror. It would be more accurate to define insurgency as an organized movement to overthrow a government *from within the borders of the state* through a combination of subversion, terror, and guerrilla warfare. Insurgency typically arises when a government so fails to meet the basic needs of its citizens that a significant number of them seek, or are willing to support, an alternative outside the legitimate political process. Insurgents exploit this discontent through information operations designed to highlight government failures and explain how the insurgents can do a better job of governing. The insurgent organization conducts terrorist acts to disrupt government activities and intimidate government supporters, which can include ordinary citizens who try to go to school or conduct official business. Insurgents use terror in a highly selective manner. Because they need to win popular support, they rarely try to cause mass casualties outside of the police or army. They want people to understand that they can strike whenever and wherever they wish, but they also want people to know what behaviors (e.g., supporting the government) will make them a target.

Insurgent *guerrillas* (Spanish for "small wars") operate in organized cadres out of uniform, forming for operations and then often melting back into the general population. They attack police outposts and small military units, dispersing in the presence of superior force. Guerrillas seek to wear down conventional security forces and/or provoke them into indiscriminate retaliation that increases popular support for the insurgents. The Vietcong dubbed U.S. bombing raids communist "recruiting drives."[7] The bombs killed innocent civilians along with the insurgents living among them, inducing more people to join the insurgent movement or at least to support it. The Kosovo Liberation Army employed a provocative strategy against the Yugoslav People's Army from 1998 to 1999. Knowing that it could never hope to defeat the security forces, it provoked them into an overreliance on repressive force that ultimately prompted the North Atlantic Treaty Organization, led by the United States, to intervene on behalf of the Kosovar Albanians.

Chronic Insurgency

Classical insurgencies, the series of wars that ushered Europeans out of their empires during the decades following World War II, ended cleanly. The insurgents fought the colonialists and the puppet governments for control of the emerging state. They either succeeded, as in the case of Palestine and Algeria, or lost, as in the case of Malaya. The conflicts dragged on for years, but they ended in victory for one side or the other.

Since the early 1990s, a new pattern of insurgency has emerged. Some insurgent movements no longer seek to overthrow and replace the existing government, but to carve out living space for themselves and their followers. Their original goal may have been to win control of the country through force, but at some point survival itself becomes their primary motivation. They fight to achieve a kind of stasis with the government of the country in which they operate. Whereas classic insurgencies lasted years, chronic insurgencies drag on for decades.

The FARC (Revolutionary Armed Forces of Colombia) provides the best contemporary example of a chronic insurgency. The movement began in the 1960s as a Marxist insurgency to replace the oligarchic Colombian government and address the legitimate grievances of an impoverished peasantry. To fund their activities, the insurgents became involved in the narcotics trade. Aided in part by Plan Colombia, a massive U.S. aid program to assist the Colombian government in breaking up the Cali and Medellin drug cartels, the FARC gained control over much of the country's coca production.[8] The movement has no chance of gaining power, but it now controls major drug-producing regions and enjoys a safe haven across the Venezuelan border. Several regions of Africa have been devastated by chronic insurgencies that, although they might have their roots in the anticolonial movements of the 1960s, have degenerated into heavily armed smuggling and drug gangs, whose only purpose is self-perpetuation. (For a more detailed look at one of Africa's insurgencies, see Chapter 17, on Somalia.)

Shadow Governance

Extremist organizations flourish where governments have little control, and border regions are particularly susceptible to exploitation. "Shadow governance" occurs when nonstate actors exercise the functions of governance, either in opposition to the established government or parallel to it. Political scientist Robert Cribb notes the proliferation of "spaces on the globe that are, for practical purposes, outside the formal international system."[9] Insurgent movements such as the Taliban in Afghanistan (which controlled the Afghan government from 1996 until the U.S. invasion in 2001) provide security, tax opium production and smuggling, and run a system of alternative courts. By 2008, the Taliban's thirteen "guerrilla courts," hearing civil and criminal cases based on their version of strict sharia law, had a reputation for greater fairness than did the official courts run by the Afghan government.[10]

The number of areas in which state sovereignty has so weakened that nonstate actors can exercise shadow governance has increased dramatically since the end of the Cold War. One analyst estimates that forty to sixty states with a total population of two billion "are either sliding backward or teetering on the brink of implosion or have already collapsed."[11] According to the Fund for Peace's annual "Failed States Index," based on twelve broad social, economic, and political indicators, thirty-eight states fall into the highest "alert" category, and another ninety-three scored in its next highest concern category, "warning."[12] Thus, of the approximately 195 countries in the world, some two-thirds are ineffectively governed at best. Fragile and failing states are where terrorism thrives.

Terrorism

Few terms are so problematic and as emotionally loaded as *terrorism.* Even within the U.S. government, agencies use different definitions, and no two nations define it exactly the same way. The United Nations has been trying for years to reach agreement on an international definition. Its efforts falter in the face of demands that any definition include state terrorism, and the insistence that it acknowledge the notion that "one man's terrorist is another man's freedom fighter."[13] If the United Nations ever does come up with a universally acceptable definition of terrorism, the definition is likely to be so broad as to be of little value. The current U.S. military definition of terrorism illustrates the problem:

> The calculated use of unlawful violence or the threat of unlawful violence to inculcate fear; intended to coerce or to intimidate governments or societies in the pursuit of goals that are generally political, religious, or ideological.[14]

Although technically correct, this definition could be applied to almost any use of terror. According to British law and international norms of the day, the rebellion of the thirteen American colonies was "illegal" and included acts of terror. However, it was not terrorism.

Terrorism is a phenomenon more easily described than precisely defined. From the description a useful functional definition can be derived, provided that we constantly reassess and revise it. In the contemporary world the term *terrorism* is best reserved for extremist organizations whose ideology is so utopian as to be unachievable. Convinced of the absolute rightness of their cause, they kill indiscriminately, making no distinction between military and civilian, man, woman, or child. They can perpetrate acts of terror but can do little else. Unlike insurgent groups, they seldom negotiate with the state to achieve limited results when their ultimate goal is thwarted.

The difference between a terrorist group and an insurgent movement can be illustrated by a simple comparison. Asked in the 1970s what he wanted, a member of the Irish Republican Army would have responded clearly and unequivocally: "I want the British security forces to leave Northern Ireland so that the province can unite with the Irish Republic." (For more on the IRA, see Chapter 21.) Ask a contemporary Al Qaeda member what he wants, and you will get a laundry list of goals, including the establishment of a worldwide caliphate. The testament of London bomber Mohammed Sadique Khan illustrates this point: "Until we feel security, you will be our targets. . . . Until you will stop the bombing, gassing, imprisonment and torture of my people, we will not stop this fight."[15] These demands are cosmic, not concrete.

Types of Terrorist Organizations

Terrorist organizations may be classified according to two broad characteristics: structure and ideology. Traditional terrorist organizations have been organized on the hub-and-spoke model. Cells of various sizes are linked to a central committee or even a single charismatic leader. If any one of these autonomous cells is destroyed, the larger organization remains intact because only one member of the compromised cell knows anyone in the central committee, and no one in the cell knows anything about the other cells.

Hub-and-spoke organization combines the advantages of centralized decision making and decentralized execution. However, it does have one great vulnerability. Targeting the leadership, the hub of the wheel, can disrupt the entire organization. The Peruvian security forces conducted just such a decapitation strike against the extremist group *Sendero Luminoso* (Shining Path). Once they captured leader Abimael Guzmán in 1992, the organization collapsed. In the late 1990s, Al Qaeda, which at the time had a hub-and-spoke organization with a central council (Shura) and committees dealing with various tasks, was vulnerable to such a blow.[16]

Terrorist organizations today are increasingly configured as loose, decentralized networks of operational cells and leadership groups rather than as cells tightly linked to a central hub. Networks have many of the advantages of a hub-and-spoke system without the vulnerability to decapitation. Cells can be specialized or general. They can be linked for a specific operation, decoupled afterwards, and recombined for a different mission. Cells may also receive a broad mandate to strike whenever and wherever opportunity allows without further instructions from the leadership.[17] Networks have proven to be resilient and tenacious. "The Analyst's Notebook," a sophisticated software package, allows law-enforcement and intelligence personnel to map networks, identifying "critical nodes" whose removal can disrupt an operation. Unfortunately, most terrorist networks have redundancy built into them. An operational grouping of cells may have more than one node performing the same crucial function.[18]

Al Qaeda ("the base" in Arabic) has grown from a hub-and-spoke organization into a network of networks. It provides strategic direction and lends expertise and resources as necessary and appropriate, but it allows subsidiaries to operate autonomously. Affiliates such as Al Qaeda in Iraq, Al Qaeda in the Arabian Peninsula, and Al Qaeda in the Islamic Maghreb sometimes act in concert with Al Qaeda "central," Osama bin Laden's group, which is now believed to be in the Pakistan–Afghanistan border region, but they frequently work alone. Each of them has its own network of operational and support cells.

Terrorist organizations can also be categorized according to ideology. Every individual has a worldview, a system of conscious beliefs and unconscious assumptions about the proper ordering of society. Terrorist ideology is countercultural, expressing profound unhappiness with the status quo and seeking to change it by violent means. This ideology may be political, cultural, or religious. Marxist terrorists such as the Red Army Faction (also called the Baader–Meinhof Gang) in Germany during the 1970s embraced a political ideology. Their goal was to overthrow the West German government and replace capitalism with communism.[19] Ethnic nationalism motivates groups such as the Basque separatist organization ETA and the IRA. Such ideologies continue to motivate some terrorists, but religion forms the basis for most terrorism in the contemporary world. David Rapoport contends that a wave of religious terrorism began in 1979, when the Ayatollah Khomeini seized power in Iran, and it continues to this day.[20]

Any discussion of religious terrorist ideology must be prefaced by consideration of the relationship between such ideology and the religion from which the terrorists derive it. None of the world's great religions are inherently violent; indeed, all of them preach peace. However, each of them has been perverted to promote extremism. The Hutaree Militia espouses a militant form of Christianity that predicts the imminent end of the world and a coming battle with the Antichrist, represented by the U.S. federal government.[21] In April 2010 the FBI arrested nine members of the group for plotting to kill police officers. Timothy McVeigh and Terry Nichols espoused a similar ideology when they blew up the Murrow Federal Building in Oklahoma City, in 1995. Shoko Asahara claimed to be preparing for Armageddon when his religious cult Aum Shinrikyo released sarin gas into several areas of the Tokyo subway system in 1995, killing thirteen and injuring hundreds (a detailed account of this attack appears in Chapter 18).[22]

Judaism also has its extremists. The ultraorthodox Kaf Party has engaged in vigilante violence against Palestinians in the West Bank. In 1996 Baruch Goldstein entered a mosque in Hebron during Friday prayers and opened fire, killing twenty-nine people. When he ran out of ammunition, the survivors beat him to death. His supporters later erected a monument to him in their settlement as though he were the victim in the incident.[23] Kaf's parent organization in the United States, the Jewish Defense League, has been designated a hate group by the Southern Poverty Law Center.[24]

Much recent terrorism has been motivated by perversions of Islam. Like Christianity, Islam is a proselytizing religion. Historically, it has used violence against nonbelievers, though generally not against Jews or Christians, who, as "people of the Book," trace their descent through Abraham as do Muslims. However, contemporary mainstream Islam no longer espouses violent conversion, just as Christians no longer conduct crusades against Muslims or burn heretics. The ideology motivating radical Muslim terrorism is sometimes called *Jihadist-Salafism*.[25] Often mistranslated as "holy war," *jihad* really means "holy struggle." The Prophet Mohammed identified two types of jihad. The greater jihad is the spiritual struggle that each Muslim undergoes to live a righteous life. The lesser jihad is warfare in defense of Islam. *Salafi* means "revered ancestor." Salafism is a broad revival movement seeking to return Islam to the envisioned purity of the first *ummah*, the community of the Prophet Mohammed.[26]

Al Qaeda distorts these two ancient concepts by elevating the lesser jihad above the greater and by propounding that terrorist attacks qualify as warfare in defense of Islam. It also ignores the Prophet Mohammed's injunctions to spare women, children, and noncombatants. Al Qaeda further breaks with tradition by validating the killing of Muslim apostates, or *taqfirs*. For this reason, Muslim terrorists have also been called *taqfirs*. Because all religious designations present problems, however, mainstream Muslims prefer the term "religious extremists" to describe Al Qaeda. Although it would be a mistake to equate Al Qaeda's warped ideology with Islam, it would also be inaccurate and simplistic to dismiss radical Islam as a mere aberration. It can be understood only within a larger reform movement known as Islamism, also called "the new Islamic discourse"—an effort to find a uniquely Muslim solution to the problems of modernity.[27] What Westerners call "moderate Islam" rejects terrorism but is nonetheless fairly conservative and shares Al Qaeda's rejection of secularism.

Causes of Terrorism

Ideology mobilizes but does not cause discontent. Terrorist organizations exploit the discontent within a society and focus it on a specific target, usually the government. In the absence of a terrorist or insurgent organization, angry young men (and, increasingly, young women) will often join gangs or other nefarious groups. Lack of economic opportunity and structural racism can produce the anger and alienation that fuel terrorism. Ethnic separatism, the desire of a minority group concentrated in one area to secede from a state, can also fuel insurgency and terrorism. Globalization and the communications revolution exacerbate all these problems. Multinational corporations extract raw materials from African and Asian countries at a fraction of their value. Little of the compensation paid to corrupt regimes benefits the general public, who bear the brunt of pollution and degraded resources. The widespread availability of cell phones, the Internet, and satellite television have linked the world together, making its disadvantaged people keenly aware of how much they lack. The new means of communication also broadcast secular values that threaten traditional societies.

Terrorist Recruits

Dissatisfaction, mobilized and focused by ideology, explains why terrorism and insurgency exist. However, it does not explain why some unhappy individuals join terrorist organizations and others do not. The answer to that vexing question lies more in the realm of psychology than in the fields of history, political science, or sociology. Behavioral analysts seek to understand what personality traits and life experiences motivate people to engage in certain types of criminal activity. Their insights have proven helpful in understanding what motivates terrorists.

Conventional wisdom has it that terrorist organizations recruit their foot soldiers from the impoverished angry young men living in the world's slums and refugee camps. The leadership of these organizations has been on average older, better educated, and of a higher social class than those they deploy to fight and die. However, the 9/11 attacks challenged the simplicity of this profile as they did many other assumptions about terrorism. The nineteen hijackers came from a range of socioeconomic backgrounds. Some were very well educated and solidly middle class. Osama bin Laden comes from one of the wealthiest families in the world.[28] Previous notions about who becomes a terrorist are not so much wrong as incomplete.

Some scholars believe that life experience provides more insight into why an individual becomes a terrorist than does his or her socioeconomic background or level of education. Dan Korem describes many terrorists as "random actors," individuals who have experienced some profound loss or trauma that leads them to engage in antisocial behavior. Some nurse a grievance that overwhelms other aspects of their lives. Depending on circumstances, such individuals may shoot up their place of employment or join a terrorist group.[29]

Suicide Bombers

Suicide bombers are a subset of terrorist recruits. Although most members of extremist groups are willing to die for the cause, few actually do so. Like conventional military organizations, terrorist groups accept the expendability of human life. They engage in the brutal calculus of war, deciding who is essential to the organization and who can best serve as cannon fodder. The leaders do not lack the courage to die, but they are pragmatic enough to understand that they may best contribute to the success of the organization by staying alive. Osama bin Laden is a case in point. He journeyed to Pakistan hoping to become a martyr in the holy war against the Soviet invaders of Afghanistan during the 1980s. However, his family wealth and connections made him too valuable an asset to waste, so his handlers for the most part kept him out of harm's way. He went on to help found Al Qaeda. Although he has all the character traits of the ideal suicide bomber, bin Laden has proven far too valuable as a demagogue to waste on a one-way mission.[30]

Considerable research on why individuals volunteer for suicide missions has been done, but the evidence is far from conclusive, and the data reveal variations based on location and gender. The majority of Palestinian terrorists, for example, are eighteen to thirty-eight years old, come from a range of socioeconomic backgrounds, and have a strong desire to do something dramatic to promote their cause.[31] Hamas generally turns down volunteers who are sole breadwinners or only sons, as well as those with families.[32] In addition to religious zeal or ideological conviction, profound personal reasons motivate female suicide bombers. The Chechen "Black Widows" lost husbands or fathers and sometimes children in their struggle with the Russian Federation. One Palestinian woman volunteered for a suicide mission when she learned she could not have children.[33]

Cooperation Among Illicit Organizations

Conventional wisdom and some scholarship glibly conclude that terrorists and criminals are natural allies. Nothing could be further from the truth. Criminal organizations, like businesses, want to make money, and killing people indiscriminately and in large numbers is bad for business. On the one hand, criminal and terrorist organizations may form temporary alliances of convenience under certain circumstances. In Afghanistan, for example, the Taliban taxes and protects opium cultivation, refinement, and shipment to fund its war against the Hamid Karzai government. Terrorists may also outsource certain services, such as document forging, to criminal enterprises. On the other hand, terrorists seek the publicity that criminals wish to avoid. Criminal organizations understand that they should operate below a threshold of public tolerance. If they rise above that threshold, the state will devote more resources to suppressing their activity. For this reason, what the Irish call "ordinary decent criminals" usually avoid getting too cozy with terrorists.

Al Qaeda

Considerable ink has been spilled over the question of Al Qaeda's apparent uniqueness.[34] Whether its methods and targeting reflect past terrorist practices or represent the culmination of historic trends, its organization *is* unique. Al Qaeda is not a single organization but a network (or a network of networks) akin to a holding company or brand name with franchises around the world.

The original organization developed out of the Afghan Services Office, set up by Abdullah Assam and Osama bin Laden to assist mujahedeen traveling to Afghanistan to fight the Soviets in the 1980s. Once that conflict was over, Al Qaeda aimed to continue the struggle on behalf of Muslims in places such as Chechnya and Somalia. After the murder of Assam, bin Laden fell increasingly under the sway of Dr. Ayman al-Zawahiri, an Egyptian who encouraged bin Laden to take up the cause of jihad against heretical regimes such as the governments of Saudi Arabia and Egypt, and their backer, the United States.[35]

Until 2001, Al Qaeda organized itself in the traditional hub-and-spoke fashion, albeit on a global scale. A central council (Shura) directed functional committees (devoted to fund-raising, information, and so on) linked to cells in approximately sixty countries.[36] The 2001 U.S. invasion of Afghanistan disrupted but stopped short of destroying Al Qaeda central, which moved to the border area of Pakistan to regroup. The organization became flatter, relying more and more on its network of cells and affiliates to plan and carry out attacks with minimal guidance from the center. The decade after 9/11 also saw the appearance of affiliates loosely tied to the parent organization. Groups such as Al Qaeda in the Land of the Two Rivers (Al Qaeda in Iraq) and Al Qaeda in the Arabian Peninsula began to conduct terrorist operations on their own initiative. In Chapter 22 Lawrence Cline details the evolution of this latter group.

There is also evidence that terrorist groups not originally affiliated with Al Qaeda are joining the franchise, in part to improve their fund-raising and recruitment profile. A prominent example is the Algerian Islamist organization formerly styled the Salafist Group for Preaching and Combat (GSPC in French), which began as a fairly traditional anticolonial insurgency. Once the French pulled out, GSPC turned its violence against the postcolonial regime for being too pro-European. The group, which officially allied with bin Laden's organization in 2006 and changed its name to Al Qaeda in the Islamic Maghreb (AQIM), has spread throughout the Northwest Sahara region. Its goals seem to have broadened from regime change to the more amorphous anti-Western jihad. There is strong evidence that AQIM cells are spreading in Western Europe and that its fighters have infiltrated Iraq.[37]

Conclusion: Combating Terrorism

Terror is used from time to time by threatened states and nonstate actors for a variety of purposes, but terrorists use it consistently. The line between terror and terrorism is sometimes difficult to find, but it is found at the point where terror becomes the overriding characteristic of the organization, used as a *strategy* for political or ideological ends.

The remainder of this book addresses in great detail how governments can counter terrorist strategies with well-conceived strategies of their own. A few general conclusions here can help frame that discussion. Winning the struggle against insurgency, organized crime, and terrorism does not entail defeating nefarious organizations but reducing them to an acceptable level. Flexible networks cannot be eradicated, but they can be contained and their operating space increasingly constrained to the point where they remain a nuisance but pose no serious threat to national or international security.

Achieving this result requires a strategy of attrition implemented over years and perhaps decades. Such a strategy must be comprehensive, employing all elements of national power.

Notes

1. President George W. Bush, "Address to the Nation," 20 September 2001, *Congressional Record,* H5859-H5862.

2. David K. Shipler, *Arab and Jew: Wounded Spirits in a Promised Land* (New York: Penguin, 1987), 84.

3. Thomas P. Thornton, "Terror as a Weapon of Political Agitation," in *Internal Wars: Problems and Approaches,* ed. Harry Eckstein (Westport: Praeger, 1964), 72–73.

4. For information on these munitions and the campaign to ban them, see http://www.clusterbombs.us.

5. Humbert S. Nelli, "Italians and Crime in Chicago: The Formative Years, 1890–1920," *American Journal of Sociology* 74, no. 4 (1969): 387.

6. "Department of Defense Dictionary of Military and Associated Terms," Joint Publication 1-02, http://www.dtic.mil/doctrine/jel/doddict/data/i/02689.html.

7. Thomas R. Mockaitis, *British Counterinsurgency, 1919–1960* (London: Macmillan, 1990), 56.

8. For an assessment of Plan Colombia, see Julia E. Zweig, "Challenges for U.S. Policy Toward Colombia: Is Plan Colombia Working—The Regional Dimensions?" U.S. Council on Foreign Relations, Washington, D.C., 2003, available at http://www.cfr.org/publication/6511/challenges_for_us_policy_toward_colombia.html%20.

9. Robert Cribb, "Introduction: Parapolitics, Shadow Governance, and Criminal Sovereignty," in *Government of the Shadows: Parapolitics and Criminal Sovereignty,* ed. Eric Wilson and Tim Lindsey (New York: Pluto, 2009), 1–12. See also Scott Jasper and Paul Giarra, "Disruptions in the Commons," in *Securing Freedom in the Global Commons,* ed. Scott Jasper (Palo Alto: Stanford University Press, 2010), 1–17.

10. Cribb, "Introduction," 76.

11. Ibid., 3.

12. "Failed States Index 2009," http://www.fundforpeace.org/web/index.php?option=com_content&task=view&id=99&Itemid=140.

13. Mark Burgess, "The UN and Terrorism: Defining the Indefinable?" Center for Defense Information, 16 September 2005, http://www.cdi.org/friendlyversion/printversion.cfm?documentID=3140.

14. "Department of Defense Dictionary."

15. Statement of Mohammad Sidique Khan, quoted in Paul Reynolds, "Bomber Video 'Points to al-Qaeda,'" *BBC News,* 2 September 2005: http://news.bbc.co.uk/2/hi/uk_news/4208250.stm.

16. Rohan Gunaratna, *Inside Al-Qaeda, Global Network of Terror* (New York: Colombia University Press, 2002), 54–94.

17. Christopher Harmon, *Terrorism Today* (London: Frank Cass, 2000), 96–101.

18. Information on "The Analyst's Notebook" is available at http://i2group.com/us/products—services/analysis-product-line/analysts-notebook.

19. See the Baader–Meinhof Gang Web site: http://www.baader-meinhof.com/index.html.

20. David Rapoport, "Four Waves of Modern Terrorism," in *Attacking Terrorism: Elements of Grand Strategy*, ed. Audrey Kurth Cronin and James S. Ludes (Washington, D.C.: Georgetown University Press, 2004), 61.

21. See the Hutaree Web site: http://hutaree.com.

22. Jessica Stern, "Terrorist Motivations and Unconventional Weapons," in *Planning the Unthinkable*, ed. Peter R. Lavoy, Scott D. Sagan, and James J. Wirtz (Ithaca: Cornell University Press, 2000), 205–06.

23. Ariel Glucklich, *Dying for Heaven: Holy Pleasure and Suicide Bombers, Why the Best Qualities of Religion Are Also Its Most Dangerous* (New York: HarperOne, 2009). The author argues that religious ecstasy also motivates terrorists.

24. "Jewish Defense League," Southern Poverty Law Center, http://splcenter.org/get-informed/intelligence-files/groups/jewish-defense-league.

25. Thomas R. Mockaitis, *The "New" Terrorism: Myths and Reality* (Westport: Praeger, 2007), 219.

26. Ibid., 74.

27. Ibid.

28. For a detailed discussion of Osama bin Laden's background and motivation, see Thomas R. Mockaitis, *Osama bin Laden: A Biography* (Santa Barbara: Greenwood, 2010).

29. Dan Korem, *The Rage of the Random Actor* (Richardson: International Focus, 2005).

30. Mockaitis, *Osama bin Laden*, 115.

31. Nasra Hassan, "Are You Ready? Tomorrow You Will Be in Paradise . . .," *Times Online*, 14 July 2005.

32. Ibid.

33. Brian Handwerk, "Female Suicide Bombers," *National Geographic News Online*, 13 December 2004.

34. I take up this question at length in *New Terrorism*.

35. For the evolution of Al Qaeda, see ibid., 54–57.

36. Gunaratna, *Inside Al Qaeda*, 54.

37. Andrew Hansen and Lauren Vriens, "Al-Qaeda in the Islamic Maghreb (AQIM) or L'Organisation Al-Qaïda au Maghreb Islamique (Formerly Salafist Group for Preaching and Combat or Groupe Salafiste pour la Prédication et le Combat)," Council on Foreign Relations, updated 21 July 2009: http://www.cfr.org/publication/12717.

3 Terrorist Networks

Phil Williams

IN EARLY JULY 2010 A *NEWSWEEK* ARTICLE SUGGESTED THAT Al Qaeda had become little more than a brand name and that the organization which had been able to "orchestrate attacks like the one of September 11, 2001, is now hunted and fragmented."[1] Ironically, only the previous day, the U.S. Department of Justice had filed charges alleging that three Al Qaeda leaders had helped organize a plot in which Afghan immigrant Najibullah Zazi and several coconspirators were to carry out bomb attacks on the New York City subway in September 2009. One commentary described the new charges as "the strongest evidence yet that the subway-attack plot . . . was an operation conceived and directed by elements of what remains of the so-called core, or central leadership, of Al Qaeda, believed to be based mainly in Pakistan."[2] These divergent assessments reflected an ongoing debate in the counterterrorism community about whether Al Qaeda remained a formal organization or had become merely a social movement, and whether terrorist attacks were directed from the top down or emerged spontaneously at the local level. In effect, the indictments reignited the debate between those who argue that Al Qaeda has morphed into a leaderless jihad and those who argue that Al Qaeda is alive and well and still directing terrorist activities from the Afghanistan–Pakistan border. The first school of thought is represented by Marc Sageman and Scott Atran, the second by Bruce Hoffman.[3] This debate has implications for both intelligence analysis and for national security strategy.

Yet there is another debate that is perhaps more academic but also has important strategic implications. This concerns the threat posed to nation-states by transnational networks. Even before 11 September 2001, some observers were arguing that globalization had brought with it the rise of the network society and had provided both new forms of empowerment and new opportunities for illicit networks formed by drug traffickers, transnational criminals, and terrorists. The notion of the network society was developed by Manuel Castells but was articulated most fully with regard to national and international security by John Arquilla and David Ronfeldt in *Networks and Netwars*.[4] Starting from the premise that "the rise of networks means that power is migrating to non-state actors, because they are able to organize into sprawling multi-organizational networks . . . more readily than can traditional, hierarchical, state actors," Arquilla and Ronfeldt suggested that "networks tend to be redundant and diverse, making them robust and resilient in the face of attack."[5] Consequently, they argued, "it takes networks to defeat networks."[6]

The proposition that networks inevitably have advantages over hierarchies, and the idea that they can be defeated only by other networks, have been challenged by Mette Eilstrup-Sangiovanni and Calvert Jones, who contend that "the prevailing pessimism about the ability of states to combat illicit networks is premature. The advantages claimed for networks vis-à-vis hierarchical organizations . . . are often not well characterized or substantiated. Although they tend to enjoy flexibility and adaptability, networks have important and often overlooked structural disadvantages that limit their effectiveness."[7] The authors also argue that many of these disadvantages are inherent in the clandestine nature of "dark networks," something that imposes "a unique set of constraints that distinguish them from their legal commercial counterparts."[8] On the other side, the "disadvantages claimed for hierarchies are often based on bad management and are not inherent to form; law enforcement agencies enjoy several advantages over clandestine networks, such as centralized information processing, monitoring of activities, formal training, and reliable organizational memory. All this, combined with a significant force advantage, implies that states can inflict costs on illicit networks with a greater efficiency, and for longer periods of time, than illicit networks can with regard to states."[9] For Eilstrup-Sangiovanni and Jones, it does not take a network to defeat a network because hierarchies are quite capable of doing it themselves.

Against the background of these two debates, this chapter will briefly summarize the nature of networks and identify some of their key dimensions and characteristics. It will then offer a net assessment of the threat posed by transnational terrorist networks to global and national security. The next part of the chapter will focus on Al Qaeda's network structure and delineate the ways in which this has evolved over time, paying particular attention to the weaknesses that the Al Qaeda network in Europe exhibited from the late 1990s through to 2002 or 2003, and the adjustments that its members made to overcome or rectify these deficiencies. Finally, the chapter will identify the key elements of a counter-network strategy and assess the achievements and limitations of U.S. efforts to combat Al Qaeda.

The Nature of Networks

In recent years the network concept has been popularized by physicists who see it as a critical component of complexity, by management gurus who view networks of relationships as a way of making formally structured organizations more effective, and by Internet devotees who regard Twitter as the latest form of postmodern communication.[10] Despite all the rhetoric, however, networks are very simple. They consist of various kinds of entities (or nodes) and the linkages among them. The difficulty is that such a definition is loose and somewhat amorphous. Yet in some ways this is appropriate because networks are a ubiquitous phenomenon: Sometimes they refer to distinct organizations that lack hierarchy and are horizontal in nature; at other times they imply an absence of organization altogether. The entities can be things such as computers, firms, or individuals; relationships among those in the network can be strong or weak, direct or indirect. Some networks are large, and some are small; some are concentrated geographically while others are widely dispersed; some are governed by explicit norms and rules, but others are much more informal; some endure while others are short term in nature. Some networks are dense in terms of their connectivity while others are sparse. Moreover, although networks are generally regarded as the antithesis of hierarchies, in some networks certain nodes are much more important than others. Sometimes network boundaries are clear and well defined; in other cases the boundaries are ragged or blurred. Because networks are ubiquitous, they often overlap with other networks—sometimes marginally and at other times very substantially. Some networks rely heavily on trust; others are based much more on pragmatic considerations. The ultimate paradox, though, is that a network can be both a type of organization and something that transcends organizations.[11]

Partly because of their ubiquity, partly because of the growing scholarly and analytic work on networks in disciplines ranging from sociology to physics and mathematics to economics, and partly because of the enormous importance of the Internet, networks have taken on a certain aura and mystique. Indeed, they are generally described as more agile than hierarchies; as twenty-first-century, postindustrial organizations; and as exhibiting a capacity for adaptation and resilience that more traditional structures have a hard time matching. Networking has become a necessity for twenty-first-century society, and networks are increasingly understood in terms of social and political capital. All this has been underlined by a sense that in an era of globalization, interdependence, and increasing reliance on distributed technology, distributed social and political organizations have advantages over centralized hierarchies and bureaucracies. In some cases, such as transnational advocacy networks, this is generally seen as a benefit. However, the emergence of what have come to be called *dark networks* has reflected the other side of the coin.[12] Generally this term is used to refer to terrorists and criminals, but it is with transnational terrorist networks that this chapter is concerned.[13]

Transnational Terrorist Networks and States: A Net Assessment

The new archetype of terrorism, and the dominant successor to the three earlier waves of terror identified by political scientist David Rapoport, is the so-called global jihadi movement, in which Al Qaeda has acted as vanguard, inspiration, and—to one degree or another—organizer.[14] Although terrorism has a long history, the events of 11 September 2001 gave both the phenomenon in general and particularly Al Qaeda, as its most virulent current manifestation, an unprecedented prominence. Led by wealthy Saudi heir Osama bin Laden, Al Qaeda's major objective appears to be the replacement of existing regimes in the Middle East with new governments that will espouse sharia law, be religious rather than secular in outlook, and focus on tradition rather than modernization. Propelled by a rejection of both globalization and the cultural and social predominance of the United States, Al Qaeda's leadership regards the existing regimes (especially the Saudi royal family and that of former

President Hosni Mubarak in Egypt) as the "near enemy." The United States is designated the "far enemy" because of its support for these governments and Israel, as well as its larger geopolitical and economic role. In many respects Al Qaeda can be understood as the most serious challenger to U.S. hegemony yet to emerge. Indeed, it is the first time that a transnational network has challenged the dominant power in the international system. In many ways the challenge remains quixotic. It is certainly not a contest of equals, even though Al Qaeda has been assisted by U.S. missteps, such as the invasion and occupation of Iraq.[15] Ironically, the Iraq intervention stemmed in part from the Bush administration's sense of frustration with the inability to quickly capture or kill bin Laden. Frustrated in dealing with an elusive enemy, the U.S. government reverted to what it does best, which is to use large-scale conventional forces in conventional warfare against a static and fixed, state-bound enemy.

Part of the reason for the frustration was that Washington found it difficult to respond effectively to a transnational terrorist network. This is not surprising. Network structures are ideal organizations for terrorist operations in a globalized world. Transnational networks are distributed across multiple jurisdictions, and this makes them very difficult to counter. Within Europe in the late 1990s and for several years thereafter, for example, Al Qaeda structured its European cells "not . . . country by country but rather on a free-floating, cross-border basis, some being multinational, others mononational."[16] Moreover, network organizational forms have a high degree of flexibility, a capacity for adaptation, and a resilience that make them difficult for hierarchical and bureaucratic structures to counter. These factors had both strategic and tactical implications. At the strategic level it was not even clear which countries "owned the problem" or, in other words, were the major targets of terrorist activity. At the operational level it meant that the cell levels were harder to track—although as suggested below this was offset to some degree by the fact that when arrests were made in one country, they aided law enforcement in other European states.[17]

Al Qaeda's transnational distributed-network structure is one of the reasons that the United States has not comprehensively defeated Al Qaeda in spite of the initial—although not necessarily permanent—success in 2001 at taking away bin Laden's sanctuary in Afghanistan. This certainly hurt Al Qaeda, putting it on the defensive in ways that made further terrorist spectaculars more difficult to plan and implement. The initial removal of the Taliban regime from power was important in the short term because it also eliminated Al Qaeda's training camps. These camps were critical not only in the development of terrorist skills and capabilities but also in their creation of social capital.[18] In effect, the camps and the indoctrination and training process created networks of individuals who could subsequently be encouraged to coalesce more or less independently in cells to carry out attacks. Therefore, the destruction of the camps was an important and indispensable part of the U.S. response to September 11. In retrospect, however, it appears that Al Qaeda was able to reestablish at least some kind of training and planning base in Pakistan—although on a smaller scale and with far less effect than the Afghan camps of the late 1990s.

The other factor contributing to Al Qaeda's resilience is its success at waging what Arquilla and Ronfeldt describe as the "battle of the story."[19] Bin Laden and his followers are adept at fanning a sense of cultural dislocation and social disenfranchisement among the young into extremist ideology and moral outrage that easily justify violence against "outsiders." (For a closer look at what motivates terrorists, see Chapter 2, by Thomas Mockaitis.) This guarantees a stream of recruits, and even though fewer have access to the level of training that was available prior to the U.S. intervention in Afghanistan, there is little indication that Al Qaeda is hurting for volunteers. None of this is intended to suggest that Al Qaeda is invincible, nor is it to claim that networks will always triumph over hierarchies. In this connection, however, it is necessary to look more closely at the argument that the network threat has been overstated.

Octopus Versus Leviathan?

The critique of the network threat offered by Eilstrup-Sangiovanni and Jones has resonated in the academic security-studies community and parts of the policy community. This is perhaps not surprising in disciplines that are highly state-centric. Yet it also reflects some good empirical evidence revealing that networks are sometimes slow to respond to countermeasures by governments, and as a result are more easily degraded and dismantled than is often assumed.[20] Even though the argument is well articulated, however, it remains problematic for several reasons. First, historical networks did not have the technological opportunities and advantages available to contemporary terrorist networks. Second, there is a danger of equating the capacity to inflict harm on a network with the capacity to defeat or destroy it. The transnational, distributed nature of Al Qaeda ensures that even when a single state can hurt one part of the network, other segments are out of reach and relatively immune from the effects. This enables Al Qaeda to absorb significant damage without in any way jeopardizing its continued existence.[21] Third, members of Al Qaeda and other terrorist networks are also socially embedded in particular societies, enabling them to overcome some of the information limitations and communications failures described by Eilstrup-Sangiovanni and Jones. Closely related to this, networks tend to be "edge organizations" that are far closer to the environment in which they operate than are hierarchical, bureaucratic organizations.[22] This gives networks certain advantages in the acquisition and exploitation of information.

Another problem is that Eilstrup-Sangiovanni and Jones seem almost blind to the pernicious consequences of bureaucratic structures and organizational cultures that erode flexibility, reward conservatism, and stifle innovation. All too often, these structures—even a decade after the attacks on New York and Washington—continue to operate through standard procedures that inhibit cooperation with other agencies even at the domestic level, let alone with bureaucratic organizations in other nations. By simultaneously extolling the virtues of bureaucracy and ignoring organizational pathologies, bureaucratic parochialism, and deeply embedded but highly dysfunctional legal and cultural norms, Eilstrup-Sangiovanni and Jones assume an ideal type of rational decision making and implementation within bureaucracies. This approach has roots in strategic rationality, but it largely ignores conceptual models that highlight the ways in which bureaucratic politics and organizational processes actually inhibit rationality.

Closely linked to this, Eilstrup-Sangiovanni and Jones exhibit the same kind of selection bias that they criticize. Whereas those who emphasize the network threat focus on the strengths rather than the weaknesses of these networks, Eilstrup-Sangiovanni and Jones focus on unsuccessful or failed networks. By and large, they ignore the possibility that these particular networks are often the most unsophisticated and inept of their kind. There is little recognition in their analysis that efforts by government agencies to counter terrorist and criminal networks—to the extent that they are successful—inadvertently act as a Darwinian selection mechanism. They weed out the weakest and most vulnerable, reduce the competition, and in a perverse way aid the survival of the fittest. Indeed, what is often portrayed as government or state success is really nothing more than picking the low-hanging fruit.

Perhaps most important, however, Eilstrup-Sangiovanni and Jones downplay the power differentials between states and illicit networks. Given these differentials, the ability of networks to present states with serious and persistent problems suggests that other factors than power are at play, and it seems likely that one of these is the network form. Networks support an ideal way of conducting asymmetric warfare, in which the weak avoid direct force-on-force confrontations with powerful adversaries. Networks do not provide easy targets for strategic planners who are much more attuned to think in terms of decapitating hierarchical organizations than removing various kinds of critical nodes from networks.

None of this is meant to deny that terrorist networks suffer from certain deficiencies and weaknesses, nor is it to ignore the inescapable tradeoffs between, for example, security and efficiency.[23] However, such tradeoffs are not unique to terrorist networks. They also exist in business networks, where there are inherent tensions between the brokerage and external linkages essential for cooperation and vision, and the insulation necessary for trust and cohesion.[24] Tradeoffs between the redundancy needed for resilience and the financial benefits from streamlining also confront both licit and illicit networks. Of course, different kinds of networks deal with these tradeoffs in different ways, with terrorist and criminal networks often accepting the costs of redundancy. In sum, Eilstrup-Sangiovanni and Jones are justified in emphasizing that networks are not invincible, that their strengths can be neutralized and their weaknesses exploited, but they are also in danger of throwing the baby of realistic danger out with the bathwater of overwrought fear by underestimating the strengths—and especially the adaptive capacity—of Al Qaeda. The next section examines the evolution of Al Qaeda in ways that highlight this capability.

The Evolution of Al Qaeda

It has become fashionable to claim that Al Qaeda has evolved from a hierarchy into a network since the United States destroyed its safe haven in Afghanistan. Some observers go even further, arguing that Al Qaeda has transformed from terrorist network to social movement, inspiring sympathetic individuals and groups but not controlling them. On the contrary, what seems clear is that the overall structure of Al Qaeda has remained largely the same but that the various components of the overall network structure have evolved in ways that reflect both the partial success of counterterrorism strategies and the adaptability of Al Qaeda.

Several observations are worth making in this connection. First, Al Qaeda has always had a network quality. Indeed, a key part of bin Laden's strategic genius is the way he established himself as a bridge builder or boundary spanner, infusing groups as different as Jemaah Islamiya in Indonesia and the Salafist Group for Call and Combat in Western Europe with a common sense of purpose, and bringing them all under a common strategic umbrella. The Al Qaeda leadership was able to do this because of its effectiveness in developing and selling a powerful narrative that helped create a common sense of identity across large parts of the Muslim world.[25]

Second, a useful way of understanding Al Qaeda is in terms of concentric circles, with the leadership at the center, radiating outwards to include terrorist organizers, terrorist members, and terrorist supporters.[26] However, it is important to emphasize that linkages run both across the concentric circles and along the periphery itself, and that the nature and extent of these linkages vary over time. The difficulty, as Clive Williams has pointed out, is the vagueness of the term *linkage*.[27] Indeed, linkages can range from command and control or operational linkages at one end to merely moral support, symbolic backing, and legitimization at the other. Linkages can also be direct or indirect, dense or sparse.

Third, following this, Al Qaeda can be understood in terms of a hybrid network with a core and a periphery connected by a set of intermediaries. At the center is a small group providing leadership and direction and a unifying ideology for Al Qaeda. The hub of the network has a high degree of stability and considerable continuity, although it has had to be replenished in the face of attrition. At the periphery is a pulsating, dynamic, loose network with people moving in and out all the time. This is the recruitment pool, often clustered around radical mosques, religious schools, and secular recruiters, and sometimes coalescing into distinct cells. The participants in this outer network include those who flirt with radicalization, those who become militants, and those who become part of operational and support cells. In some cases, people will join and then leave; some of those who join will go to training camps and then become members of operational cells; others will become part of support cells, assisting with financing or simply providing encouragement and moral support. This amorphous and fluid network at the periphery offers few, if any, critical nodes whose removal could cripple the network. Significantly, the core and the periphery are connected by a set of intermediaries or brokers, who can encourage individuals to radicalize, facilitate the development of cliques or cells, and provide a degree of insulation for the core.

During the late 1990s and even for a year or two following the 2001 invasion of Afghanistan, Al Qaeda had a distinct structure in which the core provided overall direction, key intermediaries acted as recruiters and played a major role in funding and implementing specific terrorist operations, and its cells in Europe were very closely connected with one another. The intermediaries included people such as Abu Doha, based in London, who reportedly supervised the attempted bombing of Los Angeles Airport by Ahmed Ressam and was linked to a cell in Frankfurt that planned an attack in December 2000. Another key figure was Jamal Beghal, a thirty-six-year-old French-Algerian who recruited both Richard Reid, the "shoe bomber," and Zacharias Moussaoui, often characterized (wrongly) as the "twentieth hijacker" of 9/11. Beghal was the key figure in a planned attack on the U.S. embassy in Paris and a NATO base in Belgium. Details of this plot were exposed as a result of his arrest in July 2001 in Dubai. Beghal's interrogation provided considerable information about the plot and helped to avert a major terrorist incident in Europe. After his extradition to France, Beghal recanted many of his confessions. Nevertheless, and somewhat ironically in view of events the following day, on 10 September 2001 French authorities began a clampdown on terrorist groups and individuals they had been monitoring for some time.

This clampdown was helped because Al Qaeda in Western Europe was characterized at the time by dense interactions among key figures from individual cells in France, Britain, Italy, and Spain. Face-to-face meetings among cell leaders supplemented frequent telephone calls. In effect, the cells were tightly rather than loosely coupled.[28] This tight coupling was a major vulnerability. When one key figure was identified and subsequently arrested, there tended to be a cascading effect through portions of the network. Indeed, the dismantling of a cell in one country almost invariably generated information about cells elsewhere.[29] The result was a domino effect that, until the 2004 Madrid and 2005 London bombings, proved very effective in preventing attacks.

In December 2000, for example, German police arrested a group of Muslim militants in Frankfurt who planned an attack on the famous Strasbourg Christmas market.[30] Three members of the cell were Algerians who had gone to an Al Qaeda camp in Afghanistan for training in 1998. In early 2000 they returned to Europe, and in summer 2000 they went to Britain, where many of the plans for their bomb plot were conceived with the help of Abu Doha. In fall 2000 they moved to Frankfurt. Their preparations for the attack in Strasbourg included the use of a stolen credit card supplied by a cell in Milan, video surveillance of possible targets, and the acquisition of materials for explosives from forty-eight separate pharmacies in various parts of Germany. As well as receiving support from the Milan cell, the Frankfurt group obtained some funds from low-level drug dealing. Some reports suggested that the plot was foiled when British intelligence intercepted a call by a cell member to Abu Doha in London and passed the information to German authorities.[31] Another source emphasized the role of French undercover work in forestalling the planned attack.[32] Whatever the precise circumstances, the disruption of the Frankfurt cell was followed over the next twelve months by similar arrests in Italy, Spain, Britain, France, and Belgium.

The intelligence and law-enforcement successes provided important insights into both the structure and operations of Al Qaeda in Europe. In Italy and Spain, in particular, the electronic surveillance of suspected Muslim extremists revealed considerable details about the ways in which terrorist cells operated, the links among them, and the broader links to Al Qaeda. By the end of 2001, a picture had also emerged of the kinds of people who provided leadership and acted as critical nodes in the European terror network, as well as the kinds of followers they were able to recruit. Most of the organizers and cell leaders had been through the camps in Afghanistan, where they had obtained specialized skills relating to activities such as recruiting potential terrorists and suicide bombers, transportation of the recruits to the camps, secure use of communications and computers, document fraud, and the financing and organizing of specific operations. Jamal Beghal, Abu Doha, Tarek Maroufi, and Ben Khemais can all be understood as critical nodes in both structural and functional terms. In terms of structure, they acted as an intermediary set of links between the core of the networks in Afghanistan and the operational periphery of cells, supporters, and "wannabes." In terms of function, they acted as planners, coordinators, and paymasters for operations. They communicated extensively with one another and with those in their cells and those involved in their operations. The cells themselves had a division of responsibility, with some providing logistic and financial support for those planning operations. For example, the Milan cell under Ben

Khemais provided logistic and financial support for the cell in Frankfurt that was planning the Strasbourg attack. The intercepted communications revealed that in some respects the network was denser and more clustered than expected. None of the cells were clearly autonomous and isolated, features that were essential to the classical Leninist model of revolutionary cells.

The removal of the intermediaries clearly hurt Al Qaeda in Europe, as did the dismantling of the interconnected cells. Moreover, after September 11 the United States attacked Al Qaeda with a ferocious intensity, seriously depleting the network core. The capture of several key figures, such as Abu Zubayda, Khalid Sheik Mohammed, and Abu Masri, and the killing of others such as Mohammed Atef, significantly degraded the organization, making it more difficult for Al Qaeda to plan and implement large-scale spectacular attacks. Nevertheless, the resilience of Al Qaeda remains remarkable, and the leadership ranks seem to have been replenished, even if Al Qaeda's ability to maintain command and control linkages has diminished. The core leadership still represents the organization, symbolically and substantively.

On the periphery of the network, replenishing cells was certainly not a problem. Providing a new set of intermediaries and critical nodes between core and periphery was more difficult, but also seems to have been accomplished. In both these areas Al Qaeda also proved adept at learning from its mistakes. Both the Madrid and London attacks suggest that interconnections among cells, while not completely abandoned, were much fewer. Moreover, in the Madrid attack, known jihadist and Al Qaeda affiliate Amer Azizi seems to have played an important, if indirect, intermediary role.[33] In other words, after the damage and setbacks in Europe, Al Qaeda moved to more insulated autonomous cells, or at least to a more loosely coupled arrangement than the closely enmeshed structure that characterized its network in Europe both prior to and immediately after the September 11 attacks. This has meant some loss of operational flexibility, although this might be more than outweighed by the gains in organizational security.

The conclusion here is that these three components—core leadership, various levels of adherents with differing degrees of commitment, and a network of intermediaries who tie them together—are all still part of Al Qaeda. The linkages between core and periphery have become somewhat looser, and the intermediaries are playing a less direct and obvious role. There is also somewhat greater reliance on bottom-up initiatives. Yet it seems likely that the core leadership is still able to set priorities and even plan distinct missions for those on the periphery. The extent to which the intermediaries continue to play the role they did in Europe a decade ago is unclear, but it seems likely that even at this level there is also some continuity. At the cell level, there are probably fewer connections with other cells, but this most likely enhances security and makes the cells difficult to identify.

Combating Terrorist Networks

It is clear from this discussion that counterterrorism strategies have had considerable impact on the ability of Al Qaeda to function. The United States in particular recognized the need for a counter-network strategy; the National Strategy for Combating Terrorism, released by the Bush Administration in 2003, emphasized the need to disrupt, degrade, and destroy "a flexible transnational network structure, enabled by modern technology and characterized by loose interconnectivity both within and between groups."[34] This strategy, which was encapsulated in what were called the "four D's"—defeat, deny, diminish, and defend—incorporated a comprehensive attack on terrorist organizations through targeting not only the networks themselves but also their leadership, sanctuaries, and finances.[35] The articulation of the strategy was impressive and has seen considerable success. Yet attacking networks has not proven an easy task, and Al Qaeda has not yet been reduced to a law-enforcement threat rather than a national-security threat, which is the central aim of the strategy.

Intelligence agencies and military services have not found it easy to think in network terms rather than revert, at least implicitly, to hierarchical state-centric thinking. Moreover, it is arguable that (1) a counter-network strategy has to be even more comprehensive than what has been done so far, (2) network thinking has to be embraced and extended throughout the national-security establishment, and (3) increasingly sophisticated software tools such as i2's Analyst's Notebook, or systems by Palantir and Semantica—widely used at the tactical level—need to be used strategically to map networks and identify points of vulnerability. Not all nodes in a network are created equal, and one of the keys to success is to target critical nodes—that is, those nodes that are high in importance and low in redundancy. There are at least four kinds of critical nodes in networks:

- **Leadership nodes.** These are particularly important in a hub or core network. Successfully attacking the leaders in a core network can leave the network without clear direction.

- **Nodes with a high degree of actor centrality.** In some networks, some members have a high concentration of direct links and are often critical in terms of communications and facilitation of flows within the network.
- **Connectors.** These connect across structural holes, act as "boundary spanners" and link terrorist groups in different countries, or provide access to human or financial resources that would otherwise not be available.[36]
- **Critical function nodes.** These are critical assets in terms of the substantive tasks or functions that the network has to carry out to ensure success. A bomb maker in a terrorist network would fit into this category.

Although a counter-network attack strategy appears largely a matter of identifying and then systematically removing critical nodes, the task is actually more difficult and complex. For example, there are inescapable tradeoffs between monitoring and exploiting key communications nodes, on the one hand, and destroying and removing them, on the other. Moreover, where there is redundancy or a "functional equivalence" of nodes, their removal has to be an iterative process, in effect turning subcritical nodes into critical nodes. It is only when this is done that the elimination of these nodes can have real impact. The key is to map the network as accurately as possible, subject it to stress, and undermine its adaptive mechanisms. In other words, a counter-network strategy requires iterative attacks, a capacity for network damage assessment, and appropriate adjustments in targeting.

Experience with Al Qaeda, however, reveals that the issue is not simply one of targeting. If a network is to be permanently disabled rather than temporarily disrupted, it is essential to undermine trust in the leadership, destroy the legitimacy of the movement, and neutralize the capacity to mobilize new recruits and replenish the membership. This requires a more comprehensive and holistic approach than has yet been enunciated by the United States. Unfortunately, the vagaries of bureaucratic politics, the inhibitions of organizational culture, the tendency to rely excessively on the military dimension of counterterrorism policy, and the West's failure to win the "battle of the story" ensure that Al Qaeda continues to pose a formidable threat. It would be encouraging to conclude that terrorist networks are weak, dysfunctional, and susceptible to rapid defeat by hierarchical governments. Unfortunately, the evidence thus far suggests that this is patently not the case.

Notes

1. Ravi Somaiya, "Is Al Qaeda Now Just a Brand?" *Newsweek*, 8 July 2010, http://www.newsweek.com/2010/07/08/is-al-qaeda-now-just-a-brand.html.

2. Mark Hosenball, "New Charges Link Qaeda Biggies to N.Y. Subway Plot," *Newsweek*, 7 July 2010, http://www.newsweek.com/blogs/declassified/2010/07/07/new-charges-link-al-qaeda-biggies-to-n-y-subway-plot.html.

3. For a good summary, see Elaine Sciolino and Eric Schmitt, "A Not Very Private Feud over Terrorism," *New York Times*, 8 June 2008, http://www.nytimes.com/2008/06/08/weekinreview/08sciolino.html.

4. See Manuel Castells, *The Rise of the Network Society* (Oxford: Blackwell, 1996); and John Arquilla and David Ronfeldt, eds., *Networks and Netwars* (Santa Monica: RAND, 2001).

5. Arquilla and Ronfeldt, *Networks and Netwars*, 13.

6. Ibid., 15.

7. Mette Eilstrup-Sangiovanni and Calvert Jones, "Assessing the Dangers of Illicit Networks: Why Al-Qaida May Be Less Threatening Than Many Think," *International Security* 33, no. 2 (Fall 2008): 8.

8. Ibid., 11.

9. Ibid., 42–43.

10. See in particular, Albert-Laszlo Barabasi, *Linked: The New Science of Networks* (Cambridge: Perseus, 2002).

11. Carlo Morselli quoting Klaus Von Lampe in *Inside Criminal Networks* (New York: Springer, 2009), 10.

12. For a good analysis, see H. Brinton Milward and Jörg Raab, "Dark Networks: The Structure, Operation, and Performance of International Drug, Terror, and Arms Trafficking Networks," paper presented at the International Conference on the Empirical Study of Governance, Management, and Performance, Barcelona, Spain, 4–5 October 2002.

13. A nexus between terrorist organizations and organized crime syndicates is commonly postulated, partially owing to the belief that dark networks often merge in mutually beneficial ways. Such a nexus is elusive at the strategic level, although tactical "marriages of convenience" are discovered all the time. Terrorists and criminals have different motives (the former wish to gain support for a cause, while the latter seek profits), but the relationship is complicated by evidence that some terrorist organizations make extensive use of criminal activities to fund their campaigns of violence, while some criminal organizations use terror against governments and citizens.

14. David C. Rapoport, "The Four Waves of Modern Terrorism," in *Attacking Terrorism: Elements of a Grand Strategy*, ed. Audrey Kurth Cronin and James M. Ludes (Washington, D.C.: Georgetown University Press, 2004), 46–73.

15. See Richard Norton-Taylor, "Former MI5 Chief Delivers Damning Verdict on Iraq Invasion," *Guardian*, 20 July 2010, http://www.guardian.co.uk/uk/2010/jul/20/chilcot-mi5-boss-iraq-war.

16. Rohan Gunaratna, *Inside Al Qaeda* (New York: Columbia University Press, 2002), 130.

17. The importance of understanding who owns the problem was brought home to me in several very helpful discussions over many years with Dr. Paul Y. Hammond, professor emeritus, University of Pittsburgh.

18. The importance of social capital for insurgencies is discussed in Vanda Felbab-Brown, *Shooting Up* (Washington D.C.: Brookings, 2009).

19. Arquilla and Ronfeldt, *Networks and Netwars*, 20.

20. Eilstrup-Sangiovanni and Jones, "Assessing the Dangers of Illicit Networks," 43.

21. As discussed below, this was not always the case in Europe, where terrorist cells in different countries were closely linked to one another and where there were cascading costs.

22. David S. Alberts and Richard E Hayes, "Power to the Edge," CCRP Publication Series, National Defense University, Washington D.C., 2003.

23. This is one of the themes in Michael Kenney, *From Pablo to Osama* (College Park: Pennsylvania State University Press, 2007).

24. Ronald Burt, *Brokerage and Closure: An Introduction to Social Capital* (New York: Oxford University Press, 2000).

25. There is also evidence that Al Qaeda stepped in with offers of money and personnel for the Salafists at a time when the group had lost its purpose and was in danger of dissolving. In return, Al Qaeda got access to training bases hidden deep in the southern Sahara, as well as new connections in Europe. In 2007 the Salafists changed their name to Al Qaeda in the Islamic Maghreb. See David Sharrock, "Al-Qaeda in the Islamic Maghreb Is a Remnant of Algerian Civil War," *Sunday Times* (London), 3 June 2009, http://www.timesonline.co.uk/tol/news/world/africa/article6421523.ece.

26. This theory has been developed by a number of analysts. See, for example, April Isaacs, ed., *Critical Perspectives on Al Qaeda* (New York: Rosen, 2006), 265.

27. Clive Williams, "The Question of 'Links' Between Al Qaeda and Southeast Asia," in *After Bali: The Threat of Terrorism in Southeast Asia,* ed. Kumar Ramakrishna and See Seng Tan (Singapore: World Scientific and the Institute of Defense and Strategic Studies, 2003). The author is grateful to Luke Gerdes for this reference.

28. The concept of tight and loose coupling is drawn from Charles Perrow, *Normal Accidents* (New York: Basic, 1994).

29. Michael Evans, Daniel McGrory, and Philip Webster, "Al-Qaeda Cells Spread Across Europe," *Times* (London), 19 November 2002; and Giles Tremlett, Nick Hopkins, and Richard Norton-Taylor, "Terror Arrests Sweep Europe," *Guardian*, 25 January 2003.

30. Paul Harris, Burhan Wazir, and Kate Connolly, "Al-Qaeda's Bombers Used Britain to Plot Slaughter," *Observer,* 21 April 2002.

31. Ibid.

32. This is based on a December 2003 author interview in Cormayeur, Italy, with an Italian magistrate who has particular knowledge of the case.

33. Fernando Reinares, "Al-Qaeda Is Back," *National Interest,* 8 January 2010, http://www.nationalinterest.org/Article.aspx?id=22744.

34. "National Strategy for Combating Terrorism 2003," The White House, 2003, 8.

35. Ibid., 15.

36. The author is grateful to Dr. Kevin Kearns of the University of Pittsburgh for the term *boundary spanners.*

4 Terrorist Financing

Phil Williams

PRIOR TO THE TERRORIST ATTACKS OF 11 SEPTEMBER 2001, little was known about terrorist financing, and finding out more was not a high priority "for either domestic or foreign intelligence collection. As a result, intelligence reporting on the issue was episodic, insufficient, and often inaccurate."[1] In the aftermath of the attacks on New York and Washington, however, shutting down terrorist finances became a priority for the United States. Money was characterized as the "lifeblood" of terrorism, and it was hoped that choking off the flow would ensure success in the "war on terror." The lifeblood metaphor itself was powerful and compelling. A decade later, however, efforts to stop terrorist finances, while having had some success, remain in most respects frustrating and unsatisfactory. Moreover, although the knowledge gap has been reduced, particularly in relation to fund-raising, deficits persist in knowledge, intelligence gathering, and understanding. As a result, the finances of terrorism are often obscured by myths and misconceptions.

Against this background, this chapter examines the three major dimensions of terrorist finances—fund-raising, transfer, and spending—and then provides a brief outline and assessment of efforts to combat and disrupt the flow of money to terrorists. Its goal is to provide a succinct yet comprehensive analysis that focuses largely, although not exclusively, on Muslim terrorist organizations, especially Al Qaeda. It also gives some consideration to the financial dimensions of insurgency in Iraq and Afghanistan, where in both cases Al Qaeda is deeply involved. Throughout, the analysis attempts to go beyond the mythology to the reality and to dispel persistent misconceptions.

Terrorist Fund-Raising

Money is critical for terrorist groups. It not only enables them to carry out successful attacks, but it is also used for recruiting, training, travel, propaganda, and the acquisition of weapons and explosives. As the Financial Action Task Force noted, "financing is required not just to fund specific terrorist operations, but to meet the broader organizational costs of developing and maintaining" terrorist networks and "to create an enabling environment necessary to sustain their activities."[2] Not surprisingly, therefore, terrorists have typically adopted an eclectic and opportunistic approach to fund-raising, especially after the precipitous decline in the levels of state support that existed during the Cold War.[3] In some cases they look primarily to sympathizers and supporters for funding to support their campaigns of violence; in other instances they are compelled to become more directly involved in fund-raising, often through crime. The mix changes over time and is influenced sometimes by whether the cause is nationalist or religious—although in both instances diaspora communities can be a source of support. In addition, fund-raising can occur at the local level, at the strategic level, or at all levels of a terrorist organization.

For Al Qaeda, prior to the attacks of 11 September, the main basis of financial support seems to have been donations by sympathizers in Saudi Arabia and the Persian Gulf region, and diversions of money from Islamic charities:

> Contrary to common belief, bin Laden did not have access to any significant amounts of personal wealth (particularly after his move from Sudan to Afghanistan) and did not personally fund Al Qaeda, either through an inheritance or businesses he was said to have owned in Sudan. Rather, Al Qaeda was funded, to the tune of approximately $30 million per year, by diversions of money from Islamic charities and the use of well-placed financial facilitators who gathered money from both witting and unwitting donors, primarily in the Gulf region.[4]

In some instances an element of extortion was present, and it is possible that bin Laden had a tacit understanding with Saudi Arabia that as long as the kingdom provided financial support, Al Qaeda would take its terrorist activities elsewhere.[5] In other instances, however, the donors were quite possibly true believers, knowingly supporting a terrorist organization that pursued objectives that they admired. In yet other instances donations were completely innocent and given by devout Muslims honoring their religious obligation to give alms (*zakat* in Arabic, meaning "purification"), who had no idea that the money would be used for terror. As one report noted, "some individual donors knew of the ultimate destination of their donations, and others did not."[6] In part this was because of the key role played by "facilitators, fund-raisers, and employees of corrupted charities, particularly during the Islamic holy month of Ramadan."[7] These facilitators acted as cutouts and intermediaries, providing plausible deniability to those who knew where the money was going and legitimate-looking fronts to those who did not.

Sometimes, Al Qaeda obtained or diverted funds close to the origin or source, particularly when it involved a degree of coercion, as it seems to have done in Kuwait and Saudi Arabia. In other instances, however, the diversion was further downstream as Al Qaeda "penetrated specific foreign branch offices of large, internationally recognized charities," a process aided by lax oversight and control.[8] In such cases the charity was guilty of sins of negligence and omission rather than sins of commission. There were also instances when "entire charities from the top down may have known of and even participated in the funneling of money to Al Qaeda. In those cases, Al Qaeda operatives had control over the entire organization, including access to bank accounts."[9] The Wafu Humanitarian Organization, the International Islamic Relief Organization, al Haramain, and the Holy Land Foundation were among the charities that came under suspicion for supplying funds to Al Qaeda or other Middle East terrorist organizations. In the aftermath of 11 September, a number of these charities were identified, investigated, and in some cases shut down. Moreover, Saudi Arabia eventually succumbed to pressure and took steps to regulate its charities and make them less vulnerable to abuse and misuse. As a result, charities became a less central source of Al Qaeda funding.

Yet the valve was not completely shut. Some of the charities simply became less direct in their support for terrorist organizations, while some of those that were shut down simply reopened with new names.[10] The close relationship between Islamic charities on the one side and Al Qaeda and its affiliates and offshoots on the other was certainly not severed. For example, one British report noted that in 2006, a "significant proportion" of terror finance investigations revealed continuing links to charities.[11] Indeed, despite the initiatives taken since 11 September 2001, "the risk of exploitation of charities" remained "a significant aspect of the terrorist finance threat."[12] The Financial Action Task Force subsequently acknowledged that "the misuse of non-profit organizations for the financing of terrorism" remained "a crucial weak point in the global struggle to stop such funding at its source."[13] In short, scrutiny, pressure, and oversight have all fallen short of their goals.

Not all support for terrorist organizations is provided through charities, however. Contributions to the cause also come from sympathetic communities overseas and can be obtained from legitimate businesses, given voluntarily, given under duress, and obtained through crime. Funding support for the Liberation Tigers of Tamil Elam (LTTE) among the Tamil diaspora in Western Europe and Canada has encompassed all these categories. During the 1980s the "Tamil connection" became an important source of heroin moving from Burma to Europe. Gradually, however, the LTTE moved into a broader range of criminal activities. According to some reports, by the mid-1990s the LTTE had cells in as many as thirty-eight countries in Europe, the Middle East, and North America. Donations given by Tamils with real sympathy for the nationalist cause were accompanied by "donations" obtained through extortion and intimidation. In Canada, which has the largest population of Tamils outside South Asia, a front organization called the World Tamil Movement made extensive use of threats to ensure that Tamil communities in Montreal and Toronto provided financial support, some of which was portrayed as assistance for orphanages and schools.[14] Investigations in Canada also reveal that LTTE supporters have engaged in extensive credit card fraud, social security fraud, counterfeiting, and other criminal activities to provide revenue streams for the LTTE.

A similar situation has occurred with Hezbollah supporters in the Lebanese diaspora. Although Hezbollah has significant financial support from Iran, it also receives considerable money from Lebanese expatriates in Europe, North America, Latin America, Australia, and Africa. Much of this is freely given to an organization that, despite its terrorist activities, evokes a high level of sympathy and support from many Lebanese. Both Hezbollah's resistance to Israel and its social-welfare activities enhance its status and legitimacy among Lebanese across the world, and it is not coincidental that "wealthy Shias" provide significant donations.[15] Hezbollah reportedly has received "a significant amount of financing from the Shiite populations of West Africa and Central Africa," particularly from Lebanese merchants involved in the diamond business and other commercial sectors.[16] The donations often "are in the form of religious donations and paid in cash," which make them "difficult to track."[17] They are "collected by Hezbollah couriers transiting the region."[18]

If some of the money is the result of legitimate business, other funds are obtained through criminal activities. In the United States, for example, Hezbollah supporters have been arrested for smuggling cigarettes from North Carolina to Michigan, where the taxes are much higher and profits larger. In other cases, Hezbollah supporters involved in drug trafficking were sending at least a portion of the proceeds back to Lebanon. Perhaps the most infamous example of using criminal proceeds to support Hezbollah involved Assad Ahmed Barakat and the Barakat clan in the tri-border region of South America, where Brazil, Argentina, and Paraguay come together. Based in Ciudad del Este, Barakat ran a diverse mix of licit and criminal businesses, including the smuggling of contraband and counterfeit goods from Hong Kong. In many ways he was a traditional criminal entrepreneur, but one with political sympathies and affiliations. He sent significant amounts of money to Hezbollah, some from his own profits and some from other Lebanese business owners whom he had pressured into donating. Barakat was imprisoned in Paraguay, but it is likely that the family businesses have continued, along with the flow of funds to Hezbollah.[19]

Other groups also rely on sympathetic populations elsewhere. For example, the Irish Republican Army (IRA) has obtained significant support from the Irish immigrant population in the United States, much of it channeled through the Irish Northern Aid Committee (NORAID), a group that helps the families of imprisoned IRA members and that has been accused of acting as a front for gunrunning into Northern Ireland. The IRA also engaged in a wide range of criminal activities to enhance its funding base, including extortion, bank robberies, video piracy, pig smuggling (which exploited the European Union's system of subsidies), building-site scams, fraud, trade in counterfeit goods and illegal fuel sales, and quasi-legitimate business activities such as the operation of black (unlicensed) taxis and drinking clubs.[20] The IRA also became involved in kidnapping, although its efforts in this area, for the most part, were inept and unsuccessful.[21] The organization was more successful in exploiting new opportunities such as the Internet; in 2003, "approximately 25 percent of the cases undertaken by the Police Service Northern Ireland Computer Crime Unit related to terrorism."[22] With such a broad portfolio of criminal activities, many IRA members were able to respond to the peace process by moving away from terror and engaging in criminal activities for personal profit. Indeed, John Horgan and Max Taylor have suggested that the IRA has morphed directly from terrorist organization to criminal conspiracy.[23]

One of the most notable things about the IRA is its relative lack of involvement in the drug business. This is in marked contrast to many other terrorist organizations that became heavily involved in the drug trade. For example, the Kurdish separatist organization the Kurdistan Workers' Party (PKK) became deeply involved in drug trafficking in Europe. The involvement started when the organization began to impose "transit taxes" on Kurdish drug-trafficking organizations. After the PKK built up its own competence and created drug-trafficking substructures, it sought to replace Kurdish criminal networks in Western Europe. This sparked a series of turf wars in heroin markets in Europe that the PKK mostly won.[24]

If PKK involvement in drug trafficking is indisputable, the involvement of Al Qaeda has been a more controversial issue. Suffice it to say here that although there is little evidence that Al Qaeda as an organization has trafficked drugs, Al Qaeda allies and affiliates, and even Al Qaeda members, seem to have been involved at various levels. During the late 1990s, for example, the Islamic Movement of Uzbekistan directly engaged in opium and heroin smuggling through Central Asia, under the direction of Juma Namangami, the organization's military commander. The Madrid railway bombings in March 2004 were also funded by drug money. Leader Jamal Ahmidan and other members of a Moroccan drug-trafficking group used the proceeds from hashish and ecstasy sales to fund the attacks.[25] However, perhaps the most serious use of drug proceeds to fund terrorism or insurgency has occurred in Afghanistan, where the Taliban, when it was in power, imposed taxes on the opium business to help fund the government.[26]

In 2000 the Taliban banned opium production, but its motivation for this has never been clear. Some observers suggest the ban was simply a device to increase prices, given the large stockpiles the Taliban had accrued; others argue that it was an effort to establish legitimacy with the international community.[27] Whatever the case, since 2003 the Taliban insurgency has been fueled in large part by profits from involvement in the opium and heroin industry. Precise amounts of money are difficult to pinpoint because there are so many uncertainties involved. The Taliban raises money from *ushr* (a 10-percent tax on agricultural products levied at the farm gate), from *zakat* (a 2.5-percent transit tax on opium and other merchandise), and from protecting convoys of traders.[28] It is also possible that the Taliban earns additional money from the trade in precursor chemicals for illegal drug production, and from some direct involvement in the trafficking of opium and heroin. According to estimates by UNODC, between 2005 and 2008 the Taliban annually earned between $90 million and $160 million from *ushr* and transit taxes, as well as unknown additional amounts from precursor and processing profits.[29] Such estimates are significantly higher than the annual $75 million to $100 million the Taliban is believed to have made between 1995 and 2000.[30] What makes this even more important in Afghanistan is that it blurs the lines between insurgency and terrorism on the one side and the Afghan government on the other. Indeed, in Afghanistan opium is common currency, a source of power and influence, and a driver of symbiotic relationships. The drug business is also a place where corrupt government officials, tribal networks, Taliban insurgents, Al Qaeda terrorists, and transnational drug-trafficking organizations overlap and intersect.

In Iraq, by contrast, drug trafficking has been a much smaller factor. However, other criminal activities have contributed significantly to funding the various insurgencies, including Al Qaeda in Iraq (AQI). If the dominant commodity in Afghanistan is opium, in Iraq it is oil. Indeed, the theft and smuggling of oil and petroleum products have been a major moneymaker for black marketeers. The extortion of Iraqi businessmen, including those who have had contracts as part of the U.S. reconstruction effort, has also proven very profitable. Indeed, extortion has remained particularly important to AQI in the city of Mosul, where "merchants in every conceivable sector give a levy to al-Qaeda. Payments to the group enable the local economy to function, keeping markets stocked with essential goods and guaranteeing the passage of construction materials and farm produce across the nearby borders."[31]

Another major revenue source in Iraq has been kidnapping, aided by cooperative relationships between criminals and those involved in political violence. Reports indicate that "hostages, in particular foreign nationals, taken by criminal gangs" were subsequently "handed over to armed political groups in exchange for money."[32] Some of those hostages were then ransomed to governments and businesses. The kidnapping of foreigners has been extremely lucrative: The French, German, and Italian governments paid somewhere in the region of $45 million for the release of fewer than a dozen hostages.[33] In addition, the kidnapping of Iraqis (an estimated forty per day in 2006), even on conservative assumptions about ransom payments, could easily have yielded about $140 million per year at its peak—although how this was distributed between political and purely criminal actors is uncertain.[34] The portfolio of criminal activities used by terrorist and insurgent groups includes car thefts, smuggling of illicit antiquities, and trafficking in women. This is not really surprising. Although the stream of volunteers from Saudi Arabia, Libya, Morocco, and other countries brought some funding, the Sinjar records (data captured from Al Qaeda in western Iraq) suggest that even the Saudi volunteers carried with them only an average of $1,000 per person, while those from other countries brought significantly less.[35] From this perspective, AQI's reliance on criminal activities for funding is essential.

Yet in some senses there is nothing new in this. In Southeast Asia, for example, "most terrorist organizations . . . have a strong tradition utilizing the same techniques as organized crime."[36] This really began during the 1990s, when "criminality became the most pragmatic avenue to secure finances for future operations" and was

> facilitated by weak regulatory financial systems, porous borders, and a thriving underground remittance system particularly in Cambodia, the Philippines, Vietnam, and Thailand. The passive compliance by government officials in various countries and the co-optation of corrupt political and judicial authorities have also been conducive for the diversification of terrorist groups into a wide variety of criminal activities and the rapid and covert movement of funds derived from those activities.[37]

The Philippines' Abu Sayyaf Group has used smuggling, extortion, kidnapping, and even piracy as fund-raising methods; the Moro Islamic Liberation Front, also in the southern Philippines, has relied on drug trafficking, illegal logging, arms trafficking, and the imposition of "taxes"; while even Jemaah Islamiya, which received some funding from Al Qaeda, has used robberies of the infidel as a source of money for its operations in Indonesia.[38]

Involvement in criminal activities has become increasingly important as Al Qaeda has become more decentralized. With less direction and support coming from the core network, local, largely autonomous, and bottom-up forms of fund-raising have become more significant. And to the extent that self-financing at the cell level is successful, there is less need for any transfer of funds. Yet ten years after 11 September 2001, Al Qaeda itself retains a variety of options for transferring funds whenever necessary.

Transferring Money

Terrorist financial transfers are very normal looking and are difficult to distinguish from legitimate transactions. They are, as it were, hidden in plain sight. In spite of all the discussion of how terrorist organizations use *hawala* (described below) or other informal transfer systems to move money, the main channel probably remains the banking system. Certainly this was the case for Al Qaeda prior to 11 September:

> The . . . hijackers used U.S. and foreign financial institutions to hold, move, and retrieve their money. The hijackers deposited money into U.S. accounts, primarily by wire transfers and deposits of cash or travelers checks brought from overseas. Additionally, several of them kept funds in foreign accounts, which they accessed in the United States through ATM and credit card transactions.[39]

Financiers in the UAE and Germany provided funds transfers, but for the most part these appeared innocuous. The anti-money-laundering measures in place had little impact. Although at least one suspicious transaction report might have been filed, it is hard to disagree with the September 11 Commission task force report on terrorist finances, which noted that "the controls were never intended to, and could not, detect or disrupt the routine transactions in which the hijackers engaged."[40] Much the same remains true today, "as money sent from one country to another can be disguised behind false name accounts, charities or businesses."[41] Canada's Financial Intelligence Unit, known as FINTRAC, has acknowledged that "financial transactions associated with terrorist financing tend to be in smaller amounts than is the case with money laundering, and when terrorists raise funds from legitimate sources, the detection and tracking of these funds becomes more difficult."[42]

Terrorists sometimes move money through informal financial systems, particularly *hawala* networks. Sometimes *hawala* is described as a system designed specifically for funding terrorist organizations rather than simply a channel through which remittances are transferred. However, these networks are extensively used for remittances from emigrant populations back to their home countries, and most of the transfers are perfectly legitimate. The system, legal in most places, works through trust and typically involves a customer asking a *hawaladar* (dealer) in Kabul, for example, to transfer money to a specific recipient via another *hawaladar* in, say, London. The recipient merely has to provide some kind of agreed-upon password to the London *hawaladar* to receive the money. Significantly, there is no actual transfer of money from one place to another by the dealers; they build relationships and simply keep a running tally of what they owe to whom; periodically they will deal with inequalities in the flow by settling up via the formal banking system or, in some cases, payment in goods. Many *hawaladars* keep records, but tracing transactions through the system is difficult for law-enforcement and intelligence agencies.[43] Consequently, terrorists can sometimes exploit the system to keep their financial transfers under the radar.

Another way of doing the same thing is through intra-organizational funds transfers. Within a charity, for example, money can be moved from the head office to branches without necessarily raising any suspicions. Similarly, trade-based money transfers using over-invoicing or under-invoicing through either legitimate or front companies are difficult to detect.[44] On occasion, however, terrorists—like criminals—simply move and smuggle bulk cash. As long as the couriers are trusted and the amounts are relatively modest, this is a very easy and simple way to transfer money. In some instances they might use commodities such as diamonds and gold as alternatives, although the extent to which terrorists have actually done this is a matter of considerable controversy.[45]

Most specialists on the financial dimensions of terrorism have emphasized both the adaptability and opportunism of terrorist organizations when it comes to fund-raising and transfers. Indeed, the Financial Action Task Force has concluded that terrorists raise and move money in "any way they can."[46] The September 11 Commission report put it somewhat more elegantly, noting that "sources and conduits are resilient, redundant, and difficult to detect."[47]

Spending Money

Although terrorism is ultimately about campaigns of violence, getting to the operational point requires spending on recruitment, training, and travel, as well as on efforts to mobilize support. In some instances terrorist groups have been heavily engaged in service provision. This is particularly true of the Palestinian group Hamas, which has evolved into a paradoxical blend of legitimate political party, social-service provider, and terrorist organization. Hezbollah is also deeply involved in welfare provision, which demands significant resources.[48] Moreover, operations or attacks, while starkly asymmetrical in terms of their modest financial costs relative to the losses they inflict on the target, are nevertheless more costly than is often assumed. Because terrorist networks operate covertly, however, it is very difficult to obtain good information about how they allocate resources, and in particular about the costs of attacks. As a result, initial estimates are often wrong. For example, the operational cost of the 2004 Madrid train bombings was initially estimated by the UN Monitoring Group at about $10,000. Many commentators on terrorism still use this figure even though it proved a serious underestimation of an attack that actually cost somewhere between €41,000 and €54,000 ($51,000–$67,000 U.S.) to pull off.

A similar underestimation seems to have occurred with the U.S. embassy bombings in Kenya and Tanzania in August 1998. The UN estimate for these two attacks was $50,000. As Joshua Prober suggests, however, this estimate is almost certainly too low. Trial transcripts and government reports indicate that Al Qaeda "incurred a wide array of costs well in excess of $50,000."[49] According to Prober's study, these included

- travel for senior Al Qaeda members to visit Nairobi.
- training of East African Al Qaeda operatives at either Al Qaeda camps or Hezbollah camps in Lebanon. (One operative reportedly spent $6,000 on high-explosives training.)
- rental payments for residential estates in Nairobi and Dar es Salaam, where the bombs were made.
- the maintenance of a communications network—including using satellite phones costing $80,000 each—between Osama bin Laden and the operational cells.
- bribes for local border officials.
- the purchase of surveillance equipment from China and Germany.
- the acquisition of the Nissan and Toyota trucks used in the bombings.
- payments for the bomb materials.[50]

The difficulty, of course, is determining what costs can reasonably be allocated to the operations as distinct from the more general overhead costs for maintaining the network. Nevertheless, Prober's argument that the accepted figure is an underestimate certainly fits with what happened in the Madrid case.

The other difficulty is that attacks themselves vary a great deal in both the level of sophistication and the level of cost. At the top end, the September 11

Commission estimated that the attacks on New York and Washington "cost al Qaeda somewhere in the range of $400,000–$500,000, of which approximately $300,000 passed through the hijackers' bank accounts in the United States" and was used "primarily for flight training, travel, and living expenses (such as housing, food, cars, and auto insurance)."[51] At the other end of the scale are the London bombings of 7 July 2005. In this case most of the living expenses seem to have been covered by the bombers themselves. Moreover, the devices were relatively primitive. One estimate suggests that the overall cost was £72,035 ($133,265), which covered the construction of the bombs, travel, and training weekends.[52] Even if this is an underestimate by several thousand dollars, the London bombings were remarkably cost-effective, leading to losses of several hundred million pounds in tourism and other economic revenue damage, as well as the need for massive investment in security for the 2012 London Olympics. The 11 September attacks cost half a million dollars to carry out but cost the United States billions of dollars in direct costs and billions more in indirect costs.

Even if we go beyond the costs of specific attacks to examine the overall costs of running a terrorist organization, the figures are substantial but still relatively modest. According to one assessment, the Provisional IRA was able to mount a significant campaign of terror in the 1980s and 1990s "with an annual operating budget" under £5 million per year.[53] For a transnational network with global aspirations, the costs will be higher. Nevertheless, when terrorist organizations are clearly differentiated from insurgencies, it is obvious that they can operate effectively on a modest budget and obtain enormous "bang for the buck." This makes the campaign against terrorist finances particularly difficult, and it is hard to avoid the conclusion that the systematic attacks on terrorist finances initiated after 11 September 2001 have had limited success. The final section of this chapter looks more closely at the reasons for this.

Attacking Terrorist Finances

In the months following the 11 September attacks, the United States and its allies made energetic efforts to dismantle Al Qaeda's financial infrastructure. Some Islamic charities and *hawala* networks operating in the United States were closed down, charities elsewhere were subject to much stricter regulation, and considerable attention was given to freezing terrorist funds and appropriating terrorist assets. It appeared for a short while that the Achilles heel of terrorism had been identified and exploited. Ten years later, however, the situation looks very different. Although it would be overly pessimistic to suggest that targeting terrorist finances has been a dismal failure, the effort can by no stretch of the imagination be described as a success.

The effort to shut down terrorist finances, particularly but not exclusively those of Al Qaeda, has operated at several levels: national, bilateral, regional, and global. Most initial efforts were based on UN Security Council Resolution (UNSCR) 1267 (passed in 1999), designating Al Qaeda and the Taliban members and associated individuals as targets for three kinds of sanctions—asset freezing, travel restrictions, and an arms embargo. UN Security Council Resolution 1373, passed in late September 2001, obligated all member states to take measures to prevent and suppress the financing of terrorism. Although there have been adjustments and refinements in subsequent resolutions, 1267 and 1373 provided the essential framework for the efforts to combat terrorist finances.

A second strand in the effort to attack terrorist finances was the broadening of the Financial Action Task Force (FATF). An intergovernmental body established by the G-7 in 1989 to deal with money laundering, in October 2001 the FATF extended its mission to encompass terrorist finances. The organization, which was important in establishing norms and standards in the financial sector with its original forty anti-money-laundering recommendations, added eight (subsequently amended to nine) recommendations specifically designed to combat terrorist finances. Subsequently, the World Bank and IMF took on a complementary role in crystallizing "a single, comprehensive . . . assessment methodology" to target money laundering and terrorist finances by building institutional capacity through training conferences, technical assistance, the provision of handbooks and reference materials for financial intelligence units, and educating officials about informal financial transfer systems.[54] In February 2010 the FATF publicly identified more than twenty countries that remain deficient in developing, passing, and implementing appropriate laws to combat money laundering and terrorist finances.[55]

As well as using these global agencies, the United States articulated a distinct set of mechanisms of its own to combat terrorist finances. Domestically, the Federal Bureau of Investigation established a number of joint terrorism task forces, which focused partly on tracking and seizing money.[56] Operation Green Quest, a multiagency financial enforcement initiative begun in

October 2001, was led by the U.S. Customs Service. These efforts seem to have played a part in disrupting some terrorist plots and, along with the shutting down of several Islamic charities and a major *hawala,* had some effect in constricting financial flows to Al Qaeda and other terrorist organizations. Although there was considerable duplication and overlap of efforts by U.S. agencies, this was more acceptable than allowing indications of terrorist fund-raising or, even worse, of an impending attack, to slip though the seams and remain unnoticed as they had done prior to 11 September.

In addition to undermining terrorist fund-raising, the United States determined that the freeze strategy had to be accompanied by an attempt to follow the money and monitor terrorist financial flows. This was deemed important both in terms of enhancing the capacity to disrupt terrorist organizations and to provide financial indicators of possible attacks. Although there are facets of this activity that were completely covert, some details of what was known as the Terrorist Finance Tracking Program gradually leaked out. The United States, not surprisingly, sought to monitor global financial transactions to detect terrorist activities, and to this end obtained records from the Society for Worldwide Interbank Financial Telecommunication (SWIFT), a global financial-messaging system headquartered in Belgium. The importance of SWIFT is difficult to overestimate. Along with the Clearing House for International Payments and the U.S. Federal Reserve's electronic payments system known as FEDWIRE, SWIFT forms the backbone of the global financial infrastructure for payments and transactions. Details of the tracking program were published in the *New York Times* in June 2006, sparking a major controversy in the United States and Europe that was to render an already complex task even more difficult.[57]

In addition, the United States pressured a number of countries, including most significantly Saudi Arabia, to adopt stringent measures to crack down on terrorist finances through more careful regulation of charities as well as more scrutiny of financial transactions. The Saudi government initially resisted such measures, but after the Al Qaeda attacks in Riyadh in May 2003, it became much more cooperative and compliant. In 2010 Saudi Arabia's Council of Senior Scholars issued a fatwa condemning the financing of terrorist activities.[58]

In sum, the United States and the international community initiated a multipronged effort to combat terrorist finances that in some respects was quite remarkable. Moreover, this effort initially seemed to be having considerable success. The more egregious charities were shut down, $100 million was seized or frozen by the end of 2001, and the tracking program reportedly led to the arrests of key figures in terrorist networks. Yet the effort does not seem to have inhibited terrorist attacks in Europe or Southeast Asia, or the insurgencies in Iraq and Afghanistan. A decade after 11 September 2001, it is evident that problems inherent in the efforts to combat terrorist finances have combined with the adaptive capacity of terrorist organizations to undermine what initially appeared to be a very promising approach.

Part of the promise itself was illusory, however. The multipronged effort was a series of disparate, hastily conceived measures rather than a holistic, carefully crafted strategy. The United States in particular, and the international community in general, failed to develop a strategic approach to dealing with terrorist finances. The purpose of the campaign was never fully articulated beyond the rhetorical level, in part because of the inherent tension between the "freeze and seize" approach preferred by law enforcement and the "follow the money" approach of the intelligence community. An early emphasis on seizing or freezing terrorist assets encountered diminishing returns, and it took several more years after 2001 to add another $50 million to the amounts initially seized or frozen.[59]

The second problem, particularly at the global level, was the gap between standards and implementation. With the adoption of UNSCR 1373, all members of the United Nations accepted formal obligations to take measures against terrorist finances. Yet a significant number of governments were unwilling or unable to meet these obligations. In many instances the issue was simply a lack of capacity; in others it was a lack of will. After 11 September, combating terrorism became a driving theme of U.S. national-security strategy; for many nations in the developing world, however, this remained a low priority and a distracting sideshow from core issues of economic development and public security.

In too many cases, conformity with the U.S.-led global regime to undermine terrorist finances was merely cosmetic, and some countries did not even pretend to adhere to these global norms. Currently, in spite of the efforts of the multilateral agencies discussed above, it does not appear that much has changed. As one Treasury official candidly acknowledged in early 2010, "compliance with UNSCR 1373 is quite spotty. In fact, my colleagues and I spend a good deal of time traveling the globe to encourage states to come into compliance with this Resolution."[60]

A third and closely related problem has stemmed from divergent priorities. Even close allies have not gone along with all the elements of the U.S. approach, particularly after the public disclosures about the monitoring program. Differences between the EU and the United States came to a head in early 2010, when the European Parliament rejected an agreement that would have allowed the United States continued access to the SWIFT transactions database, causing a hiatus in cooperation. However, EU and U.S. negotiators worked out a compromise agreement that was accepted by the European Parliament in a 484-to-109 vote.[61] Although the program resumed on 1 August 2010, many Europeans are still concerned about privacy rights, whereas Washington would prefer to err on the side of comprehensive coverage.

A fourth difficulty stems from the fact that the campaign against terrorist finances was modeled on efforts to combat money laundering by organized crime. As a result, the initiatives "did not grow within a realm sensitive to the unique challenges posed by terrorism."[62] In effect, they extended an approach that had achieved limited success to an area where it was even less appropriate or effective. Attacking profits challenges the purpose of organized crime; for terrorists, in contrast, money is merely a means to an end. Terrorist finances overlap to some degree with criminal proceeds, especially in the desire to avoid detection and interdiction by law enforcement. Yet, unlike criminal proceeds, terrorist financing rarely goes through a comprehensive laundering process in which dirty money is cleaned and made to appear legitimate. Much of the money used by terrorists comes from legitimate sources in the first place, so there is no need to disguise its origins. When terrorists do use criminal activities for funding, the proceeds are often spent locally and rapidly rather than moved through a laundering cycle. Finally, the effort to combat terrorist finances mimicked the anti-money-laundering system in its emphasis on reporting requirements and flagging suspicious transactions.[63] Unfortunately, these approaches are much better at generating data than they are at sparking successful investigations or providing effective warning.

The upshot of all this is that although efforts to shut down terrorist finances have had some positive impact, they also suffer from "strategic deficiencies."[64] The initiatives that have been taken are impressive in both scope and reach, yet they also reflect the inherent shortcomings of multilateralism and many of the pathologies of bureaucratic politics. Moreover, the system to counter terrorist finances, dynamic though it is, has lagged behind the terrorist capacity to morph and adapt, in terms of both fund-raising and organizational structures. Therefore, perhaps the best we can hope for is that the efforts to combat terrorist finances, while they will not stop attacks like London and Madrid, will at least make it more difficult for Al Qaeda to carry out another attack on the scale of 11 September 2001.

Notes

1. John Roth, Douglas Greenburg, and Serena Wille, "Monograph on Terrorist Financing: Staff Report to the Commission," National Commission on Terrorist Attacks upon the United States, Washington, D.C., 2004, 4, www.9-11commission.gov/staff.../911_TerrFin_Monograph.pdf.

2. "Terrorist Financing," Financial Action Task Force (FATF), Organization for Economic Co-operation and Development (OECD), Paris, 29 February 2008, 4. The FATF is a policy-making body set up by the OECD specifically to combat international money laundering and terrorist financing.

3. For an excellent overview, see David E. Kaplan, "Paying for Terror," *U.S. News and World Report*, 27 November 2005, http://www.usnews.com/usnews/news/articles/051205/5terror.htm.

4. Roth et al., "Monograph on Terrorist Financing," 4.

5. For a balanced and useful discussion see Christopher M. Blanchard and Alfred B. Prados, "Saudi Arabia: Terrorist Financing Issues," *Congressional Research Service*, updated 14 September 2007.

6. Roth et al., "Monograph on Terrorist Financing," 20.

7. Ibid., 20–21.

8. Ibid., 21.

9. Ibid.

10. Matthew Levitt, "Charitable Organizations and Terrorist Financing: A War on Terror Status-Check," draft paper presented at the Workshop on the Dimensions of Terrorist Financing, University of Pittsburgh, 19–20 March 2004.

11. Quoted in Matthew Levitt, "Anti-Money Laundering: Blocking Terrorist Financing and Its Impact on Lawful Charities," *Counterterrorism Blog*, 26 May 2010, http://counterterrorismblog.org/2010/05/anti-money_laundering_blocking.php.

12. Ibid.

13. "Terrorist Financing," 11; see also note 10.

14. "Tigers Collecting Funds in Canada: Sri Lanka Tamil Tigers Use Pressure to Raise Funds, Canadian Police Say," US Bureau, *Asian Tribune* 10, no. 81 (11 May 2007), http://asiantribune.com/node/5681.

15. See Matthew Levitt, "Hezbollah: Financing Terror Through Criminal Enterprise," testimony before the Committee on Homeland Security and Governmental Affairs, United States Senate, 109th Congress, 1st session, 15 May 2005, 5.

16. "Hezbollah 'an Octopus' with Tentacles Around World, Officials Say," from America.gov, Bureau of International Information Programs, U.S. Department of State, 28 September 2006.

17. Ibid.

18. Ibid.

19. "Hizballah Fundraising Network in the Triple Frontier," Office of Public Affairs, U.S. Treasury Department, 6 December 2006, http://paraguay.usembassy.gov/hizballah_fundraising_network_in_the_triple_frontier2.html.

20. Laura K. Donohue, "Anti-Terrorist Finance in the United Kingdom and United States," *Michigan Journal of International Law* 27 (2006): 315.

21. Ibid., 320.

22. Ibid., 321.

23. John Horgan and Max Taylor, "Playing the 'Green Card'—Financing the Provisional IRA: Part 1," *Terrorism and Political Violence* 11, no. 2 (Summer 1999): 1–38; and Horgan and Taylor, "Playing the 'Green Card'—Financing the Provisional IRA: Part 2," *Terrorism and Political Violence* 15, no. 2 (Summer 2003): 1–60.

24. See Behsat Ekici, Phil Williams, and Ayhan Akbulut, "The PKK and Kurdish Drug Networks: Cooperation, Convergence or Conflict?" forthcoming.

25. This is discussed more fully in Chapter 19, on the Madrid train bombings.

26. Two very helpful studies on this are Gretchen Peters, *The Seeds of Terror* (New York: St. Martin's, 2009); and Vanda Felbab-Brown, *Shooting Up* (Washington, D.C.: Brookings, 2009).

27. Amnesty International report, 25 July 2005, quoted in Home Office (UK), "Country of Origin Information Report: Iraq," 31 October 2006.

28. "Addiction, Crime and Insurgency: The Transnational Threat of Afghan Opium," United Nations Office on Drugs and Crime (UNODC), Vienna, October 2009.

29. Ibid., 108.

30. Ibid., 2.

31. Saad al-Mosuli, "Al-Qaeda Turns to Mafia Tactics in Mosul," IWPR (Institute for War and Peace Reporting), 9 June 2010, http://iwpr.net/report-news/al-qaeda-turns-mafia-tactics-mosu.

32. Amnesty International report, 25 July 2005.

33. Daniel McGrory, "How $45m Secretly Bought Freedom of Foreign Hostages," *Times* (London), 22 May 2006, 8.

34. For a fuller analysis, see Phil Williams, "Criminals, Militias, and Insurgents: Organized Crime in Iraq," Security Studies Institute, Carlisle Barracks, 2009.

35. Joseph Felter and Brian Fishman, "Al-Qa'ida's Foreign Fighters in Iraq: A First Look at the Sinjar Records," Combating Terrorism Center, West Point, New York, July 2008, http://ctc.usma.edu/publications/publications.asp.

36. Aurel Croissant and Daniel Barlow, "Following the Money Trail: Terrorist Financing and Government Responses in Southeast Asia," *Studies in Conflict & Terrorism* 30 (2007): 135.

37. Ibid.

38. See ibid., 135–36, for a fuller analysis.

39. Roth et al., "Monograph on Terrorist Financing," 3.

40. Ibid.

41. "Terrorist Financing," 21.

42. "What Is Terrorist Financing?" Financial Transactions and Reports Analysis Centre of Canada (FINTRAC), 23 August 2007, http://www.fintrac.gc.ca/fintrac-canafe/definitions/terrorist-terroriste-eng.asp.

43. For a more detailed explanation of how *hawala* networks function, see Patrick M. Yost and Harjit Singh Sandhu, "The Hawala Alternative Remittance System and Its Role in Money Laundering," Interpol General Secretariat, January 2000, http://www.interpol.int/public/financialcrime/moneylaundering/hawala/default.asp.

44. Ibid., under the heading "How Does Hawala Work?"

45. See Douglas Farah, *Blood from Stones: The Secret Financial Network of Terror* (New York: Broadway, 2004).

46. "Terrorist Financing," 21.

47. Roth et al., "Monograph on Terrorist Financing," 17.

48. See Alexus G. Grynkewich, "Welfare as Warfare: How Violent Non-State Groups Use Social Services to Attack the State," *Studies in Conflict & Terrorism* 31, no. 4 (2008): 353.

49. Joshua Prober, "Accounting for Terror: Debunking the Paradigm of Inexpensive Terrorism," *Policy Watch* (Washington Institute for Near East Policy) 1041 (1 November 2006).

50. Ibid.

51. Roth et al., "Monograph on Terrorist Financing," 3.

52. Simon Dilloway, "7/7 Attack—London Bombings," http://www.lophamconsultancy.co.uk/London%20Bombings.pdf.

53. Donohue, "Anti-Terrorist Finance in the United Kingdom," 312.

54. See "Factsheet: The IMF and the Fight Against Money Laundering and the Financing of Terrorism," International Monetary Fund (IMF), 5 April 2010; and "Reference Guide to Anti-Money Laundering and Combating the Financing of Terrorism," second edition and supplement on special recommendation IX, World Bank and IMF, Washington, D.C., 2006, http://siteresources.worldbank.org/EXTAML/Resources/396511-1146581427871/Reference_Guide_AMLCFT_2ndSupplement.pdf.

55. The relevant statements were updated in June 2010 and are published in "FATF Public Statement," 25 June 2010, http://www.fatfgafi.org/dataoecd/17/5/45540828.pdf; and "Improving Global AML/CFT Compliance: On-Going Process," 25 June 2010, http://www.fatf-gafi.org/dataoecd/34/28/44636196.pdf.

56. See "Protecting America Against Terrorist Attack: A Closer Look at the FBI's Joint Terrorism Task Forces," Federal Bureau of Investigation, 1 December 2004, http://www.fbi.gov/page2/dec04/jttf120114.htm.

57. Eric Lichtblau and James Risen, "Bank Data Is Sifted by U.S. in Secret to Block Terror," *New York Times*, 22 June 2006.

58. Donna Miles, "Petraeus Lauds Saudi Fatwa Condemning Terrorism Financing," *American Forces Press Service*, 22 May 2010.

59. Paul J. Smith, "Terrorism Finance: Global Responses to the Terrorism Money Trail," in *Countering Terrorism and Insurgency in the 21st Century: International Per-*

spectives, Volume 2: *Combating the Sources and Facilitators*, ed. James J. F. Forest (Santa Barbara: Praeger, 2007).

60. David S. Cohen, U.S. Treasury Department Assistant Secretary for Terrorism and Financial Intelligence, remarks to the Washington Institute for Near East Policy, 7 April 2010.

61. James Kanter, "Europe Resumes Sharing Bank Data with U.S.," *New York Times*, 8 July 2010.

62. Donohue, "Anti-Terrorist Finance in the United Kingdom," 307.

63. Ibid. I have long argued that the FATF places too much emphasis on procedural norms (i.e., what institutions and procedures are in place) rather than substantive norms (i.e., what works most effectively). See, for example, Phil Williams, "Transnational Organized Crime, Illicit Markets, and Money Laundering" in *Challenges in International Governance,* eds. P. J. Simmons and Chantel Ouderen (Washington, D.C.: Carnegie Endowment, 2001), 106–50.

64. Cohen, remarks.

5 Cyber Terrorism

Timothy J. Doorey

THE TERM *CYBER TERRORISM* HAS BECOME A RORSCHACH TEST for government officials and concerned citizens alike. For many, it conjures up images of shadowy killers armed with both bombs *and* keyboards. This version features traditional attacks against people, along with digital attacks against a nation's critical infrastructure (the commercial and financial sector, air-traffic-control system, electric power grid, medical-information network, rail transport, water and sewage-treatment systems, emergency-response services, etc.). Some fear that by skillfully combining these kinetic and virtual weapons, terrorists will be able to inflict unprecedented physical destruction, economic damage, and psychological harm. This vision is perhaps best expressed by the FBI Director, Robert Muller, who warned in 2010 of the following: The threat of cyber terrorism is "real and . . . rapidly expanding." Terrorists look "toward combining physical attacks with cyberattacks." In the last decade, "Al-Qaeda's online presence has become as potent as its physical presence."[1]

But for others, cyber terrorism is nothing more than a hyped menace, a "doomsday" threat peddled by sensationalist journalists, so-called security "experts," and cyber-security software companies hoping to profit from the growing irrational fear. Joshua Green articulated this point of view in 2002:

> [T]here is no such thing as cyberterrorism—no instance of anyone ever having been killed by a terrorist (or anyone else) using a computer. Nor is there com-

pelling evidence that al Qaeda or any other terrorist organization has resorted to computers for any sort of serious destructive activity.[2]

Using a broad definition of cyber terrorism, including all terrorist uses of the Internet, this chapter will attempt to separate myth from reality. First, it will describe how terrorists currently employ the Internet to support their global operations. Second, it will introduce a hierarchy of cyber-terrorism threats ranging from malicious hacking to other forms of online criminal activity, from remote surveillance and espionage, to recruitment and indoctrination, and to potentially devastating direct attacks on a nation's critical infrastructure. Third, it will identify disturbing trends that terrorism scholars, law-enforcement professionals, and intelligence officials are just now beginning to understand and fully appreciate. Among these are the emerging threats of virtual recruitment and self-radicalization. Finally, this chapter will offer suggestions on how governments can better deny terrorist groups unrestricted access to and use of this digital sanctuary.

A Paradigm Shift for Terrorism

Although the scourge of terrorism has existed since ancient times, it was not until the late twentieth century that individual terrorists and small terrorist groups acquired the weapons necessary to conduct attacks beyond the assassination of individuals or a small group of victims. In the past, with a narrow range of weaponry and limited media coverage available, terrorist groups were forced to place a great deal of emphasis on target selection in order to have maximum political and psychological impact. Examples of this specialized target selection include the June 1914 assassination of the heir to the throne of the Austrian–Hungarian Empire in Sarajevo (an attack credited as the catalyst for World War I) and Black September's attack against Israeli athletes at the 1972 Summer Olympic games in Munich. Despite those dramatic operations, terrorism did not have a significant global impact until satellite television and widespread use of the Internet brought even minor attacks to the world stage.[3]

The "democratization" of information over the past two decades has in effect taken a monopoly away from governments and placed ever-more-powerful information technologies into the hands of private individuals. Terrorists—as well as international criminals and other nonstate actors—

now have the ability to communicate and collaborate globally with minimal government interference. They can recruit, train, raise money, transfer funds, collect intelligence, and distribute propaganda, even under the most repressive regime. Because governments can no longer effectively censor content or limit its distribution, the terrorist's list of potential targets—both "hard" and "soft"—has expanded greatly.

Today, governments are routinely placed on the defensive, forced to respond to a terrorist group's proclamations, online postings, or attacks. For example, a simple Google search of the term *beheading videos* in November 2010 produced 124,000 results. It is unlikely that any government would endorse the posting of such content—especially when it depicts the authorities as impotent to stop it—yet governments around the world are now in the awkward position of explaining to their frightened publics why they are unable to prevent such acts of brutality.

The Growing Terrorist Presence Online

With more than two billion global Internet users already online, and many more new users added daily, it is not surprising that terrorists have a significant presence online. In his book *Terror on the Internet,* Gabriel Weimann, professor of communications at Haifa University, reports that by 2005, four years after the 11 September attacks, all forty terrorist organizations on the State Department's list of foreign terrorist organizations had established a presence online. A thorough and extensive scan of the Internet between 2003 and 2005 uncovered more than 4,300 Web sites serving terrorist groups and their supporters.[4]

In September 2010, Interpol's Secretary General, Ron Noble, addressing a conference of police chiefs in Paris, echoed Weimann's findings. Noble claimed there were only twelve Islamist extremist-related Web sites in 1998, but by 2006 the number had grown to 4,500.[5] Some terrorism experts believe that even those high numbers are too low. Alexander Meleagrou-Hitchens, a researcher at the International Centre for the Study of Radicalisation in London, claimed that the number of radical online sites—in English alone—is well into the thousands. He also noted that governments have been unable to make a dent in the number of radical sites. According to Meleagrou-Hitchens, "As soon as you knock out one, another pops up. It's like playing 'whack-a-mole.'"[6]

Terrorists and terrorist groups use the Internet in ways not unlike the rest of the world's users: to communicate; to exchange ideas and information with like-minded individuals from around the world; to research, to train, and to educate; to raise and transfer funds; to advertise their organization's prowess, accomplishments, legitimacy, and capabilities; to recruit and indoctrinate new members; and to advocate for continued support of their cause. The Internet's low cost and extensive reach are extremely attractive to individuals and groups with a dwindling number of physical sanctuaries. For many terrorist groups—especially Al Qaeda and its affiliates—the Internet has become a "virtual sanctuary" where they can communicate, train, and keep their movement alive in relative safety. The Internet has allowed what would have been small national or regional terrorist groups in the pre-Internet era to become global movements.

The Hierarchy of Cyber-Terrorism Threats

When discussing cyber terrorism, it is essential to understand that there is a continuum, or hierarchy, of cyber threats. Several questions loom. Are terrorist groups and their supporters operating primarily at the low end of the cyber-threat spectrum, where hackers deface official Web sites and engage in various forms of cyber vandalism? At the other end of the spectrum, are terrorists focused on conducting direct cyber attacks against a nation's critical infrastructure in order to inflict serious economic, physical, and emotional harm to millions? Or are terrorist groups content to use cyberspace for what Weimann refers to as "instrumental uses of the internet for terrorism"? This middle-range cyber-threat area includes data mining, networking, recruitment and mobilization, training, planning and coordination, and fundraising.[7] Understanding how terrorists are using the Internet is now a critical element of threat assessment. This knowledge is also a factor in establishing counterterrorism priorities, as well as in allocating limited monitoring and response resources. Ultimately, however, governments must be able to develop appropriate strategies and tactics to counter *specific* cyber threats.

Malicious Hacking and Cyber Crime

At the lower end of the cyber-threat spectrum, terrorists and their supporters engage in various forms of cyber vandalism. These attacks, such as defacing official Web pages, are a nuisance and can be costly to repair in terms of lost time and money. They are akin to nonterrorist hackers spreading viruses and other malware online. In May 2000 Professor Dorothy Denning, a computer science expert at Georgetown University at the time, testified before the U.S. House of Representatives on the threat of cyber terrorism. In her testimony she highlighted a number of examples of cyber vandalism. In one instance ethnic Tamil guerrillas bombarded numerous Sri Lankan embassies in 1998 with 800 e-mails per day over a two-week period. The messages read, "We are the Internet Black Tigers and we're doing this to disrupt your communications." According to Denning, intelligence authorities characterized this episode as the first known attack by terrorists against a country's computer systems.[8] Many sympathizers around the world of terrorist organizations will engage in similar disruptive activities with little fear of being caught. However, most have no intention of engaging in more serious cyber attacks or supporting actual acts of violence.

The next step up is the rapidly expanding threat of cyber criminal activity. Law-enforcement organizations have struggled to adapt in the fight against cyber criminals and online threats. In the 1990s many national law-enforcement agencies, including the FBI, were slow to recognize and respond to the emerging cyber-crime threat. On June 26, 1991, a hacking-induced crash of the central telephone network in Baltimore, Maryland—along with simultaneous losses of telephone service in parts of Los Angeles—forced the U.S. government's hand.[9] This relatively small incident (later traced back to a teenage computer hacker) shut down all telephone service, including 911 calls to police, fire, and ambulance services, for hours, until engineers could restore the networks. These and other criminal events in the early 1990s prompted the FBI to build a cyber-crime investigative capability from scratch.[10]

Fund-Raising

The next rung on the cyber-terrorism ladder is fund-raising to support violent attacks. The Internet has become an efficient, low-risk means to obtain funds for terrorist activities. Money can be solicited directly through appeals to ideology and outrage. Funds can also be supplied by stealing credit card information online to fund various terrorist activities.[11] Money can be obtained through deception, tricking unsuspecting individuals who believe they are supporting legitimate causes, especially Islamic charities. Sophisticated terrorist groups know how to make strong online appeals for donations, usually accompanied by heart-wrenching images and videos of people suffering, to convince donors to send funds to their charity front organizations.

Credit card fraud and other forms of identity theft cost U.S. businesses and consumers $50 billion per year. Because of the difficulty of pinpointing the sources of such activity, it is likely that some of that money ends up in terrorist coffers.[12] British authorities traced a massive credit card theft ring to three British citizens who had used the cards to purchase night-vision goggles, tents, global-positioning-satellite (GPS) devices, hundreds of prepaid cell phones, and 250 airline tickets, all for use by terrorists. In total, the trio made $3.5 million in fraudulent charges from a database of 37,000 stolen credit cards.[13]

Another example of terrorists using credit card fraud to finance their operations is Imam Samudra, the Indonesian who was convicted and eventually executed for masterminding the Bali bombing in 2002 that killed 202 people. While awaiting execution, Samudra wrote a "how-to" manifesto on funding terrorism. In a chapter titled "Hacking, Why Not?" he directed fellow Muslim radicals to use Indonesian-language Web sites and chat rooms to post instructions on how to commit online credit card fraud and money laundering.[14]

Surveillance and Reconnaissance

For many terrorists, the Internet is a powerful yet inexpensive tool for conducting pre-attack surveillance of potential targets without fear of detection or capture. From the safety of a dusty Internet café thousands of miles from the actual target site, a terrorist can learn a tremendous amount about his or her intended target without compromising operational security.

In the summer of 2001, the Web site coordinator for the city of Mountain View, California, noticed an unusual spike in activity from various Middle Eastern countries. The significance of this activity was not apparent until after the attacks on September 11, 2001. Subsequently, the FBI found similar examples of "multiple casings" at other sites in cities throughout the United States. The suspicious activity appeared to be related to the remote probing of public utilities, including electrical and water systems.[15]

Ron Dick, the former director of the FBI's National Infrastructure Protection Center (NIPC), reported that, at the time, the NIPC was unable to link the Mountain View activity to any specific terrorist organization or pre-attack planning.[16] There have also been numerous examples of pre-attack surveillance on the U.S. electrical grid. This activity appears to be pervasive, not targeting a particular company or region. Said a former Department of Homeland Security official, referring to electrical systems, "There are intrusions, and they are growing."[17]

Cyber Espionage

The next level above remote online surveillance and reconnaissance by terrorists is cyber espionage—the penetration of private or sensitive computer networks, cell-phone systems, and official tracking devices. Cyber espionage could improve the odds for successful physical attacks. The evidence of terrorists actually conducting such complex operations is limited, but more can be expected as sophisticated cyber-espionage tools continue to proliferate on the Internet.

In March 2000 Japan's Metropolitan Police Department learned that a software system that it had procured to track 150 police vehicles, including unmarked cars, had actually been developed by Aum Shinryko, acting in its legitimate business role as a software developer. (Aum's terrorist activities are profiled in Chapter 18, by Ed Hoffer.) By the time the police discovered the security vulnerability, this terrorist organization had received classified tracking data on 115 vehicles. Without breaking any laws, Aum placed itself in an ideal position to install rogue software that would have permitted unauthorized access to sensitive systems and data.[18]

Other recent examples of sophisticated cyber espionage with terrorism implications include the "Athens Affair" and "Ghostnet." In both cases criminal or foreign intelligence organizations managed to place rogue software on sensitive computer networks by hacking into those systems, infiltrating the commercial networks with a trusted agent, or tricking unwitting authorized users into downloading malicious code onto their systems. In March 2005 the Greek prime minister, the mayor of Athens, and more than one hundred high-ranking Greek government and business leaders were notified that their individual mobile phones had been bugged since 2004.[19]

In March 2009 Canadian computer specialists published a report on their two-year investigation into a massive cyber-espionage effort they labeled "Ghostnet." The Ghostnet operation had managed to "infiltrate at least 1,295 computers in 103 countries, including many residing in embassies, foreign ministries, and other government offices. Also targeted were the Dalai Lama's Tibetan exile centers in India, Brussels, London and New York."[20] The sophisticated Trojan horse software used in these penetrations allowed the perpetrators to take complete control of the infected computers, including access to all of the computers' files, microphones, and Web cameras.

Propaganda, Recruitment, and Radicalization

In the physical world (with the possible exception of drug trafficking), criminal and terrorist organizations are reluctant to cooperate because of differing motives and incentives. Criminals are primarily profit motivated and are reluctant to bring unnecessary media attention to their nefarious activities for fear of provoking a strong government crackdown. Terrorists have no such qualms. In fact, because terrorists are primarily ideologically driven, they actively seek media attention to spread fear and to enhance their perceived power at the expense of the state.

The Internet's rapid and global expansion in the last decade of the twentieth century and the initial decade of the twenty-first—combined with a parallel growth and expansion of satellite television—allows even small terrorist groups to get their message out to all corners of the globe and classes of society, including to those who are semiliterate or illiterate. With the increasing availability of greater bandwidth, the Internet now permits wide dissemination of text, images, and streaming videos—unimpeded and uncensored by most governments—directly from the terrorist group to its intended audience.

In this virtual world the lines between criminal and terrorist activity are often blurred. For example, Mexican drug cartels have adopted Al Qaeda propaganda techniques, regularly posting videos on YouTube of cartel rivals, journalists, and even government officials being tortured and executed. As with Al Qaeda, such gruesome propaganda is designed to warn rival gangs, the authorities, and the general population not to challenge the group's authority or business territory.[21] Indeed, the Internet has enabled the most violent criminal syndicates to become *de facto* terrorist organizations.

Terrorist groups now have the ability to communicate directly with millions of disaffected young people around the globe, offering them convincing explanations of the causes of their dissatisfaction and, more importantly, possible solutions. For many, especially the unemployed and desperate, such appeals can be irresistible and intoxicating. Demographics in the developing world are prone to "youth bulges" that provide clusters of frustrated young people and potential terrorists. Within a very short time, a sufficient number of these individuals can be recruited, radicalized, and sent on missions.

A terrorist group's appeal for action—combined with images of their ethnic brethren being brutalized and humiliated—can be quite compelling.

Professor Mohamed Hafez, in his research on suicide bombers in Iraq from 2003 to 2006, discovered that most of the bombers were not Iraqis but mainly foreign volunteers.[22] Hafez characterizes the Internet as a source of "non-relational diffusion of movement ideology, strategy, and tactics." He further explains the critical role that the Internet played in recruiting and motivating these individuals to leave their families and countries, travel to Iraq, and commit the ultimate act of sacrifice.[23]

The Iraq war was a watershed event for terrorist use of the Internet, especially for recruiting and motivating extremists to join the fight. In addition to his legendary brutality, Jordanian terrorist leader Abu Musab al-Zarqawi was a master of online public relations. According to Susan B. Glasser and Steve Coll, "Never before has a guerilla organization so successfully intertwined its real-time war on the ground with its electronic *jihad,* making Zarqawi's group early practitioners of what experts say will be the future of insurgent warfare. This is a world where no act goes unrecorded, and atrocities seem to be committed in order to be filmed and distributed nearly instantaneously online."[24]

There is mounting evidence that radical Islamist groups have so improved their methods of Internet recruiting and radicalization that physical contact between recruiters and recruits may no longer be essential. Recent testimony by U.S. military and counterterrorism officials reinforces the notion that some militant groups have also compressed the time it takes to radicalize an individual. In the case of Umar Farouk Abdulmutallab, the so-called "underwear bomber," the process from initial contact to full readiness was compressed to only six weeks.[25]

Terrorist organizations' skillful use of the Internet has led to what some experts refer to as "self-recruitment" online, where disaffected youths can plug into the global jihad without traveling abroad. Recent examples include Nidal Malik Hasan, the Palestinian–American psychiatrist and active-duty U.S. Army major who shot and killed thirteen of his fellow soldiers at Fort Hood, Texas, in November 2009. Hasan's attack followed almost a year of e-mail exchanges with a radical, American-born cleric in Yemen, Anwar al-Awlaki. According to al-Awlaki's Web site, Hasan asked al-Awlaki for guidance on killing U.S. military personnel in his first e-mail.[26]

Online self-recruitment and radicalization are not limited to one ethnic group. In October 2005 Mirsad Bektasevic, a Bosnian raised in Sweden, was arrested with forty-two pounds of explosives, a suicide vest with detonators, martyr videos, and a silencer-equipped pistol.[27] Using evidence obtained from safe houses in Sarajevo and other parts of Bosnia, police across Europe and North America arrested more than thirty suspects, all members of a network that had planned attacks in Washington, Toronto, London, and Sarajevo. Surprisingly, most of the suspects had never met face-to-face.

In March 2010 a suburban Philadelphian woman, Colleen Renee LaRose, who used the online name "Jihad Jane," was indicted on four counts, including aiding a terrorist group.[28] She allegedly traveled to Sweden in an attempt to kill a Swedish man selected for assassination by her online handlers.[29] If such diversified online recruitment and radicalization become widespread, a new dimension and level of difficulty in the struggle against international terrorism will be added.

Direct Cyber Attack

At the high end of the cyber-threat spectrum is a devastating direct attack against a nation's critical infrastructure. Such cyber attacks are more likely as an increasing share of control of the digital systems migrates to the Internet (much of it protected by questionable safeguards). Mainframe computers were first "networked" together via ARPANet in the 1960s for research purposes; commercial use was introduced only in 1988. This technical lineage has left us with a magnificent yet fragile information network. The Internet we have today is not built for security; it is rather the creation of a "wild west" or laissez-faire approach to regulation, where access was valued over information assurance. Not surprisingly, cyber crimes ranging from malicious hacking to credit card and identity theft, and from industrial espionage to sabotage, have proliferated over the past two decades. As the Internet grew in scope and commercial importance in the 1990s, cyber-related crimes began to appear in greater number and severity, many of them extremely costly and disruptive to essential government and public services.

Former White House Director of Cyberspace Security Richard Clarke and others have been vocal advocates for governments to do more to protect their critical infrastructure from cyber attacks.[30] To date, however, there has been little evidence of terrorist groups planning direct cyber attacks against a nation's critical infrastructure (although some nation-states have likely engaged in such activity). Will terrorists resort to massive cyber attacks as either a substitute for, or adjunct to, physical attacks? Such a scenario depends on a terrorist group's capabilities and intentions, as well as a target country's vulnerability to cyber attack. As FBI Director Robert Muller has pointed out, some of these terrorist groups already have—or can acquire—the necessary cyber talent.[31] Do they intend to use these unique skills? Are our cyber infrastructures vulnerable?

Over the past few years there have been a number of successful cyber attacks, the origins of which are difficult to attribute. In the spring of 2007 the small Baltic nation of Estonia suffered a serious attack on its administration of government services, heavily dependent on cyber systems.[32] In the following year the Republic of Georgia was hit by a prolonged cyber attack while it was also under military attack by Russia's conventional armed forces.[33] In the summer of 2010 a sophisticated cyber worm, dubbed "Stuxnet," infected millions of computers around the world, most significantly those associated with Iran's uranium-enrichment process. This worm was different from its predecessors: It was built specifically to infect software used by supervisory control and data acquisition (SCADA) systems, the central nervous system of our postindustrial word.[34]

The recent attack by the cyber-anarchist movement called "Anonymous" against the Web sites of multinational companies and governments that are opposed to Wikileaks and its founder, Julian Assange, is a crude example of what is possible. This leaderless global network of sympathizers managed to execute coordinated distributed denial of service (DoS) attacks against the credit card companies Visa and MasterCard, as well as the online payment service PayPal.[35]

For terrorists who seek the massive disruption of a society they loathe, there could be no sharper tool than cyber attack. And using that tool will be tempting, especially given the weakened economic position of most countries around the world. Thanks in part to enhanced security measures adopted by the United States and its partners, Al Qaeda and its affiliates have struggled to repeat their earlier spectacular terrorism successes in North America and Europe. Despite numerous attempts, they have not conducted a successful major terrorist attack in North America since September 2001, or in Europe since the London bombings in July 2005. Perhaps frustration, along with the need to maintain credibility, will drive them to take this tactical quantum leap into digital warfare.

Fighting in Cyberspace Is Not a Choice

How can governments, armed and ready to fight terrorists in the physical dimensions, also fight them in cyberspace? Most governments have figured out that *all* their institutions have at least a small role in fighting terrorism. How should nations balance roles and resources to empower those institutions to fight in the physical *and* the virtual battlespace? They cannot simply choose one over the other. State strategies must guide long campaigns on both fronts at the same time; physical attacks can have far-reaching cyber consequences, while cyber attacks can produce catastrophic physical effects.

Since 11 September 2001, the United States and its coalition partners have expended tremendous resources in just two countries—Afghanistan and Iraq—the combined populations of which total only sixty million. But the 1.5 billion Muslims who live outside of the two countries are linked together, observing these physical wars via satellite television and the Internet. Missteps by the West are often seen as reinforcement for the belief that both wars are being waged against *all* Muslims. The physical and the virtual have merged. Final political victory in such an environment is not possible. But there are lessons here for all governments, not just those in the West. No regime can now afford to govern badly while its citizens watch and listen (the current wave of popular revolutions in the Middle East is ample evidence).

In October 2010 Britain's new coalition government unveiled its long-awaited Strategic Defence and Security Review. The review's list of prioritized threats declared that cyberspace deserves greater attention. Indeed, it listed cyber threats and terrorism as two of the top four "Tier One" threats facing the United Kingdom in the years ahead. (Tier One threats are the most serious of the sixteen threats considered in the review.) By implication, such threats deserve immediate, increased attention and resources.[36] However, most of the subsequent government commentary and media attention focused on cuts to twentieth-century platforms and personnel. Old thinking dies hard. Like the United Kingdom, all nations need to continually reevaluate their physical and virtual terrorist threats and redistribute their limited resources accordingly among defense, intelligence, law enforcement, and other institutions.

Conclusion

Despite the many advantages that cyberspace provides, it remains a hostile environment, with terrorists only one of numerous bad actors. For terrorists, the Internet provides a global command and control system, recruitment platform, fund-raising network, distance-learning capability, and propaganda outlet, with minimal cost or risk to its operatives and supporters. The debate on whether terrorist groups will attack in this way has shifted from capabilities to intentions. It's just a matter of time. Given the mastery of the medium by terrorists—coupled with the increasing reliance that modern societies place on cyber systems—the leap from using the Internet for support services to employing it against critical infrastructure may be closer at hand than many skeptics would like us to believe. Of the many vulnerabilities out there, the globalized financial system, with its extreme dependency on computers for moving money between and among countries, ranks high.

Will cyber attacks reach or surpass the lethality and destructiveness of conventional attacks? Or will terrorist groups continue to use the Internet primarily as a low-cost support system for their traditional tactics? Only time (and good intelligence) will tell. It is difficult to predict a terrorist leader's intentions, which are also subject to change. Groups such as Al Qaeda and its affiliates have learned how to leverage the Internet's unique capabilities in ways that expand their global reach and effectiveness. These developments continue to frustrate national law-enforcement and intelligence agencies that must operate within agency, geographic, legal, jurisdictional, and political boundaries. National, regional, and international institutions can damage terrorist networks by constraining their use of cyberspace. They will have to confront terrorist organizations in both the physical and virtual dimensions with equal energy and imagination. It is imperative that government officials and counterterrorism professionals fully understand the terrorists' virtual world, then develop strategies to deny them the digital sanctuary that they now enjoy.

Notes

1. Ellen Nakashima, "FBI Director Warns of 'Rapidly Expanding' Cyberterrorism Threat," *Washington Post,* 4 March 2010, accessed 20 July 2010, http://www.washingtonpost.com/wp-dyn/content/article/2010/03/04/AR2010030405066.html.

2. Joshua Green, "The Myth of Cyberterrorism," *Washington Monthly,* November 2002, accessed 8 August 2010, http://www.washingtonmonthly.com/features/2001/0211.green.html.

3. Imagine how much impact the 1979 seizure of 100,000 hostages in Mecca would have if it took place today. See "1979: Remembering 'The Siege of Mecca,'" National Public Radio, accessed 23 November 2010, http://www.npr.org/templates/story/story.php?storyId=112051155.

4. Gabriel Weimann, *Terror on the Internet* (Washington, D.C.: United States Institute of Peace Press, 2006), 15.

5. BBC News Europe, "Extremist Websites Skyrocketing, Says Interpol," 21 September 2010, accessed 5 October 2010, http://www.bbc.co.uk/news/world-europe-11382124.

6. Ibid.

7. Weimann, 111–48.

8. Dorothy M. Denning, "Testimony Before the Special Oversight Panel on Terrorism," Committee on Armed Services, U.S. House of Representatives, 23 May 2000, accessed 2 November 2010, http://www.cs.georgetown.edu/~denning/infosec/cyber terror.html.

9. David H. Freedman and Charles C. Mann, *@Large: The Strange Case of the World's Biggest Internet Invasion* (New York: Simon and Schuster, 1997), 26.

10. Ibid., 26–27.

11. Weimann, 134–41.

12. Clay Wilson, "Botnets, Cybercrime, and Cyberterrorism: Vulnerabilities and Policy Issues for Congress," CRS Report for Congress, 29 January 2008, accessed 13 November 2010, http://www.fas.org/sgp/crs/terror/RL32114.pdf, 10–11.

13. Brian Krebbs, "Terrorism's Hook into Your Inbox: U.K. Case Shows Link Between Online Fraud and Jihadist Networks," *Washington Post,* 5 July 2007, accessed 4 November 2010, http://www.washingtonpost.com/wp-dyn/content/arti cle/2007/07/05/AR2007070501153.html.

14. Jon Swartz, "Terrorists' Use of Internet Spreads," *USA Today,* 20 February 2005, accessed 18 November 2010, http://www.usatoday.com/money/industries/technology/2005-02-20-cyber-terror-usat_x.htm.

15. Barton Gellman, "Cyber-Attacks by Al Qaeda Feared," *Washington Post,* 27 June 2002.

16. Interview with Ron Dick in "Cyberwar!" *PBS Frontline,* 18 March 2003, accessed 2 November 2010, http://www.pbs.org/wgbh/pages/frontline/shows/cyberwar/interviews/dick.html.

17. Siobhan Gorman, "Electricity Grid in U.S. Penetrated by Spies," *Wall Street Journal,* 8 April 2009, accessed 8 January 2010, http://online.wsj.com/article/SB123914805204099085.html.

18. Denning, "Testimony."

19. Vassilis Prevelakis and Diomidis Spinellis, "The Athens Affair: How Some Extremely Smart Hackers Pulled Off the Most Audacious Cell-Network Break-in Ever," *IEEE Spectrum,* July 2007, accessed 23 March 2010, www.spectrum.ieee.org.

20. John Markoff, "Vast Spy System Loots Computers in 103 Countries," *New York Times,* 28 March 2009, http://www.nytimes.com/2009/03/29/technology/29spy.html.

21. Mica Rosenberg, "Mexico Drug Cartels Use Gory Videos to Spread Fear," Reuters, 4 August 2010, accessed 5 November 2010, http://www.reuters.com/article/idUSTRE6734E720100804.

22. Mohammed M. Hafez, *Suicide Bombers in Iraq: The Strategy and Ideology of Martyrdom* (Washington, D.C.: United States Institute of Peace, 2007).

23. Ibid., 169–70.

24. Susan B. Glasser and Steve Coll, "The Web as a Weapon," *Washington Post,* 9 August 2005, accessed 2 November 2010, http://washingtonpost.com/wp-dyn/content/article/2005/08/08/AR2005080801018.html.

25. Gordon Lubold, "Internet Aids Terrorist Recruiting, Radicalization, Pentagon Says," *Christian Science Monitor,* 10 March 2010, accessed 14 October 2010, http://www.csmonitor.com/USA/Military/2010/0310/Internet-aids-terrorist-recruiting-radicalization-Pentagon-says.

26. Mark Schone and Reheb El-Buri, "Fort Hood: Hasan Asked Awlaki if It Was Okay to Kill American Soldiers," *ABC News,* 23 December 2009, accessed 14 November 2010, http://abcnews.go.com/Blotter/FtHoodInvestigation/fort-hood-hasan-asked-awlaki-kill-american-soldiers/story?id=9410718.

27. Sebastion Rotella, "A World Wide Web of Terrorist Plotting," *Los Angeles Times,* 16 April 2007, accessed 12 November 2010, http://articles.latimes.com/print/2007/apr/16/world/fg-net16.

28. Sam Jones, "Muslim Convert Colleen LaRose, aka Jihad Jane, Faces Terror Charges," *Guardian,* 10 March 2010, accessed 5 November 2010, http://www.guardian.co.uk/world/2010/mar/10/colleen-larose-jihad-jane-charges.

29. Ibid.

30. "Cyberwar!" Public Broadcasting Corporation, *Frontline,* 24 April 2003, accessed 16 July 2010, http://www.pbs.org/wgbh/pages/frontline/shows/cyberwar; Richard Clarke, *Your Government Failed You: Breaking the Cycle of National Security Disasters* (New York: HarperCollins, 2008), 302.

31. Nakashima, "FBI Director Warns."

32. Clay Wilson, "Botnets, Cybercrime, and Cyberterrorism: Vulnerabilities and Policy Issues for Congress," CRS Report for Congress, 29 January 2008, 7–8.

33. Brian Krebs, "Report: Russian Hacker Forums Fueled Georgia Cyber Attacks," *Washington Post,* 16 October 2008, accessed 3 November 2010, http://voices.washingtonpost.com/securityfix/2008/10/report_russian_hacker_forums_f.html.

34. Richard Adhikari, "Stuxnet: Dissecting the Worm," *TechNewsWorld,* 16 August 2010, accessed 4 November 2010, http://www.technewsworld.com/story/70622.html?wlc=1290297541.

35. Cassell Bryan-Low and Sven Grundberg, "WikiLeaks' Supporters Launch Cyber Assault," *Wall Street Journal,* 9 December 2010, A19.

36. See "Securing Britain in an Age of Uncertainty: The Strategic Defence and Security Review," November 2010, http://www.direct.gov.uk/prod_consum_dg/groups/dg_digitalassets/@dg/@en/documents/digitalasset/dg_191634.pdf; and *BBC News,* "Cyber Attacks and Terrorism Head Threats Facing UK," 18 October 2010, accessed 10 November 2010, http://www.bbc.co.uk/news/uk-11562969.

6 Maritime Terrorism

Peter Chalk

WITH THE COLLAPSE OF THE SOVIET UNION AND THE European Communist bloc in the late 1980s, many analysts confidently assumed that the international system was on the threshold of an era of unprecedented peace and stability. Politicians, academics, and diplomats alike increasingly began to forecast the imminent establishment of a "new world order" that would be managed by liberal democratic institutions and that would develop within the context of an integrated global economy based on the principles of the free market.[1] As this unprecedented interstate structure emerged and took root, observers predicted that destabilizing threats to national and international security would decline commensurately.

However, the initial euphoria that was evoked by the end of the Cold War has steadily been replaced by a growing apprehension that global stability not only has not been achieved but has, in fact, been decisively undermined by transnational security threats, or so-called "gray-area phenomena." These threats, which cannot be readily defeated by the traditional defenses that states have erected to protect their territories and populaces, exploit the remarkable fluidity that currently characterizes international politics—a setting in which it is no longer exactly apparent who can do what, to whom, and with what means. Moreover, it has become increasingly apparent that in the contemporary era the readiness to inflict violence and death is being used by the politically and ideologically weak not so much as a means of expressing identity but more intrinsically as a way of creating it.[2]

In simple terms, the geopolitical landscape that presently confronts the global community lacks the relative stability of the linear Cold War division between East and West. Today's dangers, rather than having the familiar character of overt military aggression stemming from a clearly defined, state-based source, by contrast have become increasingly opaque, diffuse, and amorphous.[3]

The "maritime commons" is particularly conducive to these types of nonstate threat contingencies, given its vast, relatively opaque, and largely unregulated nature.[4] Covering 139,768,200 square miles (more than two-thirds of the Earth's surface), most of this environment is designated as "high seas," beyond the strict jurisdiction of any one state and therefore, by definition, anarchic. These "over the horizon" oceans are fringed and linked by a complex lattice of territorial waters, estuaries, and riverine systems that are, in many cases, poorly monitored and exist in terms of internationally recognized jurisprudence as entirely distinct and independent entities.[5] Combined, these various traits and practices have imbued the planet's oceans with the unpredictable and lawless qualities that can make life on the world's oceans, as Thomas Hobbes once famously wrote, "nasty, brutish, and short."[6]

One particular threat that security officials have begun to take more seriously in the past several years is the exploitation by terrorist groups of the maritime commons to further their logistical and operational designs. Indeed, analysts in various countries now appear to believe that the next major strike against Western interests is as likely to emanate from sea, space, or cyberspace as from land.[7]

This chapter will examine the scope and dimensions of maritime terrorism in the modern age. It will discuss the reasons why militant extremists have traditionally shunned non-land-based theaters, and the factors that appear to have caused a shift in this operational calculus. The chapter goes on to examine specific terrorist scenarios, including the use of the maritime environment to exact mass-casualty attacks, cause economic disruption, and enable the movement of weapons and personnel.

Maritime Terrorism: A Changing Operational Calculus?

Historically, the world's oceans have not been a major locus of terrorist activity. Part of the reason for this has to do with the fact that most terrorist groups are either not located near coastal regions or do not have the means to extend their physical reach beyond purely local theaters. There are also several practical problems associated with carrying out waterborne strikes. Most intrinsically, operating at sea requires terrorists to have mariner skills, access to appropriate assault and transport vessels, and certain specialist capabilities (for example, surface and underwater demolition techniques).[8] Limited resources have traditionally made such options unavailable to most groups.

Closely related to these obstacles is the inherently conservative nature of terrorists in terms of their chosen attack modalities. Precisely because groups are constrained by limited access to finance and skill sets, most have deliberately chosen to follow the course of least resistance, adhering to tested methods that are known to work, offer a reasonably high chance of success, and the consequences of which can be relatively easily predicted.[9] Stated more directly, in a world of finite human and material assets, the costs and unpredictability associated with expanding into the maritime realm have typically trumped any potential benefits that might be garnered from initiating such a change in operational direction.

A further consideration has to do with the nature of maritime targets themselves, which generally are out of sight on the open ocean and therefore removed from immediate public and media attention (something that is particularly true of commercial vessels). An attack on a ship is simply less likely to elicit the same publicity, either in scope or immediacy, as strikes on land-based targets, which are far more accessible to public view and the media (although, as is discussed below, this may not hold with respect to contingencies involving heavily laden cruise liners and ferries).[10] This consideration is important because terrorism, at its root, is a tactic that can be effective only if it is able to *visibly* demonstrate its salience and relevance through the "propaganda of the deed."[11] Rather like the philosopher's tree falling in the forest, if no one observes the event, does it have any real significance?

In spite of these considerations, over the past decade there has been a modest yet clearly discernible spike in high-profile terrorist incidents at sea. Just as importantly, a number of significant maritime terrorist plots have either been aborted or prevented prior to execution. This heightened level of activity has galvanized fears in the West that terrorists, especially militants connected with Al Qaeda's international jihadist network, are developing the capability and intent to conduct highly damaging attacks at sea. If this is in fact the case, why might terrorists be seeking to expand their operational agenda to the maritime environment?

Three possible rationales would seem to have relevance. First, attacks at sea, especially on passenger vessels, constitute a viable means for inflicting "mass coercive punishment" on enemy populations. Second, maritime strikes offer terrorists an additional way to cause economic destabilization—by closing sea lanes, interrupting oil and gas production and transport, and the like. Third, in several respects the global shipborne container system provides extremists and militants with a ready logistical channel for the covert movement of weapons and personnel. Each of these potential motivational drivers is discussed in more detail below.

Maritime Terrorism as a Means of Causing Mass Casualties

Ever since the attacks of 9/11, the common wisdom that terrorists were prepared to draw the line on mass casualties has been turned on its head.[12] The suicide strikes on the Pentagon and World Trade Center, which collectively killed nearly 3,000, have been followed by a series of devastating bombings around the world, where the intent has clearly been to inflict as much death and suffering as possible. Although most concern for security has focused on land-based venues as the most fruitful targets for this objective, maritime assets could realistically be targeted in an act of mass-casualty terrorism.

Passenger ships, like aircraft, concentrate large numbers of people in a single confined space, which theoretically makes ships ideal venues for carrying out attacks that are intended to maximize civilian casualties. However, not all vessels have the same vulnerabilities in this regard. Cruise liners, while large and highly visible symbols of Western wealth, are constructed with safety as the foremost priority. Hulls are double-constructed, and in most cases, interiors are compartmentalized with largely (though not fully) watertight bulkhead systems in place.[13] Overcoming these safeguards to sink such a ship would require, at a minimum, several highly powerful bombs, as well as a sophisticated understanding of the structural integrity of the intended target, particularly in terms of being able to identify locations where simultaneous explosions could be expected to cause the most damage. As a result, most authorities agree that attempting to sink a cruise ship would be an extremely difficult proposition that is probably beyond the existing capabilities of known terrorist groups.[14]

By contrast, ramming a large ship using a fast inshore attack craft has a far greater prospect of causing extensive damage. Such vessels are cheap, easy to handle, and anonymous enough to mingle with other marine traffic, particularly at ports of call where harbor patrols or surveillance are not extensive.[15] Even in these instances, however, the prospect of causing a critical breach is questionable. As the attacks against the *USS Cole* in 2000 and the *MV Limburg* in 2002 highlight, if the site of the impact is not at a weak point in the craft's skeletal design, critically damaging a large, oceangoing vessel is unlikely.[16]

If a cruise ship were to be the subject of a terrorism attack, the most likely scenario would be an onboard assault. Although not as catastrophic or spectacular as sinking the entire vessel, a strike of this sort could still elicit considerable damage if properly timed and executed. The 1985 hijacking by Palestinian terrorists of the Italian cruise ship *Achille Lauro* is an example of such an attack, although in this instance only one person was killed. Several scenarios are possible, including bombing venues where passengers routinely congregate for relaxation or recreation (such as restaurants, cinemas, and casinos); staging a series of random killings or hostage takings using weapons that had been pre-deployed on the ship; carrying out localized acts of arson in areas where fire doors are absent or where sprinklers and alarms have been disabled; or contaminating the food supply with easy-to-grow toxins and bacteria such as salmonella, *E. coli,* and botulism (all of which are colorless, odorless, and tasteless).[17] Several recent instances of widespread viral illnesses and food-borne diseases aboard cruise ships show just how vulnerable a large group of closely confined people can be, even when the infection is unintentional. A well-planned attack could easily be devastating.

The most obvious point of vulnerability for a cruise ship in terms of an onboard attack would be when it stops at a port of call. It is a routine practice for major operators to thoroughly vet and clear their crew and maintenance staff, but many shore-based service employees who have access (in some cases unhindered) to ships at overseas docks may not have undergone any comprehensive background checking. These personnel, who are generally not paid well and therefore may be receptive to bribes, offer terrorists a ready conduit through which to smuggle aboard and stash weapons and explosives or plant contaminants for a subsequent attack. In the words of one ex-defense intelligence official, "Overseas ports of call represent the single biggest, but mostly overlooked threat to the cruise line industry."[18]

Passenger ferries constitute a different danger altogether: As potential mass-casualty targets, these vessels represent the "softest of the soft." Moreover, many of the ships currently in operation cater to a customer base in the tens of hundreds, if not thousands, and, at least in the developing world, sail at, or well over, design-capacity limits. Overburdened and unwieldy, they therefore provide an ideal target for attacks that are designed to maximize the body count.

What differentiates passenger ferries from cruise ships in terms of potential mass-casualty attacks is that ferries' levels of safety and security leave them acutely susceptible. Several factors account for this inherent vulnerability. First, current security measures at passenger terminals vary greatly and, even in developed littoral states such as the Netherlands, Canada, the United Kingdom, and the United States, are not nearly as extensive as those for cruise liners (much less those for aircraft). The simple reason for this is the need to move high volumes of traffic as quickly and efficiently as possible, which necessarily precludes carrying out extensive checks on baggage, cars, trucks, and people.[19] Indeed, even the institution of minimal precautionary measures can generate huge delays and backlogs. The popular Dover–Calais ferry provides a case in point. In the immediate aftermath of the July 2005 London Underground bombings, all motorists bound for Calais were subjected to a slightly more rigorous regime of predeparture scrutiny. Although individual inspections and questions generally took no more than a few minutes per vehicle, combined they served to create traffic backups that extended over four miles.[20]

Second, the vetting of those who work on board ferries is ad hoc and partial, reflecting the seasonal and highly transient nature of these personnel. Background checks, to the extent that they occur, are generally aimed at verifying past employment and rarely entail wider criminal investigations. Throughout much of Asia and Africa, it is unlikely that any consistent form of examination takes place at all, largely because owner/operators lack the means (and frequently the willingness) to do so, largely for reasons of cost. Maritime experts generally concur that the absence of effective screening of staff and crew represents a significant point of vulnerability for commercial ferry companies, providing extremists with an ideal opening to covertly place insiders on board vessels for strike or logistical purposes. Several commentators warn that these dangers are further exacerbated—at least in the context of the post-9/11 international Islamist threat—by the overwhelming numbers of North Africans, Arabs, Filipinos (Catholic and Muslim), and Indonesians that owner-operators typically hire to fill service positions on their ships. This employment bias is viewed as potentially worrisome in that it affords Al Qaeda cohorts and affiliates with a perfect cover and allows them to take advantage of one of the key principles emphasized in jihadist field-training manuals: to "hide in plain sight" whenever possible.[21]

Third (and in common with cruise liners), ferries sail along predefined routes according to set departure and arrival times. By definition, these schedules have to be made widely available to the paying public through a broad array of media, ranging from travel guides and port terminals to the Internet.[22] Itineraries are, in short, both fixed and highly transparent, providing terrorists with a reasonably accurate cartographic picture that can be used to gauge the point at which vessels are most susceptible to attack and interception. The Abu Sayyaf Group in the southern Philippines provides a good example of an organization that has conspicuously planned many of its maritime assaults around information of this sort.[23]

Finally, there are certain features in the specific construction of ferries that serve to weaken their wider structural integrity and safety, something that is particularly true of those that transport vehicles. Colloquially known as "ro-ros" (roll on, roll off), these ships are deliberately built with large, open car decks on the lower level for the efficient embarkation and disembarkation of cars, trucks, vans, and other vehicles. Crucially, this particular design format makes these vessels acutely sensitive to subtle shifts in their center of gravity, largely because they necessarily lack stabilizing bulkheads on their lower sections. Undue movements of improperly secured automobiles or sudden accumulations of even small amounts of water are especially likely to trigger such effects and could, depending on the severity of the situation at hand, cause a ship to list or even to capsize.[24]

The 2004 bombing of *SuperFerry 14* in the Philippines graphically underscores the potential ease with which mass casualties could result from a planned attack against a passenger ferry. The operation left at least 116 people dead yet involved a total planning cycle of only a couple of months. It was executed with a crude improvised explosive device (sixteen sticks of dynamite secreted in a hollowed-out television set) and cost approximately U.S. $400 to pull off. As one senior official with the Philippine Anti-Terrorism Task Force remarked, the incident demonstrated the acute vulnerability of ferries to sabotage and caused fears of copycat strikes by other groups intent on maximizing civilian damage with the least amount of expenditure.[25]

Maritime Terrorism to Cause Economic Destabilization

Besides mass casualties, it has been suggested by some researchers that the maritime realm offers terrorists a feasible theater in which to execute attacks that are designed to trigger mass economic destabilization.[26] This has particular relevance to the global Al Qaeda network, which has repeatedly affirmed that carrying out attacks that can deliver a crippling blow to the Western financial, commercial, and trading systems is the most effective way of waging its self-defined jihad against the United States and its partner nations. This tactical bent was given concrete expression in 2004, when Osama bin Laden, Al Qaeda's leader, announced a "bleed to bankruptcy" strategy that was explicitly aimed at destroying the financial and commercial lifeline of the global capitalist system:

> This in addition to our having experience in using guerrilla warfare and the war of attrition to fight tyrannical superpowers, as we, alongside the mujahidin, bled Russia for ten years, until it went bankrupt and was forced to withdraw in defeat . . . so we are continuing this policy in bleeding America to the point of bankruptcy.[27]

A number of scenarios have been posited by which an act of maritime terrorism could generate negative, cascading economic effects. One of the most commonly postulated is to scuttle a ship in a narrow sea lane of communication (SLOC) in order to disrupt the mechanics of the "just-enough, just-in-time" international trading system.[28] Several choke points have been identified as possible locations for such an attack, including the Panama Canal, the Suez Canal, the Malacca Straits, the Singapore Straits, the Strait of Hormuz, the Bab el-Mandeb passage, and the Bosporus and Turkish straits. Commenting on the economic impact that could result from delivery delays due to the closing of one of these SLOCs, Michael Richardson of the Singaporean Institute for Southeast Asia Studies points out the following:

> The very nature and scale of the globalized trading system makes it vulnerable to terrorist attack. Seaborne trade and its land connections . . . have become increasingly open . . . built on integrated supply chains that feed components and other materials to users just before they are required and just in the right amounts. That way, inventory costs are kept low. . . . [I]f [these supply chains] are disrupted, it will have repercussions around the world, profoundly affecting business [stability].[29]

Another possibility often highlighted is the explosion of an oil tanker, or the detonation of a radiological dispersal device (aka "dirty bomb") hidden inside a container ship, to shut down a major commercial port. The assumption here is that halting the operations of a prominent import–export terminal would disrupt supply lines, trigger rapid price increases, and ultimately damage consumer confidence both nationally and internationally. In 2002 the consulting firm Booz Allen Hamilton sponsored a simulation exercise to estimate the economic damage that would result from the shutdown of all American seaports for a period of twelve days. The scenario showed that the United States would lose roughly $58 billion in revenue and that there would be significant disruptions to the movement of trade, both within the country and internationally.[30] That same year, a two-week lockdown of twenty-nine ports along the western American seaboard due to a labor dispute resulted in cargo delays of $467 million, in addition to removing between 0.4 and 1.1 percent of nominal gross domestic product from major Asian exporters such as Hong Kong, Singapore, and Malaysia.[31] The residual effects of a terrorist attack would likely last much longer.

Finally, analysts have suggested that terrorists might look at blowing up pipelines, tankers, and offshore platforms as a means of causing widespread economic damage.[32] The suicide strike on the oil tanker *M/V Limburg* in 2002, in which a small boat rammed the ship's hull while it was in port, is taken as a case in point. Despite the fact that the attack caused only minor damage to the ship, the incident immediately caused a short-term increase in the price of Brent crude oil of forty-eight cents a barrel and, due to the tripling of war premiums levied on ships calling at Aden, resulted in a 93-percent drop in container terminal throughput that cost Yemen $3.8 million a month in lost port revenue.[33] More telling was a statement released by bin Laden in the aftermath of the attack, which confirmed Al Qaeda's intention to target Western oil interests as part of a protracted campaign of asymmetric economic warfare:

> If a boat that didn't cost US$1,000 managed to devastate an oil tanker of that magnitude, so imagine the extent of the danger that threatens the West's commercial lifeline, which is petroleum. The operation of attacking the French tanker is not merely an attack against a tanker, it is an attack against international transport lines.[34]

Although all of these scenarios are certainly possible, an attempt to decisively disrupt the contemporary international trading system through a campaign of terrorism would face obstacles on numerous levels. With the exception of the Suez Canal, very few SLOCs truly have no detours, and most would impose, at most, only one or two days' extra transit time in the event of a closing.[35] Effectively blocking a choke point would be an extremely tall undertaking and even in the case of very narrow straits would require several vessels to be scuttled at once—a formidable and technically demanding task, one that would be very hard to keep secret long enough to carry through.[36] Contingencies involving oil tankers, either as targets in their own right or as floating bombs, also pose problems. These vessels are hard to critically damage if they are not struck exactly at a weak point (as was demonstrated in the suicide attack on the *MV Limburg*), and the weapons potential of oil is questionable. Unless it vents in liquid form and mixes with air in the correct ratio, the probability of it fully igniting is low.[37] Even if this did occur, the lateral force of any subsequent explosion would likely be contained by the tanker's hull, thus forcing the destructive energy upwards. There would be little (if any) prospect of such an event closing down a major port.[38] Equally, while it might be feasible for a group to smuggle a dirty bomb in an empty container (assuming that the necessary material could be procured in the first place), the ensuing damage and fallout from such an attack would be mostly localized and unlikely to affect all import–export operations, especially from geographically expansive terminals such as Long Beach, Los Angeles, or Rotterdam.[39]

In sum, although maritime attacks have the theoretical potential to deliver a strategic blow to the global economy, the likelihood of this occurring is not high. At most, the effects would probably be localized and short term, as indeed they were in the case of the *MV Limburg* as well as the assaults on the Khor al-Amaya and al-Basra oil terminals two years later.[40] Moreover, it is arguable whether purely economically oriented attacks truly animate the minds of terrorists, their public rhetoric notwithstanding. In the absence of human fatalities, such strikes would do little to satisfy the desire for immediate, visible, headline-grabbing effects—not to mention the bloodlust—that has become so intrinsic to militant extremist action in the post-9/11 era.

Use of the Maritime Commons to Move Weapons and Personnel

Approximately 112,000 merchant vessels, 6,500 ports and harbor facilities, and 45,000 shipping bureaus constitute the contemporary international maritime transport system, linking roughly 225 coastal nations, dependent territories, and island states.[41] This expansive network, which handles around eighty percent of the world's commercial freight, has been the focus of considerable attention from maritime security analysts and intelligence officials, largely because it can be a viable logistical conduit for the covert movement of terrorist weapons and personnel. There are at least six factors that support this perception of vulnerability.

First, the sheer volume of commercial freight that is moved by container ships effectively eliminates the possibility of comprehensive checks once cargo reaches its port of destination. Experts universally acknowledge that trying to inspect all incoming cargo, or even a significant random sample, is neither logistically practicable nor economically tenable given the sheer numbers of crates involved.[42] Even in those few facilities with advanced X-ray and gamma scanning technologies, inspection rates remain relatively minimal. In the United States, for instance, a mere 10 percent of the roughly six million containers that arrive in the country every year can be expected to undergo some sort of scrutiny; this equates to roughly one to two containers out of every twenty.[43]

Second, the highly complex nature of the containerized supply chain creates a plethora of opportunities for terrorist infiltration. Unlike other cargo vessels that typically handle payloads for a single customer loaded at port, a given container ship will deal with goods and commodities from hundreds of companies and individuals, most of which are received and transported from inland warehouses that have widely varying levels of on-site security. For even a standard commercial consignment, numerous agents and parties would be involved: the exporter, the importer, the freight forwarder, warehouse workers, a customs broker, excise inspectors, commercial trucking firms and/or railroads, dockworkers, possibly harbor feeder craft, and the ocean carrier itself. Each point of transfer along this continuum represents a potential source of vulnerability for the overall security and integrity of the cargo, providing terrorists with numerous openings to "stuff" or otherwise tamper with the crates.[44]

Third, and directly bearing on the above, is the rudimentary nature of the locks that are used to seal containers. Existing devices offer little, if any protection, and often consist of nothing more than a plastic tie or bolt that can be quickly cut and then reattached using a combination of superglue and heat.[45] Most commercial shipping companies have been reluctant to develop more-resistant mechanisms given the costs involved. A standard plastic seal can be purchased for a few cents if ordered in bulk, whereas more robust versions might run to several hundreds of dollars. Moves to develop so-called "smart boxes," which are equipped with global positioning system (GPS) transponders and radio-frequency identification devices that emit signals if they are interfered with, have run into similar problems and had not, at the time of writing, been embraced with any real degree of enthusiasm by the international maritime transport industry.[46]

Fourth, the effectiveness of point-of-origin inspections for containerized freight is highly questionable. Many resource-constrained states in Asia and Africa fail to routinely vet dockworkers, do not require that truck drivers present valid identification before entering an off-loading facility, and frequently overlook the need to ensure that all cargo is accompanied by an accurate manifest. Even richer nations in Western Europe and North America are not devoid of these types of deficiencies. For instance, privacy regulations in the Netherlands require that dockworkers grant their permission for a comprehensive security vetting. In the words of one Dutch expert, "I would be amazed if harbor employees at Rotterdam, Antwerp, or Amsterdam were required to undergo any form of mandatory background criminal check."[47] In the United States some 11,000 truck drivers regularly enter and leave the Long Beach terminal in Los Angeles with only a standard commercial license. Even Singapore, which runs arguably one of the world's most sophisticated commercial maritime terminals, does not require shipping companies to declare goods on their vessels if they are only transiting through the country's port, meaning that the government does not know what is being transported on the vast bulk of carriers that transship through the city-state.[48]

Fifth, commercial shipping is a well-tested means of smuggling people around the world without being detected. Illegal migrants and stowaways have frequently been able to enter a third country posing as sailors, which gives them the right to go ashore (while their vessel is docked) without being subjected to the types of identity checks and procedures that are used for normal passengers. The fear is that terrorists could exploit this modus operandi to aid the placement of their own cadres around the world.[49] The 2002 apprehension of eight Pakistani militants in Trieste, Italy, after they presented false papers showing them to be crew members of the freighter *Twillinger* illustrates the potential.[50]

Finally, the inconsistent and ad hoc procedures governments use to register ships arguably allow terrorists an opportunity to build and consolidate their own network of oceangoing vessels. Roughly 50 percent of the world's fleet sails under so-called flags of convenience (FoCs), the eight principal ones being Panama, Liberia, the Bahamas, Malta, Cyprus, Belize, Liberia, and

Honduras. A ship can be registered in any one of these countries from the high seas, all provide specific mechanisms that allow anonymity, and each offers extremely cheap annual tonnage fees.[51] Western intelligence and security analysts have repeatedly warned that this lack of transparency and regulation works to the direct advantage of terrorists, and in many ways mimics the use of tax havens and offshore bank accounts to hide financial assets.[52]

Over the last several years there have been a number of publicized cases in which terrorists have transported weapons and personnel by sea. One month after 9/11, an Egyptian was found in a container bound for Halifax, Nova Scotia. The stowaway, who was carrying U.S. airport maps and security passes, had transformed his crate into a sophisticated living space complete with bedding, cooking facilities, and a latrine system. He disappeared after being granted bail in Italy, the country where he was initially arrested.[53]

In 2002 the Palestinian Authority used a 4,000-ton freighter, the *Karine A,* to smuggle a wide assortment of Russian and Iranian weapons, including Katyusha rockets (with a range of twenty kilometers), antitank missiles, long-range mortar bombs, mines, sniper rifles, ammunition, and more than two tons of high explosives. The shipment, which was seized off Sinai on the Red Sea and estimated at $100 million, was allegedly to be used for attacks against Jewish targets in Israel and the Occupied Territories.[54]

A year later, the owner of an Egyptian-registered fishing trawler, the *Abu Hassan,* was recruited by the Lebanese organization Hezbollah to carry out support missions. When Israeli naval commandos intercepted the vessel thirty-five nautical miles off the coast from Haifa, they discovered a complex weapons and logistics consignment composed of fuses for 122-mm Qassam rockets, electronic time-delay fuses, a training video for carrying out suicide attacks, and two sets of CD-ROMs containing detailed bomb-making information.[55]

In 2004 the Palestinian groups Fatah and Hamas used a specially modified marine cargo container to covertly deploy two operatives for a suicide attack against the Port of Ashdod in Israel. The cadres, who were smuggled into Israeli territory from the Gaza Strip, were hidden inside a secret compartment that also contained their weapons, food, water, and sleeping accommodations.[56]

In addition to these known instances, there have been repeated claims that various terrorist movements have used FoCs to build their own maritime network. U.S. and other officials believe that at its height, Al Qaeda owned at least fifteen and possibly as many as thirty vessels, all of which were flagged under so-called "open-registry" countries.[57] While it remains unclear whether bin Laden actually controlled any ships directly, it is known, for instance, that the Liberation Tigers of Tamil Eelam (the "Tamil Tigers"), an insurgent group in northern Sri Lanka, operated its own fleet of oceangoing container carriers.[58] Referred to as the *Kadalpura* (literally "sea pigeons"), these vessels were mostly registered out of Panama, Honduras, or Liberia and played a critical role in transporting weapons and other war-related material back to the Sri Lankan war theater.[59]

These cases reflect the ubiquitous nature of the container supply network and the relative ease with which it can be diverted for terrorist purposes. As international trade grows more dependent on maritime freight, and as this system increases in complexity, one can expect subversive actors to exploit maritime transport for logistical purposes more and more regularly. Such a trend will likely be further encouraged by the continued reluctance of the shipping sector to accept greater regulation and oversight for fear that this will reduce cost efficiency. The use of FoCs exemplifies this mind-set, creating what Stephen Flynn, a senior security advisor on the Council of Foreign Relations and a former Coast Guard officer, has aptly described as "managed anarchy."[60]

Conclusion

In many respects the maritime environment constitutes a useful theater for terrorist operations because of its expanse, lack of regulation, direct access to wide-flung parts of the world, and general importance for global trade. However, it is essential that the overall level of threat is put in context. Numerous attack scenarios are possible, but relatively few are likely or fall within the purview or capacity limits of known groups. Spectacular events such as sinking a cruise ship, simultaneously scuttling vessels to block critical choke points, or exploding an oil tanker as a floating bomb seem to be more in the realm of fantasy than fact. By contrast, scenarios involving exploitation of the supply chain for logistical purposes, or the critical breach of a passenger ferry to cause mass casualties, do represent realistic dangers. It is these contingencies that security analysts need to focus on in terms of threat mitigation and consequence management.

Notes

1. See, for example, *World Economic Outlook* (Washington, D.C.: International Monetary Fund, 1991), 26–27.

2. "Terrorism and the Warfare of the Weak," *Guardian*, 27 October 1993.

3. Peter Chalk, *Non-Military Security and Global Order: The Impact of Extremism, Violence and Chaos on National and International Security* (London: Macmillan, 2000), 1–2.

4. See Chapter 1 for a definition of the global commons.

5. Rupert Herbert-Burns, "Terrorism in the Early 21st Century Maritime Domain," in *The Best of Times, the Worst of Times: Maritime Security in the Asia-Pacific*, ed. Joshua Ho and Catherine Zara Raymond (Singapore: World Scientific, 2005), 157.

6. Thomas Hobbes, *Leviathan* (New York: Macmillan, 1904), 84; facsimile from Google Books, http://books.google.com.

7. This assertion is based on author interviews conducted in Singapore, the United States, London, and Amsterdam between August and September 2005. See also Michael Richardson, *A Time Bomb for Global Trade* (Singapore: ISEAS, 2004); and Gal Luft and Anne Korin, "Terrorism Goes to Sea," *Foreign Affairs* (November/December 2004).

8. Author interviews, Institute of Defense and Strategic Studies (IDSS), Singapore, September 2005. See also Paul Wilkinson, "Terrorism and the Maritime Environment," and Brian Jenkins, Bonnie Cordes, Karen Gardela, and Geraldine Petty, "A Chronology of Terrorist Attacks and Other Criminal Actions Against Maritime Targets," both in *Violence at Sea*, ed. Eric Ellen (Paris: International Chamber of Commerce, 1986).

9. This point is directly taken up by Bruce Hoffman in "The Contemporary Terrorist Mindset: Targeting, Tactics and Likely Future Trends," *Intelligence and National Security* 11, no. 2 (1996).

10. Wilkinson, "Terrorism and the Maritime Environment," 34; Jenkins et al., "A Chronology of Terrorist Attacks," 65.

11. For a discussion on this aspect of the terrorist phenomenon, see Peter Chalk, *West European Terrorism and Counter-Terrorism: The Evolving Dynamic* (London: Macmillan, 1996), Chapter 1.

12. This wisdom was perhaps most famously summed up in Brian Jenkins's assertion that "terrorists want a lot of people watching, not a lot of people dead," cited in Bruce Hoffman, *Inside Terrorism* (London: Victor Gollancz, 1998), 198. See also Brian Jenkins, *The Likelihood of Nuclear Terrorism* (Santa Monica: RAND, 1985), 6.

13. It would be impossible to construct a cruise liner that has a fully compartmentalized watertight system in place because the recreational and luxury-oriented nature of these vessels requires an onboard configuration that is as open and accessible as safety limits allow.

14. Author interviews, maritime security analysts, London and Kuala Lumpur, September 2005.

15. Martin Murphy, "Maritime Terrorism: The Threat in Context," *Jane's Intelligence Review* (February 2006): 23. In the United States and most European ports, these small, fast craft would have somewhat less opportunity to cause damage compared to in other areas of the world, for the extensive activity around cruise ships as they enter and leave dock provides an effective outer layer of defense against this type of attack.

16. See, for instance, Herbert-Burns, "Terrorism in the Early 21st Century," 164–65.

17. Author interviews, government officials and security analysts, London, September 2005. See also Joshua Sinai, "Future Trends in Worldwide Maritime Terrorism," *Connections* 3, no. 1 (March 2004): 65, http://wwwcianoet.org/olj/co/co_mar04e.pdf; and Eric Watkins, "Shipping Fraud Heightens Terror Threat," *BBC News*, 6 February 2002, http://news.bbc.co.uk/2/hi/asia-pacific/1804146.stm.

18. Author interview, ex-defense intelligence official, London, September 2005.

19. In Britain, for instance, cars and coaches are inspected on a random, selective basis. Freight vehicles are rarely if ever checked. As one former defense intelligence official opined, "Ferries are their own worst enemies: [The industry is] designed to transport a high volume of people as conveniently, cheaply and quickly as possible. Most operators simply do not have the infrastructure—or willingness—to carry out a comprehensive regimen of security checks" (author interview, former UK defense intelligence official, London, September 2005).

20. Ibid.

21. Author interviews, maritime analysts and intelligence officials, Singapore, London, Amsterdam, and Washington, D.C., August and September 2005.

22. In the United Kingdom, for instance, the schedules and itineraries of all ferry companies operating out of the country can be accessed at www.ferries.com.

23. Author interviews, Ministry of Home Affairs and Ministry of Foreign Affairs, Singapore, September 2005.

24. According to one U.S.-based maritime security analyst, as little as a foot of water accumulated in a single location could upset a ship's center of gravity through the so-called "free-surface effect" (author interview, Washington D.C., August 2005). It should be noted that certain countries have moved to address this specific structural vulnerability. In the UK, for instance, ferries are now constructed with drains in their car decks to prevent the free-surface effect. Many also have additional buoyancy devices, such as air-filled tanks strapped to either side of the vessel (author interviews, UK Customs and Excise officials, London, September 2005).

25. Author interview, Philippine Anti-Terrorism Task Force, Manila, November 2005.

26. Richardson, *Time Bomb;* Herbert-Burns, "Terrorism in the Early 21st Century"; and Catherine Zara Raymond, "Maritime Terrorism—a Risk Assessment: The Australian Dimension," in *The Best of Times,* ed. Ho and Raymond.

27. Bin Laden statement, reproduced in "Full Transcript of bin Laden's Speech," *Aljazeera.net*, 1 November 2004, http://english.aljazeera.net. See also Matthew Hunt, "Bleed to Bankruptcy," *Jane's Intelligence Review* (January 2007): 14–17; "Bin Laden:

Goal Is to Bankrupt the US," *CNN.com*, 1 November 2004, http://www.cnn.com/2004/WORLD/meast/11/01/binladen.tape; and Douglas Jehl and David Johnston, "In Video Message, bin Laden Issues Warning to U.S.," *New York Times*, 30 October 2004.

28. Author interviews, Control Risks Group and Lloyd's, London and Amsterdam, September 2005. See also Raymond, "Maritime Terrorism—a Risk Assessment," 179; and Murphy, "Maritime Terrorism," 20.

29. Richardson, *Time Bomb*, 6–7.

30. "Supply Chain Security," General Accounting Office (GAO) Report to Congress (GAO-08-538), August 2008, 8.

31. Richardson, *Time Bomb*, 66; "Report on Maritime Transport: Risk Factors and Economic Impact," Organization for Economic Cooperation and Development (OECD), Paris, July 2003, 17–18; "Global Issues Brief on the Economic Costs of Terrorism," Department of Foreign Affairs and Trade, Economic Analytical Unit, Canberra, 7 April 2003.

32. See, for instance, Martin Murphy, *Small Boats, Weak States, Dirty Money: Piracy and Maritime Terrorism in the Modern World* (New York: Columbia University Press, 2009), 201–07; Christopher Blanchard, "Al Qaeda: Statements and Evolving Ideology," CRS Report for Congress (RL372759), 20 June 2004, 12; and Herbert-Burns, "Terrorism in the Early 21st Century," 165. It has been estimated that a 4-percent global shortfall in daily supply would result in a 177-percent rise in the price of oil.

33. Ben Sheppard, "Maritime Security Measures," *Jane's Intelligence Review* (March 2003): 55; Richardson, *Time Bomb*, 70; Herbert-Burns, "Terrorism in the 21st Century," 165; Murphy, *Small Boats, Weak States*, 203; and Rashmi Jain, *Securing the Port of New York and New Jersey: Network-Centric Operations Applied to the Campaign Against Terrorism* (New Jersey: Stevens Institute of Technology, 2004), 4.

34. Al Qaeda communiqué, cited in Richardson, *Time Bomb*, 50. See also Brian Whitaker, "Tanker Blast Was Work of Terrorists," *Guardian*, 17 October 2002, http://www.guardian.co.uk/yemen/Story/0,2763,813411,00.htm.

35. By contrast, rerouting around the Cape of Good Hope as opposed to transiting through the Suez Canal would lengthen a vessel's journey by around three weeks, adding an estimated $1.5 to $2 million to an average shipment in terms of extra fuel, time, and labor.

36. Sinking any sizable vessel with a high waterline would require the perpetrating group to have access to a large quantity of explosives, the time and means to transport this material, and the expertise to know where to place bombs to cause a critical breach. These logistical and knowledge barriers would pose formidable barriers for a single attack, much less an assault that targeted two or three ships.

37. This is also true of liquefied natural gas, which has also been posited as a potential improvised explosive device (IED) of the sort that could be used to down a major port. The real threat from such an attack would not be an explosion, but rather a "pool fire" resulting from the deliberate or catastrophic spillage of very cold liquid onto the surface of a harbor.

38. See Murphy, "Maritime Terrorism," 21.

39. The level of contamination from a radiological dispersal device (RDD) would obviously depend on the size of the device and prevailing weather conditions and terrain. However, most analysts have concluded that radiation emitted from an average RDD would be unlikely to kill more than ten people in a sparsely populated area (a city would be a different matter), the majority of whom would die at the immediate site of the blast. See Murphy, *Small Boats, Weak States*, 260; Peter Zimmerman, "Seize the Cesium," *New York Times*, 1 August 2007; and James Ford, "Radiological Dispersal Devices: Assessing the Transnational Threat," *Strategic Forum* 136 (March 1998).

40. In the Khor al-Amaya and al-Basra attacks, two suicide boats were driven toward the terminals but exploded before they made contact. Following the incident, the price of oil rose but quickly fell back, as it did after the *Limburg* incident. See Murphy, *Small Boats, Weak States*, 207; and "Oil Prices Rise on Fears of Attacks on Iraqi Resources," *Taipei Times*, 27 April 2005.

41. Author interviews, Lloyds of London, London, September 2005. See also Herbert-Burns, "Terrorism in the Early 21st Century," 158–59; Sinai, "Future Trends"; "Security in Maritime Transport: Risk Factors and Economic Impact," OECD, Paris, July 2003; and Catherine Meldrum, "Murky Waters: Financing Maritime Terrorism and Crime," *Jane's Intelligence Review* (June 2007): 36.

42. Author interviews, maritime experts and intelligence officials, Singapore, London, and Rotterdam, September 2005. See also John Fritelli, "Port and Maritime Security: Background and Issues for Congress," CRS Report for Congress (RL31733), 30 December 2004, 4; Catherine Zara Raymond, "Maritime Terrorism, A Risk Assessment," in *The Best of Times, the Worst of Times*, ed. Ho and Raymond, 187; N. Brew, "Ripples from 9/11: The U.S. Container Security Initiative and Its Implications for Australia," *Current Issues Brief* 28 (2003): 5; and "Fact Sheet: Cargo Container Security—U.S. Customs and Border Protection Reality," Customs and Border Protection (CBP), October 2004, http://www.cbp.gov/linkhandler/cgov/newsroom/fact_sheets/2004/5percent_myth.ctt/5percent_myth.doc.

43. Robert Block, "Security Gaps Already Plague Ports," *Wall Street Journal*, 23 February 2006.

44. Fritelli, "Port and Maritime Security," 9; James Hoge and Gideon Rose, eds., *How Did This Happen* (New York: Public Affairs, 2001), 188; "Supply Chain Security," 7.

45. See, for instance, J. Saunders, "Marine Vulnerability and the Terrorist Threat," International Chamber of Commerce, International Maritime Bureau, London, 2003, 4.

46. Author interviews, Department of Homeland Security liaison officials, U.S. Embassy, Singapore and London, September 2005. In bulk-order form, these types of technologies would cost at least U.S. $500 per container. Shipping companies have also been reluctant to make such investments given that even more-advanced boxes cannot offer anything approaching one-hundred-percent infallibility.

47. Author interview with a senior analyst from the Control Risks Group in Amsterdam in August 2005. Name withheld by request.

48. This is largely due to a fear that if declarations on all cargoes were made mandatory irrespective of whether or not Singapore was the final port of call, the resulting

red tape would deflect trade north to Malaysia (author interviews, maritime security analysts and government officials, Amsterdam and Singapore, September 2005). See also Block, "Security Gaps Already Plague Ports."

49. Author interviews, maritime security analysts, London, September 2005.

50. Murphy, *Small Boats, Weak States*, 348; "Al-Qaeda's 'Navy'—How Much a Threat?" Centre for Defense Information, 20 August 2003, accessed 2 June 2004, http://www.cdi.org/friendlyversion/printversion.cfm?documentID=16422; John Mintz, "15 Freighters Believed to be Linked to Al Qaeda," *Washington Post*, 31 December 2002; and Meldrum, "Murky Waters," 37.

51. An owner need not be physically present to submit an application to register in such countries; as long as the money is transferred, all registration paperwork can be completed by fax. Ownership can be kept anonymous by permitting corporate ownership of vessels and using nominee shareholders and directors, in addition to having no formal reporting, meeting, or even proof-of-identity requirements.

52. See, for instance, Meldrum, "Murky Waters," 36–39; James Boutilier, "The Best of Times, the Worst of Times: The Global Maritime Outlook 2004," in *The Best of Times, the Worst of Times*, ed. Ho and Raymond, 26–27; and "Brassed Off," *Economist*, 16 May 2002. For a detailed critique of FoCs, see "A Brief Guide to Flags of Convenience," *Global Policy Forum*, International Transportation Federation, 2004.

53. Sinai, "Future Trends," 57; Philip Shenon, "After the War: U.S. Widens Checks at Foreign Ports," *New York Times*, 12 June 2003; Meldrum, "Murky Waters," 39.

54. "IDF Seizes PA Weapons Ship: The *Karine A* Affair," *Jewish Virtual Library*, 3 January 2002, http://www.jewishvirtuallibrary.org/jsource/Peace/paship.html; "Israel's Navy Steps Up to Security Challenge in Wake of Gaza Pull-Out," *JINSA Online*, 31 May 2006, http://jinsa.rg/articles/print.htm; Murphy, *Small Boats, Weak States*, 299.

55. Herbert-Burns, "Terrorism in the Early 21st Century," 165–67; Murphy, *Small Boats, Weak States*, 299–300; Greg Myre, "Israel Says Explosives Expert on Fishing Boat It Seized," *New York Times*, 23 May 2003; "Navy Seizes Hizbollah Bomb Expert and Explosives-Making Materials on Boat," *Israel Insider*, 23 May 2003, http://www.freereoublic.com/focus/f-news/917286/posts.

56. Charles Reinhardt, "Case Study—Attack on the Port of Ashdod," presentation given during an executive training course, "Protecting the Maritime Domain," presented by the U.S. Naval Postgraduate School's Center for Civil–Military Relations, Manila, Philippines, 5–9 February 2007.

57. Meldrum, "Murky Waters," 38; Murphy, *Small Boats, Weak States*, 347–48; David Osler, "Nato Unmasks al-Qa'eda Fleet," *BNET*, 2 February 2002, http://findarticles.com/p/articles/mi_qa3738/is_200202/ai_n9044121/?tag=content;col1; "Al-Qaeda's 'Navy'"; Mintz, "15 Freighters."

58. At their height, the sea pigeons numbered ten to twelve vessels, which procured weapons from a variety of sources in Eastern Europe, Northeast and Southeast Asia, and Southern Africa. Some of the ships known to be in the Liberation Tigers of Tamil Eelam (LTTE) inventory included the *M/V Sunbird* (aka the *Illiyana, Francis,* and *Ichulite*), the *M/V Amazon*, the *M/V Golden Bird* (aka the *Baris, St. Anthony,*

Sophia, and *Parham*), the *M/V Ivy B,* the *M/V Swanee,* the *M/V Julex Comex 3* (aka *Comex-Joux 3*), the *M/V Venus,* the *M/V Emerald,* and the *M/V Point Pedro* (information supplied to author between 2002 and 2007).

59. For more on the sea pigeons and their role in the LTTE terrorist insurgency in Sri Lanka, see Daniel Byman, Peter Chalk, Bruce Hoffman, William Rosenau, and David Brannan, *Trends in Outside Support for Insurgent Movements* (Santa Monica: RAND, 2001), 119–22; Peter Chalk, "Liberation Tigers of Tamil Eelam (LTTE) International Organization and Operations: A Preliminary Analysis," *Commentary* 77, Canadian Security Intelligence Service, 17 March 2000, http://www.csis-scrs.gc.ca/eng/comment/com77e.html; Rohan Gunaratna, "International and Regional Security Implications of the Sri Lankan Tamil Insurgency," Bandaranaike Centre for International Studies, Colombo, Sri Lanka, 1997, 26–29; David Osler, "The Tiger Shipping Empire," *The Island* (Sri Lanka), 31 March 2000, http://www.upali.lk/island/sun/politics.htm; and Murphy, *Small Boats, Weak States,* 349–58.

60. "Brassed Off"; Boutilier, "The Best of Times," 26.

7 Weapons of Mass Destruction and Terrorism

Edward E. Hoffer

SINCE THE TERRORIST ATTACKS OF 11 SEPTEMBER 2001, CONCERN has been rising about the possibility that terrorist groups may get their hands on nuclear, biological, or chemical weapons and use them to carry out attacks of a catastrophic scale against targets in the West. As states find their ability to guarantee the security of their territory under increasing challenge from violent nonstate actors, the security of these highly dangerous weapons and materials stockpiles also seems less and less certain. To weigh the validity of such concerns, however, we must first answer several basic questions.

What really *are* weapons of mass destruction, and how much attention and resources should we direct towards countering their possible use? Are weapons of mass destruction, as often portrayed, an overwhelming threat? Can we prevent their use? Is it possible to respond effectively to them if they are used? These are questions that all leaders in government, business, public institutions, and private institutions, as well as emergency responders at all levels, should focus on. Unfortunately, this is rarely the case. Too often the potential use of a weapon of mass destruction by terrorists, as presented in the media and expounded on by supposed experts, is portrayed by the most unrealistic and worst-case scenarios. This causes many leaders to inappropriately invest scarce resources in measures that do little to prevent the use of these weapons or mitigate their effects. Citizens are also negatively influenced by the same misleading information and too often come to the conclusion that there is little they can do to protect themselves from such weapons.

This chapter discusses the fact that although weapons of mass destruction are now a threat and will remain so for the foreseeable future, they are by their very nature difficult to make, acquire, or use effectively. Thus, their use by terrorist groups is not only highly unlikely, but if they are used, their effects are not likely to be overwhelming. Moreover, by applying consistent and realistic practices at the local, national, and international levels, we can significantly reduce the opportunities for terrorists to acquire and use such weapons.

Changing Definitions

So what *are* weapons of mass destruction? After all, as many commentators have noted, the "mass destruction" that was inflicted on the United States on 11 September 2001 was initiated by weapons no more sophisticated than box cutters. This is an important point that we should not forget as we closely examine our technologically advanced, but potentially lethal, modern environment. This realization has caused the term "weapons of mass destruction (WMD)" to undergo constant review and revision since the 11 September attacks. The term first arose during the latter part of the Cold War and referred specifically to the chemical, biological, and nuclear military weapons developed by the Soviet Union, the United States and its allies, China, and other nations. The emergence of international terrorism, coupled with the demise of the Soviet Union and the fear that scattered sources of highly radioactive materials were no longer secured, resulted in the addition of radiological weapons to the definition.[1] As an example, the United States Department of Defense presently defines WMD as "chemical, biological, radiological or nuclear weapons capable of a high order of destruction or causing mass casualties. . . ."[2]

Even today, the definition of a weapon of mass destruction continues to evolve. Based on the devastating terrorist attacks using conventional high explosives that the twenty-first century has already seen, most analysts now include conventional high explosives on the list of WMD. Reflecting this trend, the FBI goes even further in its definition of what constitutes a weapon of mass destruction by appropriately focusing on the intended outcome and motive of the weapon's use. If it was designed or intended to cause death or serious bodily injury to large numbers of people, then it can be categorized as WMD. Using this expanded approach, the FBI includes the three original weapon types but specifically allows for the addition of other kinds of weapons, such as explosive and incendiary devices, to its definition.[3] Even though this definition correctly identifies explosives as the most common terrorist weapon, and the one most likely to be used in the future, the world's long and unfortunate history and familiarity with explosives tends to diminish our focus on them as the weapon of choice for terrorists. Conversely, our fear of the relatively unknown effects of chemical, biological, and radiological weapons has led many to overemphasize their danger to us. And although we have a good idea of how destructive nuclear weapons can be, the ability of terrorists to acquire and successfully deploy such a weapon is far less certain. An examination of each of these weapons will show that although they continue to be a potential threat, their usability and effectiveness are so limited that terrorists will continue to pursue relatively simple, creative methods of using high explosives in their efforts to achieve a mass-casualty attack.

Many leaders today are often startled to learn that humanity's use of biological and chemical weapons is much older than our use of high explosives. One of the first recorded uses of a biological toxin was in 600 BCE, when the Athenians used the toxins contained in the hellebore plant to contaminate the River Pleithenes. Drinking from the river gave the defenders of Kirrha debilitating stomach cramps and diarrhea, making them unable to defend the city.[4] Roman siege warfare often relied on a chemical weapon created by using sulfur and pitch-soaked wood fires to produce poisonous sulfur dioxide gas. In the eighteenth century the British army deliberately gave blankets contaminated with smallpox to Native American tribes opposing them during the French and Indian War, wiping out a large portion of the population.[5]

The Evolution of Chemical Weapons

Modern chemical weapons initially appeared during World War I. In an attempt to break the deadlock of trench warfare, both sides resorted to the use of chlorine and phosgene gas, and then a combination of the two, named "mustard gas" after its color. Mustard gas liquefies on contact with moist skin and the membrane tissues of the nose, eyes, and lungs, causing the exposed tissue to burn and blister. Soldiers were often permanently blinded by mustard gas, and when it was inhaled in high enough concentrations, their lungs would fill with fluids, causing them to die of suffocation. Because it can suffocate victims, mustard gas falls into a category of chemical weapon agents called choking or pulmonary agents. This is one of five categories used to classify existing chemical weapons—four of which have the potential to be lethal weapons. Along with choking agents, the other lethal categories are blister agents, blood agents, and nerve agents. The fifth category describes chemical weapons that are nonlethal and are called irritant agents. Antiriot chemicals such as tear gas and pepper spray are in this category. Because they are nonlethal, these are of little value to terrorists. Blister agents are named for the large and deep blisters they make when they remain in contact with exposed skin. Exposure to this category of agents often causes injuries, but they are rarely fatal.

Blister agents can remain in a liquid form for many weeks, and when they do evaporate, the relatively dense gas tends to settle in low areas. During the Cold War era, this category of chemical weapon was viewed as an "area denial weapon" because it kept an opponent from traveling through or occupying the exposed ground. However, its limited lethality makes it a poor terrorist weapon. Blood agents such as hydrogen cyanide, cyanogen chloride, and cyanogen bromide are lethal when a high enough concentration is inhaled. The ability of these agents to prevent a victim's red blood cells from releasing oxygen to the body causes severe injury and death. Nerve agents, also referred to as organophosphate nerve agents, are chemically similar to commercial insecticides, which are very highly diluted nerve agents. Three of the most widely known of these agents are sarin, soman, and tabun. Exposure to a nerve agent may be via droplets making contact with the exposed skin or inhalation as a gas. These agents block vital nervous-system muscular functions such as breathing and heartbeat. Of all the categories of chemical agents, nerve agents are the most lethal.[6]

Therefore, are chemical weapons likely to be used by terrorists? The reality is that effective use by terrorists of a chemical weapon presents numerous difficulties. The first of these is the sheer volume of agent that must be used to achieve lethal concentrations over a large area. Sunlight, wind, distance from the release point, and time rapidly diminish an agent's concentration and thus its effectiveness. During World War I it was determined that kilogram for kilogram, high explosives caused more casualties than chemical weapons. This is the primary reason that the opposing forces ceased using chemical agents and the reason that they were not used on the battlefield at all during

World War II.[7] Or, as a thorough study of the threat from weapons of mass destruction by the United States' Gilmore Commission explained, it would take a full ton of sarin gas released under favorable weather conditions for the destructive effects to be distinctly greater than those that could be obtained by conventional explosives.[8]

The 20 March 1995 sarin attack by the Aum Shinrikyo cult in the Tokyo subway system illustrates the limitations that terrorists face in trying to effectively use chemical weapons. At five different subway stations, individuals punctured pre-deployed plastic bags of sarin with umbrella tips and then quickly left the trains. The attack ultimately claimed the lives of twelve people.[9] The low number of fatalities even in the confined spaces of subway cars is attributed to the sarin's impurity and the way in which it was released. The twelve people who died were perhaps knocked to the floor, where they came into contact with some liquid sarin or inhaled a fatal concentration of the gas. Unfortunately, Tokyo subway authorities were mentally unprepared to deal with any type of attack, let alone a chemical attack, and further spread the sarin gas by allowing the trains to continue operating, until more than 1,000 subway riders and responders were eventually affected. The difficulty that even the highly trained Aum chemists faced in order to produce a proper sarin formula and then effectively disperse it shows the very real limitations these weapons have when compared to conventional explosives, such as those used in the 11 March 2004 Madrid train bombing, which left 191 dead and 1,800 seriously injured.[10]

Therefore, can terrorists unleash a massive attack by first manufacturing and then dispersing large amounts of chemical agents? This scenario is highly unlikely. However, what terrorists can do is use toxic industrial chemical agents found in our own backyard to attack us. An event that starkly illustrates this is the tragic explosion that occurred at a pesticide plant in Bhopal, India, on the night and early morning of 2–3 December 1984. The explanation by the plant owner, Union Carbide, holds cautionary lessons for our approach to countering potentially realistic terrorist threats. According to Union Carbide's own investigation, the event was not an accident caused by poor plant maintenance or faulty safety equipment, as had initially been assumed by many.[11] There were adequate operational safety devices and procedures in place that made an accidental release of gas impossible. The event was apparently a deliberate act of terrorism or sabotage by a single disgruntled employee, who removed a safety flow meter and then forced water into a large tank of methyl isocyanate, causing it to heat up, vaporize, and—under tremendous pressure—spew out nearly forty tons of toxic gas into the atmosphere. During the night and early morning the gas killed thousands in the surrounding neighborhood, primarily because warning and evacuation procedures either were not in existence or were not executed.

The lesson from this tragedy is that we must pay closer attention to safeguarding our industrial facilities that store and use toxic chemicals, as well as those that produce or store highly flammable fuels. No chemical weapon carries a payload approaching the forty tons that the single plant in Bhopal released. We need to ensure that terrorists cannot externally attack and threaten such facilities and that they cannot exploit or infiltrate the workers who operate them. Alongside robust automatic and backup safety systems for accident or sabotage, plants must have adequate warning systems and well-rehearsed evacuation plans in place, not only for their workers but also for nearby communities. As corporate and government interests continue to intersect, public–private partnerships are an important element of protecting critical infrastructure as well as citizens.

Biological Agents

Of all the WMD agents this chapter discusses, humanity has had by far the most experience dealing with, controlling, and—in most instances—overcoming biological agents. Natural pathogens in the form of bacteria, viruses, yeast, and fungi have been causing disease among humans as long as humans have existed. Bacteria are the smallest organisms capable of independent reproduction, and they exist virtually everywhere, including as vital symbionts within our bodies. Some common examples of deadly bacteria are anthrax, cholera, pneumonic plague, and typhoid fever. Unlike bacteria, viruses are not capable of independent reproduction and must infect and use a host cell to reproduce successfully. Some of the most well-known dangerous viruses are smallpox, yellow fever, Ebola, Marburg virus, and Rift Valley fever. Certain kinds of yeasts and fungi produce toxins that can cause sickness and death. Despite our long history of studying and dealing with natural pathogens, however, most people continue to have an exaggerated fear of bioterrorism. This may be a product of popular culture in the form of novels and films in which terrorists unleash a biological agent that spreads quickly, is resistant to any known treatment, and results in painful death within hours of exposure. Unfortunately adding to this fear are those who hope to profit from the intentional and exaggerated portrayal of potential biological-terrorist threats by selling their expertise or some product to counter biological terrorism.[12]

However, biological weapons are extremely difficult to develop and disperse. And even terrorists know that once dispersed, they are impossible to control. When assessing the difficulties a terrorist organization would have gaining access to a deadly pathogen, then maintaining rigorous isolation while handling and growing it, and then processing and dispersing it effectively, biological weapons experts such as Milton Leitenberg conclude that "The less the commentator seems to know about biological warfare the easier he seems to think the task is."[13] Another disadvantage of biological agents for terrorists is that their debilitating potential can be limited by medical treatment.

The production and refinement of a pathogenic agent present numerous obstacles. The foremost is the need for rigorous isolation and containment of the agent, and the protection of those developing it. Furthermore, for a biological weapon to achieve any degree of effectiveness, it must be dispersed in an extremely fine aerosol form, at very high concentrations, close to the intended target audience, where it can be inhaled or otherwise absorbed. During the actual dissemination process most of the biological organisms would be destroyed, while subsequent exposure to sunlight, humidity, and temperature changes would further the destruction—thus the need for a highly concentrated medium. Dispersal is another enormous hurdle: how to aerosolize gallons of deadly agent in a public space without attracting attention? Any method that uses explosives would kill almost all the biological agent off the bat. If this problem were overcome, it is very likely that anyone carrying out the mission would be heavily exposed, thus effectively making this a suicide mission. However, it is one thing to steel oneself to instantaneous death through an explosion; it is quite another to willingly face protracted pain and suffering, along with the very real possibility of rescue, survival, and prosecution. Adding to the problem of using a biological weapon is the difficulty not only of producing the agent but also of storing it. Biological-weapon agents, with the exception of anthrax, have a very limited storage life even when kept at ideal temperatures.

The primary pathogen candidates for a biological weapon are anthrax, smallpox, and pneumonic plague, all of which, if identified early, can be medically countered. Anthrax can be treated with antibiotics, including prophylactically for those known to be exposed but not yet symptomatic. Smallpox can be prevented with the smallpox vaccine; vaccination within three days of exposure will completely prevent illness or greatly reduce symptoms, and vaccination within seven days can still offer some protection or mitigation. Antibiotics are also effective for preventing disease in individuals exposed to pneumonic plague and can greatly reduce the incidence of death or serious illness when administered within twenty-four hours to patients exhibiting the first symptoms of plague.

If societies can, through good public information and education, remove the fear factor associated with the use of biological weapons, such weapons become a very poor choice for would-be terrorists. Terrorist groups may in the future be able to overcome all these difficulties with advances in knowledge and technology, but only if those in positions of responsibility do not protect and secure such knowledge and technology. All of our present-day efforts to prevent, monitor, and treat naturally occurring pathogens can also, if expanded, ensure a robust response capability to counter terrorist use of biological weapons. The recent worldwide cooperative efforts to identify, monitor, and contain the outbreak and spread of the SARs, H5N1, and H1N1 viruses are directly applicable to dealing successfully with a terrorist biological attack. Ongoing programs that have developed vaccines capable of immunizing whole populations against viral pathogens must continue and grow. Integrated worldwide epidemiological tracking and information sharing must also improve. By openly reporting and sharing information about potential pathogenic outbreaks caused either by nature or by terrorists, countries can quickly identify, treat, isolate, or quarantine those exposed, thus saving lives and significantly reducing long-term effects. Finally, societies must work to expand the surge capacities of their medical care facilities and hospitals to handle large numbers of patients. Such actions prepare us for both natural pandemics and potential terrorist attacks.

Radiological Devices: The "Poor Man's Nuke?"

Radiological weapons are often referred to as the poor man's nuclear weapon, an unfortunate exaggeration of their actual effectiveness. Unlike thermonuclear weapons, these devices do not have the blast or thermal power to inflict much immediate damage, but instead use a conventional explosive or some mechanical means to spread radioactive materials such as cobalt 60 or cesium 137 through the immediate target area. The more appropriate names given to this type of weapon are "dirty bomb" or "radiological dispersal device" (RDD). Most analysts, including this author, consider RDDs to be more appropriately termed weapons of mass "disruption" rather than destruction, given their low lethality but very high likelihood of causing widespread fear and panic. More people would likely become casualties from the conventional explosives used to spread the radiological material than from exposure to the material itself. It is true that the successful use of a radiological weapon would raise radiation levels in the target area to unhealthy levels, but immediate evacuation of the contaminated area and thorough cleaning of all those exposed to radiological contaminants would reduce the number of immediate and long-term victims. Even so, citizens (and their offspring) who do experience the lingering effects of radiation can be expected to blame the government rather than long-forgotten terrorists.

Radioactive material that could be used as a "dirty" weapon could come from any number of sources. Both old and new industrial X-ray scanning equipment and medical equipment used to treat cancer and for diagnostic imagining are also widespread potential sources of highly radioactive materials. Throughout the world much of this equipment is poorly secured, while old, obsolete equipment typically was never disposed of properly. An incident that took place in the town of Goiania, Brazil, illustrates this global problem and also the realistic potential for danger from a radiological weapon. Starting on 13 September 1987, more than 240 people were exposed to dangerous levels of radiation when a junkyard dealer in Goiania broke open an abandoned radiation-therapy machine and removed a small amount of highly radioactive cesium chloride, a salt made with the radioisotope cesium 137. Family members and other adults, intrigued with its brilliant blue color and with the blue glow it gave off at nighttime, handled the material. Children, attracted to the bright blue residue that came off the cake, rubbed it on their skin. After fifteen days, one family member who became alarmed by the increasing sickness of those who had handled the material took some of it to a physician, who correctly suspected that it was dangerous. By the time authorities mounted a proper response and decontamination, some 249 people were seriously contaminated; 4 eventually died, and more than 200 were diagnosed with radiation poisoning. Several city blocks had to be completely removed to reduce the radioactive contamination.[14] In this incident the involvement of local law-enforcement officials in early detection and decontamination could have precluded any deaths and prevented the majority of radiation poisonings. Worldwide cooperation in tracking and securing all significant amounts of radioactive materials would go a long way towards preventing this type of accident from happening again. This would also certainly limit the opportunity for terrorists to gain easy access to enough radioactive material to produce an effective radiological weapon. As with chemical weapons, it is important to bear in mind that should terrorists use this type of weapon, it still would not be as outright destructive as the use of conventional explosives.

All societies need to be aware of the large amounts of potential radiological contaminants that legally reside in their own communities. The major area of concern is the security of nuclear facilities from terrorist attack. Such facilities throughout the world have both greatly increased their security from direct and indirect attack, and also incorporated major safeguards to prevent a nuclear-core meltdown if terrorists should gain control of the reactor. These efforts make a "terrorist Chernobyl" extremely unlikely. The diversion of material such as spent reactor fuel rods or uranium and plutonium from dismantled nuclear warheads has been another cause of international concern. Since the breakup of the Soviet Union, large radioactive materials stockpiles have been scattered among a number of small countries without secure borders. Several reports of would-be smugglers attempting to divert material into Europe or elsewhere cropped up in the 1990s, but to date most such fears have proved groundless. At the same time, bodies such as the International Atomic Energy Agency have stepped up efforts to work with governments to secure their materials.[15]

Of great concern are the large pools and storage containers, found at nuclear facilities, used to hold spent nuclear fuel. For example, in the United States such nuclear waste continues to build up at sixty-six commercial and fifty-five military sites. A terrorist attack that emptied a pool or breached some containers could produce a high-temperature fire that would release large quantities of radioactive material into the environment. Centralized storage in a highly secure facility away from population centers would go a long way towards reducing this potential threat. Of course, such an attack would almost inevitably expose the attackers to lethal radiation doses as well.

The Ultimate Nightmare? Nuclear Weapons in Terrorist Hands

Unlike chemical, biological, or radiological weapons, the detonation of a nuclear weapon in a populated urban area would, under any circumstances, produce massive destruction and death. But how would terrorists come to possess a nuclear weapon? The Gilmore Commission, a special advisory commission to the President and the Congress of the United States, stated that building a nuclear weapon requires overcoming numerous "Herculean challenges."[16] First, acquiring enough weapons-grade material, either plutonium or highly enriched uranium 235, would be extremely difficult. No terrorist organization has the huge, complex, and highly technical facility necessary to produce such material, so terrorists would have to buy or steal it from a nuclear facility or several facilities, in a large enough quantity and at a high enough concentration, to make a crude nuclear device. It would take over 100 kilograms of highly enriched uranium, HEU, or over 400 kilograms of 20-percent enriched uranium to make a crude nuclear weapon.[17]

The next hurdle for terrorists would be to properly mill and shape the weapons-grade material. Lacking the protective facilities normally used to manufacture these weapons would mean that the highly trained technical specialists making the weapon would have to expose themselves directly to the material's radiation, which would within a matter of hours kill them. Finding and recruiting the necessary cadre of highly skilled and knowledgeable "suicide technicians" is also a problem (although the United States and others have been concerned enough about the fate of former Soviet physicists who suddenly found themselves without a job to step in with employment initiatives).[18] Next, assembling the material in such a way that a critical mass of it can be brought together in a millionth of a second before heat from the early chain reaction blows the material apart is technically challenging. If all these difficult tasks are not fully achieved, the weapon will simply not function.

The best way to eliminate the potential for terrorists even to attempt to make their own weapon is to ensure that they cannot get their hands on weapons-grade material. Present efforts to increase the safety and security of nuclear-storage sites and research reactors worldwide that use highly enriched uranium must continue. Another program, sponsored by the United States, assists nuclear-research reactors throughout the world in converting their operations to the use of low-enriched uranium and is an even better solution to prevent weapons-grade material from falling into terrorist hands.

Some commentators have suggested that if it is so difficult for terrorists to make their own nuclear weapons, then perhaps they will steal one, buy one, or have one given to them by a sympathetic nation. Stealing a weapon from a secured military site and then transporting it successfully to a location where it could not be found would be nearly impossible. However, even possession of a nuclear weapon does not mean that it is usable. Most if not all of the nine or so nations that actually possess nuclear weapons have designed the warheads with locking mechanisms that require a code to unlock them. Forcefully removing such a device will render the weapon inoperable. The scenario of terrorists directly receiving a weapon from a nation is even more unlikely than the successful theft of a weapon. For more than sixty years no nation has ever sold or given a nuclear weapon to another country—not even to one that is a close ally. The fear that a terrorist organization would use the weapon against an undesirable target or, worse yet, that the terrorists might turn against the providing state, remains a strong disincentive for this kind of proliferation. Furthermore, the development of "nuclear-weapon forensics" that can identify a warhead's nation of origin opens a rogue supplier nation to the threat of direct military retaliation.

Political instability is seen as probably the greatest current risk factor for weapons or materials diversion, particularly in Pakistan and India, which are not parties to the Nonproliferation Treaty and so are not required to adhere to its safeguards, although India voluntarily observes most international standards (all four nuclear successor states of the former Soviet Union joined the treaty). Both countries are dealing with violent insurgencies and terrorism, as well as a tenuous state of peace between them. The United States and the international community are undertaking extensive diplomatic and practical measures to help both the Indian and Pakistani governments ensure their nuclear security.[19]

Even if a terrorist organization could overcome all of these considerable hurdles and found itself in possession of a functional nuclear warhead, there is one more major obstacle to deal with, and that, as with all WMD, is the delivery system. Most nuclear weapons of any size are designed to be delivered by some kind of projectile, usually a surface-to-surface or air-to-surface missile, or dropped from a bomber. Thermonuclear weapons cause the most destruction when they explode at a distance of hundreds or thousands of feet above the ground. This requires highly sophisticated technology, and either a launch vehicle or an airplane, both of which are going to be hard to come by and readily traceable. The so-called "city busters" of the size used in World War II need either a specially outfitted heavy bomber or a sophisticated launch facility the size of a factory, rendering reported terrorist threats to "carry out a 'Hiroshima' on America" absurd.[20] In short, it is virtually impossible for terrorists to send a nuclear warhead into the United States or anyplace else without inviting immediate, catastrophic retaliation on themselves and wherever the launch was made from. Even smaller tactical weapons need launchers, and these are not likely to have the spectacular effect that terrorist organizations such as Al Qaeda are after.[21]

Conclusion

This chapter has attempted to show that although weapons of mass destruction are, and will be for the foreseeable future, a potential threat, they are by their very nature difficult to make, acquire, or deploy effectively. Thus, their use is either highly unlikely or in most instances less deadly than the effect that terrorists could achieve by using conventional explosives. Our present preoccupation with fears that terrorists will wield a weapon of mass destruction against us should be replaced by practical measures to secure the potential weapons in our own backyard. By applying realistic practices locally, nationally, and internationally, governments can significantly reduce the opportunities for terrorists to acquire such weapons. By securing the potentially dangerous materials and facilities that are a part of everyday life, such as the toxic chemicals and materials industries; energy production, transport, and storage infrastructure; nuclear-power plants and research centers; and industrial and medical radiological equipment, societies can greatly reduce the opportunities for terrorists to use them. Citizens and first responders, properly informed and educated by government officials, can significantly reduce the harmful effects of these weapons. Most importantly, an educated public can counter the fear that terrorists are trying to instill by the threat of using a weapon of mass destruction. The better that ordinary people are informed and trained to respond to any such event, the less likely it is that present and future terrorists will use them.

Notes

1. Radiological weapons inflict damage to living things through the spread of radioactive material rather than the actual explosion. Nuclear weapons destroy everything in the vicinity, living or not, primarily through the force of the blast wave, while their radioactive fallout is essentially a side effect.

2. "Joint Publication JP 1–02, DOD Dictionary of Military and Associated Terms," U.S Department of Defense, 12 April 2010, as amended through April 2010, http://www.dtic.mil/doctrine/dod_dictionary/index.html. These weapons are often referred to as "CBRN," an especially useful phrase given the visceral association of "WMD" with the 2003 Iraq war.

3. "Weapon of Mass Destruction Definition," Federal Bureau of Investigation, National Security Branch, http://www.fbi.gov/hq/nsb/wmd/wmd_definition.htm.

4. Jeffrey K. Smart, "History of Chemical and Biological Warfare: An American Perspective," in *Medical Aspects of Chemical and Biological Warfare*, Textbooks of Military Medicine Series, ed. Frederick R. Sidell, Ernest T. Takafuji, and David R. Franz (Washington, D.C.: Borden Institute, Walter Reed Army Medical Center, 1997), 11, http://www.bordeninstitute.army.mil/published_volumes/chemBio/Ch2.pdf.

5. "History and Potential as a Bioweapon," Smallpox Information Center, http://smallpox.phages.org.

6. Without disputing this conclusion, it is worth pointing out that the lethality of even blister agents is going to be quite a bit higher in a civilian population than on the battlefield because civilians do not have the same training, equipment, and preparation as troops; furthermore, many of those exposed will be young, elderly, pregnant, or already in compromised physical health. Iraq's use of chemical weapons in Kurdish areas during the Iran–Iraq war (1980–1988) is the best example, though what happened even in those towns will be different from the consequences in a large city.

7. Thomas L. McNaugher, "Ballistic Missiles and Chemical Weapons: The Legacy of the Iran–Iraq War," *International Security* 15, no. 2 (Fall 1990), 19–20.

8. "First Annual Report to the President and the Congress: Assessing the Threats," the Advisory Panel to Assess Domestic Response Capabilities for Terrorism Involving Weapons of Mass Destruction (known as the Gilmore Commission), U.S. Government Printing Office, 15 December 1999, 28, http://cip.gmu.edu/clib/GilmoreCommissionReportsandDocuments.php.

9. Kyle B. Olson, "Aum Shinrikyo: Once and Future Threat?" *Emerging Infectious Diseases* 5, no. 4 (July–August 1999), 513–16. See also "Aum Shinrikyo," Country Reports on Terrorism, Office of the Coordinator for CounterTerrorism, U.S. Department of State, updated 30 April 2008, http://www.state.gov/s/ct/rls/crt/2007/103714.htm.

10. "Timeline: Madrid Investigation," *BBC News*, 28 April 2004, http://news.bbc.co.uk/2/hi/europe/3597885.stm.

11. Union Carbide Corporation, "Statement of Union Carbide Corporation Regarding the Bhopal Tragedy," http://www .bhopal.com/ucs.htm. Whatever the cause, it is apparent that backup safety systems were inadequate for the size of the plant and

the potential catastrophic result of a worst-case-scenario event, such as what actually occurred.

12. This is the author's personal observation based on his experience as the senior training advisor for Joint Task Force Homeland Defense, United States Army Pacific, from 2003 to 2005. During this period the United States spent wastefully on ineffective and now discarded civil-defense biological-weapons monitors and on a perishable and unnecessary anthrax vaccine. In 2005 more than 700 scientists, including 2 Nobel Prize winners, publicly criticized the ongoing major shift of research funds from pathogens of high public health importance to obscure organisms of biodefense and low public health importance. See Jon Mueller, *Overblown: How Politicians and the Terrorism Industry Inflate National Security Threats, and Why We Believe Them* (New York: Free, 2006), 30–31.

13. Milton Leitenberg, *The Problem of Biological Weapons* (Stockholm: Swedish National Defense College, 2004), 35–39.

14. "The Radiological Accident in Goiania," International Atomic Energy Agency (IAEA), Vienna, September 1988, http://www-pub.iaea.org/MTCD/publications/PDF/Pub815_web.pdf.

15. The Center for Nonproliferation Studies' Nuclear Threat Initiative (NTI) provides a wealth of information on the trafficking of nuclear materials, particularly from the Soviet Union's successor states. Go to http://www.nti.org/e_research/e3_special_nuctrafficking.html. On IAEA involvement, see "Security of Radioactive Sources: Implementing Guide," IAEA Nuclear Security Series No. 11, IAEA, Vienna, 2009.

16. Gilmore Commission, "First Annual Report," 31.

17. Alexander Glaser and Frank N. von Hippel, "What Nuclear Terrorists Would Need," *Scientific American* (February 2006), 59.

18. There have been several public and private initiatives to employ highly skilled former Soviet scientists and physicists in nonweapons research. For example, see "Stabilizing Employment for Nuclear Personnel: Civilian Research and Development Foundation," Nuclear Threat Initiative (NTI), http://nti.org/e_research/cnwm/stabilizing/crdf.asp.

19. Arian L. Pregenzer, "Securing Nuclear Capabilities in India and Pakistan," *Nonproliferation Review* 10, no. 1 (Spring 2003).

20. See "The Nature of the Threat: Nuclear," at the NTI Web site: http://nti.org/j_features/j4_threats.html.

21. For more on this subject, see Graham Allison, *Nuclear Terrorism: The Ultimate Preventable Catastrophe* (New York: Times, 2004).

II COMPREHENSIVE GOVERNMENT RESPONSES

8 Risk Assessment

James Petroni

THE PROTECTION OF CITIZENS IS THE FIRST RESPONSIBILITY of government and, indeed, forms the basis of the Westphalian state. Over time, the primary duty of government has expanded from defending against invasion to creating a *climate* of security, an environment within which individuals can safely raise families and construct an orderly civil society. Generating this climate requires more than the use of coercive force against enemies; it requires good governance. That is, security is a product of the relationship between a government and its people.[1] Traditional security, which operates at the state level, has been overshadowed in much of the world by "human security," which operates at the community and individual levels. Governments, faced with the rise of transnational threats such as terrorism, must establish and maintain both kinds of security.[2]

To prove itself worthy of the people's trust, any government must have a method of analyzing risk. Governments must do more than merely announce that they are ready to guard against risk; they must decide *how* to do it. For that, they need a transparent decision-making process that the public can understand. Citizens must know that government officials are using the resources available to them to manage the deadliest risks. In the early days of the nation-state, Frederick the Great of Prussia (1712–1786) is reputed to have said, "He who defends everything defends nothing." That dictum is just as true in a world where human security takes center stage. No government has enough resources to protect its society against all risks. Each must engage in a process of risk triage.[3]

Compared with most of the things governments are obliged to do, deciding which risks are the most deadly sounds easy. But that decision is more complicated than is generally supposed. For instance, deadliness does not take into account frequency or vulnerability. Frequency can be measured (at least with hindsight), but how do we measure vulnerability? Intuitively, we know that risks can be reduced through generating some level of capability to offset them. But we also know that risk is relative. There are countless hazards in the world, ranging from natural events and accidents to deliberate violence and disorder. But hazards are not necessarily disasters. That is, they do not always cause harm to human beings.

Any risk-assessment methodology must distinguish between *hazards* and the *potential* for harm. At the same time, it must take into account the inevitability of cascading effects. Some hazards, such as most hurricanes, take place in isolation from human populations and do not have the potential to cause harm. By contrast, those hazards that *do* cause harm should be expected to cause more disruption than the initial event due to second- and third-order effects. Hurricane damage comes primarily from wind and tide, but follow-on effects can include social unrest and disease. A terrorist attack is meant to create fear, but its effects can include loss of public services and the curtailment of citizens' civil rights.

However, terrorism has blurred the distinction between hazard and risk. It is a hazard that is so unpredictable (and potentially so deadly) that it cannot be dismissed as the low-probability event that it actually is.[4] Aided by media coverage, terrorist attacks fuel public outrage, and that emotion increases the public *perception* of risk. Citizens are comfortable with death rates from automobile accidents; they are not comfortable with something as arbitrary as car bombings. The *fear* of terrorism has become more hazardous than the reality. And that is exactly the point.

From a government perspective, then, it would not be useful to evaluate the risk of terrorism separately from other risks or to allow a climate of irrational fear to emphasize terrorism over other risks. Governments must distribute a finite amount of resources over a whole spectrum of hazards and threats to their citizens. The institutions that manage the consequences of deliberate and natural disasters are largely the same. Governments are forced to do the analysis, letting the chips fall where they may and the resources accrue where they must.

Risk for any given threat, then, can be defined by the vulnerability of people to that risk and the government's ability to offset the risk. This reduces to a simple equation:

$$\text{risk} = (\text{threat} + \text{vulnerability}) - \text{capability}$$

In other words, risk can be *managed*.

Managing Risk

There are five basic phases to risk management, beginning with the identification of possible threats, all the way through the difficult process of recovery from a disaster. Although they are presented here as a linear flow, it is more accurate to think of these phases as points on a wheel, each of which is linked to the others in a constant iterative process of planning, preparation, evaluation, and more planning. Although the response and recovery phases are the most visible to the public and get the most media attention, governments need to be sure that they are committing sufficient attention and resources to the pre-event phases as well. Neglect on one side damages the other.

I. Analysis. This first step, also called "awareness," is the foundation for the whole process. It is at this stage where data of all types are gathered and evaluated—by local authorities, by provincial emergency-management task forces, and by national-level institutions. Analysts trained in risk management consider all realistic threats. They evaluate governmental and societal vulnerabilities, inventorying capabilities available (or needed) to mitigate the dangers. It is during the analysis phase that risks are identified and ranked, providing the raw material for the remainder of the process.

II. Planning. Using data acquired in the analytical phase, the president's office, the ministry of the interior, or another department in charge of domestic security now assigns lower-level government institutions the roles and responsibilities appropriate for their capabilities. With input from these various actors, the lead ministry will develop a strategic plan to identify actions that will minimize vulnerabilities and maximize capabilities. Operational-level plans, which require the coordinated responses of multiple institutions, undergo testing with integrated command-and-control systems to make sure that all flaws and obstacles have been dealt with well before the plans are actually needed. At the tactical level, responders develop, test, and then exercise event- and site-specific plans.

III. Mitigation. Often the least developed part of the process, mitigation offers the greatest opportunity for the reduction of risk. Here the strategic plan should guide the implementation of specific measures to prevent disasters in the first place or to minimize their potential consequences should they occur. Actions in this phase can be *physical* (structural reinforcement, flood control), *legal* (land-use regulations, criminalization of terrorist activities), *economic* (insurance regulation, direct relief programs), or *human* (public education, first-responder training).

IV. Response. Although the response phase normally receives the most attention, few people understand the limits of what can be accomplished after a disaster occurs.[5] The rapid development of situational awareness and the creation of a common operating picture for all responders are critical first steps that depend to a large degree on how well command and control was set up and exercised in the planning stage. This system must be able to integrate all institutions and their capabilities right from the start. In an effort to manage natural disasters more effectively, for example, California developed the Incident Command System during the 1980s. This system, a multi-institutional adaptation of the military command structure, has been adopted as the U.S. national standard and has spread to many governments around the world.[6]

V. Recovery. The minimum goal of this final phase is restoration of the affected area and its inhabitants to *status quo ante* (or better). Combined with sensible mitigation efforts, the recovery can vastly improve the resilience of a building or system relative to recurring catastrophic events such as flood or earthquake. This phase is often segmented into three subphases—short, middle, and long term—of which the long-term measures can sometimes last for decades.

As noted above, the risks first identified in the analysis phase, coupled with damage assessments from the response phase, drive future planning, mitigation, and recovery efforts in a constant feedback cycle. Two examples from the U.S. experience underline the importance of beginning this cycle with good analysis: the Los Angeles riots in 1992 and Hurricane Katrina in 2005.

In 1992 four white police officers were acquitted by a mostly white jury (there were one Latino and one Asian juror, but no African Americans) of brutality during the arrest of Rodney King, a young black man. Large portions of the city of Los Angeles exploded in racially targeted assaults, looting, and arson. Over the course of four days fifty-three people died, and damage estimates would eventually reach $1 billion. Surprisingly, the city appeared totally unprepared for the public disorder.[7] In the aftermath of the riots it was determined that the city's excellent emergency-response services had prepared almost exclusively for earthquakes (a recurring threat). They had not anticipated, nor had they exercised, the very different command-and-control requirements for rapidly spreading urban violence—despite the fact that the city was no stranger to violence and there were warnings of racial tension before the verdict was announced. Since that time, Los Angeles has taken a much broader, all-hazards approach to emergency planning, with good results and few surprises.

In the wake of the World Trade Center attacks of 2001, the U.S. government decided to establish the Department of Homeland Security. The new department brought twenty-two separate institutions together under one cabinet official. One of those was the Federal Emergency Management Agency (FEMA), which had previously enjoyed a high public profile, with adequate funding and a good track record. As the priority and culture of the new mega-department skewed heavily toward terrorism as the all-consuming threat, FEMA lost funding and key personnel, including a director experienced in disaster preparation and response. When Katrina, a Category 3 hurricane, struck New Orleans on 29 August 2005, the weakened FEMA could not manage a disaster that it had originally been created for, and a disaster that was known to be a high-probability event. A realistic, comparative evaluation of risk in advance of the hurricane season would have resulted in far less damage and loss of life.

These examples illustrate the difficulty of getting risk assessment right. In Los Angeles, preparation was guided by the incorrect assumption that earthquakes and wildfires were the only disaster threats; in New Orleans, officials at all levels refused to consider the worst-case possibilities of a recurring threat that appeared all too familiar. Such mistakes do not bode well for protecting against terrorism. The modern terrorist is a smart and adaptable enemy who can imagine endless ways to hurt governments and the citizens they represent. Although probabilities are a central factor in assessing risk, it is now imperative that public officials think beyond probabilities to what is *possible*. For instance, it was not probable that airplanes piloted by suicide terrorists would fly into buildings, but it certainly was possible. The tragedy of 9/11 is that it was a failure of *imagination* as much as a failure of intelligence.[8]

With the foregoing in mind, it becomes clear that all governments require a system for continuously analyzing both recurring and emerging threats, one that can assess the risks from terrorism alongside those from fire, flood, and earthquake. That system must also balance probability against possibility while tracking changes in vulnerabilities and capabilities. What planners need is an easy-to-use tool that fuses the dearth of available objective data with the judgment of experienced emergency-management officials, is comprehensive in scope, yet simple enough to be adaptable for a spectrum of government institutions. In short, planners need a *dynamic* system with the flexibility to encourage imaginative thinking. All government institutions must be on the same page, and such a tool would provide the mechanism for getting them there.

A system that does all of this was developed in the 1970s in Northern California to assess the risks of natural disaster (particularly fire and earthquake).[9] The system features a matrix-based analytical tool that fuses hard and soft data on threats with the judgment of experts to yield raw numerical scores for carefully chosen "assessment criteria." Those scores can be combined to yield overall totals that can be compared. In other words, we already have a tool that is designed to prioritize threats in terms of risk to the public from natural disasters. In today's world it makes sense to add terrorism to that list of threats.

Quantifying Assessment Criteria

The evaluation of public risk starts with a listing of all threats (hazards judged to have a potential for harming people). All countries experience natural disasters of one kind or another, and all are susceptible to accidents and deliberate violence. As we have argued in Part I, the threat of terrorism now belongs on every government's list of security risks.[10] Because threats are not uniform throughout the territory of an entire country, threat lists and risk assessments will have to be tailored for provinces and cities as well. Indeed, the risk-assessment process should *begin* at the local level, where risk-management resources are needed first. It should culminate at the national

TABLE 8-1 "Demosland" All-Hazards Risk Comparison

Criteria Threat	*History (×2)*	*Vulnerability (×5)*	*Maximum Threat (×10)*	*Probability (×7)*	*Total*
Earthquake	(7) × (2) = **14**	(5) × (5) = **25**	(6) × (10) = **60**	(5) × (7) = **35**	**134**
Wildfire	(10) × (2) = **20**	(4) × (5) = **20**	(2) × (10) = **20**	(8) × (7) = **56**	**116**
Flood	(6) × (2) = **12**	(3) × (5) = **15**	(3) × (10) = **30**	(8) × (7) = **56**	**113**
Terrorism	(8) × (2) = **16**	(10) × (5) = **50**	(4) × (10) = **40**	(10) × (7) = **70**	**176**
Epidemic	(1) × (2) = **2**	(9) × (5) = **45**	(8) × (10) = **80**	(2) × (7) = **14**	**141**
Transit Accident	(8) × (2) = **16**	(2) × (5) = **10**	(2) × (10) = **20**	(10) × (7) = **70**	**116**
Civil Disorder	(4) × (2) = **8**	(1) × (5) = **5**	(1) × (10) = **10**	(2) × (7) = **14**	**37**
Drought	(9) × (2) = **18**	(4) × (5) = **20**	(2) × (10) = **20**	(7) × (7) = **49**	**107**

level, from where most of those resources are distributed. Working risk assessment at both ends simultaneously, with a reliable mutual feedback link, will ensure that requirements and resources remain in balance over a wide spectrum of local- and national-level threats.[11]

Wherever it is compiled, the threat listing should be produced by an advisory group comprising experts who are empowered to think critically and speak openly. Such a group, large enough to be diverse but small enough to be creative, would have to include technical experts, industry representatives, operations research specialists, and emergency-management officials. Such collaboration can be expected to produce the kinds of disagreement, and even conflict, that are part of the creative process. Group "brainstorming" is a regular feature of successful companies and should have a place in government institutions, especially when it comes to evaluating risk.[12]

The initial product of the advisory group would ideally be a consensus list of threats to be analyzed with respect to risk. In the absence of consensus, the group would present a compilation of members' views to the appropriate decision makers. The proceedings of such a group could be made available to the public, but posting on the Internet risk-assessment information for terrorist attacks would set up a liberty–security debate in any democratic country. A hypothetical example of such a list forms the basis of the "all-hazards" risk-comparison matrix in Table 8-1 for the fictional country of "Demosland."

The second product of the brainstorming group would be an analysis of the assessment criteria as they apply to each threat. However, it is important to keep in mind that the four criteria used in this methodology are not equally important in determining relative risk. Therefore, weighting factors are assigned to each criterion, based on the judgment of those who designed the system (but subject to modification as necessary to suit new conditions).[13] This is where the process transforms inherently qualitative judgments into hard numbers that can be used to evaluate risks.[14] It is the *combination* of assessment criteria, weighted individually, that adds power to the methodology; it is the creative tension of informed debate that adds value to the analysis.

Assessment Criteria

A complete understanding of how the various assessment criteria influence overall results requires some explanation.

History This criterion is based on the premise that if it happened before, it will happen again. To make the data useful to decision makers, a standardized time perspective is needed. For geological threats, for example, a one-hundred-year historical sample might be realistic, but for other threats that span would be unwieldy. Terrorism has evolved too much, and response factors such as emergency medicine have advanced too far, to validate historical samples of greater than thirty years for those threats. For the purposes of this discussion, then, the sample standard will be thirty years. Because history is not as important as the other analytic criteria, it is normally assigned a low weighting factor (2). The assigned value representing a particular threat would be a number between 1 and 10, reflecting the occurrence data. As with all assessment criteria, the group number for history is derived from the recommendations of individual experts, based on their unique experience and judgment. The number assigned to the threat/history box, then, would be this value, weighted by a factor of 2.

Vulnerability As an assessment criterion, vulnerability can be defined as the susceptibility of a population to harm resulting from a particular threat. As the risk equation tells us, vulnerability can be mitigated. For instance, susceptibility to epidemic can be mitigated with a robust health care system, reliable pharmaceutical industry, and generally healthier population. The threat of terrorism can be mitigated through public education that teaches citizens to be more aware of what is happening in their own neighborhoods and to report what they see.[15] Vulnerability is more important than history in assessing risk because it measures the progress that a government is making to reduce susceptibility to harm. The weighting factor for vulnerability most often used in this system is 5, meaning that the initial score (1–10) would be multiplied by 5 to yield a number for the threat/vulnerability box.[16]

Maximum Threat This is the worst-case scenario for a particular threat. The weighting factor of 10 indicates that if this event happens, the country will suffer significant losses. Maximum threat is the most misunderstood assessment criterion. The number does not measure a government's capability to prevent the event, but it does provide an indication of how prepared that government is to contain the effects of the event. As Hurricane Katrina showed, the city of New Orleans is not just *vulnerable* to hurricanes; it is vulnerable to the worst effects a hurricane can possibly generate. The risk-assessment methodology therefore must account somehow for the difference between New Orleans (large sections of which are below sea level) and other hurricane-prone cities such as Houston (which lies just far enough inland to be relatively protected). Although the ports of New York and Los Angeles are both vulnerable to terrorist attack, a strong case can be made that Los Angeles has a "worse" worst-case scenario because there are fewer alternative ports on the West Coast.[17] The weighting factor of 10 indicates how important it is for governments to take a high-impact event seriously, even if there is a low probability of occurrence.

Probability The *likelihood* that something will happen in a given location is distinguishable from the history of its happening and that location's vulnerability to it. History tells us what *has* happened, but vulnerability is a measure of how ready we are to withstand the effects of an event if it does happen. Mathematics can suggest probabilities based on observable trends, while the scientific method helps us distinguish between what is real (climate change) and what is fantasy (Martians). Intelligence can give us a useful idea of how likely it is that Al Qaeda will attack Los Angeles. Forecasting events such as fires and floods may be relatively easy in some regions because of the rhythms of nature, but predicting a terrorist attack requires a high degree of skill and access to many inputs, including politics, culture, national history, the terrorist group's characteristics, and the behavior of individual terrorists. A weighting factor of 7 reflects the importance of accurate probability forecasting.

The risk-comparison tables can now be filled in, using a combination of data and judgment. But what do the numbers mean?

Assessing Risk in "Demosland"

The president of a small fictional country called "Demosland" has asked a diverse group of trusted advisors to brainstorm together and then provide her with a realistic picture of risks to the country. Tables 8-1 and 8-2 display some numbers filled in by this hypothetical group, based on the criteria and weighting values discussed above. With this information, the government of Demosland would now be in a position to make decisions on how to distribute its risk-management resources in the most effective and efficient ways. There is no space here to provide a complete profile of Demosland, but the risk-comparison numbers can tell us a lot about the country. Looking at the "all-hazards" data in Table 8-1, we can conclude that the country has a dry climate and is subject to a yearly drought/flood cycle. Judging from the high numbers for terrorism and low numbers for civil disorder, the country is likely to have robust law-enforcement institutions (it could be that the swift suppression of civil disorder is one of the root causes of terrorism in Demosland). In presenting this table, the advisory group would be telling the government to invest a lot of resources in preparing for and managing the most likely threats.

However, the all-hazards table does not reflect much emphasis on low-probability threats. The values for earthquake suggest that Demosland has had occasional earthquakes but that those events have not been near major population centers. The values further suggest that the government might be willing to bet (by withholding resources) that its cities will remain untouched by earthquake. The values for epidemic tell a different story. It is clear that Demosland is vulnerable to epidemics and that the worst-case scenario is cause for grave concern. Although the probability of epidemic is rather low, the maximum-threat value has placed the risk of epidemic almost as high as that of terrorism (which is apparently quite common). From what we see in the data, this government is doing what most governments do—it is making the best cost–benefit choices it can based on what resources it has.

TABLE 8-2 "Demosland" Terrorism-Risk Comparison

Criteria Threat	*History (×2)*	*Vulnerability (×5)*	*Maximum Threat (×10)*	*Probability (×7)*	*Total*
Small-Arms Attack	(7) × (2) = **14**	(8) × (5) = **40**	(2) × (10) = **20**	(3) × (7) = **21**	**95**
Suicide Bombing	(6) × (2) = **12**	(8) × (5) = **40**	(5) × (10) = **50**	(3) × (7) = **21**	**123**
IED/Car Bomb	(8) × (2) = **16**	(8) × (5) = **40**	(4) × (10) = **40**	(3) × (7) = **21**	**117**
Cyber Attack	(0) × (2) = **0**	(10) × (5) = **50**	(8) × (10) = **80**	(2) × (7) = **14**	**144**
Biological Attack	(0) × (2) = **0**	(5) × (5) = **25**	(6) × (10) = **60**	(2) × (7) = **14**	**99**
Chemical Attack	(0) × (2) = **0**	(4) × (5) = **20**	(7) × (10) = **70**	(3) × (7) = **21**	**111**
"Dirty" Bomb	(0) × (2) = **0**	(3) × (5) = **15**	(2) × (10) = **20**	(2) × (7) = **14**	**49**
Critical Infrastructure Attack	(8) × (2) = **16**	(5) × (5) = **25**	(7) × (10) = **70**	(8) × (7) = **56**	**167**
Ship Attack	(0) × (2) = **0**	(9) × (5) = **45**	(6) × (10) = **60**	(4) × (7) = **28**	**133**

Looking at Demosland's terrorism-risk comparison in Table 8-2, we see a history of conventional terrorist activity but none involving cyber, biological, or chemical weapons. Critical infrastructure is vulnerable and has been attacked often, which indicates that Demosland may be facing an active terrorist group waging a campaign of attrition and that the conflict is at stalemate. The government may have small-arms attacks under control, but its people seem quite vulnerable to suicide bombings and improvised explosive devices. The advisory group has listed cyber attack as a category separate from critical infrastructure, even though cyber systems constitute part of that infrastructure. This may indicate that one or more of the advisors brought expertise in cyber security to the table and wanted to make sure it was addressed.

The advisors have correctly avoided overinflating the potential effects of a radiological device, however, perhaps with the understanding that such devices cause more fear than death. Table 8-2 suggests that Demosland's government should reexamine what looks like a failing strategy against its domestic terrorists, perhaps by using nonlethal inducements to bring them into the political process, and begin to address emerging threats such as maritime terrorism.

The advantage of this methodology is that it displays relative risk in a form that can be understood immediately by decision makers. Although the values are based largely on judgment, the fact that available data are debated freely by advisory groups with wide collective experience offers a high probability of valid results. The tables present a framework for discussing what threats are important enough to warrant government resources, and then for assigning values to the assessment criteria. The value of the methodology lies in its flexibility. It is a *framework* for analysis, yielding not a perfect solution to end all threats but an evaluation of relative risk that can guide the rational application of scarce resources.[18]

Conclusion

The need to enhance human security against natural and deliberate disasters comes at the same time that most governments find themselves with fewer resources in the midst of a widespread global recession. As citizens become accustomed to better levels of security, they tend to expect more, but their leaders can deliver only less as resources must be spread further. This is a formula that cannot lead to the sustained prosperity needed to immunize a society from the harm wrought by an overwhelming number of potential hazards. Nature does not care about human security, but terrorists exploit these trends to achieve their aims. If governments do not develop creative and successful strategies to mitigate and respond to terrorist threats, there will be fewer incentives for disaffected citizens to seek nonviolent ways to achieve their political goals.

Without good strategy to counter them, ideologically driven terrorists will continue to use terror as an instrument for destroying domestic and international order. Risk assessment is the first step on the path to good strategy. The next chapter will take us further down that path, examining how governments can use all their resources to develop strategies that enable the state to thrive in its primary role of protecting citizens.

Notes

1. For further insight into the relationship between a government and its people in the context of security, see Thomas C. Bruneau and Scott D. Tollefson, eds., *Who Guards the Guardians and How* (Austin: University of Texas Press, 2006).

collective fight. The world is a big place, and global efforts against terrorism are slow to implement. Once governments master the art of developing their own strategies, they must go the extra mile and work with their neighbors to apply that art to a set of regional strategies. In the long run, *regions* are where civilized nations will win against terrorism.

Now and forever, governments must balance liberty and security in ways that satisfy their own legal frameworks and popular expectations. Skilled leaders understand that this balance is dynamic. However a government decides to treat terrorism and terrorists, having a comprehensive set of strategies like the ones suggested here is an absolute requirement. An open question is whether time is on the side of terrorists or governments. A partial answer would be to observe that democracies are more vulnerable to terrorism in the short term but that they are *less* vulnerable over time. Terrorists have the advantages of speed and surprise, but violence against innocent civilians will never give them the long-term legitimacy they seek—either from ordinary citizens or from their own constituents. By pursuing strategies that replace fear with security, governments can earn the loyalty of all their citizens. Of all the tools against terrorism that governments have, ordinary citizens are, in the end, the most powerful.

Notes

1. For governments trapped in a cycle of violence, the war image certainly fits. Terrorism is also a crime, but how governments describe it makes a difference in how they fight it.

2. Colin S. Gray, "Schools for Strategy: Teaching Strategy for 21st Century Conflict," monograph, Strategic Studies Institute, U.S. Army War College, November 2009.

3. John Arquilla and David Ronfeldt, *Networks and Netwars: The Future of Terror, Crime, and Militancy* (Santa Monica: RAND, 2001), 15.

4. The U.S. government sometimes uses the acronym "DIMEFIL" to refer to the "seven instruments of government power." To this list we have added emergency services, civil society, and moral factors, all critical tools for combating terrorism.

5. Paul Berman explains this war of ideas particularly well in his book *Terror and Liberalism* (New York: Norton, 2003).

6. The best example of this may be Great Britain's response to the London bombings of July 2005. Historical experience and government policy had prepared British citizens to return to their daily lives very quickly. As Andy Trotter, the senior British transport police officer, announced on the day after the bombings, "London is back in

business." "'Business as Usual' After Bombs," *BBC News*, 11 July 2005, http://news.bbc.co.uk/2/hi/uk_news/england/london/4669831.stm.

7. The term *soft power* has been popularized in the American context by Dr. Joseph S. Nye, Jr., in *Soft Power: The Means to Success in World Politics* (New York: Public Affairs, 2004). A creative mix of hard and soft power has been described more recently as "smart power." For more on this concept, go to the Center for Strategic and International Studies Web site: http://csis.org/program/smart-power-initiative.

8. Edward Luttwak, *Strategy: The Logic of War and Peace* (Harvard College, 1987). Written for the context of large-scale conventional war, his vertical breakdown includes grand strategic, strategic, operational, tactical, and technical. For the purpose of explaining counterterrorism (CT) strategy, the political and operational levels will suffice.

9. It must not be forgotten that "successful" terrorist organizations and networks also have both political and operational strategies. By definition, terrorist operations are subordinate to political objectives.

10. The nonspatial dimensions of counterterrorism (CT) strategy are taken from the lectures of Tim Heinemann.

11. Carl von Clausewitz, *On War*, trans. Michael Howard and Peter Paret (New Jersey: Princeton University Press, 1976), 595–96. Clausewitz describes "center of gravity" as the "hub of all power and movement, on which everything depends." It is my belief that terrorist organizations have multiple centers of gravity that should be attacked simultaneously.

12. One can only imagine the amount of fear that terrorists could generate in California with just a book of matches (and a series of video clips) in the dry season.

13. The term "WMD" conjures George W. Bush's 2003 invasion of Iraq. A far better descriptive term would be "chemical, biological, radiological, nuclear, explosive" (CBRNE). This eliminates the nuclear and U.S.-centric imagery, thus helping governments face this broad spectrum of risks more intelligently.

14. See Anne Clunan and Harold Trinkunas, eds., *Ungoverned Spaces: Alternatives to State Authority in an Era of Softened Sovereignty* (Palo Alto: Stanford Security Studies, 2010).

15. The Revolutionary Armed Forces of Colombia (FARC), which began as a Marxist insurgency but now exists in large part as a violent transnational drug-smuggling operation, is the best example of this. FARC manages to keep the border regions in turmoil and occasionally carries out an ostensibly political attack, but the insurgency has been a *de facto* stalemate for years. See "Revolutionary Armed Forces of Colombia" at GlobalSecurity.org: http://www.globalsecurity.org/military/world/para/farc.htm.

16. Ian O. Lesser, Bruce Hoffman, John Arquilla, David Ronfeldt, Michele Zanini, and Brian Michael Jenkins, *Countering the New Terrorism* (Santa Monica: RAND, 1999), 126–38.

17. The U.S. government has at least twelve strategies against terrorism, both operational and political. These are broken down into specific campaigns rather than

the typology suggested here. It is indeed difficult to determine how these individual strategies were synchronized or whether there is an overarching political-level strategy at all.

18. See Mark S. Granovetter, "The Strength of Weak Ties," *American Journal of Sociology* 78, no. 6 (Fall 1973): 1360–80.

19. This mandate often takes the form in the United States of "joint task forces" that mix together the planning and operational elements of several institutions, such as the National Guard, Immigration and Customs Enforcement, and the Federal Bureau of Investigation.

20. Another element of vertical compression is the explosion of communications technology. It is now possible (indeed probable) that a commanding general will descend to the tactical level whenever he wishes.

21. Charles C. Krulak, "The Strategic Corporal: Leadership in the Three Block War," *Marines* (January 1999). Awareness of this at both ends of the chain of command compresses vertical levels of strategy even more.

22. Andrew J. Bacevich, *The Limits of Power: The End of American Exceptionalism* (New York: Metropolitan, 2008), 168.

23. Peru and Sri Lanka offer examples of operational success against domestic terrorism, but political victory still eludes both governments, primarily because they have neglected to develop core strategies that would obviate the grievances that drove the insurgencies in the first place.

24. Two centuries ago piracy, slavery, and genocide were common. Through the collective efforts of most governments, all of those phenomena have been reduced in frequency, and where these threats have rebounded, governments are acting in coalition against them. Terrorism is currently in a rebound, and it is through collective action, particularly within regions, that terrorist activity will be forced below the threshold of popular fear.

25. Audrey Kirth Cronin, "No Silver Bullets: Explaining Research on How Terrorism Ends," *CTC Sentinel* 3, no. 4 (April 2010): 16–18.

10 Building Effective Counterterrorism Institutions

Paul Shemella

AN INSTITUTION IS AN ORGANIZATION FOUNDED AND operated for a specific long-term purpose, usually having a logo, a building, and a Web site. Organizations are simply groups of people who work together for a common purpose, with widely varying degrees of interaction, guided by a set of rules or principles. A network is a group of things or people interconnected in some way that permits interaction among the members. In order to fight terrorism effectively, governments, both in whole and in part, must be institutions, organizations, *and* networks, all at the same time. But governments have almost never operated this way, especially while trying to develop national security. Bureaucracy, as a system for organizing the administration of government services, yields the advantages of deliberation and advocacy, guarding against knee-jerk responses to immediate problems and offering citizens better transparency in public operations. When it comes to fighting terrorists, however, too many layers of government can increase response times and politicize operational alternatives. Each government, taking into account its own unique geographic, historical, cultural, and political circumstances, must work out the balance between too much and too little bureaucracy.

Since the Peace of Westphalia (1648) ended decades of war in Europe, threats to the security of nation-states have come mostly from governments organized into parallel institutional structures with similar decision-making processes. Guided by Carl von Clausewitz's dicta and the Law of Armed

Conflict, the conduct of wars between nation-states has been more or less predictable and the actions of war leaders fairly rational, if not always wise.[1] The outcomes of war have usually depended on which governments accumulated more allies and more resources. Much of that has now changed. While governments are still organized vertically, in a traditionally hierarchical manner, the most likely opponents of governments are organized horizontally, in a networked or hub-and-spoke configuration.[2] Terrorist organizations, insurgent groups, and organized-crime syndicates defy the established rules and frustrate our traditional institutions. They are smart, adaptable, and fast—much faster than governments. Terrorists and other networked adversaries operate inside our decision-making cycles, along our physical borders with other states, within the global commons, and in the jurisdictional gaps among our institutions.

The world has spawned a so-called "fourth generation" of warfare, in which nonstate actors use asymmetric attacks to target the political will of a state rather than its military or economic power.[3] The slow decline of the nation-state as the world's organizing principle has led some observers to describe the emerging security environment as "the New Middle Ages," while Phil Williams suggests a possible return to the Dark Ages.[4] These threats are forcing governments to continually restructure themselves in four basic ways: first, by considering whole new concepts of security; second, by redesigning their decision-making processes; third, by integrating new technologies; and fourth, by modifying organizational designs. Organizational designs get the most attention in restructuring; the standard approach has been to redraw the boxes and the lines that connect them. It is time to concentrate on what is inside the boxes and how the institutions they represent can be reengineered to develop the capacity for countering new threats more effectively. This chapter will focus on fighting terrorism across the range of government capabilities, but much of what is prescribed applies to insurgency and organized crime as well.

What Is Terrorism?

To evaluate the institutional capacity to prevent or counter terrorism, we need a common understanding of what terrorism is. This is not a definition; as Thomas Mockaitis notes in Chapter 2, the U.S. government alone has multiple definitions of terrorism, reinforcing the old Washington axiom "Where you stand depends on where you sit." Such definitional fragmentation has resulted in a predictable dearth of institutional cooperation. We suggest a practical, characteristics-based examination of violence—a litmus test of five pillars—to give us some common ground on which to build a useful concept.

The first pillar is the recognition that terrorism is an act of violence to advance a specific political or ideological agenda. Second, it intends to incite fear in a wide audience—that is, beyond the immediate victims of the act. Third, terrorism deliberately targets civilians. Fourth, the act is associated with a particular group.[5] The fifth pillar identifies terrorism as the *systematic* use of calculated violence—violent acts linked together in a strategy of coercive intimidation. This is what distinguishes terrorism from "terror," which is a tactical action used by threatened states, insurgent groups, and criminal syndicates.

If we accept the five pillars as our basis for analysis, they can help us decide whether or not a genre of violence (in a given scenario) is indeed terrorism. A major advantage of this test is that it characterizes terrorism by the nature of the action rather than who does it or why. But a government's political and legal calculations inevitably influence its decisions. On the political front, governments label certain violent groups as terrorist based on the ideological bent of the leadership, the demands of partner countries, and the expectations of their own citizens.[6] On the legal side, most governments define terrorism in their domestic laws, as opposed to following an international standard. The diversity of domestic characterizations of terrorism is an obstacle to international cooperation, which the five-pillars analysis can also help reconcile.[7]

Terrorism scenarios, witnessed or imagined, can inform legislation and policy. With these in place, clear roles for combating terrorism can be assigned to specific institutions. It is in institutions where capabilities are generated and capacity is built.

What Is Capacity?

U.S. government officials talk incessantly about "building capacity," both at home and in the governments of partner nations. However, not every official who talks about it actually understands what *capacity* is and why it must be distinguished from that other favorite word, *capability.* But first it is important to fully grasp yet another term—*competency.* Competency is simply the ability to accomplish a given task, normally conferred on an individual through training. Institutions often describe their "core competencies" as a means of telling other institutions what they do well, when what they should be talking about is capabilities. Competency describes individual potential; it does not produce a measurable effect. For that, an institution must develop capability.[8]

All government institutions should think of their performance in terms of capabilities, broken down into expected missions, and then further broken down into tasks that can be demonstrated under real-world conditions, according to realistic standards, with whatever specialized equipment will be needed to perform each task. Developing competency requires basic resources, including manpower and material costs. A single capability requires a set of mutually reinforcing competencies, the outcome of which can be combined with other capabilities and their outcomes. Institutions are where capabilities are developed and incubated. But capabilities are still not enough; our institutions must generate *capacity.* Figure 10-1 illustrates this process by tracing

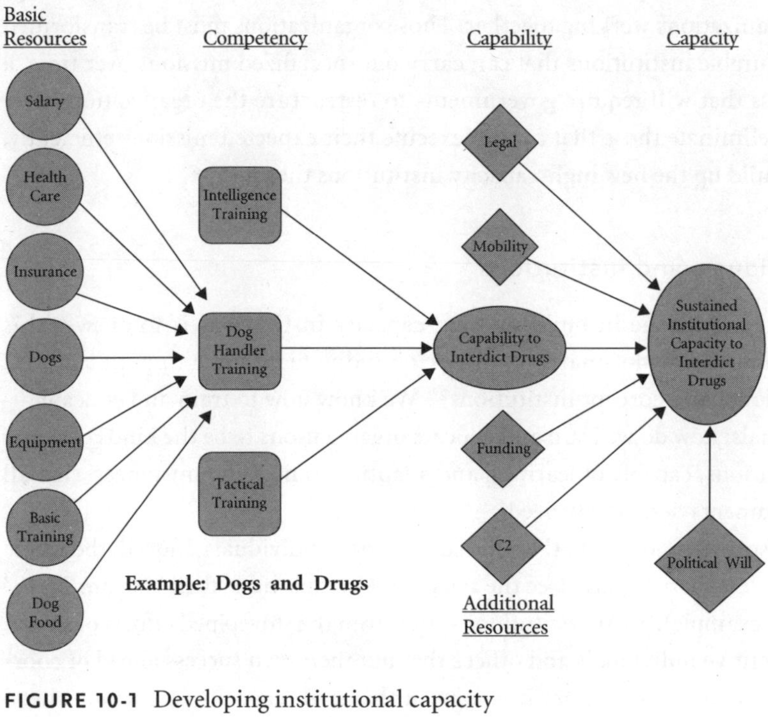

FIGURE 10-1 Developing institutional capacity

the development of institutional capacity for interdicting drug shipments by using sniffer dogs.

Capacity is capability fortified with additional resources, which might include a legal framework, adequate funding, and—perhaps most importantly—political will.[9] Capacity is also the ability to maintain and deploy capabilities again and again over time. No institution can fulfill its roles in government without developing capacity. For example, the United States military has been trying to transform itself since the end of the Cold War from a threat-based force to a capabilities-based force. What it needs to be is a "capacity-based force." Looking beyond its shores, flush with good intentions, the United States regularly helps other governments develop competency and capability but leaves them on their own to develop capacity. Ongoing engagement is critical to this further step, and that means a considerable commitment of time and money.

Even beyond providing resources over the long term, however, building the institutional capacity to oppose terrorism requires us to look *inside* the organizations charged by their leaders with specific roles. Terrorism policy is a good case in point because successful outcomes depend on a wide range of organizations working together. Those organizations must be transformed into durable institutions that can carry out specialized missions over time, a process that will require governments to restructure the organizations they have, eliminate those that cannot execute their expected missions efficiently, and build up the new high-capacity institutions they need.[10]

Individuals and Institutions

The key challenge in building high-capacity institutions is to answer this question: "How do smart, hardworking individuals come to populate dysfunctional and corrupt institutions?" We know how to train and educate individuals; how do we train and educate organizations to be the kinds of smart institutions, capable of learning and adapting to new circumstances, that all governments desperately need?

Institutions are more than the sum of their individuals; indeed, the whole can be less than its parts (see the 2004 U.S. Olympic basketball "Dream Team" for an example). Most institutions suffer from the stovepiped efforts of smart, competitive individuals and offices that put their own success ahead of coordination and cooperation. It is a given that high-capacity institutions need quality human resources, but to combat a smart, networked, and nimble opponent, they need a lot more. Smart individuals are now confronted with a real challenge: They must enable their own institutions to operate more effectively without diminishing the effectiveness of the government's *constellation* of institutions. When fighting terrorism, there must be a consensus that it is not the performance of single institutions that counts but the broader institution of government that must succeed.

Robert Michels diagnosed the problem perfectly a century ago with his "Iron Law of Oligarchy," which describes the increasing centralization of organizations through bureaucracy and specialization. According to Michels, sooner or later all organizations become too centralized, concentrating power in the hands of just a few people.[11] Adding personal charisma to this tendency often exacerbates the problem. The paradox here is that good people can ruin institutions, and better people can ruin them *faster.* With success and added power comes the conviction that one's own institution can do everything better than its "competitors." The ultimate expression of that power is the authority to hire and fire. Most governments promote those who have demonstrated effectiveness within a particular institution when they *should* be promoting those who understand the central role of institutional coordination while building capacity within their own.

If Western democracies could design their institutions from scratch, what might they look like? Let us hope they would look quite different from the stovepiped, sclerotic bureaucracies inherited from the Cold War. There are five essential qualities with which to build the foundation of effective institutions: good leadership, zero tolerance for corruption, right-sizing, decentralization, and self-organization.

Good leadership is the obvious place to begin, but what is "good" when it comes to generating the capacity to deal with terrorism? In this context the good leader is one who recruits and retains well-trained people, issues clear guidance, and then gets out of the way. When all members of the institution know that their own operational decisions will have some influence on the outcome, they respond by making better decisions.[12] The good leader understands complexity and appreciates the power of networks to find solutions quickly. He or she places a premium on critical thinking and maintains a cadre of "loyal contrarians" who are not afraid to question the conventional wisdom—or the wisdom of the leader.

Traditional leadership relies on the ideas of just a few high-level individuals (Michels' oligarchy); to defeat terrorists, leaders must rely on the ideas of *every* member of the institution. When people trust their counterparts within and outside their own offices, key decisions will be taken in coordination with other stakeholders. The result is an institution that looks in all directions, not just inward and upward.[13] This "institutional situational awareness" cannot develop unless leaders diminish their personal importance and focus on creating a climate within which strong working relationships among subordinates can flourish. If those relationships are right, the actual work often takes care of itself.[14]

But trust-based relationships cannot be sustained within corrupt institutions. The cancer of corruption takes many forms, and all governments harbor it. Bribery, nepotism, and organized crime are no more—and no less—crippling to an institution than the less obvious sins of political abuse and lack of transparency. Human nature is rooted in the competition for resources, and we are still a greedy species.[15] Thus, trust-based relationships are important in *deterring* corruption. The ideal climate within an institution discourages corruption with the same mechanism used in tribal societies—shame. Without such a mechanism, individual greed spills over into institutional greed. Many institutions have replaced the goal of contributing to the government's overall effectiveness with the goal of controlling ever more resources for themselves. This form of "legal" corruption, often masked in patriotism and purposeless activity, denies a government its full potential power. In order to achieve the goal of contributing to collective effectiveness, individual institutions must learn to share resources and credit (the former often depending on the latter).

What is the right size for a "combating terrorism (CT)" institution? Every institution has an optimum size, and most institutions, through unchecked bureaucratic growth, are much bigger than they need to be.[16] Since the Stone Age, the most effective human groups have averaged around 150 people. It is no accident that a military company has about 150 soldiers. Beyond that number, the personal relationships that serve to bind a group together cannot be maintained.[17] If an institution becomes too large, nothing the leadership can do will make it more effective. We can learn a lot from the business world here. At Gore-Tex, a horizontally organized company, managers try to keep each work group capped at 200 individuals. Other companies have experimented with common-area "nodes" in the office to force employees to interact with one another.[18] At General Electric, CEO Jack Welch dealt with gargantuan size by breaking the company into smaller businesses, each with its own inputs and outputs, along with responsibility for its bottom line.[19]

Given the truism that creativity is maximized at the threshold of chaos, how do leaders take their institutions to the brink without going over the edge? They do it through decentralizing their institutions and promoting self-organization.

Decentralization and self-organization, the final pillars of the high-capacity institution, are highly interdependent. In order to work, decentralization requires coordination at all levels, which in turn means that individuals must be able to operate with a minimum of control.[20] For business executives and terrorist leaders alike, small, flat, networked organizations staffed with smart, empowered individuals have become the business model for success.[21] Governments have always operated on the opposite model (big, highly centralized, rigidly hierarchical); they must now figure out how to transform themselves into small-unit, horizontal, networked, and, yes, *self-organized* enterprises. When attacked, centralized institutions tend to become more centralized, for which there is no better example than the formation of the U.S. Department of Homeland Security after the 11 September 2001 attacks.[22] When *de*centralized institutions are attacked, they tend to become more decentralized. This is certainly what happened to Al Qaeda after the U.S. government retaliated by nearly destroying its core in Afghanistan. The outcome of these two developments is not what we had in mind: The United States is arguably less capable, and Al Qaeda is arguably more capable.

Institutional Roles

Taking the comprehensive approach to terrorism that we suggest would require a government to assign specific roles in planning, prevention, mitigation, response, and armed intervention to most of its institutions.[23] The traditional "security sector" of armed forces, law enforcement, and intelligence does not suffice. Depending on how broadly a government defines terrorism, the list of institutions could include the Ministries of Foreign Affairs, Emergency Management, Health, and Agriculture; specialized civilian and military centers for countering terrorism; and so on. If the threat is bioterrorism, the minister of Health may suddenly become the most important CT official in the government. If a government were preparing to manage the consequences of terrorism, the director of emergency services (or the equivalent) would become the key official. What becomes clear is that *all* government officials are key to preventing and preparing for acts of terrorism. Figure 10-2 presents a short list of the institutions most likely to be assigned a CT role, along with some of the CT roles that most governments must organize.

The careful matching of institutions with roles lays the foundation for both effective strategy and the ability to develop and sustain capacity. Terrorists study their targets carefully and will exploit any gaps they detect between and among institutions. Governments may, in fact, make deliberate decisions to maintain certain overlaps between institutions, creating redundancy in the most important capabilities. Resilience, a by-product of capacity, is sometimes worth the extra cost, but it should be created deliberately rather than as a result of competition for funding or turf.[24] In cases where an institution is given multiple roles, decision makers must determine whether or not

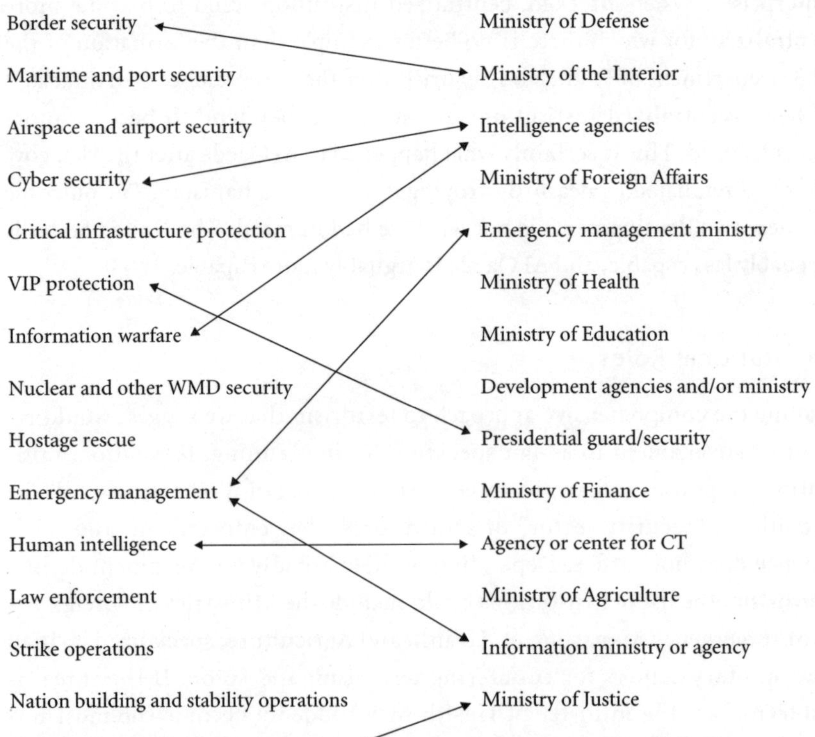

FIGURE 10-2 Which roles for which institutions?
NOTE: Some roles will be shared between more than one institution, while some institutions will have more than one role.

those roles are in conflict. Such a conflict lingered at the U.S. Federal Aviation Administration, even after 11 September 2001.[25]

Once roles are clarified, governments must provide the resources their institutions need to develop the capabilities and capacities to fight terrorism collectively.[26] No government has enough resources to give all its institutions everything they say they need, but government institutions can also be *over*-funded. As reflections of the human beings that populate them, institutions often tend to reach beyond their stated roles and demand more resources to feed growing bureaucracies. In a self-sustaining cycle, new roles draw more resources, and more resources enable institutions to take on new roles. To curb runaway growth, decision makers may be forced to limit resources and actually narrow the roles of their security institutions. Paradoxically, under-funded institutions may have greater incentive for interagency coordination and collaboration. Many governments with more-than-adequate resources are unconsciously providing *dis*incentives for their component institutions to work together by feeding the endless-growth dynamic. If one or two institutions can do it all, why cooperate?[27]

Beyond Institutions

The imperative of information sharing has, by this time, become a cliché. While it is certainly important to share information between and among individuals and the agencies they represent, there is a whole spectrum of interactivity required for effectiveness beyond the simple act of making information available to others. First there is *cooperation,* which reflects the attitude needed to engage in joint activities. If a cooperative attitude pervades an institution, either naturally or inspired through good leadership, then the systematic *coordination* of roles and missions becomes possible.[28] However, this coordination does not require institutions to actually work together to produce something new. That is the aim of *collaboration,* which can be described as a mechanism for mixing the best capabilities from multiple institutions into a better strategy, or perhaps faster and more effective operations. An interagency "task-force" approach has worked well to increase levels of cooperation, coordination, and collaboration for some governments, but it may not obviate the need to create permanent multiagency institutions. However this transformation is accomplished, greater interactivity of the kind suggested here can lead from high-capacity *institutions* to high-capacity *governments.*

However, even the best integrated high-capacity government will still not be able to eliminate terrorism alone. That end can come only through the collective efforts of multiple governments. Because there is ample evidence that global approaches are too politically complicated to be viable, national leaders must turn to regional approaches as the key to success. The way that governments can create high-capacity regional security institutions is by breaking the fight against terrorism into functional areas, a reflection of the government "tool kit" introduced in the preceding chapter. The most common functional coalitions are clustered around law-enforcement, intelligence, financial, and military efforts.

The notion of collective security has changed with the threat. It is no longer enough to promise that an attack on one is an attack on all; counterpart institutions from regional governments must be cooperating, coordinating, and even collaborating every day.[29] That requires policies, strategies, and operational plans to be aligned toward a set of common ends, ways, and means—by *region*. Effective regional strategies against terrorism are the only way that governments can achieve lasting success at home.[30]

Conclusion: Let's Build Something Together

Now that we know what our own CT institutions would look like if we could reengineer them, perhaps national-security officials from resource-rich countries can help other governments design *their* institutions—in some cases from scratch—so they can generate the capacity they need to be effective. However, we cannot expect that the institutions we are helping our partners build should necessarily look like ours—or any other, for that matter. Although every government faces the same challenges, each government has a unique context within which to place its institutions. Governments comfortable with institutions of civil law or a gendarmerie should not have to remodel themselves after one based on common law or the National Guard. To help build real institutional capacity to fight terrorism, supporting countries must be not only able to assess other governments in terms of what works for them, but also be willing to realistically assess their own capacity to help others achieve their full potential. Every government's capacity to fight terrorism is now an important component of every other government.

The Cold War was about the "containment" of one principal threat to the Western block of nations; the new century is about the integration of governments worldwide against a common set of global threats, including terrorism.[31] In the process of helping other governments build CT capacity, the supporting government's officials often end up learning just as much as their counterparts. These officials benefit their home institutions the most when they are candid about their own capacity gaps. Those especially close to the origins of international terrorism should be especially clear about what they think that the United States and other major powers can do better. No country is so small that it cannot make major contributions to the efforts against terrorism. There are plenty of lessons learned and best practices to share among all participants. The critical step is to translate these lessons, learned at the personal level, into better structures and processes in all governments and their institutions. Capacity at the institutional level is the fundamental building block for successful strategies against terrorism, both nationally and regionally. If governments help one another build institutional capacity, and then share in the application of the results, terrorist organizations have no chance in the long term. We know it, and they know it.

Notes

1. See Carl von Clausewitz, *On War*, trans. Michael Howard and Peter Paret (Princeton: Princeton University Press, 1976). The Law of Armed Conflict, also called the Laws of War, refers to the body of law promulgated mostly since World War I to codify and govern permissible actions by combatants in wartime. For a fairly exhaustive list, see the University of Minnesota's Human Rights Library online: http://www1.umn.edu/humanrts/instree/auoy.htm.

2. Thomas Mockaitis describes contemporary terrorist organizations in Chapter 2.

3. See Thomas X. Hammes, *The Sling and the Stone* (St. Paul: Zenith, 2004), 31. The whole book is dedicated to this proposition.

4. See John Rapley, "The New Middle Ages," *Foreign Affairs* (May/June, 2006); and Phil Williams, "From the New Middle Ages to a New Dark Age: The Decline of the State and U.S. Strategy," Strategic Studies Institute, U.S. Army War College, 3 June 2008, http://www.StrategicStudiesInstitute.army.mil.

5. Group identity is less characteristic than it used to be, but terrorism is still a social activity. "Lone-wolf" terrorism is becoming more of a concern, but most terrorists still cluster together in tight formations or sprawling networks.

6. Hamas and Hezbollah are two examples. These organizations are more than just terrorism factories; they are also humanitarian organizations that govern large portions of their societies. Labeling them terrorist organizations may reduce flexibility in dealing with them effectively.

7. A good example of discontinuity between governments will be witnessed during the U.S. trial of 9/11 hijackers, whenever and wherever that takes place. Germany will be asked by the prosecution to provide evidence that may lead to death penalties

for the defendants, but because German law prohibits the death penalty, that evidence could conceivably be withheld. For a good summary of the issue, see John Goetz and Marcel Rosenbach, "9/11 Trial Puts German–US Relations Under Strain," *Spiegel*, 23 November 2009, http://www.spiegel.de/international/world/0,1518,662814,00.html.

8. *Capability* is not just a military term; it describes anything governments do.

9. For example, Pakistan has the *capabilities* to defeat its Taliban insurgency but may lack the political will.

10. Joseph Schumpeter's concept of "creative destruction" could be applied to government institutions as well as private economic enterprises. Without constant innovation, government can lose its effectiveness as circumstances change. An excerpt from Schumpeter's *Capitalism, Socialism, and Democracy* (1942) appears in *Harper's*, 1975: 82–85.

11. Michels's work is well summarized by Darcy K. Leach, "The Iron Law of What Again? Conceptualizing Oligarchy Across Organizational Forms," *Sociological Theory* 23, no. 3 (September 2005): 312–37. Some critics have suggested that small organizations can avoid becoming oligarchies but that the potential is always there.

12. One reason that we see so many good leaders in the world of sports may be that players continue to play within rules established beforehand. Coaches and managers on the sidelines must watch their players make split-second decisions on the field. Those coaches who try to micromanage their players destroy the spirit of independence needed to win.

13. Combat pilots still use Colonel John Boyd's "OODA Loop" framework (Observe, Orient, Decide, Act). A copy of Boyd's last briefing can be found at http://www.chetrichards.com/modern_business_strategy/boyd/essence/eowl_frameset.htm. Institutions can be trained to operate in the same way.

14. The concept of gravitation describes the effect that strong leaders sometimes have on their institutions, drawing all attention to them, making the organization vulnerable to isolation and groupthink.

15. Institutions compete in a Darwinian environment, where funds are scarce and those who should be team players can become existential threats.

16. Some institutions are too small to marshal the resources needed to fulfill their assigned roles. Leaders of these organizations should request more resources or demand a reduction in roles.

17. One of the best discussions of these findings can be found in Malcolm Gladwell, *The Tipping Point* (New York: Little, Brown, 2003), 179.

18. These anecdotes are drawn from a profile of author Keith Sawyer in Justin Ewers, "No Ideas? You're Not Alone," *U.S. News & World Report* (18 June 2007), 50–52.

19. See Ori Brafman's and Rod A. Beckstrom's brilliant but simple book, *The Starfish and the Spider: The Unstoppable Power of Leaderless Organizations* (London: Portfolio, 2006), 175.

20. Retired General Paul Van Riper coined the phrase "in command, but out of control," quoted in Malcolm Gladwell, *Blink: The Power of Thinking Without Thinking* (New York: Little, Brown, 2005), 118.

21. With proper guidance and training, individuals on the fringes of their institutions should be the main players against terrorism.

22. Branfman and Beckstrom, *The Starfish and the Spider*, 21.

23. A role is the broad and continuing purpose for an organization. Missions, which are often confused with roles, are operational tasks given to specific commanders, to be completed in the short to medium term.

24. Planned redundancy leads to resilience; *unplanned* redundancy—a sure indication that an institution is dysfunctional—leads to waste.

25. The FAA had been given the role of making airline flight more attractive to customers, while at the same time its core regulatory role would inevitably make flying *more* inconvenient for passengers. This conflict of roles may have caused the FAA to compromise security for convenience. Similar conflicts can be expected whenever governments set up regulatory institutions.

26. Institutions should focus on developing capabilities, then build capacity. Too many institutions develop new capabilities without generating enough capacity to sustain performance.

27. A good example of this is the Mexican Army. Well-funded and well regarded, that institution does just about everything the government must do (especially police work). Mexico's challenge is either to build other institutions capable of relieving the army of its law-enforcement role or to restructure the army for long-term operations against drug-trafficking organizations.

28. To maximize the possibilities, institutions must tap the power of liaison, assigning good people to other institutions to expand their own capacity without growing too large.

29. Ironically, the invocation of Article 5 by NATO member states did not become necessary until the terrorist attacks of September 2001. NATO is now facing the tougher challenge of collaborating every day in Afghanistan.

30. The same rule applies to other transnational threats, including maritime piracy. The collective efforts of Southeast Asian governments against piracy offer a prime example of what works, one initiative being the "Eye in the Sky" agreement, allowing officers from several countries to share surveillance aircraft. For more, go to http://www.marinetalk.com/articles-marine-companies/art/Eye-in-the-sky-Initiative-BIM003102745IN.html.

31. Richard M. Haass, *The Opportunity: America's Moment to Alter History's Course* (New York: Public Affairs, 2005). Haass uses the word *integration* to propose a doctrine to succeed containment. He places great emphasis on the importance of integrating U.S. institutions with international bodies.

11 Interagency Decision Making

Lawrence E. Cline

INTERAGENCY COORDINATION AND COOPERATION CONTINUE TO be a hot topic among analysts of governmental-security processes, particularly when dealing with issues surrounding terrorism. In many ways the plethora of study groups, think tanks, and commissions that deal with improving interagency processes have become a virtual cottage industry, producing a continuous spate of analyses that identify specific and general problems, along with recommendations for resolving these problems. However, perhaps the first and most critical point to make about improving interagency coordination is that the best interagency processes in the world cannot make bad policies and strategies succeed. Focusing exclusively on the process rather than broader strategic issues is a recipe for overall failure. Conversely, major blockages in interagency processes can lead to the failure of even well-crafted strategies. There is a fine line to be walked between the extremes of full coordination to the point that agencies lose sight of their specific mandates, and strict "stovepiping" to the point that knowledge vital to the mission fails to reach those who need it most.

The first half of this chapter will review some of the major problems in interagency cooperation identified by several studies and then assess the utility and practicality of some proposed solutions. These solutions fall into two "families": those that can improve coordination among existing organizational structures and those that would require extensive shifts in current procedures. The chapter's second half consists of a case study of the U.S. federal agencies that deal with terrorism and how well, or poorly, they are working together to carry out the executive branch's strategies and policies.

Reasons for Interagency Failure

A number of factors complicate or potentially block effective interagency cooperation within any country's government. In general, these factors can be divided into two major clusters. The first group of obstacles revolves around the internal dynamics of the governmental actors themselves. The second group involves the sorts of specific crisis environments that seem to create the "deer-in-the-headlights syndrome" for governmental and agency leaders, and the overall capabilities of senior leaders—e.g., presidents or prime ministers—to actually control the activities of the agencies beneath them. Furthermore, as analysts William Mendel and David Bradford note, "A fundamental issue in conducting coordination among government agencies is that each agency must first understand its own objectives, concepts for operating, and the resources it has available."[1] In other words, unless the different actors have a clear idea themselves of what they bring to the table, and where their limits for cooperation are, it will be very difficult for them to coordinate planning, strategy, and operations in any meaningful way.

Internal dynamics involve the interests and characteristics of both government agencies and their individual members. It is fair to surmise not only that individuals will be drawn into different kinds of agencies according to their own interests and personality traits, but also that the path to success within a given agency typically can reinforce particular behaviors. Most organizations tend to socialize their members in particular behaviors, and likewise will promote those individuals who best fit the corporate culture. This approach can result in disparate, self-reinforcing organizational cultures even within a larger department or ministry.

On a more practical bureaucratic level, agencies almost inherently have competing interests that can pose real obstacles to coordination and cooperation. This translates into competition for funding. Given finite governmental resources, each agency has a vested interest in maximizing its influence and visibility within the government because doing so typically leads to increased funding. This dynamic can go even further than the agency budget process.

In many countries, including the United States, agencies can and do go outside of normal organizational channels, particularly to national legislatures, to plead their cases for more resources.

Technical capabilities can vary widely between agencies, making coordination difficult and even impossible. In many cases, this can be as simple—but potentially catastrophic—as various security services not having common computer operating systems or common databases. Most typically, the problem arises because ministries or agencies contract individually for information-technology systems and support from private companies rather than depending on a common mandated source or standard. As a result, they operate on systems that are not mutually compatible or, due to staggered purchases, on different generations of similar systems that might or might not function well together. In other cases agencies simply have not kept pace with newer technology, either because of funding constraints or because their leaders are technophobes. As younger workers who are comfortable with information technology move upward through the bureaucratic ranks, however, this latter problem should gradually dissipate.

Larger environmental issues also play a key role in how well organizations will be able to coordinate their counterterrorism work. At the national level in particular, command arrangements between agencies are typically either weak or nonexistent. Perhaps one of the most critical issues involving the interagency process is to answer the question of who is in charge. This issue is usually exacerbated by a lack of clear communications between agencies. Because internal bureaucratic processes differ significantly among many agencies, their methods of communication can at times be a very difficult code for other agencies to break. At the operational level during crises, this largely has been resolved in the United States through mechanisms such as the Incident Command System, but such a system is typically nonexistent during routine operations. At the national level, establishing lines of authority remains a huge problem, which some countries have addressed by establishing new offices, directorates, and the like. In some cases this kind of move has met with success. In others, however, simply establishing a new directorate has had minimal impact because it has not actually addressed the critical question of practical authority.

To complicate matters further, the United States and some other countries have policies in place that deliberately preclude close interagency cooperation in some cases. These "firewalls" tend to be particularly strong between military and civilian agencies, and between foreign and domestic intelligence operations, although since 2001 they have been reduced significantly within the U.S. government. Such limits have been considered necessary to protect the constitutional rights of citizens and to prevent particular security services from gaining excessive power. Governments should establish legal systems to preclude cooperation that is viewed as potentially harmful either to the government or the citizenry, but such restrictions should not be set in stone, and governments should routinely examine their structures and functions to adapt interagency systems as the security environment changes. Clearly, this can be a complex situation, usually necessitating changes to regulations, standard operating procedures, and in many cases laws, but such adaptability is necessary to make sure that lines of communication and authority are clear in an emergency.

Ultimately, without better interagency communication, agencies can disagree not only on what their responses should be but also on what the underlying problem actually is. Obviously, without a common operating picture—which certainly is not always present among agencies at the national level—solutions are very unlikely to be found except by trial and error, at great cost in time, resources, and—ultimately—lives. This need for a common understanding of the situation is closely associated with the importance, mentioned earlier, of having an effectively crafted government-wide strategy that can be operationalized across agencies.

These series of obstacles to coordination and cooperation can easily result in overlapping responsibilities between agencies or in situations in which one agency has the primary authority for a response but another has the resources. The United States presents a good example of this problem. As noted by analyst Gabriel Marcella, the Defense Department has the "resource barons"—agencies replete with people, money, expertise, and equipment. Most other Cabinet departments simply do not have the resources or institutional capability to handle very many disparate programs, and they tend to lack long-term coordination.[2] Because preventing and responding to terrorism require many different actors with a wide range of expertise, governments will need to be diligent about avoiding duplication of effort between agencies to ensure both effectiveness and efficiency. Most importantly, however, governments must ensure that no aspect of the security equation is overlooked and that there are no gaps between agencies where threats can fester unnoticed.

General Approaches to Improving Interagency Coordination

The three main elements to improving interagency coordination systems and processes are leadership, planning, and specific coordination measures. Much of the impetus for interagency improvements typically comes from the leadership level, although many of the practical aspects of cooperation commonly bubble up from the bottom (whether or not sanctioned by senior management). This section examines the roles and responsibilities of planners and leaders, and suggests concrete ways in which they can improve interagency communication and cooperation.

Finding, Making, and Keeping Leaders

Specific measures at the leadership level include executive workshops and other structured forms of senior-leader interagency development. Interestingly, although workshops and similar interagency training at senior levels would seem to be one of the simplest measures to improve coordination, in practice they can be some of the most difficult because corralling senior officials for regular, sustained interagency training and practice can be extraordinarily frustrating. The "I'm too busy; send an aide" syndrome is all too common. These programs usually require reinforcement (preferably positive and, if necessary, negative) from even more senior leaders to ensure their success.

In the long term, education is even more important than specific training for interagency operations. If used properly, existing education programs (such as military staff colleges, in-house governmental programs for civil-service staff, and seminars and programs at civilian universities and colleges) can provide valuable venues for developing individuals with the skills to use interagency methods and tools. These efforts are more likely to succeed if there is cross-fertilization of both students and faculty between these various institutions, combined with programs to strengthen civilian academic and subject-matter expert ties with governmental agencies. However, there are clearly some significant issues with increasing the levels of cooperation between security agencies and military services and civilian academic institutions. These potential problems include academic distrust of security services and the traditional independence that civilian universities and colleges maintain from government influence (with notable exceptions), government personnel policies that dissuade easy entrance to and exit from short-term civil service, and access to classified information. Nevertheless, in today's complex security environment, no government can possibly retain all the varied expertise required for successful counterterrorism "in house."

Concepts for strengthening civilian support have included various forms of civilian reserve for stabilization-type missions. Many of these missions are very analogous to other counterterrorism efforts. In an ideal system a civilian reserve would be composed of specialists on call for specific missions or longer-term augmentation for critical agencies. Similar to military reserve forces, they would draw small monthly stipends in return for guaranteed availability when required. Given the seemingly endless need for specialties such as linguists, area specialists, development experts, and intelligence specialists, such a reserve system could help provide flexibility for both crises and longer-term contingency operations. The numerous difficulties that allied forces are facing in Iraq and Afghanistan as they try to cope with very complex environments have sharply increased interest in these types of new structures for tapping other sources of expertise. Proposals have ranged from simply maintaining national-level databases on former military and government civilians who have the desired expertise and who could be recalled on a short-term contract basis, to a formalized reserve system similar to that of the military.

However, there are some practical difficulties with these types of proposals. Most broadly, a civilian reserve corps would require a probably extensive series of new legal structures. Military reservists now are covered by an umbrella of laws protecting everything from reemployment rights to health benefits. Tailoring these types of laws to civilian reservists—who would seem to be equally deserving, especially if serving in combat zones—might be a somewhat tougher political sell both within Congress and among the public. Funding such a system could also be problematic. As demonstrated by the various legal issues surrounding the extensive use of contractors in Iraq, simply hiring contractors to bring in necessary skill sets can present some interesting political and diplomatic issues, particularly regarding legal jurisdiction, chain of command, and terms of service. At the more operational level, the integration of either "reservists" or contractors into existing bureaucratic structures does not always go smoothly and almost always takes time to become effective. Also, with several of the proposals, the odds are good that some of these reserve civilians would be fairly senior, leading to the question of whether they would be appointed to key leadership positions; in the nature of the bureaucratic beast, this situation could lead to a fair degree of organizational upheaval—the very opposite of the intended outcome.

Somewhat more broadly, leadership must provide an environment in which interagency cooperation is actually rewarded. In fairness to the U.S. system, several agencies (especially the intelligence services) have begun to increase their emphasis on this, albeit after considerable prodding by Congress. Among other measures under the rubric of the "information sharing environment," employee evaluations include how well the employees share information with partner agencies, while an awards system recognizes improvements in information sharing.[3] Although this particular initiative focuses only on sharing information while paying little attention to other forms of interagency cooperation, the underlying concept could be adapted to broader coordination systems.

Planning to Win

At the planning level, it should be obvious that workable plans must be in place *before* a crisis strikes. The baseline for any plan involves identifying all those agencies that will be involved in implementing it, and creating a clear picture of their roles and contributions. Planners must not only specify the hierarchies for the flow of authority but also ensure that each agency understands its own role in implementing the plan. An important component of any plan (and one that frequently is overlooked due to its difficulty) is to identify potential obstacles to its successful implementation. This essentially boils down to asking—and answering—the question "What if?"

For the initial stages of planning, senior steering groups (primarily for planning and establishing broad guidelines) have proven to be a useful tool, particularly for establishing mutually agreed-upon concepts, planning tools, and constructs. Both senior and operational leaders must agree ahead of time on roles and missions for the various agencies that will be working together. A more informal step, but at least as important, is fairly unstructured brainstorming and war-gaming sessions, which can provide a useful start for the planning process, which can then be followed by more-structured interagency planning exercises. It is also critical for each agency to develop baseline knowledge of the other agencies' capabilities and limitations, which will help determine the information and support that any of them might require from the others. After the planning process, participants will need practice and rehearsal to validate and, if necessary, change the plans. Plans must also be reviewed regularly to ensure that they remain valid as the security environment changes. All too often, once plans are put on paper, those responsible for their implementation tend to assume that all they need to do is to pull the plans off the shelf at the right moment and then implement them. The development, rehearsal, updating, review, rehearsal, and further updating of plans must be routine for all agencies.

Some specific procedures to improve coordination that have proven successful include formal interagency exchanges. As with other steps, these need to be crafted somewhat carefully. The exchange officers should be highly qualified and have a broad knowledge of their home agencies' operations. They should also be fairly senior, with enough authority to represent their agencies' interests. The time length for such tours can vary but should probably be in terms of a year to a few years, rather than months: Too little time means such exchanges can add little value; too much time and the exchange officer can lose touch with his or her own agency.

At the operational level, reliable and knowledgeable liaison teams between agencies may be the most useful tool. As with exchange officers, these liaison teams must have solid knowledge of their own agency and be able to rapidly acquire knowledge of the agency to which they are posted. The most critical capability of such liaison teams is solid communications, both technical and personal, between the team, their home agency, and the attached agency. One issue with liaison teams is that they typically must be "taken out of hide," meaning that the sourcing institution is investing resources for an undefined payoff. All too frequently, this can result in choosing liaison officers who are readily at hand or who are viewed as being the most easily spared. One technique used by some organizations to alleviate this problem has been to add allotments of personnel (and supporting equipment) specifically formed as liaison teams, which can help both to reduce the selection of "spare" personnel (unlikely to be of the highest qualification) for the teams and to permit liaison team personnel to become more skilled in their roles.

The United States as a Case Study

A good way to evaluate the practicalities and potential problems that can arise from efforts to improve the interagency process is through a case study. The enormous U.S. government bureaucracy, which is continuously looking for ways to recast its processes to be more effective and efficient, may provide some useful examples for countries that find themselves facing similar obstacles.

Counterterrorism planning that involves interagency coordination among U.S. government actors begins at the National Security Council (NSC) staff, a non-Cabinet agency directed by the President's "national security advisor." One difficulty during the initial development of national-security policy is that the exact role of the NSC staff remains fluid. It most typically is the coordinating body for national interagency policy development, but this has varied significantly based on the nature of the administration; the relative strengths of the national security advisor (who is appointed directly by the President), the secretary of State, and the secretary of Defense; and in some cases on the particular issues at hand.[4] At least in theory, the national security advisor and the NSC staff corporately should have more power over national-security policy than other agencies because of the NSC's proximity to the President, but experience has not always supported this.

Beyond the normal bureaucratic turf battles with other departments, the NSC staff must also compete with a variety of other "czars" and special presidential advisors for particular policy issues. Bureaucratic shifts based on administration reorganizations and changing priorities also affect the staff's ability to coordinate national-security policy. For instance, some elements that were previously handled through the NSC staff have gravitated to the National Economic Council. The more recently established Homeland Security Council must also be factored in, especially for transnational terrorism, which affects both domestic and overseas government activities.

Several major changes to the strategic interagency planning process were made under both the William Clinton and George W. Bush administrations through presidential decision directives. These directives have tried to institutionalize integrated civil–military implementation plans and interagency rehearsals, after-action reviews, and training. Although such efforts bore some fruit, resource allocation, cultural variations, and actual authority have remained problematic.[5] Also, while these directives did provide improved guidance for coordination in specific situations, they did not cover the widest range of environments in which the interagency process is required. Gabriel Marcella describes some basic bureaucratic mindsets that affect how U.S. policy translates into action:

> The reality is that a presidential directive is not a permanent guide to the actions of agencies. Rarely is it fully implemented. The cultures of the various executive departments will modify how directives are interpreted. For example, for the military oriented Defense Department, a directive is an order to be

carried out. For State, a directive may be interpreted as the general direction a policy should take. Presidential policy can be overtaken by new priorities, new administrations, and by the departure of senior officials who had the stakes, the personal relationships, know-how, and institutional memory to make it work. A senior NSC staffer, Navy Captain Joseph Bouchard, Director of Defense Policy and Arms Control, remarked in 1999 that one could not be sure about whether a directive from a previous administration was still in force because the government does not maintain a consolidated list of these documents for security reasons.[6]

The next layer of coordination comes at the Cabinet level, and this is where some of the most egregious problems occur. Cabinet secretaries at least theoretically are equal in rank and authority, deriving much of their influence from personal stature and their ability to gain and retain the President's ear. This creates a highly competitive environment in which a zero-sum game mentality can thrive, particularly among the major "security" Cabinet positions—State, Defense, and Homeland Security—as they vie to see who will be in charge of addressing specific security threats. This is even further complicated by occasionally contentious relations between the national security advisor and the secretaries of State or Defense.

Following 11 September 2001, the Bush administration tried to address some of these national-level coordination issues by creating two new departments: the Department of Homeland Security (DHS) and the Office of the Director of National Intelligence (DNI). Each effectively added one more layer of bureaucracy over the top of the existing structures in an effort to improve the leadership of and coordination among sub-Cabinet national agencies. Each new organization has faced significant difficulties reaching an effective operating status, however, raising questions about whether any increased internal coordination has justified the added bureaucracy.

DHS has reportedly had problems trying to meld a group of established national agencies with disparate missions, from border security to emergency management, into a coherent whole. In large part this may be ascribed to DHS leadership's view that their principal mission is antiterrorism. This was not the primary mission, or even a consideration, for many of the agencies that have been incorporated into Homeland Security. For example, the Coast Guard continues to have missions involving maritime safety, law enforcement, search and rescue, maritime and port security, and overseas support to the Navy.[7] Not all these missions fit comfortably under the rubric of homeland security. Likewise, the Federal Emergency Management Agency (FEMA) has a much broader mission than simply domestic security. These traditional missions tend to remain the most critical for the agencies, particularly because in most cases there is no other organization to substitute for them. A closely related problem for these agencies (and for some others) has been the failure of DHS leaders to adequately support the nonsecurity missions—both conceptually and financially—because of the continued stress on antiterrorism.

Several other factors influence the interagency and broader intra-agency processes within DHS. For instance, the merger of the previously separate Immigration and Customs Services into a unified Immigration and Customs Enforcement agency has reportedly not gone particularly well because of differences in institutional culture. There also continue to be overlaps in some missions between agencies, resulting in inefficiencies and probably some questions among policy makers as to which agency should take the lead.[8]

The establishment of the office of the Director of National Intelligence has also affected the national interagency process. Statutorily, the DNI is supposed to oversee the operations of sixteen intelligence agencies, a breadth of responsibility that by any established concept is excessive. The DNI also has very weak control over programming and the intelligence budget. The largest spender for intelligence programs—primarily on equipment such as satellites, unmanned aerial vehicles, electronic collection systems, and the like—is the Defense Department. The secretary of Defense certainly has shown no indications of wanting to cede his spending authority for these systems.

As the saying goes, "size matters." Although the Office of the DNI has steadily expanded, it still is miniscule in comparison with many of the intelligence agencies that it purportedly coordinates and supervises. It is far from clear that the Office of the DNI has yet developed the systems, size, or expertise to actively manage the intelligence community. Moreover, its actual analytical capabilities are still nascent. All this has coincided with a series of apparent bureaucratic turf battles between the DNI and the Director of Central Intelligence, many of whose powers (at least on paper) have been shifted to the DNI, resulting in some rather well-publicized feuds. The resignation of Dennis Blair as DNI in May 2010—the third director in the five years of the office's existence—underscored the precariousness of the position, especially when up against a strong, turf-conscious Director of Central Intelligence and weak political support from the White House.

At the macro level, one analyst correctly noted that a key player that is commonly overlooked in interagency coordination is Congress.[9] As the interagency process continues and more joint centers become operational, "Congress will need to consider its own committee structure and how to provide appropriate oversight to new arrangements, which may be hybrids, ad hoc, and require a lot of flexibility in funding and authority."[10] Executive agencies such as the Office of Management and Budget and the General Services Administration, which are involved with budgeting and resource support for other organizations, will likely face similar issues with ad hoc and emerging agencies and centers.

Still at the national level, but more on the operational side, the National Counterterrorism Center (NCTC), another subset of ODNI, thus far has presented the most positive image for interagency cooperation. According to most open-source reports, the NCTC, which was set up in 2004 to bridge what was seen as a critical gap between joint intelligence and joint operational planning after 9/11, has made considerable progress in the coordination and synthesis of multiple agencies' counterterrorism work. Cooperation with other agencies and centers is reportedly very good, and the NCTC has solid links with government decision makers through both technical and bureaucratic channels.[11] It is also linked with the Justice Department's joint terrorism task forces (JTTFs), a series of about 100 centers located in major cities across the country that bring together federal, state, and local intelligence; law enforcement; and other experts to discover and prevent planned attacks. The JTTF system has proven to be effective in its missions, despite some ongoing issues about how to merge the law-enforcement and intelligence-analysis sides of the operations, provide access to differing levels of classified material, and reduce personnel turnover.

The biggest organizational problem facing the NCTC has been somewhat extrinsic to it. Together with the JTTFs, most major security, intelligence, and law-enforcement agencies have also established internal counterterrorism centers. This proliferation of centers can greatly complicate the communications and networking grids that are basic to effective cooperation. Also, the sheer number of counterterrorism centers, although not directly undermining interagency cooperation, can dilute collective capabilities; the supply of trained, experienced analysts is a finite resource that takes time to develop and can be difficult to sustain. Finally, the NCTC and JTTFs are examples of a much larger issue: Most U.S. steps to improve the interagency process have involved creating new structures and new bureaucracies rather than rationalizing existing structures.

Below the national level, as noted earlier, interagency cooperation at the operational and tactical level has usually proven more effective. A study group that focused on embassy-level functionality concluded that "country teams"—Washington's term for the multiple agencies represented at embassies—are more likely than their counterparts back home to work toward a common purpose. These staffs regard their head, in this case the ambassador, as a unifying authority; operate on a significantly reduced scale; and likely have a sense of community as a result both of isolation from home and proximity to one another.[12] These positives are of course not guaranteed; some country teams function far better than others. In many ways the critical factor is the ambassador, whose willingness and ability to coordinate the embassy's multiple agencies' activities can vary widely. The situation can be even further complicated in countries where there is a significant U.S. military presence:

> However, the relationships among other top-level interagency officials are not as clear. In particular, the span of control and authority of both the senior civilian representative—ambassador or President's Special Representative (PSR)—and the senior military commander in the field is often hard to define. Past experience has shown that one cannot be formally subordinate to the other. By law, PSRs have authority over civilian agencies and operations in the field. Until now, relationships primarily have been personality driven.[13]

At the operational level, the U.S. Defense Department, and in particular the combatant commands have, true to form, established a number of ad hoc centers and coordinating cells at various levels within the department, which are intended to improve coordination between the military services and other agencies. Although too numerous to name individually here, it is worthwhile to address some of their common strengths and weaknesses.

First, because these operational centers and cells are Defense entities, their focus is of course skewed toward military issues. Also, they generally have been grafted onto existing relationships between government agencies and are likely to duplicate those relationships rather than simplify or clarify interagency coordination. Finally, there is no established template for how these new combatant command centers are to be structured. Whereas some flexibility may be desirable to reflect the needs of the various combatant commands, allowing too many differences in their structure, reporting chains, and specific responsibilities is more likely to increase than decrease confusion when dealing with other centers and agencies.

Some practical lessons can be drawn from ad hoc intelligence cells that were established for earlier multinational stability operations. The principal difficulty for these intelligence centers has been to find a way to turn a disparate group of "augmentees" into a functional team.[14] The author's observations in Iraq in 2007 would suggest that melding joint centers can be problematic. Individual augmentees and replacement personnel almost always require time to acclimate to the working environments of such centers because the centers' organizational structures, internal procedures, and operating cultures will normally be individualized. The augmentation personnel may or may not match the actual requirements in terms of their skills and experience. Even the information-technology systems used by particular centers may be new to augmentees, requiring even longer learning curves for new personnel and further impeding a center's effectiveness.

Final Observations

Some analysts have argued that the current stress on interagency cooperation may be overdone. Two scholars in particular suggest that the search for truly seamless interagency cooperation may be futile and that "the existence of such a solution is a chimera."[15] Also, as William Olson warns, "[C]oordination can reduce the efficiency of an individual agency to carry out task-specific, agency-specific objectives," a noteworthy downside to the present infatuation with interagency processes.[16] In the United States this has in fact been one of the criticisms occasionally leveled at the 1986 Goldwater–Nichols Act, which mandated that U.S. military officers serve in joint assignments (those that involve working with the other military services) as a way to decrease interservice rivalries and aid joint military operations.[17] These requirements can make it difficult for individual officers, who must try to "make the gates" for required joint assignments while maintaining proficiency in their primary career areas. At the systemic level, managing the rather complex statutory joint-service requirements for officers further complicated the services' personnel systems. Probably in response to these problems, the range of assignments that have been coded as "joint" has steadily expanded, seeming at times to have little to do with the practical "jointness" of the positions.

A mandatory requirement for civilian officials to serve interagency tours could have similar results.

William Olson sums up the environment very well: "Unfortunately, problems occur at the speed of light, analysis of problems occurs at the speed of sound, and responses occur at the speed of bureaucracy."[18] The speed of bureaucracy can be even further slowed by weak interagency cooperation. Problems with interagency relationships remain one of the most significant issues with regard to counterterrorism. Therefore, no matter how difficult, improving the effectiveness of the interagency process remains critical to effective planning and operations.

Notes

1. William W. Mendel and David G. Bradford, "Interagency Cooperation: A Regional Model for Overseas Operations," McNair Paper 37, Institute for National Strategic Studies, National Defense University, Washington D.C., March 1995, 25.

2. Gabriel Marcella, "Understanding the Interagency Process: The Challenge of Adaptation," in *Affairs of State: The Interagency and National Security,* ed. Gabriel Marcella (Carlisle Barracks: Strategic Studies Institute, U.S. Army War College, December 2008), 39.

3. The entire system is in Thomas E. McNamara, program manager, Information Sharing Environment, "Information Sharing Environment: Progress and Plans Annual Report to the Congress," June 2009, http://www.securitymanagement.com/news/information-sharing-environment-releases-annual-report-005871.

4. For some of these cases, see Marcella, ed., *Affairs of State,* 15.

5. For details on PDD 56, the order signed by President Clinton in 1997 that mandated education for personnel in peacekeeping missions, see William P. Hamblet and Jerry G. Kline, "PDD 56 and Complex Contingency Operations," *Joint Forces Quarterly* (Spring 2000): 92–97.

6. Marcella, ed., *Affairs of State,* 27–28.

7. These missions can be compared to the roles that DHS lists on its Web site: "Guarding Against Terrorism"; "Securing Our Borders"; "Enforcing our Immigration Laws"; "Improving our Readiness for, Response to and Recovery from Disasters"; "Maturing and Unifying the Department"; "Strengthen and Build Partnerships."

8. See Pam Fessler, "DHS Still Dogged by Questions over Effectiveness," National Public Radio, 14 January 2008, www.npr.org/templates/story/story.php?storyId=17969438. For some earlier analyses of DHS, see "The Department of Homeland Security: The Road Ahead," Testimony of Michael A. Wermuth to the Senate Committee on Homeland Security and Governmental Affairs, 109th Congress, 1st session, 26 January 2005, RAND Corporation, Santa Monica, January 2005.

9. Ellen Laipson and Olga Romanova, eds., *Improving the Interagency Process to Face 21st Century Security Challenges* (Washington D.C., Henry L. Stimson Center, 2005), 9.

10. Ibid.

11. For specific procedures being used for this system, see "Developing and Sharing Information and Intelligence in a New World: Guidelines for Establishing and Operating Fusion Centers at the Local, State, Tribal, and Federal Level (Law Enforcement Intelligence Component)," Version 1, Global Justice Information Sharing Initiative, U.S. Department of Justice, July 2005.

12. Laipson and Romanova, eds., *Improving the Interagency Process*, 5–6.

13. Neyla Arnas, Charles Barry, and Robert B. Oakley, "Harnessing the Interagency for Complex Operations," Center for Technology and National Security Policy, National Defense University, Washington, D.C., August 2005, 3.

14. Augmentees can be reserve or regular but essentially are individually assigned personnel who can either fill open slots in an existing organization or with whom completely new organizations can be built. The latter is more common for ad hoc intelligence centers.

15. Clayton K. S. Chun and Frank L. Jones, "Learning to Play the Game: The National Security Policymaking Process" in Marcella, ed., *Affairs of State*, 172. They also review the problems in cooperation: 172–214.

16. William J. Olson, "Interagency Coordination: The Normal Accident or the Essence of Indecision," in Marcella, ed., *Affairs of State*, 225.

17. Goldwater–Nichols Department of Defense Reorganization Act of 1986 (Publ.L. 99-433).

18. Olson, "Interagency Coordination," 228.

12 Defusing Terrorist Ideology

Paul Shemella

THE SO-CALLED "WAR" ON TERRORISM IS NOT A WAR AT ALL; IT is a political contest that can be won only at the political level. But terrorist attacks have the *feel* of military operations, tempting governments to respond in kind. Terrorism is not even about the action itself but rather about the *re*action it precipitates. Terrorists understand how easily governments can militarize their responses. Political leaders, especially democratically elected ones who feel pressure from their constituents to *do* something, overreact on cue. Indeed, government overreaction is a cornerstone of terrorist strategy: By provoking quick military responses, our attackers force us to make political mistakes. Terrorists have turned Clausewitz on his head; they wage war by other means.

This is not to say that coercive force should be avoided altogether. Precise and timely kinetic responses are a vital part of the government tool kit. We need ways to limit the freedom of action that terrorists bring to the fight, which includes decreasing the number of extremists eager to make their political statements with acts of terrorism. But dissuading angry citizens from resorting to violence in the first place is a strategy more challenging to execute (and more difficult to evaluate) than using brute force. How do we persuade terrorists to abandon violence while at the same time we are doing our best to find and kill them? And perhaps even more important, how do we prevent ordinary citizens from *becoming* terrorists? Governments are confronted, then, with Kafka's choices: Do we call the doctor to explain—and perhaps cure—the disease of terrorism, or do we call the locksmith to sequester terrorists from the rest of society?[1] Our leaders have to make both calls.

The Doctor Is In

Any attempt to understand the problem of terrorism begins with identifying root causes. Simply stated, root causes are conditions within contemporary societies that provide fertile ground for terrorism to germinate. These conditions operate across whole societies, influencing individuals in different ways. They do not inevitably lead to terrorism, but they are certainly the first step down that path. Each government faces its own unique set of historical, social, geographic, and political conditions, and although poverty, ignorance, and injustice often top the list of root causes, bad governance could be a more important factor (this suggests that better governance can go a long way toward defeating terrorism). In some cases a government's foreign policy could be considered a root cause, while lack of social cohesion certainly belongs on such a list—there are many possibilities from which to choose.

The second, essential step to terrorism is motivation. Acts of terrorism are carried out by individuals and small groups that are motivated by specific factors superimposed on root causes. These factors include the trinity of rage, recognition, and revenge described by Louise Richardson.[2] But sources of motivation alone cannot propel ordinary citizens to undertake extreme measures against innocent fellow citizens; they must be inspired by charismatic leaders and encouraged by similarly motivated peers. Terrorism is a *social* activity driven by group dynamics as well as root causes and motivation. Individuals do things in groups that they would never do on their own.[3]

Therefore, what motivates individuals, acting in small groups, to adopt a strategy of terrorism?[4] Frustration and fear top this list. Unhappy people anywhere, given the right circumstances, can be dangerous to the rest of society. Here it is useful to revisit Abraham Maslow's so-called "hierarchy of human needs," which places physiological requirements at the bottom and self-actualization at the top.[5] In the middle come love and esteem, both for the self and for others. It is after their most basic needs are met that human beings tend to raise their expectations for fulfillment, a condition that inevitably leads to disappointment and perhaps resorting to extreme behavior.[6] Governments cannot monitor individuals according to their places on this hierarchy, but they can create the conditions that allow their citizens to move in the direction of self-actualization. The *potential* for this mobility is what governments must explain and nurture within their societies.

However, we can go back further than Maslow, all the way to Plato, who divided the soul into three parts—reason, desire, and something the Greeks called *thymos*.[7] The word *thymos* is actually crucial to describing why terrorists behave the way they do. It translates literally as "spiritedness" and describes an innate sense of justice. *Thymos* captures the often inchoate need for self-substantiation that drives human beings to act *without* reason. Implicit in Plato's division of the soul is that each human being comprises a unique distribution of the three parts. Ironically, soldiers share a healthy dose of *thymos* with their terrorist enemies, tempting both to sacrifice their very lives for a cause. It may be that the thymotic impulse is more responsible for terrorism than anything else in the human psyche, linked as it is to recognition, power, and glory.[8]

But groups of human beings do not simply hold *themselves* together. Individuals are held together by kinship and common purpose. Setting aside kinship, which is more common in organized crime than in terrorism, shared goals are the glue that binds terrorists to one another. Goals are expressed through strongly held beliefs that present the group with an inspiring narrative and serve to legitimate acts of violence. This is extremist ideology: the DNA of terrorism, passed from generation to generation.

The Role of Ideology

Ideology is a rigid set of beliefs—a *system* of beliefs—that constrains and compels people to behave in particular ways. Ideology, especially the extremist version, does not allow for compromise; it is a Manichean system of reasoning that cannot serve as a basis for day-to-day political activity.[9] Ideology is, in fact, the antithesis of politics, a system that thrives on debate and compromise. It is also distinguishable from philosophy and religion, which guide how *individuals* choose to live.[10] Ideology is about how a few individuals think *society* should be organized. Ideologically driven behavior goes beyond merely acting on principle; it involves forcibly imposing one's rules on the larger society. The transition from principle to ideology takes place when one decides that all nonbelievers are just plain wrong.

Ideology is an attempt to make the world simple (an increasingly attractive proposition to many in the mainstream as their lives become more complex). It offers members of the group a set of basic rules, easy to follow and easy to teach others, along with a strong sense of belonging and purpose. Groups driven by ideology normally have strong leadership, but they do not need it to maintain their identification. Adherents pursue actions that fall within the parameters of their ideology, self-organizing in innovative ways that are very difficult to predict—and even more difficult to counter.[11] This is the same phenomenon that produces flocking behavior in birds and fish. These populations have no leader; they rely on a simple set of local rules, hardwired into each individual's genes, that serve to ensure the survival of the species.

There are three broad sources for ideology that motivates terrorism. The first is political philosophy. During the 1970s and 1980s Marxism was a key ideology for many European terrorist groups, while Maoism continues to motivate a number of Asian and South American groups. Environmentalism as an ideology has given impetus to the new phenomenon of "eco-terrorism." Some would include nihilism, the current manifestation of which we see in the youth gangs of Central America.[12] Significantly, the ideologies that originate in political theory are often superseded by political practice, leaving governments an opening for dialogue.[13]

The second source for extremist ideology is ethnic nationalism. The desire of small groups to earn recognition, and the resources that go with it, from the larger society often involves issues of territory and cultural integrity, while separatism continues to drive political dissent in most of the world. What transforms separatist feelings into terrorism is the ideology associated with ethnicity. This has manifested itself most famously in Northern Ireland and the Basque region of Spain, but nationalism has already done its greatest damage, provoking and justifying the conventional wars of the twentieth century. Ethnic nationalism is motivating hard-line politicians and their citizens today in places such as Iraq and Pakistan, but perhaps its ultimate expression this century has been the long civil conflict in Sri Lanka.[14]

The third source for extremist ideology is religion. Religion that has taken the evolutionary leap to ideology can be a platform for the worst kinds of atrocities. Recent examples of this phenomenon include the Oklahoma City bombing in the name of Christian identity, the expanding influence of Shia and Wahhabist extremism, and the worldwide terrorist activities of Al Qaeda in the name of Islam. Religious extremists have, throughout history, abused the power of the faith by transforming it into an ideology to guide destructive behavior.[15] Attaching religious fervor to nuclear, biological, or chemical weapons conjures some truly frightening scenarios.

The role of ideology extends beyond that of binding individuals together and legitimating their activities. Ideologies are also used to mobilize outsiders. In network fashion, terrorist organizations target the disaffected members of a population by attempting to convince them that there is an alternative way of thinking that will make their lives more meaningful (and simpler). If the population has a large number of disaffected individuals susceptible to the ideology, enough of them can be recruited to make direct action possible.[16] These recruits will be readily convinced to take part in terrorist actions, operations that validate and strengthen the ideology they share.[17]

Figure 12-1 diagrams this cycle and suggests three ways that governments can break it. The most important of the three is to establish education and antidiscrimination programs that reduce the size of the disaffected population. The second is to launch a campaign to counter the extremist ideology, severing the radical interpretation from its legitimate source. The third measure that governments must adopt is to interdict the flow of support to terrorist organizations from foreign suppliers. In the case of extremist ideology based on a legitimate religion (as in Figure 12-1), this support would include funding and teachers for schools where extremist ideology is taught.[18]

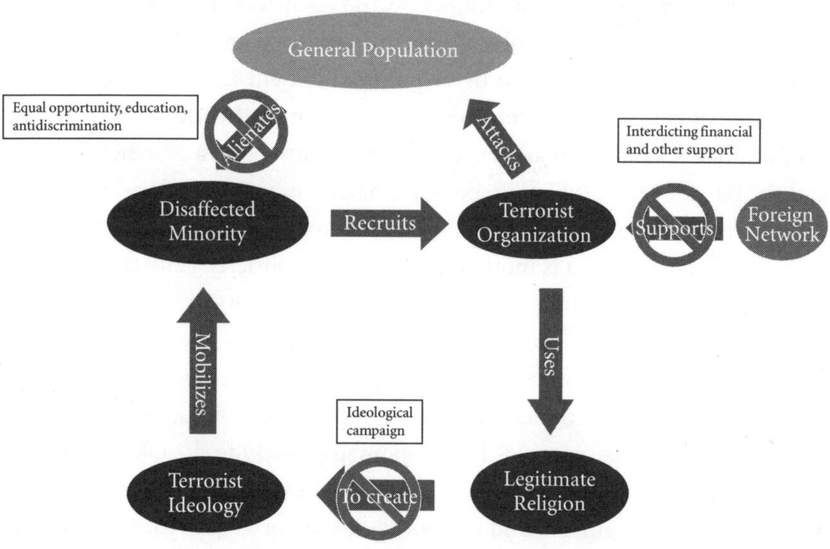

FIGURE 12-1 Disrupting ideological support for terrorism
SOURCE: This diagram was designed by Thomas Mockaitis, a contributor to this volume, and is used with his permission.

A discussion of ideology would not be complete without mentioning the concept of "fantasy ideology," best described by Lee Harris.[19] Harris has linked the historical experiences of the pre–Civil War American South, Mussolini's fascist regime, Hitler's Nazism, and Al Qaeda's quest for a pan-Islamic "caliphate"' together into a useful construct by exploring the dreamlike quality of their guiding ideologies. Fantasy ideology is the self-delusion of strong leaders who capture the mass imagination to support a vision that is either unattainable through mere political activity or unachievable through war.[20] Like other forms of ideology, it is firmly rooted in the idealized past. How do you counter a fantasy?

Linked to the concept of fantasy ideology is the enduring appeal of cults around the world. There appears to be something in the human psyche that makes many of us vulnerable to destructive messages issued by charismatic leaders. On a micro scale (though certainly not for the families involved) are examples of mass suicide among cult members, the most famous being the 1978 Jonestown disaster. On a macro scale, the frightening experience of the Japanese with Aum Shinrikyo gives us a possible prototype for the future of terrorism. Cults appear where hopelessness and lack of meaning prevail, especially in advanced societies where consumerism seems to have replaced more meaningful values, prompting some individuals to separate themselves from their families and other social groupings. They happily sacrifice their egos to the collective, vesting all power over their lives in one leader or a strict hierarchy. The root causes of cult formation, then, are very similar to the root causes of terrorism itself. Within such a context, the appearance of highly motivated individuals armed with a lust for power and lethal charisma can trigger terrorism.[21]

The Case of Violent Salafism

Since the 2001 World Trade Center attacks, officials and scholars have searched for the right term to describe the terrorists who launched them. Merely calling these people "terrorists" is correct but inadequate. To be able to counter the ideology that fueled the attacks, there must be a way to distinguish the members of this particular grouping from other terrorists with different ideologies.[22] Terrorism is terrorism regardless of who does it or why, but all terrorists are not created equal.

The term *Islamic terrorists* is an insult to all Muslims except those few to whom it applies, and is therefore counterproductive. *Islamist terrorists* does not work either because it offends many peaceful Muslims who call themselves Islamist (including the prime minister of Turkey). The term *jihadists* offends Muslims by associating terrorism with one of the most important elements of Islamic faith, while rewarding terrorists with an imprimatur of righteousness.[23] *Islamo-fascists* does not work for obvious reasons, and those U.S. officials who began using the term in 2006 withdrew it quickly. The term *Salafist* describes a portion of the Islamic community that wishes for a return to the Islamic world of Mohammed and his immediate descendants. There are pious Salafists who do not advocate violence, but there are a significant number who do. The term *violent Salafist* would appear to describe Osama bin Laden and his followers.[24]

The main goals of violent Salafism include replacing secular governments in Muslim lands with "legitimate" governments ruled by sharia. The aggregation of such governments would lead to a new "caliphate" spanning North Africa, the Middle East, Central Asia, South Asia, and Southeast Asia. Violent Salafists also intend to demonstrate the military power of motivated holy warriors and to counter the morally corrosive effect of Western secularism (and, indeed, all secularism). These are not political goals; they are ideological. This is a strategy of terrorism not as a means to an end, but as an end in itself. Terrorist acts are used to reinforce the inevitability of the dream and strengthen the power of those leading the way. It is the fantasy ideology of violent Salafism that drives the most dangerous form of terrorism today. There is no better example of the synergy between ideology and terrorism.[25]

Governments Can Help

The advent of global terrorism has forced governments, acting together, to send targeted messages to people all over the world. Those messages can be effective only when policies, strategies, and public attitudes align. With regard to violent Salafism, there are four multinational audiences to whom messages must be sent. To the opponents of secular Islam, the messages should say, "The removal of religion from politics does not dilute religious belief." To the sympathizers of Islamic renewal, "We understand and support you." To the supporters of Salafism, "You are entitled to your beliefs, but do not use violence to achieve your goals." To the terrorist core of violent Salafists, "Governments, acting together, will stop you from using terrorism against our citizens with all the means in our power."[26]

Governing is a system of incentives and disincentives to encourage or compel citizens to behave in certain ways.[27] The messages that governments send to all citizens should encourage individuals to maintain allegiance to the government (while making leadership *worthy* of that allegiance) and to foster the development of a healthy civil society through voluntary nongovernmental associations. The messages for committed and potential terrorists should be even clearer. Terrorists must know that government (and the civil society it represents) will increase the expected costs of terrorist activity while decreasing the expected benefits.

Governments can learn from business as they design foreign and domestic policies aimed at gaining the respect and allegiance that they need to govern effectively. If the government can be imagined as a doctor trying to immunize society against the virus of terrorism, it can also be imagined as a provider of services whose customers are individual citizens. Viewed from that perspective, governments need to "brand" themselves like any commercial enterprise that wishes to stay in business.[28]

Citizens of countries from Iraq to India may wonder whether terrorism is the price of democracy. Certainly, open societies are more vulnerable to terrorism than dictatorial ones, especially in the short term. In the long term, however, open societies allow citizens to express their political dissent in a wide range of nonviolent ways, thus damping the potential for political and ideological violence. Every society has a unique tolerance for violence, a different threshold, beyond which citizens feel their government can no longer protect them.[29] Each government must force whatever level of violence exists in its society below that threshold, while striving to eradicate the root causes and sources of motivation for terrorism itself.

The Pivotal Role of Civil Society

However, governments cannot do the whole job. At some point the society itself must take charge of countering ideological support for terrorism. Unless a society can develop consensus for a "zero-tolerance" approach to terrorism, its government can only achieve marginal results. But it is government's responsibility to create the *environment* in which society can, in essence, cure itself. Top-down measures have to meet bottom-up measures somewhere in the middle. This is a symbiotic relationship that depends on the existence of a healthy and active civil society.

It is civil society, the space between government institutions and individual citizens, that catalyzes the chain reaction needed for zero tolerance. Civil society contains the opinion leaders who have the ability to influence mass audiences in all sectors of a population. What is needed here is a "social epidemic," relying on citizen/messengers to spread positive ideas to friends and neighbors until everyone agrees not to support terrorism.[30] Every organization relies on super-connected individuals to make things happen; societies and the governments that protect them must take the same approach, using the power of what scientists call "scale-free networks" to spread the word.[31] Terrorism itself is now generated and sustained through networks, and so must countering terrorism be. It takes networks to defeat networks.[32]

Who are these citizen/messengers? One is Amr Khaled, an Egyptian talk-show host and Internet maven who has gained tremendous popularity in the Arab world. His philosophical model, "Lifemakers," encourages Muslims to transform their lives through Islam. Khaled has famously asked this question: "Who asked Osama bin Laden to talk for us? Nobody."[33] He is part of the growing "Islamic Renewal Movement," a loose coalition of four broad groups: Civic Islam, Islam and Democracy, Reforms Within Islam, and Culturally Modern Islam. These strains are tied together by their commitment to modernize Islamic institutions, traditions, and practices.[34]

Another citizen/messenger is Morris Dees, director of the Southern Poverty Law Center and a fierce opponent of the U.S. militia movement. Dees and his organization maintain a database on militia activities, pursue legal actions against militia groups and individuals, and communicate with the rest of U.S. society through a variety of media, including books. The Southern Poverty Law Center is not affiliated with the U.S. government, but it has been an important ally.[35]

A clear example of civil society aligning itself against terrorism can be seen in the Iraqi province of Al Anbar, where since 2006 tribal forces have come together to reject foreign terrorists. Citizen militias, properly regulated by the government, have been instrumental in defeating terrorists from Peru to Turkey. At the other end of the spectrum, groupings of motivated individuals counter terrorist ideology simply by demonstrating that society is normal and healthy. Upon winning the 2007 Asia Federation Cup in soccer (by defeating Saudi Arabia) with Kurdish, Sunni, and Shia players, the Iraqi team was profiled as a model of ethnic unity. The power of civil society can be magnified by targeting the youth bulge, particularly in Muslim populations, by using the ubiquitous information technology available to them.[36] Civil society can indeed be the terrorist's most formidable enemy.[37] The best example of this is now being playing out in the public squares of the Arab world.

With the right catalyst, whole societies can suddenly become powerful enough to destroy terrorism. Such was the case in Italy after the Red Brigades terrorist group kidnapped and murdered former Prime Minister Aldo Moro. In Jordan, after brutal attacks on three hotels in Amman in November 2005, support for extremist leader Abu Musab al Zarqawi evaporated in an avalanche of public outrage. The British, conditioned by a tradition of citizen policing, consider themselves soldiers in the war against terrorism rather than victims—the eyes and ears of a vigilant government. That attitude is the sharpest tool in the tool kit every government has for fighting terrorism. All governments must learn how to use that tool and keep it sharp.

Building an Alliance Against Radical Ideologies

Anyone attempting to counter ideological support for terrorism must realize that such efforts can succeed only from within the ideological community itself. Violent Salafism and its like-minded cousins will not be defeated by the West. The best the West can do is contain them, providing Muslim communities everywhere the space and time they need for the inside work.[38] Governments, nongovernmental organizations, and individuals from the outside can influence the debate, but they cannot finish it. A citizen/messenger such as Amr Khaled can have more effect than the entire U.S. government—but to remain effective he cannot be seen within his community to be a mouthpiece for the West (which he is certainly not).

Efforts to oppose terrorist ideologies outside one's own culture should be open and indirect.[39] That campaign should entail a careful blend of policies and practices designed to empower those within the target community to get their positive messages out. Once out, those messages will transmit themselves in a variety of ways along complex social pathways. We wish to have reasonable people say what we would say if we had the credibility. We then must report, analyze, and strengthen the positive trends we see. It is not a surprise that the United States has countered the fantasy ideology that drives its own militia movement more successfully than any other terrorist ideology. Only the Italian people—with the moral support of allies—could have countered the Marxist ideology of the Red Brigades as effectively as they did.

In a domestic context the image of an onion, with a hard core of committed terrorists at its center, clarifies the problem and suggests a solution. Overlapping the core are increasingly thick layers of active supporters, passive supporters, those who don't care either way, and by far the thickest, those who oppose the committed terrorists and their supporters. In this image the government surrounds the onion looking for ways to counter the terrorism produced in the core. Many governments, particularly those with the resources, are tempted to use a hammer to smash the onion. Other governments have developed a combination of strategies to deal with each of the layers, gently or harshly peeling the inner layers away from the core while mobilizing the periphery against the center. The most effective strategies mobilize the *moral* resources of civil society. Isolating the core allows governments to apply coercive force selectively—even surgically—without damaging the society itself. Such an approach, over time, can reduce terrorism and the ideology that underlies it.

The international context is more challenging. Domestic efforts to isolate the hard core often result in a terrorist version of diaspora, where members of one network find protection among those of another. If terrorists maintain a network of networks, then governments must do the same; success for one government cannot mean threats for another. In this world relationships are more important than capabilities. Individual governments, networked within, must reach out bilaterally and regionally to assist other governments to discredit and incapacitate extremists while winning the loyalty of their own societies. Governments which develop foreign policies that strengthen this network of networks will find themselves with improved security at home. We have come to the point where terrorism anywhere is terrorism everywhere. We should seek to move terrorism to the very fringes of human behavior. Once equally common, piracy, slavery, and genocide have been systematically diminished through collective efforts over time.[40] Most importantly, such efforts destroyed the ideologies that legitimated these behaviors. Governments must go after ideologically motivated terrorists with the same kind of collective approach.

Notes

1. In the novella *The Metamorphosis*, Franz Kafka tells the story of a young man who suddenly wakes up one morning as a bug. His parents have diametrically

opposite responses to the new reality: The mother calls on the doctor to explain what has happened, the father the locksmith to safeguard his family. Franz Kafka, *The Metamorphosis*, trans. Stanley Corngold (New York: Bantam, 1972).

2. Louise Richardson, *What Terrorists Want* (New York: Random, 2006), 71–103.

3. For a very good explanation of terrorism as a social activity, see Max Abrams, "What Terrorists Really Want," *International Security* 32, no. 4 (Spring 2008): 78–105.

4. Terrorism is understood here as a strategy involving the systematic use of violence against civilians in order to make a political *or* ideological point.

5. Abraham H. Maslow, "A Theory of Human Motivation," *Psychological Review* 50, no. 4 (1943): 370–96.

6. The concept of a revolution of rising expectations is taken from the papers of Adlai Stevenson, Volume 5 (Boston: Little, Brown, 1974), 411. Anyone wishing to place the mutual alienation of America and much of the world into some historical context would do well to read this section.

7. Plato, *The Republic* (New York: Penguin, 1955).

8. See Francis Fukuyama, *The End of History and the Last Man* (New York: Free, 1992).

9. This observation suggests two models for terrorism, one for political ends and another for ideological ends. Governments unable to distinguish between the two often apply the wrong remedies, thereby exacerbating the problem.

10. The Dalai Lama identifies the line between religion and ideology with just one sentence: "While preserving faith toward one's own tradition, one can respect, admire and appreciate other traditions" (Tenzin Gyatso, "Many Faiths, One Truth," *New York Times*, 24 May 2010).

11. The best example of this is the concept of "leaderless resistance" articulated by Louis Beam, a key American militia movement figure. Beam's ideology is well documented in Morris Dees, *Gathering Storm* (New York: HarperCollins, 1996).

12. Nihilism, the belief that nothing, including the self, matters or has purpose, is the philosophical opposite of eternalism, which postulates a deathless soul. The *maras*—extremely violent street gangs—of the United States, Guatemala, Honduras, and El Salvador are bound together by a culture of drug use and violence that is distinct from traditional organized crime. Nihilism best describes the ideology behind their actions, but the *maras* remind us that ideology can sometimes explain behavior without justifying it. For a detailed look at the *maras* phenomenon, see Thomas C. Bruneau, Lucia Dammert, and Jeanne Giraldo, *The Maras and Security in Central America* (Austin: University of Texas Press, forthcoming in 2011).

13. This strand of thinking leads back to the notion that there are two species of terrorists: those who use violence as a means to an end and those who see violence as an end in itself. Based on what they *do* rather than what they say, we call the former "political terrorists" and the latter "ideological terrorists."

14. Ethnic nationalism as an extremist ideology may have disappeared in Sri Lanka with the military defeat of the Tamil Tigers and the death of Tiger leader

Velupillai Prabhakaran. However, that does not mean that the ethnic conflict has been resolved because the original root causes are still in place.

15. In the case of Islam, extremist hijackers have more running room due to the relatively loose structure of the religion worldwide. There is a paradox here: The very nature of Islam as a simple and tolerant religion has made it more vulnerable to abuse than more dogmatic, tightly controlled religions.

16. The virus analogy would be difficult to avoid. Governments must see themselves as doctors, trying to immunize their citizen patients.

17. It may be that young people join extremist groups for primarily social reasons, but ideology—carefully reinforced by group leaders—keeps them there.

18. If the religion happens to be Islam, the government would have to separate the legitimate *madrassahs* (the Arabic word for "schools") from those that teach hatred of nonbelievers. In general, *madrassahs* in general are not the problem; certain *madrassahs* are indeed the problem.

19. Lee Harris, *Civilization and Its Enemies* (New York: Free, 2004).

20. Bolshevism as conceived by Vladimir Lenin and Leon Trotsky was fantastical, but it strived for an idealized new future rather than trying to recapture a glorious past. Many would argue that Zionism is a fantasy ideology. Others would include democracy (at least in its current evangelical form).

21. There is a chicken-and-egg argument here. Are cults formed around charismatic leaders, or do groups of believers bestow cult status upon their icons? This appears to work both ways, depending on the circumstances, with one end reinforcing the other.

22. The U.S. government has started calling Muslim terrorists *violent extremists*. Ironically, the term *Muslim terrorists* would be a generic description with minimal offense.

23. Terrorists call themselves *jihadists* for precisely the same reason; they want to wrap themselves in the legitimacy given to those who practice jihad within the tenets of Islam.

24. Osama bin Laden's deputy, Ayman al Zawahiri, brought the thinking of Sayyid Qutb together with bin Laden's Wahhabism to form a particularly lethal combination of ideology and violence. The similarities between Qutb and Karl Marx have been described by Theodore Dalrymple, "There Is No God But Politics," *New English Review* (May 2007), connecting the two most dangerous ideological strains of the last 100 years, http://www.newenglishreview.org/custpage.cfm?frm=7240$sec_id=7240. Qutb's seminal work, *Milestones*, calls for violent action to create the classless society of Islam's early history. A translation of *Milestones* by Sayyid Qutb (2005) is available at majalla.org/books/2005/qutb-nilestone.pdf.

25. In *The Accidental Guerrilla* (London: Oxford University Press, 2009), David Kilcullen uses the term *Takfiri* to describe this ideology and *Takfiri terrorists* to describe people willing to kill those (including Muslims) who disagree with it. Other terms that could be used include *neo-Salafism*. Violent Salafism captures both the fantasy ideology and the terrorism that characterize Al Qaeda and its affiliates.

26. These phrases were taken from a presentation on the subject given regularly by Dr. Thomas R. Mockaitis of DePaul University at the Center for Civil–Military Relations (CCMR) in Monterey, California.

27. The case of Anwar al Awlaki is an interesting case in point. Awlaki, who now lives in Yemen, is a U.S. citizen who broadcasts Al Qaeda's ideology to other U.S. citizens. He is linked to three alleged terrorist attacks in the United States. The U.S. government is trying to determine how to take Awlaki out of the equation: He is not in a military-style chain of command, and killing him would constitute an assassination rather than a targeted killing.

28. A very interesting view of government branding comes from a speech given by Kevin Roberts, the CEO of Saatchi and Saatchi, to a United States Intelligence Agency (a private consulting group not directly affiliated with the U.S. government) audience in New York City on 9 March 2005. The speech is titled "Loyal Beyond Reason."

29. A challenge for governments is to convince their citizens that the risk from terrorism is actually quite small. For an expansion of this theme, see John Mueller, "A False Sense of Insecurity?" *Regulation* 27, no. 3 (Fall 2004).

30. The utility of social epidemics is explained very well in Malcolm Gladwell's best seller *The Tipping Point: How Little Things Can Make a Big Difference* (New York: Little, Brown, 2002).

31. For a detailed description of scale-free networks and social connections, see Albert-Laszlo Barabasi, *Linked* (New York: Penguin, 2003).

32. For the best insight on the power of networks, both for and against terrorism, see John Arquilla and David Ronfeldt, *Networks and Netwars: The Future of Terror, Crime, and Militancy* (Santa Monica: RAND, 2001).

33. *Time* magazine profiled Amr Khaled as one of its "100 Most Influential People" in the 14 May 2007 edition. Other Muslim citizens in the Middle East region have followed Khaled's lead in what amounts to a growing movement, enabled by the Internet.

34. Abdeslam M. Maghraoui, "American Foreign Policy and Islamic Renewal," Special Report, United States Institute of Peace, July 2006.

35. For additional information concerning the Southern Poverty Law Center, see its Web site: http://www.splcenter.org.

36. Jared Cohen gives a very convincing argument for targeting youth with technology in the *Proceedings* of the symposium "Combating the Unrestricted Warfare Threat," sponsored by the Kossiakoff Center, Johns Hopkins University, Baltimore, 10–11 March 2008: 279–86. From Tunisia to Yemen, in the year 2011, social media in the hands of young people have transformed the Middle East.

37. The rise of Al Jazeera and other Arab media have provided outlets and networks for individuals to express themselves in ways that were—until recently—inconceivable. Instead of trying to counter these media, Western powers should be listening to the conversations and debates they have spawned. What we learn should inform our collective counterterrorism strategies.

38. See Philip Mudd, "Containing Terrorism," *Newsweek*, 17 May 2010, 31.

39. In U.S. policy circles one often hears the term *countering extremist ideology.* That characterization implies that we can simply substitute our own ideology for theirs. Such a course of action would be counterproductive because it would provoke resentment and strengthen the very ideology we wish to counter.

40. The current resurgence of piracy, particularly in East African waters, is a case in point. Just as the great maritime nations did in the early nineteenth century, governments are again collaborating to defend shipping and human life. The notable addition to this historical coalition is the Chinese Navy.

13 Intelligence and Combating Terrorism

Lawrence E. Cline

PERHAPS THE MOST CRITICAL ASPECT OF A GOVERNMENT'S response to terrorism is its intelligence capacity. Without a strong and accurate intelligence system, any counterterrorist campaign is almost certainly doomed to failure. Much ink has been spilled by various commissions, study groups, and individual authors on improving intelligence capabilities, with many of these studies taking place prior to 9/11. This chapter will focus on some practical issues that can further improve the intelligence system in terms of counterterrorism response and preemption.

Internal Communications—Obstacles and Solutions

One problem with intelligence systems in general is that of internal communications. U.S. intelligence agencies have frequently have been accused—usually with considerable justification—of stovepiping their intelligence reporting systems so that reporting chains travel only vertically from the lower levels of the agency to the top, with little or no horizontal coordination among agencies. This has been particularly true for "hot" intelligence reports, where agencies have stressed speed over cooperation. There certainly is justification for some intelligence products of critical importance to be treated this way. Where major breakdowns have occurred, however, has been in the seemingly more routine reporting that remains uncoordinated.

One additional specific stovepipe issue plagues the realm of counterterrorism. This is the exceptionally compartmentalized nature of counterterrorism analytic centers and sections. Some carry out their most critical work without much coordination even within their own agencies. Consequently, what could be valuable inputs and outputs at the working level with other offices in the agency may be ignored. Much of the rationale for this intense compartmentalization of counterterrorist intelligence rests with the extreme sensitivity of the sources and methods used to collect raw intelligence. Again, there are very cogent reasons for controlling access to critical counterterrorism intelligence, but at the same time, too much compartmentalization can preclude crucial interplay and cross-fertilization with other intelligence professionals.

Specific Issues in Counterterrorism Intelligence

Counterterrorism intelligence presents very specific concerns. In traditional intelligence structures there has been a relatively clear difference among the tactical, operational, and strategic levels. In counterterrorism intelligence, by contrast, there is considerable blurring of the lines among these levels because counterterrorism intelligence requirements are considerably "flatter." Using the attacks of 11 September 2001 as an example, what typically would be a tactical-level problem—tracking nineteen individuals—takes on strategic importance because those nineteen terrorists clearly had an international impact. Successful terrorist attacks in other countries provide similar examples. Ultimately, counterterrorism intelligence must succeed simultaneously at two overlapping levels: at the strategic level, where broad trends and future possibilities are identified, *and* at the tactical level—including a particularly strong and detailed indications and warning system—at which individual operations are detected and foiled, or deterred before they are launched.

In fact, in many instances the tactical level will be the most important for counterterrorism, even for national-level intelligence agencies. As noted by Condoleeza Rice, national security advisor under the George W. Bush administration, strategic intelligence on terrorist groups is in some ways rather straightforward, especially because most larger terrorist groups clearly state their strategic goals and adhere to relatively clear patterns in their operational procedures.[1] The real intelligence questions are when, where, and how terrorists will strike, which ultimately is a concern for tactical intelligence. Making the shift from worrying about "big-picture" issues to these more-tactical questions will require some major mental adjustments by analysts and national intelligence agencies.

The when, where, and how are indispensable to the most critical indications-and-warning problem: determining terrorist intent. Determining intent—whether among terrorists or more traditional adversaries—is always the most agonizing problem facing analysts because it involves trying to get inside an adversary's head, never an easy job. It is particularly problematic in dealing with terrorists. Most countries provide a "target-rich" environment, with numerous locations or national interests for terrorists to hit. Terrorist leaders frequently entertain multiple target sets and simply may not have decided the particular target that they want to attack by the time the intelligence makes its way back to analysts.[2]

To make matters worse, counterterrorist intelligence is particularly subject to the so-called paradox of warning: Successful intelligence reporting can lead to a governmental reaction that changes the operational plans of the terrorists. In practical terms, if intelligence services are able to gain intelligence on impending terrorist attacks, governments will react to the threat. In most cases this will increase visible security around the identified likely targets and will usually result in public warnings. Any reasonably smart terrorist who sees such reactions will either postpone the planned operation to a more propitious time or shift to less-secure targets. In either event, governments that receive warnings of attacks that do not happen—or worse, attacks on targets different from those they have been warned about—are quite likely to begin doubting their intelligence services and may even discount future warnings. Equally, intelligence services that receive warnings from their sources that do not pan out will probably question the sources' credibility and reliability.

There are no particularly easy answers for the paradox of warning, especially because there are two additional complicating factors. The first is that terrorist groups typically give consideration to more targets than they will actually hit.[3] As with many other things in life, timing is everything when it comes to identifying the actual targets of terrorist groups. For the intelligence to be useful for warning and prevention, it needs to identify actual planned operations rather than simply reflect whatever terrorists have thought about hitting. The second potential complication is that there is nothing to keep terrorist groups from leaking extensive lists of targets that they have no intention of attacking. Much of the intercepted "chatter" that is frequently described by various countries' security services could easily be attempts by terrorist groups to test government reactions or to stress governmental security services.

The only way that governments can avoid the paradox of warning is to initiate perfect preemption every time so that the bad guys are always killed or captured before they act. In the real world, unfortunately, this is not possible. The most practical response for governments that receive what seems to be credible intelligence on a specific target is to increase security for all those targets most likely to be attractive to terrorists, with still more security for the identified target. Beyond spreading the security cordon geographically, it can also be spread temporally to introduce enough uncertainty so that terrorists cannot simply delay their operation for a brief time until security relaxes. While increased security is obviously resource intensive and must be limited in duration, such policies are likely the best way to avoid ceding all the initiative to the terrorists.

Reforming Intelligence Services for Counterterrorism

Many, if not most, countries are currently looking at restructuring their intelligence agencies to respond to a changing environment. In some cases, plans involve only minimal changes; in others, more radical restructuring is under consideration. In either case, the mechanics of restructuring intelligence deserve some discussion.

Like any other bureaucracy, there are three aspects to how intelligence services work: (1) process—the means for acquiring and producing intelligence, (2) product—the analyses themselves, and (3) organization—the structure of the agencies that carry out intelligence functions. Many countries that are restructuring their intelligence systems in response to transnational terrorist threats have tended to focus only on the organizational aspect. In some ways this is the simplest approach for most governments to take because they understand bureaucratic organization better than anything else. Unfortunately, this is also the worst possible approach. Unless countries focus their attention and resources on what they expect the intelligence system to actually provide (the product), it will be impossible to craft an effective organization. All three aspects of bureaucratic functioning must be addressed together for restructuring to succeed.

For countries which have determined that they need extensive changes to their intelligence agencies, a significant issue is whether restructuring should be internally or externally planned and directed. Some countries have created executive commissions or special parliamentary panels to provide the impetus and guidance for intelligence reform, or even direct leadership of restructuring efforts. Other nations have relied on the intelligence agencies to restructure themselves, with minimal external direction.[4] Each of these approaches has both advantages and disadvantages.

A significant advantage of using an external commission or special panel to plan major restructuring is that it can act as a public interface. Moreover, it can focus considerable national attention on both the need for and methods of restructuring. If members of these commissions are carefully chosen for their expertise and stature and are given adequate resources (including time, funding, and qualified staff), they can provide objective, detailed plans for restructuring. However, there are two potential disadvantages in using external commissions for planning reforms. The first is that, if not chosen carefully and staffed properly, the key members' understanding of the intelligence system may be inadequate and their recommendations fall short of what is actually needed (or perhaps be counterproductive). The second disadvantage is that modern history is replete with reform commissions which produce detailed reports that are subsequently ignored by the target agency.

The advantages and disadvantages of internally planned restructuring are the converse of external commissions. The major advantage is that intelligence agencies are in the best position to know what is required to adapt their activities to changed environments. Also, if intelligence services plan their own restructuring, the leaders and members of the services are more likely to buy into the plans and decisions. The major disadvantage is that intelligence services frequently are not terribly interested in major restructuring, preferring the comfort of the status quo. Competition for recognition and resources can also color decisions when those deciding the reforms have a personal stake in the outcome. Overall, the most successful approach has been the use of commissions or other external bodies to provide impetus and guidance, provided that they receive strong executive support and the agencies are made to follow through.

Once a thorough review has identified the desired products and processes for restructuring, several organizational factors should be examined. First, it is important to know the extent to which intelligence missions can (and should) be "subcontracted" to agencies outside of government. Two of these subcontracting techniques involve sharing intelligence functions with other countries (particularly for specialized skills) and the use of civilian academics or other outside experts. For countries with multiple intelligence services, it is worth examining ways to rationalize bureaucratic structures to reduce redundancy. Normally, it is worth having more than one agency conduct analysis so that multiple viewpoints may be considered. At the same time, most intelligence agencies are similar to military services in that their administrative superstructure is very large: In military terms, the "tail" portion of the "tooth-to-tail" ratio is extensive.[5] For many countries it makes sense to consolidate some of the administrative and support services for intelligence operations so that more intelligence personnel can be used for actual collection and analysis.

Other issues to be examined during restructuring include the relative personnel and resource mix to be given to operational versus strategic intelligence; many national agencies likely need to shift more assets to the operational side. Care needs to be taken that as agencies increase their collection efforts, sufficient assets are added to the analytical side to handle the extra workload. Intelligence education systems are also likely to need restructuring to meet the new intelligence requirements.

A key issue in restructuring that is commonly not given the attention it deserves is how to improve the distribution of intelligence to users. Traditional problems in distribution are exacerbated considerably when dealing with counterterrorism. Intelligence agencies have long-established channels for distributing their products to traditional "customers" such as government officials and security forces. These channels continue to exist, but increased internal security against terrorism brings in a number of additional users, including police services, disaster-management agencies, and state or provincial governments. Currently, most intelligence agencies are not well organized to support these additional users.

The dilemma for intelligence agencies is that most of these new customers lack the required security clearances of traditional users. Intelligence personnel are inherently reluctant to share their products with uncleared personnel due to concerns for their sources and methods. As a result, the reports that are released can at times be so generic, once the sensitive information is removed, that they are of little value to those who must use them.[6] The process of "sanitizing" reports to remove sourcing can be time intensive, thereby potentially delaying the distribution of critical information until too late. As part of the overall restructuring effort, intelligence agencies should examine how well they support nontraditional users and increase their abilities to quickly disseminate meaningful information to those who need it.

Practical Steps for Restructuring

There are several actions that countries can take to improve the global intelligence system for combating terrorism. In the best of all possible worlds, intelligence agencies would convert into pure network structures because, as is frequently noted, the best structure to fight networks is another network. Given bureaucratic realities, however, a true network structure within a particular intelligence service is virtually impossible. Every intelligence service has been organized using Weberian bureaucratic models, and to expect a wholesale shift toward networks—particularly given that most of the governmental agencies which they support will continue to be organized hierarchically—is highly unlikely. Despite these constraints, some changes may help intelligence agencies respond with more agility to terrorist networks. The first is to flatten the bureaucratic pyramid that characterizes most agencies. A typical bureaucratic structure for most intelligence agencies has analysts working for senior analysts, branch chiefs who work for section chiefs, section chiefs reporting to division chiefs, and so on. It is not uncommon for there to be seven or eight levels of bureaucracy between the analyst's initial report and its release from the agency to users. Each of these levels naturally involves delays and changes, and it is far from clear that they all are needed. By removing some layers that do not add appreciably to the core skills and outcomes of the intelligence service, it can respond more quickly to the needs of its customers.

A second way to make intelligence agencies more adaptable to a networked threat is to reduce barriers between analysts and collectors. Most intelligence services do not stress close cooperation between field officers and analysts. In some ways this is cultural: Analysts generally tend to have very different personalities and interests from field officers. More importantly, services typically build bureaucratic walls between the field-officer career path and the analyst career path, which in turn gives rise to very different working cultures that tend to attract particular personalities. Switching from one side to the other is virtually impossible (or at least very uncomfortable for the individuals involved) in most cases.

Beyond the career issues, some level of separation between analysts and collectors is at least partially justified by a desire to protect sources. Also, it is useful for analysts to maintain a certain professional distance from case officers so that they can be objective when they assess the credibility and reliability of the reports that they receive from the field. Nevertheless, reducing these bureaucratic walls has many benefits. If field officers understand and can predict what information analysts are likely to want from the field (rather than limiting themselves to responding only to formalized collection requirements), they can provide better tailored reports more quickly. Likewise, if analysts have a better understanding of what is and is not realistic to demand from the field, they can focus their collection requirements and plans on what is practicable.

Networking Intelligence to Fight Networked Terrorists

What are some ways in which cooperation and coordination between analysts and collectors can be improved? The first is training. Although training time is limited for practical reasons, analysts should learn at least the basic duties of field officers, and vice versa. Second, there should be organizational structures in place to permit transfers between the analytical and field sections. Third, rather than assigning case officers who are no longer active in the field solely to training or collection-management sections—which is frequently the case in most agencies—many should be attached to analysis offices. Although typically there are cultural and personality differences between case officers and analysts, former case officers can be invaluable in terms of their "street smarts" and on-the-ground experience in particular areas. Finally, moving some portion of analysts from their headquarters closer to the field—such as in embassies or operational headquarters in theaters of operations—can greatly improve communications and reduce response time.

An example of the latter technique has been the creation in the United States of national intelligence support teams (NISTs). These small teams consist of representatives from the Central Intelligence Agency, Defense Intelligence Agency, National Geospatial-Intelligence Agency, and National Security Agency, who deploy together, along with supporting communications and computer equipment, to the field headquarters of U.S. forces during their operations abroad. The principal purpose of an NIST is to provide a multiple-source intelligence conduit for the joint task force commander. The use of the NIST, which was developed from lessons learned in Operations Desert Shield and Desert Storm, has become a routine intelligence tool during subsequent deployments.[7] The NIST system has also provided the seedbed for the organization of larger field joint intelligence task forces.

Another way to network intelligence agencies for specific missions is multiagency working groups. If established and organized with care, such groups can provide a valuable tool that crosses bureaucratic boundaries. However, one frequently contentious issue with counterterrorism intelligence working groups is the extent to which they merge domestic and foreign intelligence functions. Such joint cooperation is essential for fighting transnational terrorist groups that will not fall neatly into domestic or foreign categories, but it also raises significant legal and civil-rights issues.[8]

It is important to stress one caveat regarding working groups—and likewise field operations. Throwing assets (both personnel and funding) at the counterterrorist intelligence mission is unlikely to bring immediate results. From both the operational and analytic sides, no intelligence officer who is brought in to work in new environments or on new issues can be fully effective right away. The propensity of intelligence agencies to form working groups with the expectation that they will immediately respond with cogent and well-informed intelligence is a long-standing practice, albeit usually wrong. Once such groups have had the opportunity to work together and develop both functional relationships and levels of expertise, they typically prove their value. There is no reason to expect counterterrorist working groups or newly created intelligence centers to be any different. Similarly, field operations inevitably take time to bear fruit because developing the country knowledge, cultural expertise, and network of sources takes months, if not years.

Perhaps the most important step in networking intelligence is to improve intelligence sharing between countries. Among a number of partners, intelligence exchanges are already routine on a variety of issues, but they are becoming much more focused and extensive in the current environment.[9] There are very cogent reasons to improve the sharing of counterterrorism intelligence between countries. The first is the relative advantage of individual countries. Countries within a region will understand the intricacies of regional conditions and relationships better than outside countries and will have advantages in gaining local access to potential intelligence sources. Other countries may have significant strengths in specialized intelligence disciplines. The sheer volume of data being handled by most agencies may necessitate sharing with other countries' services just to keep up with the workload. Improved intelligence sharing may also serve larger diplomatic and political goals of regional and international cooperation. However, the biggest reason for sharing is that every country needs help with the complexities of the current international environment.

There are a number of ways to organize and conduct intelligence sharing. Agencies may provide occasional information to others on particularly "hot" issues. Countries can establish more regular exchanges that focus on particular geographic areas or on particular subjects, especially terrorism. Sharing can be broader, and it can become routine on a variety of issues. These broader exchanges can be either a form of workload sharing, in which agencies pass on finished intelligence products to other countries' services for further assessment and cross-referencing, or (more rarely) true joint operations. In the latter type analysts from two or more agencies work together directly to solve intelligence puzzles. The joint operational approach bears considerable promise because it can bring together very different assets and perspectives on specific issues.

Finally, the bureaucratic system surrounding the exchange program can be formal, with well-established procedures for how the sharing is to be conducted, or it can be informal, with participants making up the procedures more or less as they go along. In general, the more formal system is preferable because it can reduce professional hesitation over sharing and make the actual information exchanges faster. In reality, though, even exchanges that start out informal and occasional can become more formalized and deeper over time as the governments become more confident of each other. Ideally, whether formal or informal, intelligence exchanges will increasingly become multilateral (and regional) rather than remain just a series of bilateral exchanges.

Conclusion

While exchanging intelligence with other services certainly can be a very useful tool, especially against emerging transnational terrorist networks, it is important to be aware of the issues that can arise. Sharing inevitably takes additional time and effort, and managing the system can burn up scarce personnel resources. When partners have very different capacities, the flow of information itself can become problematic and can even overload a smaller intelligence agency's ability to adequately handle the data. Institutional biases, a problem even within individual governments, can make cooperation between particular agencies of different countries very troublesome. If security arrangements from each side are not adequate, the sources of one or more of the sharing agencies can be put at risk. At worst, shared intelligence can be deliberately leaked by a country for political reasons.

Beyond these issues, intelligence services will of course release only the information that is in their interest to share. Many political and diplomatic agendas are likely to shape the choice of available intelligence, and the reliability and validity of the data will almost always be suspect without further confirmation. Certainly, national intelligence services can and have "rigged" intelligence for political purposes. Also, speaking from the author's personal experience, many intelligence exchanges resemble a bartering session more than a free exchange of information, with each side trying to gain advantage over the other. This is as true of "trusted countries" as it is of other, more suspect countries.

Overall, however, intelligence sharing—together with the other measures discussed—remains an absolutely essential element of instituting a more networked intelligence system. The more integrated and cooperative national intelligence services become with each other, the more successful will be the campaign against transnational terrorist groups. Likewise, the "boundaries" of intelligence agencies need to become more permeable. Due to security constraints, most services minimize the extent of their work with nonintelligence personnel. However, such individuals, including academics, area specialists, and technical experts, can serve as a valuable resource for the intelligence system and should be incorporated into the counterterrorism network.

Ultimately, if such measures are implemented and coordinated across agencies and borders, intelligence services can form network-type structures with much greater capacity than any one country could possibly muster. In most cases the key need is to improve cross-border links. In some specialized areas, such as financial intelligence agencies, there can be better links between countries than there are between the specialist agencies and their own larger national intelligence services. Cross-national and internal linkages and cooperation are critical to the ongoing struggle against transnational terrorism. If governments cannot find ways to help one another become smarter and stronger through international cooperation, everyone risks failure.

Notes

1. "Transcript of Rice's 9/11 Commission Statement," CNN.com, 19 May 2004, http://www.cnn.com/2004/ALLPOLITICS/04/08/rice.transcript.

2. For examples of multiple targets, see Brian Michael Jenkins, *Terrorism: Current and Long Term Trends* (Santa Monica: RAND, November 2001), 6–7.

3. For one example, see Aaron A. Danis, "Al Qaeda's Surveillance Offensive Against America,

2000–2003: Implications for U.S. Homeland Countersurveillance," in *Countering Terrorism and Insurgency in the 21st Century: International Perspectives,* ed. James J. F. Forest (Westport: Praeger, 2007), 503.

4. For a general review of intelligence-reform efforts in various countries, see Larry L. Watts, "Intelligence Reform in Europe's Emerging Democracies," *Studies in Intelligence* 48, no. 1: 11–25; Alain Faupin, *Reform of the French Intelligence Services Since the End of the Cold War* (Geneva: Geneva Centre for the Democratic Control of Armed Forces, 2002); and K. G. Robertson, "Recent Reform of Intelligence in the UK: Democratization or Risk Management?" *Intelligence and National Security* 13, no. 2 (Summer 1998): 144–58.

5. This problem is noted in "Vision 2015: A Globally Networked and Integrated Intelligence Enterprise," Office of the Director of National Intelligence, July 2008, 21, available from the Council on Foreign Relations, http://www.cfr.org/publication/16890/vision_2015.html.

6. For a useful discussion of problems with release of classified reports during an earlier period, see Lt. Col. George K. Gramer, Jr., "Combined Joint Intelligence in Peace Enforcement Operations," *Military Intelligence Professional Bulletin* (October–December 1996), http://huachuca-usaic.army.mil/contlearning/infrastructure/media=mipb.

7. For a history of the NIST, see James M. Lose, "National Intelligence Support Teams: Fulfilling a Crucial Role," *Studies in Intelligence* (Central Intelligence Agency) (Winter 1999–2000), https://www.cia.gov/library/center-for-the-study-of-intelligence.

8. The FBI is responsible for intelligence activities on U.S. soil. For example, it was an FBI agent who first flagged the suspicious activities of the 9/11 terrorists once they were in the country. The CIA is forbidden by law from conducting domestic intelligence work, but it was responsible for tracing the terrorists' movements prior to their reaching the United States, and then working with the FBI to keep track of them. Coordination at all levels failed in this case. See the "Final Report of the National Commission on Terrorist Attacks upon the United States," known as the 9/11 Commission Report, official government edition, released 24 July 2003, especially Chapter 8, "The System Was Blinking Red," http://www.gpoaccess.gov/911/index.html.

9. Derek S. Reveron, "Old Allies, New Friends: Intelligence-Sharing in the War on Terror," *Orbis* 50, no. 3 (2006): 453–68.

14 Consequence Management

Edward E. Hoffer

PREVENTING A TERRORIST ATTACK FROM TAKING PLACE IS THE primary goal of any counterterrorism effort. However, the reality of the twenty-first century is that despite our best efforts to prevent such attacks, they will continue to occur. With this in mind, planners and responders must be ready with an effective and efficient consequence-management program to deal with the aftermath of these inevitable attacks. As the title of this chapter suggests, the means that we use to manage the consequences of a terrorist attack will determine to a large degree the amount of damage that the attack causes.

The purpose here is not to make the reader a trained consequence-management responder but to enable her or him to better understand what is required to develop and to sustain a successful consequence-management program. Terrorism, especially in recent practice, is intended to cause as much harm as possible to its target. While an effective consequence-management program can help to limit the damage from an attack and prevent additional harm, an ineffective one can significantly increase the damage that occurs, thus adding to the overall success of such an attack. When we examine how nations have dealt with previous terrorist attacks, it is evident that sound consequence-management plans, executed by highly trained and knowledgeable emergency managers, staff, and responders (assisted by citizens who are informed on how to help themselves in a disaster), can save lives, reduce economic loss, and quickly counter the fear that terrorists are trying to sow.

The London subway bombing of 2005 is an excellent example of a highly effective consequence-management effort. Authorities were quickly able to restore the confidence of the citizens of London in their security and safety, which enhanced people's appreciation of their government.[1] In contrast, the confused and uncoordinated consequence-management effort that occurred during and after the 2008 Mumbai attack helped to increase the fear felt by the citizens of Mumbai, and it undermined their faith in both local and national authorities.[2] Indeed, this was one of the terrorists' principal objectives.

This chapter begins with a discussion of the ways in which modern societies have become more vulnerable to the effects of disaster in general, whether deliberate or natural. Although we tend to differentiate between types of disasters—e.g., a hundred-year flood versus a terrorist bomb—preparation for managing the consequences of all disasters should take place in an "all-hazards" context rather than being compartmentalized by potential type of event. The "all-hazards" taxonomy yields more evenly distributed resources, training, and equipment, avoiding redundancy and inefficiency. The body of the chapter describes in detail the five phases of consequence management: preparation before disaster strikes, response to an actual event, recovery once the danger is passed, mitigation of future threats through the incorporation of lessons garnered from a thorough evaluation of the event, and finally a return to the preparation phase for coming events. Rather than calling for different responses, particular causes will be differentiated primarily by their emphasis on particular aspects of the response, whether it is security, in the case of suspected terrorism, or medical capacity, in the case of disease.

The main lesson to come from this discussion is that planning, preparation, and training are the keys to successful mitigation of the effects of any disaster. This is as true for the individual and family as it is for local, state, and federal disaster-response agencies. Every disaster has the potential to teach us how to be better prepared for the next one.

Disaster in the Modern Landscape

One of the most remarkable milestones we reached in the first decade of this century was that for the first time in human history, more people lived in cities than in the countryside.[3] Unfortunately, along with the benefits of urban living comes the associated reliance on a fragile urban infrastructure. The necessities of food, water, and fuel or power are no longer directly available to the city dweller as they were when people lived on the farm and in the countryside and, at least potentially, could supply these needs for themselves. Most of us rely on highly centralized commerce systems to provide us with the necessities of life, and when these systems fail or are damaged or destroyed, the efforts to restore them must be effective and efficient, or public health and morale quickly decline. This reliance on living, commuting, and working together in large numbers also makes us more vulnerable to both acts of terrorism and natural or accidental disasters. The reality is that the urban environment presents a higher potential for catastrophic damage, mass casualties, and fatalities, which can quickly overwhelm a modern urban community's disaster-response resources. All leaders, as well as all citizens, should understand what family, neighborhood, city, regional, and national consequence-management programs entail and have the knowledge to make improvements in them.

Some governments have responded to the particular threats presented by terrorism through creating and funding separate consequence-management response units and organizations that will be used only to respond to terrorist attacks. The chief problem with this approach is that we often do not know right away what caused a disastrous event. This is particularly true during the first hours after an incident, when primary responders are struggling to save lives and are dealing with immediate hazards such as fires or toxic spills. Such was the case when the author helped respond to a tragic refinery explosion and fire. In the first hours of our response we simply did not know what had caused the explosion. Was it a terrorist attack? Was it an accident or an act of nature? (In this case forensics experts determined that the explosion was the result of multiple lightning strikes.) Had the explosion been caused by terrorists planning a second strike, the entire response team could easily have been lost, along with other people nearby. This example illustrates why an all-hazards approach to consequence management is best.

Most of the challenges facing leaders who conduct consequence management are the same whether the incident is a terrorist attack, a natural disaster, or an accidental disaster. They all can occur without warning and more often than not involve mass casualties and fatalities. They may require evacuations and mass sheltering. They can produce large-scale property damage and economic loss to private businesses, homeowners, and the government; all will invariably involve strong public reactions of fear, anger, and despair. Finally, the effort to deal with their aftermath will bring together the same constellation of institutions, which may or may not be accustomed to working together.

However, there are some differences in the ways that leaders will need to respond when the incident is the result of a terrorist attack. The incident location in such a case is also the scene of a crime, or an act of war, and it now includes a major security threat that, if not handled properly, can put responders at great risk. Are terrorists still present? Will a follow-on attack occur that will endanger responders as well as the public? This security threat is often regarded as a separate and distinct response function from consequence management and is given the rubric "crisis management." According to this approach, crisis management takes place simultaneously with consequence management, but it focuses on the methods of attack and includes all activities necessary to anticipate, prevent, or resolve the threat of further attacks. Consequence management, unlike crisis management, focuses on the physical, psychological, and financial damage to lives and property. Whether a nation deals with the security threat from terrorism as part of consequence management or as a separate and simultaneous function within a broader "incident-management" program, a response leader will need to be trained for both.

Phase One: Putting a Plan in Place

What, then, constitutes a sound consequence-management program? A good program will effectively meet the five overarching objectives: First, it will ensure the survival of the maximum number of people through prompt rescue, decontamination, and medical treatment. Second, it will be capable of providing prompt emergency assistance and restoration measures to the affected local government, critical infrastructure, and citizens. Third, it will reestablish self-sufficiency and essential services as quickly as possible. Fourth, it will assist in regenerating economic activities. Fifth, and too often forgotten, it will contain, clean up, and dispose of contaminated material in an environmentally and legally correct manner. Granted, meeting these objectives can require years of hard work and significant resources, but such a program will save more of a nation's human and financial resources than it will cost to build and maintain.

There are five key program phases to address in building a sound consequence-management program: (1) preparation before a disaster, (2) immediate response, (3) recovery, (4) mitigation, and (5) preparation again following the disaster. This critical last step incorporates lessons garnered from the incident to help correct deficiencies in the existing consequence-management program so that the next time a disaster happens, the same problems will not arise. Rather than being separate and distinct activities, however, the transition between these phases can be gradual, and the phases often overlap as conditions permit or demand.

The first phase, preparation, starts with a thorough risk analysis that realistically identifies and prioritizes the threats that responders must be prepared to deal with. These risks will, of course, vary widely according to location and level of analysis—e.g., the risks that responders in rural Monterey County, California, should prepare for will be very different from those facing responders in urban Miami–Dade County, Florida. James Petroni suggests a methodology for assessing risk in Chapter 8. A properly prepared risk assessment will guide planners in the steps they should take to organize, train, and equip themselves to establish a viable consequence-management capability for the specific context in which they must work.

Train, and Train Some More

It is also a cardinal rule of a successful consequence-management program that it must have the mandate and the tools to enforce realistic and integrated training at all levels of government, from local to national. The adage that "those who refuse to train together will fail together" is axiomatic. Education certification requirements at the individual and institutional levels are one tool to help achieve this type of realistic, integrated training. Pay, allowances, and budget resource support can then be tied to the fulfillment of these certification requirements as a further guarantee that they will be taken seriously.

Equipping and staffing each level to meet its consequence-management mission often seems a daunting task because managers typically tend to believe that they do not have the equipment that their unit or section needs to function effectively. However, this is rarely the case because although there is always something else to wish for that would make the job easier, most experienced leaders can effectively use the resources that are already available to them. The following are some ideas gleaned from emergency-response exercises: using hotels as expanded hospital capacity; tying fire hoses to lamp posts to decontaminate large groups of people quickly; and recalling retired medical, police, and firefighter personnel (who can be used directly if they are still fit, or in less-demanding management assignments to free up active personnel for the more difficult tasks). Creative thinking is an indispensable asset in disaster-consequence management.

Phase Two: Responding When Disaster Strikes

In an all-hazards consequence-management program, planning for the response phase focuses on ensuring that the collective efforts of first responders will fulfill their assigned roles and missions. An effective disaster-response capability must, at a minimum, meet the following mission requirements: Responders must understand the threat, establish security, provide fire and hazard control, undertake search and rescue, provide emergency medical services, establish reliable command and control and legal emergency authority, and provide a source for public information. All of these tasks must be identified and prepared for before any event actually takes place, and then developed and maintained through a realistic and demanding exercise program. Individual responders will have to undergo separate task training to gain proficiency at their specific job, but only systematic integrated task training and operational exercises can create an efficient and effective consequence-management response capacity.

"Threat awareness" signifies the ability of first responders, in the minutes immediately following a disaster, to quickly determine what type of threat they are facing and what situational information they must provide to follow-on responders to both protect them and help them effectively conduct their missions. Accurate threat awareness is necessary to set up the conditions for subsequent success. An example of what can go wrong when first responders don't have the situational awareness they need occurred during the Tokyo subway attack of 1995, in which a domestic terrorist organization released the deadly nerve agent sarin simultaneously in several subway cars.[4] Because responders lacked the training that would enable them to identify the type of threat they were facing, the attack caused more damage than it might have otherwise. The first on-scene responders did not recognize that they were dealing with a highly toxic chemical agent and so did not immediately stop the subway trains from operating, which only exposed more people to the agent. Responders also became casualties themselves because they did not wear protective equipment or use protective procedures. Then, because victims were not decontaminated on site, secondary responders such as ambulance teams and hospital medical staff were exposed and endangered. All told, about a dozen people died, while more than a thousand required at least temporary hospitalization.[5] This case illustrates the lesson that regardless of their emergency role, police, firefighters, and emergency medical-services personnel must all be trained in threat awareness so they are able to quickly identify the threat and then provide that information to all subsequently arriving responders.

Creating a secure response environment is traditionally the role of local police, who must meet two immediate security requirements. First, if the cause of the disaster is unknown, then police must determine whether the event was criminal, an accident due to negligence, an act of nature, or the result of terrorism. They must also simultaneously secure the disaster site by establishing two concentric security perimeters. The inner perimeter is necessary to account for survivors and victims, identify witnesses, and detain possible perpetrators. The outer perimeter is established to control the entry and exit of responders and to keep out well-meaning people and frantic relatives, who would only interfere with response activities and possibly endanger themselves.

Fire and search-and-rescue operations may be performed in combined or separate organizations, but their roles and missions remain the same. Fire and hazard-suppression activities, as well as casualty and victim rescue, are conducted simultaneously. In many countries the senior firefighter present becomes the on-scene incident commander and coordinates all other response agencies and resources. In the United States the responsibility for command can be transferred as the incident grows larger, based on rank or specialty qualifications. Many nations have adopted the U.S. system; for other nations it is the senior police officer present who becomes the incident commander. The key point is to determine who will be in charge *before* an incident, thus avoiding command confusion when coordination is most desperately needed.

Effective emergency medical response requires that local medical staff and facilities be organized for and practiced at handling mass casualties. This is so different from normal day-to-day emergency medical practices and procedures that it demands separate planning and thorough training exercises to accomplish. These specialized tasks include the collection and transport of casualties, conducting mass-casualty triage, meeting sudden and greatly expanded patient treatment demands, establishing patients' identities, maintaining identification and treatment records, and communicating pertinent medical information to the incident command center and the public.[6]

Establishing Command and Control

Even this sampling of the major response tasks makes it quickly evident that there must be an agreed-upon and thoroughly understood system in place to command and control the overall response effort. That plan must include unambiguous lines of authority. The incident commander has to be supported by a trained staff and representatives from all the involved response organizations, and this group must have access to the shelter and equipment necessary to establish an incident command center. Effective command-center operations depend on having in place standard operating procedures and terminologies that all response agencies are trained in, to ensure common understanding of procedures and terminology. One of the most consistent obstacles that all response command centers face is overcoming the differences between the communications equipment used by various agencies. This difficulty can be overcome only by holding regular command-center exercises to uncover any communication incompatibility, then planning solutions, such as sending liaison teams or relying on other forms of communication. The key to successful command-center operations is prior realistic training and exercises that include all response agencies. Finding where command-and-control problems exist *before* a real disaster occurs will save lives and resources.

Legal Authority for Decision Making

To ensure an effective response, it is also important to take a close look at the legal framework that is in place before an emergency and to make sure that it is designed to assist rather than hinder the response commander and on-scene first responders. Too often, the legal authority to make crucial response decisions is not given to the designated response commander, a hurdle that invariably results in harmful, often deadly delays while responders wait for "higher authorities" to make a decision.[7] Empowering first responders and the response commander with legal emergency decision-making authority is particularly important when public safety requires responders to conduct evacuations, establish curfews and movement restrictions, isolate and quarantine sectors of the population, or carry out mandatory decontamination.

Associated with the very sensitive authority issues covered above is the difficult legal task of establishing rules covering the use of force that may be required to conduct broad measures for the safety of a community against the will of some individuals. One solution is to invoke a disaster or emergency declaration that has been preapproved by higher authority and that establishes for a limited time the legal mandate necessary for effective responder actions.

Communicating with Authorities and the Public

The final major response task for a sound consequence-management program is a professional public-information capability. Despite being listed last, however, setting up a centralized and coordinated source for public information is a critical aspect of response that must begin in parallel with the other emergency efforts. Communicating accurate and coordinated information to the public during a disaster through today's media is a demanding skill. Public-affairs personnel not only must be thoroughly knowledgeable of all consequence-management plans, terms, and procedures; they must also know how modern media operate and how to deal appropriately with all their forms, including print, radio, television, and the Internet.[8]

If improperly handled, media coverage can become a detriment to effective response. Inaccurate information, spread quickly by media looking for a "scoop," can lead to public confusion and fear, which in turn can quickly undermine the public's willingness to cooperate with accurate emergency instructions and information. By contrast, skillful and honest cooperation with the media can help ensure the proper dissemination of information, limiting the numbers of potential victims, steering victims to emergency aid, and reducing public fear. Access to good information also goes a long way towards promoting public confidence in the emergency-response system, which will make the responders' job easier next time.

One of the best ways to improve the media's cooperation with and understanding of the consequence-management response programs is to include reporters in preparatory training and exercise programs. The knowledge they gain often results in their developing, and passing along to their audience, a positive appreciation of the many difficult tasks that are taking place during an emergency and how efficient the responders are at handling them.[9] Participation in the exercise program will also enable members of the media to communicate better, more accurate information to the public when a disaster does occur. When possible, a disaster-information center should be established that allows the media and public-affairs personnel to work together, preferably in a sheltered area that allows reporters and camera crews to set up their equipment and have direct access to important response information. As an inducement to the media to participate, those who attend the exercise program can become certified to have a reserved place in the disaster-information center, where they will get the most complete information and "breaking-news stories" for their outlets. Those who undergo the training realize how to set up and where they can broadcast their stories without interfering with one another or with responders. That these reporters know how to take care of themselves is very important for their safety and the safety of those around them.

Finally, when they are working with the media, it is very important for emergency-response leaders to have the courage and discipline to always tell the truth. If the situation is bad or difficult, they should say so and then tell the media what is being done to alleviate it. If information cannot be released because it will endanger the public or responders, then the media should be told that this is why such information cannot be released. Finally, leaders should avoid saying "no comment." This phrase automatically gives the perception to the media and the public that something is being hidden from them. Sustaining people's trust and confidence in the response effort is the overall objective of the public-information mission.

These are the major response-phase tasks that are a core part of an all-hazards consequence-management program. Implementing these response tasks will save lives, reduce damage, and enhance people's confidence in their government. As always, advance training and organization are crucial to ensure proper command and control of the response effort and accurate dissemination of response and emergency information.

Phase Three: Recovery

The next consequence-management program phase is recovery. Unlike the response phase, which lasts hours or days, the recovery phase lasts much longer. In major disasters such as the 2004 Madrid train bombing, recovery can last months; in the case of severe large-scale disasters such as the Indian Ocean tsunami at the end of that same year, it might take several years. Even during the response phase, planners should immediately begin by anticipating what will be required to implement and fulfill disaster-recovery tasks. These task requirements are then integrated into the latter period of the response phase. This overlapping of planning and execution can allow for a seamless transition to a full recovery effort. As with the response phase, leaders from all agencies involved in the recovery phase must agree on a plan and train for their consequence-management missions well prior to the disaster.

Experienced consequence-management leaders know that the first priority of the recovery phase is to improve security to pre-disaster status or better. This will reassure both the affected public and the agencies conducting recovery work of their safety. Whether the disaster is natural, accidental, or the result of terrorism, this security priority does not change.

Once long-term security is reestablished, essential public services can begin the work of reestablishing communications systems, transportation, water, sanitation, and power alongside other recovery efforts. However, the primary task throughout the initial phase of recovery will be to provide shelter, food, and pure drinking water for the evacuated or homeless. While essential services are being repaired or replaced, a thorough effort to account for missing people and to reunite separated family members is paramount to successfully countering the fear and anxiety caused by the disaster.

Accounting for the missing also involves a detailed operation to locate, recover, and identify human remains. The handling of human remains, it should go without saying, must be done in as systematic and respectful a manner as time will permit; properly handled, this process also sends a psychologically positive message to the disaster-stricken community. In tandem with the recovery of remains, whether terrorism or an accident is responsible for the disaster, the appropriate investigation and forensics research must take place before debris is removed or destroyed.

One of the most difficult issues that arises during the recovery phase is when to allow displaced citizens to return to the disaster area. Medical authorities and structural engineers have to have time to conduct thorough and efficient assessments to determine both when and where it is safe to return. Making some areas safe can require the demolition of damaged structures and infrastructure, while other areas will have to be declared off limits to the public indefinitely because of safety issues. Public and, in some cases, political pressure to limit safety inspections and allow people to return to potentially unsafe locations grows quickly following a disaster, but this pressure must be resisted to avoid creating a secondary disaster on the ruins of the first.

In the latter stages of recovery, once safety issues have been dealt with, the priority among consequence-management tasks shifts to reestablishing community self-sufficiency, including the restoration of local businesses and jobs to the greatest degree possible. Every effort to effectively involve local workers and business leaders will help to generate needed work for those left unemployed by the disaster. Low-interest small-business loans from state and federal agencies are often required to repair or replace damaged goods, equipment, and structures. The actual objective of this recovery task is to make the affected population self-sufficient again, and thus free up national and regional support agencies to ready themselves for the next disaster. This managed transformation from "assisted to self-assisted" also significantly reduces disaster trauma and hopelessness.

In each of the recovery tasks discussed above, the need for helpful, open, and honest dissemination of public information continues, just as it was needed during the response phase. The public-affairs requirements also remain the same for the recovery phase. Helpful information delivered through a sound public-information system can do a great deal to shift citizens' perceptions of themselves from disaster *victims* to key players in the recovery process.

These recovery tasks obviously demand the same attention to command-and-control coordination that the response phase did, but in the recovery phase the command-and-control system has to be able to coordinate a much larger array of organizations and agencies and their personnel. Making this task even more difficult is the fact that these actors represent not only national, regional, state or provincial, and local governments, but also nongovernmental organizations and private volunteer organizations. The key to their efficient and effective integration, as it was in the response phase, is prior planning that assigns recovery responsibilities and determines who is in charge of the overall coordination effort.

Many nations have created some form of national consequence-management plan, which may be known as a national emergency-response plan or civil-defense plan that accomplishes the same objectives. Unfortunately, too many governments still do not have a nationally agreed-upon plan or, sometimes, any plan at all due to the difficult political issues involved. This lack puts them at tremendous risk of failing when a major disaster does occur. The irony of this situation is that these leaders, having avoided the political difficulties attendant to creating a plan, will face an outraged nation and possible civil unrest when the government's response and recovery efforts fail. A plan nevertheless is only half a solution for achieving effective and efficient recovery. As it was with the response phase, a sound, sufficiently funded program of training and exercises must be conducted to ensure that all responsible leaders and their supporting staff know what their assigned recovery mission is, how best to accomplish it, and how to integrate their efforts under the designated or established recovery program leader or coordinator.

Phase Four: Mitigating Further Threats

Following the recovery phase of a consequence-management program is the mitigation phase. In a perfect world, methodical programs to reduce threat risks would be in place to prevent any disaster, but the reality is that efforts to mitigate the likely harm of even known threats are often, for political or financial reasons, not carried out. Following almost every disaster, natural or deliberate, including terrorism, there is often a window of opportunity to reduce or eliminate some of the threat conditions that made the disaster more harmful than it might have been. By taking advantage of this opportunity, leaders can implement mitigation efforts so that a similar disaster will never happen again or will not be so destructive. This is the "possible silver lining to a dark disaster." In the immediate aftermath of almost every disaster, the political will and public support to undertake mitigation measures are strongest. Unfortunately, a year or two later, the return to relative normalcy allows people to believe that because they have gotten through a catastrophe, it will not likely happen to them again. In other words, the mitigation opportunity period lasts only a short time, and consequence-management leaders must be prepared to quickly seize this opportunity and implement their recommended mitigation measures. The methodical and thorough threat-risk assessment described in Chapter 8 is precisely what is needed during this consequence-management phase to prioritize mitigation efforts.

One of the most effective mitigation tasks that consequence-management leaders can undertake is simply not to repeat old mistakes. All too often the locations in which we have built our homes and communities, as well as how we have built them, are what have been called "disasters by design" or "disasters waiting to happen."[10] During the mitigation phase we need to ask hard questions before rebuilding. For instance, should we rebuild homes or businesses where they will be threatened again by historically repeating natural disasters, such as in a known floodplain? Does it make sense to replace the twin towers of the World Trade Center with another skyscraper? Should a destroyed factory that handled toxic chemicals or materials be rebuilt again so near our homes or in our city? Should we insist that buildings be designed better and built with better materials to withstand recurring natural and deliberate threats, as has been done in California through increasingly strict earthquake codes?[11]

These are just a few of the questions that we should debate and answer. If the answer is that we now need to change how and where we are building, then the mitigation phase is the time to make the changes so that we can create more disaster-resilient communities. Reducing the costs of response and recovery will be worth every penny of the up-front costs of disaster mitigation.

The last and perhaps most important task associated with the mitigation phase is that of public education. Consequence-management leaders have the public's attention following any disaster. It is at this time more than any other that people will pay serious attention to how they can become better prepared for a disaster. Simple but lifesaving steps that are explained in a clear and practical way may actually be implemented by citizens for whom disaster preparedness is suddenly a top priority.[12]

This is the time to have citizens ensure that for each family member they have five days' worth of stored drinking water, canned food, and necessary medicines; that they have available flashlights or lanterns and batteries; and that they have a battery-powered radio and know the radio frequency at which they can receive emergency information. All family members should practice how to evacuate their homes quickly and have a rehearsed rendezvous location at which to meet. Published instruction material should be available for community leaders, teachers, and families to use for educating as many people as possible on how to help themselves, their neighbors, and first responders. If leaders and individuals can accomplish these simple education goals, they will have done more to save lives the next time that disaster strikes than any other mitigation effort can achieve.

Phase Five: Preparation—Again

The last phase of a consequence-management program, preparation, brings us full circle. As with any endeavor for which the goal is to improve performance, it is now important to review all responders' performance and determine specific strengths and weaknesses. Obviously, planners want to make sure that they support the sound practices that produced those strengths. But they must also accomplish the painful task of identifying weak or failing performances, and determine why those responsible were not able to accomplish their jobs. However, lessons simply identified are not enough. All too often when serving as a training evaluator, this author has participated in disaster-response exercises that repeat the same mistakes and failures that were observed in previous exercises. It is a common error to assume that lessons identified or observed are necessarily "lessons learned." To ensure that lessons are incorporated into training and emergency operations, it is necessary to improve weak operational plans or procedures at the appropriate execution level and, where necessary, to correct the relevant organization or equipment. After any necessary changes are made, all responders must then practice and rehearse at each program level through a series of realistic, integrated training exercises. This is the only reliable way to prove whether the lessons identified are now really lessons learned.

In summary, to meet the inevitable future disasters that will affect every community and nation at some unknowable time, individuals must insist that their families and their communities have a plan in place that addresses all five consequence-management phases. Ensure that the plan is practical and easy to understand, that it is disseminated to everyone who needs it, that it is realistically exercised and practiced, and that, after an actual disaster in which the plan is executed, it is evaluated, refined, then exercised and practiced again. Government must set the tone for this process to proceed within the mutual-assistance framework upon which leaders and their societies depend.

Notes

1. Mark Easton, "Seeking Normality in the City," *BBC News,* 7 July 2006, http://news.bbc.co.uk/2/hi/uk_news/5150938.stm; "The Multi-Agency Debrief: Lessons Identified and Progress Since the Terrorist Events of 7 July 2005," London Regional Resilience Forum, Government Office for London, in *BBC News,* http://news.bbc.co.uk/2/shared/bsp/hi/pdfs/23_09_06_lrrfreport.pdf .

2. Somini Sengupta, "Mumbai Attacks Politicize Long-Isolated Elite," *New York Times,* 6 December 2008, http://www.nytimes.com/2008/12/07/world/asia/07india.html?fta=y.

3. “Urbanization: A Majority in Cities,” United Nations Population Fund, in the UNFPA Web site, http://www.unfpa.org/pds/urbanization.htm.

4. For a detailed description of the attack and its perpetrators, see Jessica Stern, “Terrorist Motivations and Unconventional Weapons,” in *Planning the Unthinkable*, ed. Peter R. Lavoy, Scott D. Sagan, and James J. Wirtz (Ithaca: Cornell University Press, 2000), 202–29.

5. Sumie Okumura, Tetsu Okumura, Shinichi Ishimatsu, Kunihisa Miura, Hiroshi Maekawa, and Toshio Naito, “Clinical Review: Tokyo—Protecting the Health Care Worker During a Chemical Mass Casualty Event: An Important Issue of Continuing Relevance,” *Critical Care* 9 (2005): 397–400, http://ccforum.com/content/9/4/397; Randal Beaton, Andy Stergachis, Mark Oberle, Elizabeth Bridges, Marcus Nemuth, and Tamlyn Thomas, “The Sarin Gas Attacks on the Tokyo Subway—Ten Years Later/Lessons Learned,” *Traumatology* (Northwest Center for Public Health Practice) 11, no. 2 (2005): 103–19.

6. For information on training for medical-disaster response, see “Emergency Room Procedures in Chemical Hazard Emergencies: A Job Aid,” http://www.cdc.gov/nceh/demil/articles/initialtreat.htm. Also see “NATO Handbook on the Medical Aspects of NBC Defensive Operations: Part II-Biological. AMedP-6(B),” http://www.fas.org/nuke/guide/usa/doctrine/dod/fm8-9/3toc.htm; and the U.S. National Institutes of Health: http://sis.nlm.nih.gov/enviro/chemicalwarfare.html#a2.

7. Please see the excellent discussion of failures in the response to the 2005 Hurricane Katrina disaster in “A Failure of Initiative: Final Report of the Select Bipartisan Committee to Investigate the Preparation for and Response to Hurricane Katrina,” the U.S. House of Representatives Select Committee to Investigate the Preparation for and Response to Hurricane Katrina, Tom Davis, Chairman, 109th Congress, 2nd session, 15 February 2006, www.gpoaccess.gov/katrinareport/mainreport.pdf.

8. The Internet became an important source of local news and information among isolated communities during the Basin Complex fire, a lightning fire that burned out of control over hundreds of square miles in California’s Los Padres National Forest for several weeks during the summer of 2008. The Firefighter Blog, for one example, helped keep people abreast of official news and fire updates, and served at times as a bulletin board for help needed and help offered among firefighters and residents. An archived page can be seen at http://firefighterblog.com/2008/07/basin-complex-fire-update-july-5.

9. The prospect for negative coverage encourages responders to do a better job, while reporters who are “embedded” from the start will be more sympathetic to the challenges that first responders face.

10. Please see Dennis Mileti’s fascinating book, *Disasters by Design: A Reassessment of Natural Hazards in the United States* (Washington, D.C.: Joseph Henry, 1999).

11. Mitigation against terrorist threats requires thinking similar to preparing for natural disaster, but with a political twist. Some would call the construction of “Freedom Tower” as a replacement for the World Trade Center towers an act of provocation.

12. A simple example of teaching the reversal of "dangerous instinctive behavior" is telling people to stay inside a building during an earthquake. Most untrained victims will immediately run out of the building and be injured by falling debris from shattered windows and broken masonry.

15 Ethics and Combating Terrorism

Robert Schoultz

Editor's Note

This book is about civilian and military responses to terrorism. As the authors have attempted to show, those actions cannot be separated at the political level. But at the operational and tactical level, military personnel often find themselves alone. Given the political authority to fight, they are faced with the personal reality of combat, a reality that—even with the most detailed political and legal guidelines—is filled with ambiguity. This chapter discusses how armed forces, as legitimate tools of democratic states, deal with that ambiguity. The implications drawn here go well beyond traditional military forces, to all state institutions with the legal authority to deliver coercive force. But the ethical dilemmas of combating terrorism with force are best discussed in a worst-case context, which is for military forces to be engaged in war against terrorist or insurgent enemies. Law-enforcement operations, whether conducted by police or military units, should also be clarified by this discussion. This chapter will use operational examples from recent U.S. experience, but the fundamentals and principles can be used by anyone who has to decide how much force to use, and when.[1]

Why Fight Ethically?

If war is about life and death, and often about national survival or destruction, and our enemies show no concern for ethical considerations in war, why should we even try to fight ethically? With the stakes that high, fighting an enemy that is eagerly killing indiscriminately to achieve its ends, does *how* we fight these evil people really matter as long as we defeat them?

These are legitimate questions that every soldier and military leader must consider and be able to answer. The premise for ethical limitations to combat is that without them, there would be no limits on how violence could be appropriately used and morally justified to seek the political, military, or personal ends of those involved. Without applying ethics to warfare, there would be no moral argument against killing entire populations in order to eradicate a few enemies or torturing and/or killing prisoners, the wounded, their families, friends, and acquaintances. Nor would we have any moral argument against our enemies using the same means against us. But we do put limits on the violence that we'll permit our soldiers to use in combat, and we do have moral arguments against what our enemies do to us. We do believe that there are actions that are generally considered "just" in warfare and actions that are considered "unjust." These moral arguments are based on fundamental civil principles that have been adapted to the unique environment of warfare, where death and destruction are necessarily part of the equation. As Michael Walzer, in his seminal book *Just and Unjust Wars,* writes,

> They can try to kill me and I can try to kill them. But it is wrong to cut the throats of their wounded, or to shoot them down when they are trying to surrender. These judgments are clear enough I think, and they suggest that war is still, somehow, a rule-governed activity, a world of permission and prohibitions—a moral world, therefore, in the midst of hell.[2]

This short chapter provides a brief background and some perspectives that should be useful to those who are "in the fight" against terrorists, subversives, revolutionaries, insurgents, criminal warlords, and other enemies who do not fight using traditional military organizations, rules, and roles, and who do not respect the rules of the customary Law of Armed Conflict or the Geneva conventions. By and large, these nontraditional enemies operate outside of internationally recognized legitimate institutions and are often referred to as "nonstate actors." In search of a single term that encompasses all of these potential enemies, and because they are violating the "laws" of war, they will here be referred to as *unlawful combatants,* as preferable to *terrorists* or *insurgents,* or an invented term such as *irregular warriors* or *nonstate fighters.* The term *honorable warrior* here refers to state-sanctioned soldiers, sailors, airmen, and marines who seek, to the best of their ability, to fight in accordance with the principles of the customary Law of Armed Conflict. The form of conflict in which honorable warriors confront unlawful combatants—that is, in which state and nonstate actors fight and struggle for legitimacy and influence over the relevant population(s)—are called here *counterterrorist* or *counterinsurgency* environments.

A Brief Background

The concept that there are limitations to what is "permissible" in combat has evolved over millennia within the traditions of chivalry, honor, and religious values on the battlefield. Only in the last 150 years, however, since the establishment of the International Committee of the Red Cross and the Geneva and Hague conventions, have these customary laws been codified in such a manner that nation-states could, at least theoretically, hold each other accountable to them.[3] The Geneva conventions provide a governance framework within international law for managing and restraining the violence of war, but the moral framework upon which the Geneva and Hague conventions were built already existed within the customary Law of Armed Conflict. These principles, in the form of chivalric codes in one form or another, have been with us for millennia; in the Western tradition they go back at least as far as the revulsion of the gods at the behavior of Achilles in the *Iliad*, and nearly as far in Eastern history.[4] About 3,000 years later, in the late nineteenth century, Jean-Henri Dunant, a Swiss banker, witnessed the carnage and suffering on the battlefield following the Battle of Solferino in northern Italy in the Austro–Sardinian War of 1859. He subsequently initiated a movement to mitigate suffering in war, which eventually led to the formation of the International Committee of the Red Cross (ICRC), and in 1901 he was awarded the first Nobel Peace Prize. The ICRC was instrumental in organizing the Geneva and Hague conventions, which established what is today the basis of international law applicable to armed conflict. The ICRC continues to be the one internationally recognized and respected organization focused on limiting the violence in warfare, seeking to protect noncombatants, and holding parties at war accountable for how they fight.[5]

The honor of showing restraint in the profession of arms has been recognized throughout history and is common across nearly all cultures. According to Michael Ignatieff, "In most traditional societies, honor is associated with restraint, and virility with discipline."[6] Mercy toward the vanquished has certainly been the exception rather than the rule, but it has always been admired. Alexander the Great was honored for his magnanimity in his treatment of vanquished foes in Jerusalem and Babylon, but history has chastised him for giving vent to his rage by setting his army loose to kill thousands and enslave nearly the entire populations of Tyre and Gaza.

Fundamental Principles

The goal of military ethics in general is to put acceptable and reasonable limits on the violence, damage, and destruction committed by warriors to achieve their objectives in war. As noted in Michael Walzer's quotation above, the concept of honorable behavior in war asserts that all is *not* fair in war. There are boundaries to what civilized and honorable human beings can accept as the legitimate prerogatives of military personnel when they fight. Arbitrary killing, violence, and destruction violate the customary Law of Armed Conflict. Civilian populations are to be protected to whatever degree possible from the violence of warfare. Obviously, the challenge comes in establishing criteria for determining "necessary" killing and destruction, as well as criteria for determining who should be treated as civilians or noncombatants, and how much effort and risk the honorable warrior should assume to protect them.

Military necessity is the first requirement for use of violence in warfare. Violence and killing must be "necessary" to fulfill some military objective that contributes to the larger objectives of the campaign or war. Any death or destruction that is intentional but that does not serve a "military necessity" is unjustifiable and immoral within the context of military ethics. Obviously, when it comes to violence that inflicts suffering on noncombatants, the question as to whether an action is truly "necessary" when weighed against alternatives is always open to debate. But the point stands: The violence of war must serve a military objective.

Noncombatant immunity requires the warrior to make all reasonable efforts to protect noncombatants from the violence and destruction of war. In order to achieve this aim, noncombatant immunity has two supporting principles: *discrimination* and *proportionality.*

Discrimination

When doling out death and destruction in warfare, the principle of *discrimination* requires the warrior to seek to discriminate between combatants and noncombatants in battle and to target only combatants. The principles of discrimination and noncombatant immunity include the prohibition against ever *intentionally* killing or harming noncombatants. In counterterrorist and counterinsurgency environments, this is a major difficulty because unlawful combatants live and hide among noncombatants, presenting themselves as and even shielding themselves with noncombatants. The greatest challenge for honorable warriors in ambiguous environments is to discriminate between a legitimate target, someone they can and should shoot or otherwise target, and someone whom they should not—someone who should be afforded the rights of a noncombatant. Until or unless a person of interest is clearly a combatant, seen to be taking action that would compromise his noncombatant status, the noncombatant and the unlawful combatant may look exactly the same. The difficulties in applying the principle of discrimination will be discussed at greater length below, but at its most basic level, the principle requires not only that warriors make every reasonable effort to target only combatants but also that they should not only not target but, if possible, *protect* noncombatants.

Proportionality

When military necessity makes harm to noncombatants unavoidable because of their proximity to "legitimate" military targets such as enemy combatants, infrastructure, or support activities critical to the enemy, the warrior must consider the principle of *proportionality.* When harm to noncombatants is unavoidable, it must never be intentional, and it should be proportional to the value of the military target. For example, it may be consistent with the principle of proportionality to cause unintended, but likely, harm to a noncombatant near a targeted terrorist, but it does not meet the stipulations of proportionality to destroy a village or neighborhood to kill a terrorist hiding there.

Noncombatant immunity and the principles of discrimination and proportionality make sense to most people, at least in theory. Clearly, the difficulty lies in applying these principles in practice. However, unlawful combatants frequently seek to use the honorable warrior's efforts to protect noncombatants as a tool to give themselves tactical advantage. This is clearly against the Law of Armed Conflict, but it does not concern unlawful combatants. Knowing that their opponents seek to avoid nonproportional responses and harm to noncombatants, they seek to look like noncombatants by hiding among crowds and in populated areas.

Vignette: Discrimination and Proportionality in Ground Combat

A story clipped long ago from the *Washington Post* illustrates in simple ground-soldier terms the common sense of discrimination and proportionality.[7] The article recounts a discussion with some marines who had been escorting a convoy in an armored personnel carrier through a contested area of Iraq about their intent to avoid civilian casualties. In the heat of a firefight, they acknowledged, their calculus is quick and imperfect. One of the sergeants described an incident in which they saw an Iraqi soldier standing among two or three civilians; the marines opened fire and saw one of the women standing near the Iraqi soldier drop. In a separate incident he said that when he saw one Iraqi soldier among a large group of women and children, he didn't take the shot.

The Moral Equality of Soldiers

The customary Law of Armed Conflict does not hold soldiers morally accountable for the decisions of their leaders to fight in a war, but soldiers are held morally accountable for *how* they fight in that war. Lawful combatants are to be considered pawns in the "game" of war and are not to be held morally responsible for the cause for or against which they are fighting. This position acknowledges that because of lack of education or access to information, many soldiers are not in a position to accurately or critically judge the proclamations of their leaders or the morality or immorality of the cause for which they are fighting. Furthermore, many soldiers are forced into combat by conscription, operational necessity, and/or fear of prosecution.[8]

This "moral equality" of soldiers is problematic in counterterrorist and counterinsurgency environments. Many terrorists, subversives, revolutionaries, and other nonstate actors are fully committed to their cause and will use any means, however abhorrent, immoral, or illegal, to achieve their ends. But not all are fanatics. In his book *The Accidental Guerilla,* David Kilcullen makes the case that a significant percentage of those fighting as unlawful combatants have been pulled into the fight by outside agitators who make the case that local grievances are merely a local manifestation of a global agenda.[9] Many recruits are uneducated, many are uninformed beyond the local injustices against which they believe they are fighting, and some are little more than children. Many are frequently intimidated into fighting by threats against family and friends. Many have been subjected to only one view of the conflict. They have essentially been brainwashed into believing they have a moral duty to use whatever means possible to fight against the state-sponsored military forces they see in their own backyard. When we look at the individual stories of some of these unlawful combatants, we realize that many are not international jihadists or political fanatics. Assigning *these* unlawful combatants the same moral accountability for their actions as insurgent or terrorist leaders makes us uncomfortable.[10]

Rear Admiral Garland Wright, after returning from Iraq, where he oversaw three major detention facilities (Camp Bucca, Camp Cropper, and Camp Taji), noted that the illiteracy rate among those who had been detained for supporting insurgents was well over double the national average in Iraq.[11] At these facilities, and in conjunction with the Iraqi Ministry of Education, the detainees were taught to read the Quran for themselves, and thereby came to realize that Al Qaeda had perverted the intent of their holy book to proselytize extremism. When these men learned the truth about what the Quran actually taught, Admiral Wright noted that many turned against Al Qaeda, and some even had to be put on a suicide watch. The point is that we should not dismiss the possibility that unlawful combatants fighting for even the most extreme causes may fit the description of many soldiers around the world—unwitting and gullible pawns in a violent game that they little understand.

Practical Considerations

As noted above, when warriors seek to discriminate between legitimate targets and noncombatants, the difference can be unclear not only to the warrior with his finger on the trigger, but also to military lawyers or even to academic theorists. This situation is complicated by the reality that there are many differing definitions of *noncombatant*, some with legal implications that may not have practical or ethical significance for the warrior in combat. For the purposes of what warriors need to know about whom they can intentionally kill or harm, a noncombatant is anyone who is not engaged in combat or violence, who is not providing support essential to that combat, and who is not part of an organization engaged in combat. What it means to be "part of an organization" is also problematic when there are no uniforms, membership cards, or other means of clearly distinguishing between those who are actively engaged in an organized effort to support unlawful combatants from those who are merely sympathetic friends, relatives, or those who have been forced or threatened into a supporting role. "Innocent" bystanders, civilians, and others not in any way engaged in combat are obvious noncombatants. Unfriendly noncombatants are not legitimate targets.

Given that they are all "civilians," those in support roles to unlawful combatants will have varying levels of association with the combat they are supporting and will inhabit an ambiguous gray area between legitimate target and noncombatant. Unlawful combatants frequently commandeer support from the civilian population with the threat of violence. It cannot be assumed that someone who has housed and fed unlawful combatants, or even driven vehicles for them, is part of the committed support infrastructure. If, when, and how to target support personnel and infrastructure will be a case-by-case judgment call that a warrior will have to make, depending on what measures are at his or her disposal and the dictates of military necessity, discrimination, proportionality, and level of risk. Walzer makes the following point: "The relevant distinction is not between those who work for the war effort and those who do not, but between those who make what soldiers need to fight and those who make what they need to live, like the rest of us."[12]

Walzer goes on to justify attacking a tank factory but not a food-processing plant, and he extends the prohibition to targeting the tank-factory workers in their homes rather than in the process of building the tanks in their factory. One might extend this analogy to permit (when such a distinction can be made) the deliberate targeting of a civilian who is carrying weapons to an enemy combatant, but not someone providing him food and shelter.

When it is unclear whether supporters are indeed part of the organization or committed to the unlawful combatants' organization and cause, they normally should not be targeted separately from the combatants they are supporting but should be treated as suspect and potentially hostile unless they are known and verified unlawful combatants, or are in the act of directly supporting and enabling combatant activity. Like anyone who *might* be an unlawful combatant, or who *might* be a supporter, such peripheral players should be treated as unfriendly noncombatants until evidence or actions prove otherwise.

If less than lethal means of neutralizing support to unlawful combatants are available, they should be used. If not, then again the principles of military necessity, discrimination, proportionality, and risk must help decide what level of violence is most appropriate. The noncombatant's right *not* to be directly targeted or harmed also applies to anyone who is under the power and control of lawful forces, and not able to take up arms to fight.

This includes prisoners, detainees, and disarmed or incapacitated unlawful combatants who are captured—even Saddam Hussein or Osama bin Laden once they are in custody. As noted above, it also includes people who *might* be, or even people who are likely to become, enemy combatants. It is the moral duty of the honorable warrior not to intentionally kill or harm these people, whether we like them or not, whether we trust them or not.

The reality is that in conflict against unlawful combatants, everyone who is not clearly on your side is a potential threat. If we were to condone targeting everyone who *might* be an enemy, there would essentially be no restrictions and no limits to the violence of war.

Vignette: Who Can We Shoot?

This was a question that U.S. Army Rangers asked Major General William F. Garrison prior to going into Mogadishu, Somalia, in 1993.[13] Master Sergeant Matt Eversmann, who was on that Ranger operation and was portrayed in the movie *Blackhawk Down,* related to me the story that after the military lawyers had briefed the Rangers on their rules of engagement, Garrison came to wish them luck. He asked if they had any questions. One of the Rangers stood up and told the general that he was confused by the rules of engagement and all the conditions they had to evaluate prior to making a shoot/don't shoot decision. The Ranger pointed out that to himself and the other Rangers, the "bad guys" in Mogadishu looked just like everybody else, and he still didn't know who he was allowed to shoot and who he was forbidden to shoot. Garrison replied that the Rangers knew that they were not to shoot anyone who was not a direct threat and that in battle they would have to make the decision themselves. When they had someone in their sights and their finger was on the trigger, they would have to decide, and this decision was between them and their God. Eversmann then told me that in the ensuing battle, this guidance came to mind on numerous occasions not only for himself, but for several of his Ranger buddies as well. In the heat of battle, with enemies and civilians mixed on the streets of Mogadishu, there was a moment when he and several of the other Rangers had their weapons trained on and were about to shoot a woman whom they believed to be ferrying weapons under her burka. None shot her, and Eversmann believed it was largely because of General Garrison's guidance—they suspected that she was supporting the enemy, but they had no other evidence. The concern that she might be merely an innocent civilian caught in the cross fire outweighed their fear that she could pose a threat to them.

Practical Justifications

The question again arises: "Why fight ethically?" War is a very practical activity, and commanders are concerned with meeting objectives as efficiently and effectively as possible. Unlike most of life's endeavors, the decisions in war deal largely with death and destruction, and the consequences can be immediate and irreversible. Choosing to fight in accordance with ethical dictates in combat may be at the expense of efficiency and effectiveness, and may require putting at risk not only some of the commander's objectives but also the lives of the warriors in the fight. So again, why bother? Is this even a realistic option?

First, the choice between fighting ethically to be "moral" and fighting simply to win is, over the long term, a false dichotomy. It is similar to the choice in business between being profitable or taking care of customers. One is a means to the other—fighting ethically, like taking care of customers' needs, may have short-term costs for meeting specific and immediate objectives; over the long term, however, there are good and practical justifications for putting restraints on violence and abiding by the principles of the Law of Armed Conflict.

First among these practical justifications is that the long-term objectives of war are to consolidate the victory and win the peace. We must remember that the vanquished foe will include civilians and former enemies, and the process of winning a lasting peace begins during the war. A brutal, take-no-prisoners approach to defeating the enemy will generate more hatred and long-term opposition than the restrained and discriminate use of violence. It is often argued that overwhelming power and violence can intimidate an enemy into quick submission, as it did in Hiroshima and Nagasaki, and that such an end to a war may in the long run cause less suffering. However, there are many examples, especially in partisan and counterinsurgency warfare, whereby the heavy-handed approach has ultimately led to defeat—France in Vietnam and Algeria, and Russia in Afghanistan and potentially in Chechnya, are examples that come to mind. In *The Accidental Guerilla* Kilcullen offers numerous examples of insurgencies that were merely driven underground to fester when the fighting had stopped.[14] The anger, resentment, grievances, and memories of barbarity remained alive in the local oral traditions and mythology, and resurfaced to contribute to new violence, sometimes decades later.

Immanuel Kant (1724–1804), one of the Enlightenment's most influential philosophers, lived and wrote in Prussia roughly during the time of Frederick the Great and Carl von Clausewitz. Kant was not a commonsense or practical philosopher; rather, he is best known for advocating principle over expediency. However, he offered a very practical justification for his advocacy of morality in war: "No state at war with another shall permit such acts of hostility as would make mutual confidence impossible during a future time of peace."[15] This argument is clearly reflected in the U.S Army's *The Law of Land Warfare,* which states that "Treacherous or perfidious conduct in war is forbidden because it destroys the basis for a restoration of peace short of the complete annihilation of one belligerent by the other."[16]

Whereas military commanders will frequently seek the most efficient means of achieving short-term military objectives, and ethical constraints seem to be a bothersome hindrance, senior military, civilian, and political leaders should keep the long-term strategic objective of "winning the peace" in focus and should insist on restraining violence to the degree that still protects both operational and strategic objectives.

Another practical argument for fighting ethically is the "hearts and minds" objective, which is always part of counterinsurgency or irregular warfare. In most of these types of conflicts, a large percentage of noncombatants are on the fence between supporting insurgents or fighting against them. These people frequently find themselves torn between support for the ideals of the cause that unlawful combatants claim to be fighting for and revulsion for the tactics they use. If those who are fighting against the unlawful combatants are regarded as equally brutal, then the ideals of the cause of the unlawful combatants can easily tip the scale to their side. Additionally, those who violate the Law of Armed Conflict become, by definition, unlawful combatants themselves; the choice then becomes between two immorally fighting forces rather than between one who fights with restraint and one who fights without. In that case a population torn between one side or the other may see the decisive factor only to be who will best serve their own short-term, parochial interests. Winning hearts and minds over the long run requires more than appealing to the immediate self-interests of the population; such calculations will change with whomever makes the most recent best offer. The support of the population will go to whichever side they trust to meet their society's needs over the long term.

Another practical consideration is what unrestricted violence and brutality do to the soldiers themselves. When a war ends, soldiers return home, and brutal and brutalized soldiers usually make poor citizens. Soldiers who are proud of how they fought, not just for their bravery and effectiveness but also for their humanity and ability to show restraint, will more readily adapt to a civilian environment that requires ethical restraints on behavior. Warriors steeped in the brutality of war adapt poorly to daily life with family, friends, and coworkers, where passions must be restrained by reason and ethical considerations. Permitting warriors to use whatever violence they desire to achieve immediate ends without limits or constraints conditions them to resort to similar behavior whenever they come under stress in more civilized settings. It is difficult enough to motivate the peaceful citizen to risk life and limb, and kill, in the uniform of a soldier; it can be even more difficult to decondition that citizen to not kill after fighting and surviving in a world of unrestrained passion and violence. The constraints of morality are necessary to distinguish legitimate killing in war from murder.

A final practical consideration is the effect that unrestrained violence has on the honor and reputation of the military profession within the society it has sworn to serve. Renaissance philosopher Niccolò Machiavelli may have said that it is better to be feared than to be loved, but over the long run, an institution that is dependent upon the goodwill of its citizens for resources, recruits, and leaders needs also to be respected for more than its ability to efficiently wield power and deliver violence. The moral authority of the government is closely tied to that of the military. None of us want to serve in, or have our sons and daughters serve in, an institution that will condone anything, no matter how vile or immoral, to achieve its ends. Honorable warriors serve in an honorable military profession, and an honorable military profession cultivates and promotes honorable warriors.

Tactical and Operational Risk

Most warriors will understand that there should be some limits to killing and destruction in warfare and will concede that killing anyone and everyone who gets in the warrior's way is probably not "right," whether from moral or practical considerations. However, warriors will frequently chafe at ethical restraints placed upon how they achieve tactical and operational objectives, and will struggle with the concept of assuming risk to themselves, their troops, or their mission in order to reduce threats and risk to noncombatants, among whom the enemy may be hiding or who may be providing support to the enemy. But in counterterrorist and counterinsurgency environments, when everyone is potentially a terrorist, suicide bomber, informant, or supporter, the assumption of risk is necessary; otherwise, warriors could justify harming or killing anyone they decide could be an enemy combatant—which could include all or most of the civilian population.

There is a natural tension between the duty to protect noncombatants and the duty to protect oneself and one's own forces. The tension between these two imperatives can frequently be seen as a zero-sum game: Reducing risk to soldiers frequently comes at the cost of increasing risk to noncombatants. According to Thomas W. Smith, "Rules of Engagement designed to protect civilians tend to place soldiers at greater risk; conversely, rules that stress force protection usually come at the expense of civilians."[17]

To achieve their strategic objectives, honorable warriors must be willing to assume more than marginal risk to their own lives and tactical and operational objectives in the effort to protect noncombatants. This is not only a moral imperative; it is also a strategic imperative to maintain the force's legitimacy. The strategic importance of accepting personal risk in order to protect noncombatants is stressed throughout the U.S. Army's "Counterinsurgency Manual FM 3-24": "Sometimes the more you protect your force, the less secure you may be. . . . If military forces remain in their compounds, they lose touch with the people, appear to be running scared, and cede the initiative to the insurgents. . . ."[18]

Vignette: Tactical and Operational Risk[19]

During the early phases of Operation Enduring Freedom in Afghanistan, Vice Admiral Robert Harward was a joint special operations task force commander. He shared a story of a senior general who, during that operation, was advised of reliable intelligence that Taliban and Al Qaeda forces were using a specific compound for planning and staging operations. The compound was on the outskirts of a town, with several other homes and compounds adjacent. The general's planners were confident that they could target this compound with a precision-guided bomb, but the general was concerned about the accuracy of the intelligence and the accuracy of the bomb. If either was not absolutely correct, many innocent people would die, which would be not only morally but also strategically untenable. He contacted then-Captain Harward and directed that he and his team put together a plan to assault the compound, which would permit his forces to use greater discrimination in whom to target within the compound and also avoid the risk of an errant bomb. There was significant risk to the assault team, but the special operations forces (SOF) team believed that with their training, they could do the mission. The bombing mission was called off, and the SOF team assaulted the target two days later. They sustained two wounded, killed several enemy, and spared a number of women and family members while also retrieving valuable intelligence within the compound.

Professional Risk

Honorable warriors may argue that their best intentions can be of little consequence when their leaders are uninterested in ethical constraints on violence. The reality is that some military leaders' sole concern is for achieving tactical and operational objectives with as little risk as possible; moral and strategic questions may not concern them. Orders from higher up to "take no prisoners," to create "free fire zones" that destroy everything in one's path, or to do "whatever it takes" to meet tactical objectives may appear to permit the fighters on the ground to set moral questions aside and to unleash their own anger, frustration, and bloodlust on noncombatants and civilian infrastructure. However, such a blind eye on the part of leadership to the dictates of honor on the battlefield creates a dilemma for honorable warriors.

Honorable warriors may be required to jeopardize their professional standing as soldiers by arguing against or choosing not to carry out unlawful or unethical orders, whether to protect noncombatants or personal honor. They may even have to argue against lawful orders that they believe do not minimize risk or harm to noncombatants or meet the dictates of proportionality. This is by no means an easy thing to do, and it requires a particularly strong sense of character and grounding in one's personal values. This is a difficult, delicate, and all-too-common dilemma for honorable warriors, and there are no easy answers. In some cases standing up to authority to minimize harm to noncombatants will involve the risk of being humiliated, fired, court-martialed, or worse for questioning orders or refusing to obey.[20]

In such cases some honorable warriors have chosen simply to not respond and to fight with as much attention as possible to the rights of noncombatants within the warriors' sphere of influence, essentially subverting rather than confronting the leader's lack of concern for military ethics. Some have responded with practical arguments, carefully demonstrating that there may be other means to achieve the stated tactical/operational objectives while still serving the strategic objective of not further alienating the population. Some have directly refused and accepted the consequences to their careers and personal lives. The honorable warrior has to make his or her own call, and there may be several possible "right" answers, but clearly the wrong answer is to feel absolved of ethical responsibility because of senior-level indifference or the need to follow orders. The honorable warrior always assumes moral responsibility for his or her conduct.

Honorable warriors may also be torn between loyalty to personal values and loyalty to fellow warriors if the fellow warriors are killing unnecessarily or engaging in unnecessary or unjustified destruction and violence. The tribal ethic inherent in most military cultures does not usually welcome or tolerate the individual who will side with higher values against the bond of loyalty that ties soldiers together. This is another aspect of the personal as well as professional risk that warriors must be prepared to assume to protect their personal honor and the lives of noncombatants. It is unfortunately an all-too-common dilemma.

Vignette: Professional Risk

A classic example in U.S. military history of assuming personal and professional risk in the face of leaders' misconduct took place during the Vietnam War's infamous My Lai massacre. Warrant Officer Hugh Thompson, a helicopter pilot, observed fellow American soldiers indiscriminately killing civilians, including women and children, as he approached the hamlet of My Lai on 16 March 1968. He landed his helicopter between U.S. soldiers and the noncombatants they were pursuing, and ordered his crewmen to protect the villagers with gunfire if necessary. The American soldiers Thompson came in contact with ceased their killing. When the incident finally came to light more than a year later, it led to the court-martial of Lieutenant William Calley, the commander on the ground, and became a significant moral black eye to the reputation of the U.S. Army. The Army's response, at least in the short term, was not supportive of Warrant Officer Thompson's moral courage in reporting this incident. He was ostracized and shunned for years by many in the Army, which to that point had been his home and family.[21]

The Soldier's Perspective and the Ethical Leader's Response

The closer the warrior is to the fighting, the greater the likelihood that a rational ethical response to the violence of war may be overcome by anger, fear, hatred, and a desire for revenge in any form. This is inevitable, and leaders must prepare for it and plan their response. Additionally, warriors may be predisposed to violate the norms of ethical combat by cultural and political messages that the warriors may have uncritically accepted and internalized. These will be strengthened by the soldiers' belief in the righteousness of the cause for which they are fighting and the immorality of the cause against which they are fighting.

Leaders will often motivate and inspire their troops with stories of enemy atrocities and immorality; emphasize that our forces are fighting for good, theirs for evil; point out that our enemies deserve the punishment we will mete out; and stress that this is a fight for our values, our future, and a greater good, against depravity, barbarity, and evil. When soldiers have seen protected noncombatants suddenly take advantage of that status and become killers and destroyers, it is understandable that the line between a legitimate target and a protected noncombatant, between legitimate and illegitimate violence, can become unclear, difficult to justify, and—to some soldiers—meaningless. Why take half measures in the name of "morality" when the fight has been characterized as an apocalyptic battle between good and evil, between civilization and barbarity?[22] The soldier has an understandable distrust of restrictions and constraints placed on him or her by strategic and political leaders who work in comfortable offices, far from the violence of war. "Tell me what you want done, but do not tie my hands, and do not put me at unnecessary risk, when you tell me what you want me to do," the soldier might say. This perspective has its own appealing logic.

How does the ethical leader respond? It is frequently fruitless to counter with moral arguments the desire for revenge against an enemy who is perceived to be evil. It is more effective to acknowledge that the unrestrained position is compelling, while also making the practical arguments offered above for the longer-term value of showing reasonable restraint. Soldiers are practical because war is practical—the cause-and-effect relationship on the battlefield is immediate and verifiable—while the morality of conduct in war is abstract, and the longer-term value of restraint may not be clear or compelling to the soldier. That said, the argument for morality in warfare must be made, despite the fact that not all will be able to understand and accept it. It is important to educate warriors on the ethical basis for the Law of Armed Conflict; some soldiers may understand immediately, others later, and some never.

Soldiers who have just seen a friend killed or who have themselves been severely injured are frequently not open to discussions about the humanity of the enemy and our moral obligation to respect their human dignity. Thus, there need to be other sanctions in place, such as the weight of law, to motivate angry or scared soldiers to control the natural impulse to act without restraint against their enemy. While it may be desirable and ideal that soldiers fight ethically because they have internalized the fundamentals underlying the Law of Armed Conflict, the Geneva conventions, and the International Human Rights conventions, it is sufficient that they simply comply and fight ethically, for whatever reasons that motivate them. As an ethics teacher once stated, though we want people to do the right thing for the right reasons, we will accept that they simply do the right thing.

Many soldiers will be motivated to comply with the conventions and principles of the Law of Armed Conflict primarily out of fear of punishment. It is the leader's responsibility to make this threat of punishment real and credible. Enforcing it will be difficult because of the bonds of loyalty between soldiers and the shared enmity toward a common foe. But if the rules are not enforced, they will be ignored, and violations will be seen as essentially sanctioned. In the full heat of battle, with all its fear, passion, rage, power, and exhilaration, the threat of punishment—immediate and certain—will often inhibit otherwise good soldiers from doing something that they would later regret. In warfare and in life, the ideal is to obey the law and "the rules" out of conviction for their value and rectitude; knowing that we will be held accountable if we fail to is also a powerful, and often more effective, motivator.

Vignette: Managing the Impulse to Violence[23]

Early in the 2003 Iraq War, a Special Operations Forces commander recognized that he and his force were unprepared for some of the problems they encountered in fighting a force mixed so thoroughly with the civilian population. The U.S. operators were increasingly angry and frustrated in their efforts to fight a deadly enemy that hid among noncombatants, emotions that manifested both during operations and later, when the soldiers were dealing with prisoners in detention. The concern was that certain operators, if left unsupervised, would act in ways that were unethical and potentially illegal. While inappropriate behavior in the field could be addressed by tactical leaders on the spot, the detention situations called for further measures. To address the issue, the commander first ensured that both the regulations and his expectations for proper detainee treatment were clearly understood by the entire unit, and the consequences if either regulations or expectations were violated. Separately, subordinate leaders and supervisors ensured that only individuals known to be trustworthy dealt with the detainees. Those who could not be implicitly trusted were still valued members of the unit, but it was clear that certain types of activities were beyond their current level of maturity and judgment.

Professional Competence[24]

While intent to minimize harm to noncombatants in war is essential to the honorable warrior, there is another facet that is critical in managing the degree and level of violence in warfare: competency in fundamental warrior skills. This is especially true in counterterrorist and counterinsurgency environments.

The combat-arms soldiers who pull the triggers, drop the bombs, and fire the artillery must be well trained and mentally ready to respond rapidly and effectively in response to perishable and actionable intelligence. The ability to get to the target quickly and provide precise and discriminate force is a sophisticated military capability. The ability to kill the enemy, but not the family next to him, to destroy the house where enemies are hiding and planning, but not the house next door, requires extensive training. Good intentions are essential, but without the complex and intensive training required to place munitions in a precise location and not in another, all while under stress, innocent people will be wounded or killed and infrastructure will be unnecessarily destroyed, consequences that are not in the interests of short- or long-term military objectives. Also, without the weapons systems that permit precision placement, honorable warriors will do the best that they can but will be frustrated and saddened to see their best efforts lead to widespread, needless death and destruction.

Highly trained combat-arms soldiers require a competent and responsive support infrastructure if they are to fight the enemy with discrimination and proportionality in ambiguous environments. They need intelligence that has been tailored to the requirements of counterterrorism and counterinsurgency, with an emphasis on culture and human intelligence. Command-and-control structures must be efficient and refined to get perishable and actionable intelligence rapidly to those who confront the enemy. The shooters are only as effective as the effectiveness of their support mechanisms enable them to be.

The training infrastructure must also prepare soldiers to fight ethically in ambiguous environments. Following the dictates of discrimination and proportionality requires experience and judgment, while the ability to make difficult shoot/don't-shoot decisions and split-second judgments requires weighing a number of context-dependent criteria, not all of which can be consciously calculated. In these cases, experience, training, and maturity are particularly important. When to use lethal force is frequently a decision that may be a "gut" call, and the warrior must quickly decide whether the situation "feels right" or not, regardless of the rules of engagement. It will be the warrior's judgment that determines whether it is best to initiate fire or wait because there will frequently be indicators to support either decision. There are numerous cases in which a warrior held fire because something didn't seem right, and in so doing avoided killing people he or she did not mean to kill. That "something" that didn't feel right was often difficult to define, even after the fact.[25] Holding fire can involve risk, but using deadly force before one absolutely must also involves risk—to the lives of innocents, to the warrior's conscience, and perhaps to the mission and strategic objectives of the war. Experience and judgment develop over time, but judgment can be improved with training.

Technology—Its Challenges and Limitations

It is important to briefly address the impact that new technologies have had on military ethics, especially in counterterrorist and counterinsurgency environments. Many of the world's most respected thinkers in the field of military ethics are addressing ethical issues associated with the deployment of unmanned vehicles and robotics in warfare, the use of standoff and non- and low-lethality weapons, and cyber warfare. The pace of technological change in warfare mirrors the pace of technological change in other human endeavors, and ethicists in all areas are struggling to keep up with the new and frequently unanticipated challenges that arise.[26]

The nuances of these discussions are beyond the scope of this short chapter, but in nearly every case the concerns boil down to the complexity of applying the fundamental principles of military necessity and noncombatant immunity to new capabilities in warfare. While technologies have continued to evolve, the fundamental ethical principles have not. The intent to minimize harm and violence to the level that is absolutely necessary to achieve military objectives remains the same.

Recent developments in standoff weapons have made it possible to deliver lethal force at a distance, with relatively low risk to the shooter. These weapons have included everything from precision-guided "smart" bombs to Tomahawk missiles to so-called drone strikes. While such weapons can be precise and effective, the fact that they are launched from remote sites without "eyes on target" increases the chance for mistakes in positive target identification, as well as imprecise target solutions that cause weapons to miss. In some cases there are concerns about shifting risk onto noncombatants to avoid risk to one's own soldiers. Autonomous and semiautonomous weapons systems, on the one hand, are able to deliver lethal force to a target that meets a specific checklist of criteria, but in so doing, they take out of the equation human judgment and the "gut feel" that could prevent unnecessary collateral damage. On the other hand, they also offer the advantage of taking fear, anger, passion, and resentment out of the equation, and thus can be more rationally programmed. Persuasive arguments have been made regarding both the advantages and disadvantages of autonomous and semiautonomous weapons.[27]

As rapid technological advances continue to give not only honorable warriors but also unlawful combatants more options for how to fight, new ethical challenges will continue to arise for the honorable warrior, who must decide how best to apply these new technologies. It is incumbent upon the professional soldier, and the honorable warrior, to stay engaged in the discussion of how to use new technologies and to stay grounded in the fundamentals of military necessity and noncombatant immunity. Honorable warriors and ethicists will struggle to find the most effective and most ethical uses for new technologies in warfare, with the goal of limiting the violence and damage to that required by military necessity and to minimize the impact of the fighting on noncombatants.

Conclusion

The fundamental quality that makes an honorable warrior "honorable" is the sincere *intent* to fight honorably and the willingness to assume risk and expend effort to protect noncombatants. This includes the intent to limit violence and destruction to what is absolutely necessary to meet the strictures of military necessity. Good intent requires tactical acumen to achieve honorable results. Without the intent to limit violence as a balance to the imperative to survive and win, however, in the heat of battle and the fog and friction of war the rights and concerns of noncombatants get lost in the interplay of violence between the competing forces. Without good intent, noncombatants are inadvertently or even intentionally slaughtered, and civilian infrastructure and whole societies can be destroyed. The intent to respect human dignity within this context is a necessary, but not a sufficient, condition to being honorable warriors. Warriors must also give *effort* to their intent, through the study of their profession, by developing tactical competence and the ability to implement this intent through ethical and honorable actions.

It is fundamental to warriors' moral maturity to understand that their moral, legal, and professional obligation requires that they *do the best they can* to protect noncombatants from malicious or ill-advised military attacks; this means that they must be ready to *assume risk* to do so. Honorable warriors who seek to hold on to their humanity while engaged in the violence of war constantly struggle to balance the duty to protect noncombatants against the dictates of the mission and the obligation to protect their fellow troops. In the heat of battle, and with the best of intentions, it is easy to make mistakes, and mistakes by even honorable warriors are inevitable. But a well-intentioned error in judgment is different from a mistake born of malice or indifference to the suffering of noncombatants. Honorable warriors do not intentionally shift the risk of war from soldiers onto noncombatants, though this may indeed occur inadvertently, through an error in judgment.

The intention to do the best one can to fight ethically and honorably is what differentiates a mistake made by an honorable warrior from a mistake made by a warrior who does not deserve the descriptor *honorable*. All warriors of conscience who have made decisions in which noncombatants have suffered, been injured, or killed have afterward asked themselves whether they really did all that they could to prevent unnecessary death and injury to noncombatants. This is healthy and necessary. And the next time, the honorable warriors will again do the best they can.

Notes

1. Much has been, and will continue to be, written on this very interesting but challenging topic. The main source for much of this chapter is Michael Walzer, *Just and Unjust Wars*, 3rd ed. (New York: Basic, 1977). It is the starting point for any informed discussion of military ethics. Anthony Hartle, *Moral Issues in Military Decision Making* (Lawrence: University Press of Kansas, 2004), is excellent and includes a discussion of the ethical imperatives associated with the idea of the military as a profession. Also, Michael Ignatieff is a seasoned and articulate scholar and journalist who has written extensively on ethical issues arising in small wars and crises in remote parts of the world. For more on the study of military ethics, see the Web site for the International Society for Military Ethics, an all-volunteer, nonprofit organization of scholars, academics, and practitioners: http://isme.tamu.edu.

2. Walzer, *Just and Unjust Wars*, 36.

3. The Hague conventions of 1899 and 1907 were among the first attempts by the European powers to codify rules of warfare between states. A third convention was canceled because of the outbreak of war in 1914. The International Committee of the Red Cross was officially founded in 1876 and formed a league with the Red Crescent Society in 1919; the Geneva conventions followed World War II in 1949. See the International Committee of the Red Cross Web site: http://www.icrc.org/web/eng/siteengo.nsf/html/genevaconventions.

4. Walzer, *Just and Unjust Wars*, 225–26. Walzer recounts how Mao Zedong, in one of his lectures in the collection *On Protracted War*, referred to the ethical code of the feudal warrior the Duke of Sung in 638 BCE as "asinine ethics."

5. Michael Ignatieff, *The Warrior's Honor: Ethnic War and the Modern Conscience* (Toronto: Viking, 1998). In the essay in this book titled "The Warrior's Honor," Ignatieff discusses the history, roles, and challenges of the ICRC in what he refers to as the "ragged wars" common since the end of the Cold War. As Ignatieff writes, "The Red Cross acknowledges that a warrior's honor is a slender hope, but it may be all there is to separate war from savagery. And a corollary hope is that men can be trained to fight with honor" (157).

6. Ibid, 127.

7. Unfortunately, I no longer have access to the author's name or the title of this article.

8. Walzer, *Just and Unjust Wars*, Chapter 3.

9. David Kilcullen, *The Accidental Guerilla* (London: Oxford University Press, 2009).

10. Ibid.

11. Speech by Rear Admiral Garland Wright to the Coronado Rotary Club 2009, verified by e-mail exchange with the author on 21 May 2010.

12. Walzer, *Just and Unjust Wars*, 146.

13. The accounts told here come from author interviews with Master Sergeant Matt Eversmann at the U.S. Naval Academy, autumn 2004.

14. Kilcullen, *The Accidental Guerilla*.

15. Anthony E. Hartle, *Moral Issues in Military Decision Making,* 2nd ed. (Lawrence: University of Kansas Press, 2004), 114–15. Hartle attributes the Kant quotation to the essay "Perpetual Peace," in *Kant's Political Writings,* ed. Hans Reiss, trans. H. B. Nisbet (Cambridge: Cambridge University Press, 1977).

16. Ibid. I owe to Hartle the connection with the quotation from "The Law of Land Warfare," U.S. Army "Field Manual FM 27-10," 22.

17. Thomas W. Smith, "Protecting Civilians . . . or Soldiers? Humanitarian Law and Economy of Risk in Iraq," *International Studies Perspective* 9, no. 2 (May 2008): 146.

18. "Counterinsurgency Manual FM 3-24," U.S. Army, December 2006: 1–27.

19. Phone interviews with Vice Admiral Robert Harward in spring 2003 and June 2010.

20. At the same time, it is important to make the distinction between refusing orders because they violate legal or ethical boundaries and doing so to make a political statement, which violates at least military standards of professionalism. It is a basic tenet of most democratic systems that the elected head of state is also commander in chief of the armed forces and that the armed forces are at all times subordinate to the state's civilian leadership.

21. This version of his story I heard from Hugh Thompson personally, when he visited the U.S. Naval Academy in 2003. It can be corroborated in many sources. The full story is available in Trent Angers, *The Forgotten Hero of My Lai: The Hugh Thompson Story* (Lafayette: Acadian House, 1999). Thompson was finally awarded a medal for valor thirty years later.

22. This overheated sort of rhetoric has been particularly prominent with regard to the most recent Iraq and Afghanistan wars, which have been called a "clash of civilizations" in reference to Samuel Huntington's coinage. See Samuel P. Huntington, "The Clash of Civilizations," *Foreign Affairs* (Summer 1993).

23. Telephone conversation with Captain Alex Krongard, U.S. Navy, 28 July 2010.

24. The idea that tactical and professional competence is fundamental to ethics in combat I owe to Captain Bill Calhoun, U.S. Navy (retired), in a 1995 discussion we had when he was Dean of the U.S. Naval War College.

25. See Malcolm Gladwell, *Blink: The Power of Thinking Without Thinking* (Boston: Little, Brown, 2005), in which Gladwell discusses immediate and intuitive decisions based on subconscious calculations that come from years of experience. In particular, the introduction gives an example of an experienced intuitive judgment that was more accurate than a judgment based on extensive analysis. The book also points to some of the pitfalls and dangers inherent in intuitive ("gut") calls.

26. This brief section is based largely on insights I gained at a conference, "New Warriors and New Weapons: The Ethical Ramifications of Emerging Military Technologies," held at the U.S. Naval Academy in April 2010.

27. For a detailed look at the issue of robotics and autonomous and semiautonomous weapons in warfare, see Ron Arkin, *Governing Lethal Behavior in Autonomous Robots* (Boca Raton: Chapman and Hall/CRC, 2009). Arkin argues primarily for the

advantages of robotics. Peter Asaro, on the other hand, expresses his strong reservations in his article, "How Just Could a Robot War Be?" available at http://www.peterasaro.org/writing/Asaro%20Just%20Robot%20War.pdf. Arkin and Asaro are frequently on panels arguing against each other's positions—though with great respect for each other's side of the argument. Recent revelations of mistargeting of civilians with drones in Pakistan and Afghanistan have considerably heated the debate. See Robert H. Reid, "Officer Reprimanded in Fatal Drone Strike," Associated Press, 1 June 2010, reprinted in the *AirForce Times*, http://www.airforcetimes.com/news/2010/05/ap_afghanistan_airforce_drone_052910.

16 Measuring Effectiveness

Paul Shemella

IN THIS VOLUME WE HAVE DISCUSSED CIVIL–MILITARY responses to terrorism within the context of political- and operational-level strategy. However, developing good strategy is only the first step to success; government officials must *execute* the ways and means needed to get them to the ends they seek. The problem is this: How do they know whether the ways and means are actually getting them where they want to go? Ultimately, the three questions they must first answer—to their publics—are "What does victory look like, does the current set of strategies take us there, and how will we know when we arrive?"

The concept of measurement has intrigued and bedeviled government officials for a long time. Interest within the United States is fueled partly by the Vietnam experience, where measuring the wrong thing (the enemy body count) led to disaster. The recognition by leaders that they must know where a strategy leads them is intuitive; the measurement of progress en route is not. Terms are important here. The technical-sounding word *metrics,* popularized by Defense Secretary Donald Rumsfeld's Pentagon (2001–2006), does not tell us *what* is to be measured. *Measure of effectiveness* (MOE) is a much better term, reminding us that it is effectiveness that counts, not simply quantity or cost. This chapter will provide insight into how we measure and why.

Measures of effectiveness do several important things. First, they give us a means to apply discipline to the execution of strategy, a road map with predetermined waypoints. Second, choosing what to measure allows us to distinguish what is important from what is not. Third, MOEs help government officials determine whether something is working or not, ideally protecting us from going too far down the path of failure. Finally, consensus regarding what to measure unifies strategic thinking and places decision makers in a position to distribute scarce resources wisely. If we are going to refine our strategies—and adjust them in execution as needed—measurement must be integrated into the strategy-development process.

Even after incorporating MOEs into the construction of strategy, three major issues present themselves. First, there are many ways to measure effectiveness, setting the stage for bitter quarrels on the government side. In addition, the terrorists we are fighting undoubtedly have their own ways to measure progress. It is indeed possible for both governments and their terrorist opponents to demonstrate progress at the same time, and ordinary citizens will hear both narratives. The second issue arises from the recognition that what we are trying to measure unfolds in a chaotic, nonlinear fashion. Terrorist actions can spring seemingly from nowhere, after years of calm for which governments have claimed credit. The third major issue centers on the differences between "hard" numbers and "soft" indicators. Measuring the wrong things, perhaps in the wrong ways, can actually lead governments and their citizens into a false sense of security. Conversely, the wrong measurements can lead to a false sense of *in*security, stoking the overwhelming fear that terrorists wish to create. How should governments decide what to measure and how?

It might be useful to think about how MOEs would be established to evaluate the effectiveness of a rival soccer team. There are many ways to evaluate the team's performance (number of goals scored, time of possession, number of shots taken, number of penalties, and even the ball-control skills of individual players). We can examine all the statistics for insight into possible weaknesses to exploit, but the most important measure is still the score. Over time, however, a different picture emerges. (For example, has this team won more games in each consecutive year, or fewer? What is its record against *us* over the last few years?) These so-called "dynamic measures" can tell us whether our long-term strategies against such a team are succeeding or not (or whether we are even playing the same game).[1]

Some researchers have suggested measuring three categories of activity related to terrorism: incidents, attitudes, and trends.[2] Measuring incidents is relatively easy, and most governments rely on these statistics to some degree.

Data points provide the raw material from which to extrapolate more information. Tracking attitudes may reveal weaknesses in our assumptions that can be strengthened before a simple decline in numbers of incidents can lead us astray. Trends over time are clearly more important than individual data points. Even so, finding things to measure, and even actually measuring them, are not enough. In the end, measurements can only inform judgment. Turning data into something that can help a leader make critical decisions requires analysis of incidents, attitudes, and trends, all of which brings us back to the question of what to measure.[3]

Efficiency and Effectiveness

Defining something is often a matter of distinguishing it from something else. The words *efficiency* and *effectiveness* sound similar and are sometimes used interchangeably by careless officials. On the one hand, efficiency is a way to express output per unit cost. An efficient operation would use the least amount of resources necessary to achieve the objective. Effectiveness, on the other hand, measures the results of an action, irrespective of cost: If an activity brought about the desired result, it was effective. An attempt to merge the two concepts into a single measure has resulted in the phrase *cost-effectiveness,* or getting the most bang for the buck. The principle of cost-effectiveness underpins long-term projects such as aircraft procurement or public health policy. But cost-effectiveness cannot be measured in the short run, and even a long campaign against terrorism cannot be canceled simply because it costs too much. When it comes to such nonelective categories as national security, we are better off examining efficiency and effectiveness as separate items, both important to measure.

Efficiency is more complicated than it first appears. In the context of an operational campaign, it can also be understood as a measure of performance. The veteran bomber pilot who follows all the procedures and the skilled surgeon who performs a delicate operation on a child are evaluated in terms of efficiency rather than effectiveness. If the target withstands the attack or the child dies, the results are not automatically seen as a reflection of poor performance. The performance could have been flawless, but countless other factors could have obstructed success. Terrorism is a complex process wherein the same caveat applies. Just because we kill the leaders or seize the funds of terrorist organizations, we cannot assume beyond doubt that particular results will flow from those actions. High levels of efficiency do not necessarily lead to the effects we wish to create.

If efficient operations do not bring us the results we want, what about more effort? If the pilot goes back again and again, the target will be destroyed sooner or later. If the doctor operates on enough children, surely he will save some of them. But what is the *result* of targets destroyed or children saved? It could be that there is no effect at all on the overall success of the campaign (destroy the terrorists, eliminate this illness). It could even be true that more effort in the wrong places could *prevent* us from attaining the result we seek (as more bombing has been shown to do). Perhaps more children could be saved by putting money into *preventing* disease rather than surgery after illness strikes. How would we measure that? It could also be true that our efforts have nothing to do with the effects we perceive. There is a difference between correlation and causation. Individuals measure their efforts because these efforts are the only thing they *can* measure, which is fine as long as we understand that it is not the same thing as measuring *results.*

Effectiveness is a description of how well something we are doing is leading us to the results we want. If our strategies against terrorism are well thought out, they will delineate those results as the "ends" for which we apply ways and means. Measuring effort comes easily at the operational level, where there are a lot of things that can be counted. But how do we measure effectiveness? An example comes from counter-drug operations in South America, where U.S. Navy and Drug Enforcement Administration (DEA) teams worked with their Latin American counterparts to build capacity to interdict narcotics moving along the region's extensive river systems. The Navy teams measured their efforts to deny use of the rivers to drug traffickers (number of patrols, number of boats on the water), while the DEA measured the amount of cocaine that it seized on the same rivers. Meanwhile, in the White House, National Security Council officials were measuring the price (which should have gone up) and purity (which should have gone down) of cocaine on the streets of Miami. Denial and seizure might have played a role in the outcome, but price and purity are measures of effectiveness for the interdiction strategy.[4]

Effectiveness and Strategy

Chapter 9 of this volume describes a "family" of strategies at both the political and operational levels as the basis for government responses to terrorism. The most successful of these strategies have MOEs built into them from the start. Deciding on what will be measured during execution will naturally shape a strategy as it is being formulated. By contrast, failure to designate MOEs during strategy development will almost certainly result in major changes early in the execution phase, wasting resources and even lives. How then do we link MOEs to specific strategies up front? At the political level the alignment of MOEs should be focused on broad political objectives, progress toward which can be measured. For example:

Core Strategy. Because this strategy will entail a long-term campaign against the root causes of terrorism, certain political objectives suggest themselves. Although always subject to debate, three such objectives might be as follows:

- Strengthen social cohesion. The fulfillment of this objective should reduce the overall number of disaffected citizens, thereby immunizing the society to some degree from the virus of extremist ideology.
- Enhance government legitimacy. Anything we can do to strengthen the government's worthiness of wide citizen support will make it harder for terrorists to recruit from within the population.
- Reduce ideological support for terrorism. Government has a responsibility to defend the values it is founded upon (if they are defensible) while discrediting the ideas aimed at changing it violently or destroying it completely.

Core MOEs. The following items are suggested as a *starting* point for measuring progress toward the political objectives listed above:

- Strengthen social cohesion: size of the middle class, literacy rate, access to education for girls, "Gini" Index[5] of social equality, number of rural villages with Internet access, crime rate, unemployment rate, number of private armies/militias, number of lawsuits claiming discrimination, number of citizens with access to health care.
- Enhance government legitimacy: number of "tips" to law enforcement by local citizens, number of citizens involved in public projects, volume of favorable press coverage, percentage of citizens who pay income taxes, percentage of citizens who vote, percentage of citizens who leave the country, military recruiting statistics.
- Reduce ideological support for terrorism: popularity of jihadist Web sites, number of youths involved in extremist violence, volume of

extremist graffiti, percentages of clerics who denounce/support religious extremism, polling data, volume of media articles supporting extremist views.

Offensive Strategy. As a series of actions against terrorist threats, attainment of the political objectives associated with this strategy usually requires the application of coercive force. Three objectives come to mind:

- Incapacitate terrorists: This could mean killing them, but it could also mean incarceration and trial. Even (especially) with terrorists, it is important to apply the law fairly to avoid making martyrs. Any attempt to circumvent the law reduces governments to the same level as their terrorist enemies and undermines the core strategy of enhancing legitimacy. Taking terrorists out of the equation is a political event as well as an operational one.
- Disrupt ongoing terrorist operations: If incapacitation is not possible, then interdiction of terrorist operations before they can succeed is critical. However, the breaking up of terrorist plots typically causes tension between politicians who wish to take credit as soon as possible and intelligence officials who wish to continue surveillance as long as possible.
- Destroy terrorist organizations: The number of terrorist organizations confronting the state is also a political issue. In some countries there is only one, but in others there are multiple terrorist organizations trying to take down the government.[6] This objective carries a lot of political weight.

Offensive MOEs. As with all the MOEs listed, the following measures fall into one of two categories: "more is better" or "less is better."

- Incapacitate terrorists: number of terrorists killed, number captured, recidivism rate for "rehabilitated" terrorists.[7]
- Disrupt ongoing terrorist operations: number of terrorist operations stopped in progress, number of operations abandoned prior to execution, number of terrorists leaving the country, number of terrorists entering the country, number of terrorist leaders incapacitated, ratio of government raids to terrorist attacks.
- Destroy terrorist organizations: number of terrorist organizations posing a threat to the government, length of time between terrorist

attacks, number of civilian casualties, number of terrorist cells/nodes rendered ineffective, volume/currency of terrorist Web sites, number of defections.

Defensive Strategy. Protecting a society against terrorist attack goes beyond the traditional notion of defense. Governments have to create a climate of security within which citizens can feel safe—whether or not they are attacked. This strategy has two parts: One is preventing terrorist attacks, and the other is building capacity to mitigate and manage the consequences of terrorist attacks that cannot be prevented. Three political objectives come to mind:

- Create a climate of security for ordinary citizens. Fear of terrorism is just as debilitating as an act of terrorism. Governments can earn the loyalty of their citizens by increasing the level of personal and public security in cities and other areas vulnerable to terrorist attack.
- Make terrorist attacks too difficult to initiate. The state must increase the expected costs that terrorists include in their decision calculus. If terrorists conclude that attacking people and property is just not worth the effort, it may force them to demonstrate their political dissent in other ways.
- Ensure the resilience of critical systems. No government has enough resources to protect all its critical infrastructure all the time. It is worth trying to convince terrorists that even if they launch a successful attack, the *system* (electricity, water, transportation) upon which citizens depend will not collapse.

Defensive MOEs. Measures of defensive progress are more difficult to identify than offensive measures. Governments may take credit for long periods of time between terrorist attacks, or the lack of any attacks at all, but it is very hard to prove that government actions (as opposed to other factors) have actually deterred terrorists from acting.[8] As above, some of the items suggested are measures of effort rather than effectiveness.

- Create a climate of security for ordinary citizens: number of civilian victims, number of public safety messages/threat warnings, amount of funding allocated to local authorities, number of threats issued by terrorists, number of violent crimes, number of police on the street, number of soldiers on the street, operating hours of local businesses, distance that a farmer will travel to bring his or her produce to market, percentage of children regularly attending school.

- Make terrorist attacks too difficult to initiate: number of terrorist attacks, volume of pessimistic or discouraged terrorist "chatter," number of police guarding critical infrastructure, number of surveillance cameras deployed, volume of press reports citing citizen assistance to law enforcement, funds expended for physical security upgrades, number of announced interagency exercises (prevention/consequence management).
- Ensure the resilience of critical systems: number of system failures because of terrorism or natural disaster, percentage of critical infrastructure systems without redundancy, volume of press reports describing system resilience, number of interagency exercises on cyber security, number of police guarding key facilities, funding allocated to high-technology alarms/controls, tracking of government/private security partnerships.

At some point MOEs begin to overlap, but rather than being a problem, it is necessary and normal to have different agencies gathering the same kinds of data. There are no hard and fast boundaries among different kinds of strategies either. A good MOE for the core strategy may also work for the defensive strategy. Selection and discussion of MOEs can provide a basis for coordination inside and among institutions. Through an uninterrupted focus on desired effects, MOEs are in fact the glue that binds together distinct strategies and the institutions that execute them collectively.

There is not sufficient space in this short chapter to suggest all possible MOEs for all strategic ends. As noted, that is an iterative process that will be unique to each actor or set of actors and to each situation. Having established a method for deriving appropriate measures, it is left to the practitioner to apply that method to specific national strategies. From there it should be extended to the operational level. At times, the national level will be forced to measure effort rather than results (until results are clear enough), but MOEs for operations will *often* be measures of effort—for example, number of small arms exchanged by a community for tools and equipment—but that is worth something. It is important for political leaders to know in detail what is being done at the operational level, by both civilian and military institutions, so they can be sure that these efforts are linked to political-level strategies. Ministers and agency directors will have their own operational strategies (with MOEs to support them), but the "effects" they create must, in the end, be political.

Leaders at the operational level should be both cautious and precise in choosing what to measure. By statement or implication, field personnel will apply the tactics required to maximize their attainment of those standards. In other words, MOEs dictate how an institution behaves. If seizures of cocaine are the overriding MOE, then DEA agents will be promoted on the basis of how much they seize. If a naval commander directs his subordinates to board and search *all* vessels, he will get reports from searches of everything that floats. Within that flood of data, the really necessary measures will be lost. Extensive discussion regarding MOEs should be integrated into every aspect of operations. Designating (and adjusting) MOEs is an exercise in creativity where every participant can play an important role.[9]

Quantum Change

Success in fighting terrorism is difficult to measure partly because terrorism defies prediction. Terrorist organizations evolve in unexpected ways. Like biological organisms, they adapt to a changing environment by making strategic choices.[10] Terrorist activities involve a set of complex actions that can lead to surprising surges. For instance, maritime terrorism represents a *qualitative* change in the way terrorists operate. Following the Limburg (2002) and Mumbai (2008) attacks, maritime terrorism is now considered by some analysts to be a quantum leap in the global threat.[11] Suicide bombings are another leap, especially given their simplicity and effectiveness. The ultimate quantum leap, of course, would be the use of chemical, biological, or nuclear weapons. Such quantum changes cannot be measured with hard data, but they can be anticipated with "soft" indicators, as those factors approach their tipping points. A Congressional Research Service report on measuring effectiveness in combating terrorism[12] suggests the following indicators, which can serve as a good starter list of things to look for when trying to predict where a terrorist organization may be going:

- Intelligence: Terrorists achieve the capability to ascertain specific knowledge critical to exploiting a nation's vulnerabilities.
- Technology: Terrorists are on the brink of access to new technology that will give them more lethal capabilities.

- Impact on Society: Terrorists cause such disruption and fear that society itself is transformed beyond what citizens consider normal.
- Targets: Terrorists shift their targeting philosophy, generally toward larger-scale attacks and higher civilian casualties.[13]
- Alliances: Terrorists form new alliances with other terrorist groups, criminal syndicates, or rogue states.
- Disruption: Terrorists step up their attacks to the point where the state is forced to concentrate a crippling level of resources on defense.
- Sophistication: Terrorists demonstrate, perhaps through new alliances, that they are capable of more complex, highly coordinated attacks.[14]
- Morale and Momentum: Terrorists gain strength and credibility as they put together a string of successful operations.

Governments wishing to measure the success of their own strategies cannot avoid measuring the success of strategies used against *them*. The idiosyncratic actions of terrorist organizations, as well as the unintended consequences of a government's actions against them, can, to a large degree, be imagined and planned for. Liberally educated and well-practiced government officials are the best insurance against terrorist surprises. But how can anyone measure something that has not happened yet, and may not happen at all?

Measuring Prevention

For some governments it may not be possible to measure terrorist incidents. If there are no terrorist attacks, governments must have a way to know whether their actions are leading to that result (causation) or the result is merely coincidental (correlation). Just as they are obliged to draw lessons from attacks they cannot prevent, governments should be cataloguing "best practices" from successful prevention efforts. These data form the basis for explaining to law-abiding citizens how public resources are being used to deny terrorists access to their targets. This is not at all an easy task, but it is an important one if governments hope to keep the confidence of their populace.

Even when the result of an intangible such as prevention cannot be measured directly, the processes and systems that lead to the desired outcome *can* be.[15] The place to begin is by identifying "desired outcomes" for each of the three strategies, at both the political and operational levels. We can then list a set of preconditions that must be in place to achieve the desired outcomes. Take the example of a hypothetical country with the usual set of root causes for antigovernment terrorism. Addressing root causes will certainly reduce the likelihood of terrorist attacks. For the core strategy at the political level, we could state one desired outcome as follows: "We have eliminated the root causes of terrorism in the country." That statement cannot be substantiated with raw numbers, but there is a process for converting the government's broad approaches into numbers that can be evaluated. The process, which could be called "institutionalizing measures of effort," deserves consideration by all governments. The interim step in this process is to identify the preconditions that enable us to reach the desired outcome. In this case the list of preconditions could include the following hopeful statements:

1. "There is a process for interethnic dialogue throughout the country."
2. "We have strengthened the justice system."
3. "We have eliminated corruption from law-enforcement institutions."
4. "We guarantee universal access to basic health care."
5. "We have ensured that every citizen can receive a basic level of education."
6. "There is a system for reviewing complaints against the government."
7. "There is a lively, open, and responsible press establishment."
8. "The armed forces are focused on external threats to the country."

For the purposes of this example, we can assume that these statements have been formulated over time by a panel of experts in our hypothetical government. The preconditions for getting to their desired outcome can now be evaluated on a scale of 0–5 (called a Likert Scale) by another (independent) panel of experts.[16] The experts will assign a "0" to statements for which nothing has been done, a "5" to statements where everything has been done, or interim values to reflect partial accomplishment. At the end of this process, the numbers can be aggregated to determine the ratio of the actual score to the maximum possible ("best") score. For eight preconditions, the maximum score in this case is 40. If the actual total comes to 20, it can be said that the government has made progress but probably not enough. This ratio is not very useful by itself, but when compared to other desired outcomes, it may show where the government needs to invest resources, as well as where its previous investments have paid off.

What is more, if the experts score each statement individually rather than by consensus, it will be possible to find an aggregate score for each item as well, which can give a more detailed picture of where the most improvement is needed and how it can be achieved. For instance, having ten experts means 50 is the best possible score. "We have strengthened the justice system" might get an aggregate score of 20 while "We have eliminated corruption from law-enforcement institutions" might score 43. It may then be argued that some methods for bringing police corruption under control can be adapted to the justice system. In a logical and methodical way, we can transform judgment into numbers.

Indirect measurement can augment direct measurement. There are some things that can be measured directly in every country (polling and statistics abound). It is useful then to think of MOEs as a broad category of direct and indirect measures that lead governments to desired outcomes. The vehicle for progress should be a well-informed strategy, executed with embedded MOEs and adjustable based on actual measurements. But the numbers alone do not lead directly to strategic adjustment decisions; they simply inform the judgment of decision makers. In the end, it is human judgment that counts, but even the most experienced decision makers are severely handicapped without measures of effectiveness. It is important for government officials to choose the right MOEs and the right *number* of MOEs. Too much data can overwhelm judgment; too few measures (or just one) can distort the analysis in the other direction. A balance of complexity and simplicity will keep government strategies on track.

Assessing Capacity

The indirect measurement technique can also be used to evaluate a government's institutional capacity to fight terrorism—what we will call a "framework" for assessment. The framework assesses capacity in four functional areas: strategy, institutional preparation, intelligence, and emergency management.[17] In order to explain the methodology, let us take a sample from the "strategy" functional area:

Strategy. Based on the discussion of strategy development in Chapter 9, we can list six "desired outcomes" for the strategy function:

1. Appropriate government institutions have clear roles in combating terrorism.

2. There is a process for coordinating strategy development among government institutions.
3. There is a process for developing an accurate and comprehensive strategic analysis.[18]
4. There is a method for measuring the effectiveness of strategies to combat terrorism.
5. There is a political-level strategy for combating terrorism.
6. Each institution with a role in combating terrorism has an operational-level strategy.

For each desired outcome above, we can list a set of preconditions that will lead a government to that outcome. To use just one example, the preconditions for desired outcome 1 should read something like this:

A. The Ministry of Interior, Ministry of Defense, Ministry of Foreign Affairs, and intelligence agencies have written guidance on their responsibilities for combating terrorism.
B. Other ministries have written guidance consistent with the government's legal definition of terrorism.
C. Institutional roles are not in conflict with each other.
D. There are no gaps between institutions in terms of responsibility for combating terrorism.

Applying the Likert Scale, we can assign a number to each precondition, based on the judgment of five experts selected for the assessment in this case. Those experts can be officials from the government being assessed, terrorism specialists from the private sector, or even officials from another government with more experience in fighting terrorism. A hypothetical set of values assigned by them might look something like this:

A. 2 out of 5
B. 4 out of 5
C. 2 out of 5
D. 2 out of 5

The total number 10 (out of a possible 20) does not tell us much by itself. The aggregation of totals for each of the six desired outcomes (and their associated preconditions) would give us a total for the strategy function (as well as a comprehensive comparison within the field of preconditions). The final number for "strategy" can then be compared to total values from the other three functional areas to indicate relative institutional capacity—and where the most resources should be invested in the future. This assessment framework is a flexible tool that can (and should) be tailored to a particular government's needs. It gives every government a place to begin building the capacity it will need to fight terrorism more effectively.

Conclusion: A Measure of Confidence

In this chapter we have left the fundamental question for last. Is "victory" over terrorism even possible, and, if so, what does victory mean? Every government, incorporating the attitudes of the society it represents, must answer this question for itself. For governments that view the fight against terrorism as a war, victory may mean the total destruction of all terrorist groups threatening that country's citizens and interests. For governments that consider terrorism a criminal act, victory could mean suppressing it to the lowest possible level. In this regard each society has different standards to satisfy. Some societies are so traumatized by unrelenting terrorist attacks that they tend to support the most aggressive use of hard power. Other societies—even some with high levels of violent crime—tend to support policies that feature robust law enforcement over time. The selection and use of MOEs can lay the groundwork for important interagency coordination and critical international cooperation. Institutions and governments that need to act together have no choice but to try to measure their effectiveness in compatible ways.

Measuring effectiveness is an essential element of both war-fighting and crime-suppression approaches to the complex problem of terrorism. Unless a government knows where it is now, the question of where it is going becomes impossible to answer. Citizens also need to know where their governments are going. MOEs give governments a way to confidently reassure people that their lives are becoming more secure, that terrorism is a receding threat. A climate of security is the antidote for the virus of fear that terrorism generates. Whatever mixture of hard and soft power a government chooses to employ, security at the personal level is the end that each one seeks. Strategies against terrorism will not produce that climate in a vacuum. Governments need feedback on what they are doing. In other words, they need to measure things, evaluate the data, and then use their best judgment to act on what they learn.

The collection of those data requires the expenditure of precious time and funding, but leaders can ensure that spending those resources increases both the efficiency and effectiveness of a campaign against terrorism.

Notes

1. The concept of "dynamic measures" is taken from Barry Crane et al., "Between Peace and War: Comprehending Low Intensity Conflict," National Security Discussion Paper, series 88-02, Harvard University, Cambridge, Massachusetts, 1987, 24.

2. See Raphael Perl, "Combating Terrorism: The Challenge of Measuring Effectiveness," Congressional Research Service Report for Congress, updated 12 March 2007, 9–11.

3. This chapter reflects much original thinking, based upon insight gained over years of research and teaching with the Center for Civil–Military Relations (CCMR) and helping foreign officials identify what to measure in their campaigns against terrorism. Within the current context there is a noticeable dearth of useful writing on MOEs.

4. Taken from the personal experience of the author in 1990 and 1991. It was pointed out at the field level that the measures of effort applied by the DEA were in direct opposition to those applied by the Navy. Seizures are a particularly bad way to measure effort because they yield a false sense of security. Denial of rivers to drug traffickers is actually a good way to measure effort, but it is still simply a measure of effort.

5. The Gini Index, named for Italian statistician Corrado Gini, is a coefficient derived from the distribution of income within a country (a perfectly equal distribution would be 0, while a perfectly unequal one would be 100). There are some surprises in the data: Values listed for 2007 score the United States (45) as less equal than Pakistan (30.6). See the Central Intelligence Agency's World Factbook: http://www.cia.gov/library/publications/the-world-factbook/fields/2172.html.

6. This number could be quite large. According to the Institute for Conflict Management's South Asia Terrorism Portal, there were 178 terrorist, insurgent, and extremist groups operating in India during 2001: http://www.satp.org/satporgtp/countries/india/terroristoutfits/index.html. There is no reason to think that this number has decreased over the years.

7. Saudi Arabia, Yemen, and Singapore have terrorist-rehabilitation programs. Saudi government sources place the recidivism rate for their program at just 2%. For a complete description of the Saudi program, see Christopher Boucek, "Extremist Reeducation and Rehabilitation in Saudi Arabia," *Terrorism Monitor* (Jamestown Foundation) 5, no. 16 (16 August 2007).

8. There have been no Al Qaeda attacks on U.S. soil since September 2001, but that could be a consequence of the stunning success of the operation itself. Al Qaeda would have nothing to gain from attacking again unless the results were even more

devastating—and spectacular—than 9/11. It seems instead to be acting as a cheerleader for amateur attacks such as the underwear bomber. But what does that tell us about progress against Al Qaeda?

9. The most important role of all may be played by the "loyal contrarian." Every institution needs members who feel secure enough to contribute bold ideas and ask tough questions. Leaders of institutions should go beyond tolerating these kinds of employees; they should actively recruit them.

10. See Martha Crenshaw, "The Logic of Terrorism: Terrorist Behavior as a Product of Strategic Choice," in *The Origins of Terrorism*, ed. Walter Reich (Washington: Woodrow Wilson Center Press 1990), 7–24.

11. "Yemen Says Tanker Blast Was Terrorism," *BBC News*, 16 October 2002, http://news.bbc.co.uk/2/hi/middle_east/2334865.stm. See Thomas Mockaitis's case study of the Mumbai bombings in Chapter 20.

12. Perl, "Combating Terrorism," 7–8.

13. Care should be exercised here not to assume that such targeting shifts indicate that a terrorist group is getting stronger. The targeting of more civilians, who are relatively easy targets, may be a signal that the group is getting desperate.

14. Al Qaeda's signature near-simultaneous explosions are a good example of this. The ability of local terrorists to execute these kinds of operations is a likely indicator of Al Qaeda support.

15. Glen Woodbury, "Measuring Prevention," *Homeland Security Affairs* 1, no. 1 (Summer 2005).

16. A Likert Scale, named for creator Rensis Likert, typically presents statements and asks the respondent to evaluate them on a five- (or more) point scale, for example from "Strongly agree" to "Strongly disagree," with gradations in between.

17. The Center for Civil–Military Relations (CCMR) has developed this framework as a tool to be used by governments that want to evaluate their own performance in dealing with the problem of terrorism. Files describing this tool can be found on the CCMR Web site: http://www.ccmr.org.

18. A proper strategic analysis would combine risk assessment (the relative risk of all threats) and net assessment (the comparison of government strengths and weaknesses to a particular threat). Risk assessment is covered in Chapter 8; net assessment is mentioned in Chapter 9.

III SELECTED CASE STUDIES

17 Somalia

Lawrence E. Cline

SOMALIA REPRESENTS WHAT IS AKIN TO THE PERFECT STORM of insecurity, from the level of the state all the way down to the individual. It has little or no governance, multiple armed groups with competing agendas, ubiquitous organized crime, and an expansionist terrorist presence. As such, Somalia may be an ideal case study for examining the growth of violent extremist movements.

The Collapse of Somalia

The history of Somalia in the early 1990s has been described in many sources, so only a brief outline will be provided here. Like so much of Africa, the territory that is now Somalia was under colonial rule until 1960, when it was first united into a sovereign state. Major General Mohamed Siad Barre came to power via a coup in 1969 and ruled Somalia as an iron-fisted dictator with the support of the Soviet Union. Siad Barre got the country involved in a disastrous insurgency against the Ethiopian government, and he was finally overthrown by a very loose coalition of armed groups in 1991. Although these movements cooperated well enough to drive Siad Barre from power, they could not then cooperate to establish a central government, and fighting broke out among them. Although it is usually described as clan warfare—and the vast majority of the fighting clearly was interclan—in many ways the violence was both the genesis and the result of emergent warlords among the clans.

Coincident with the fighting, a long, severe drought gripped Somalia and the Horn of Africa, leading to massive civilian suffering. Facing a humanitarian disaster, the United Nations authorized the United Nations Operation in Somalia (later to be known as UNOSOM I) to monitor a ceasefire between the factions and provide security for humanitarian relief operations. This mission was under-resourced from the start, and its ambit essentially did not extend beyond the port of Mogadishu. The combination of the increasing casualties taken by the Pakistani troops of UNOSOM and the inability of the UN to distribute aid to Somali civilians in dire need across the country led to calls by a number of governments, humanitarian organizations, and various pressure groups for a more robust response. Although initially resistant, the George H. W. Bush administration eventually agreed in November 1992 to send a substantially larger and better-armed force under an expanded UN mandate to Somalia to ensure the flow of humanitarian assistance countrywide.

The new mission, the Unified Task Force (UNITAF), worked in cooperation with UNOSOM I under the operational name of Restore Hope to establish enough security for the humanitarian operations to go forward. It had a fair degree of success during its existence, opening up assistance stations throughout most of Somalia and significantly reducing the level of civilian suffering.[1] UNITAF made only limited efforts at disarmament of the various factions, primarily focusing on coercing the militias to stay out of the way of the humanitarian mission. There were some incidents between UNITAF forces and the Somali militias, but these were quickly resolved in favor of UNITAF. Mostly, however, to retain control of the situation, the U.S. elements of UNITAF relied on both a very active psychological operations campaign and an image of overwhelming force and the willingness to use it if necessary.

Shortly after elections in the United States brought the administration of William J. Clinton into office, in May 1993 UNITAF was disbanded and many of the U.S. forces withdrawn from Somalia. The mission was then reestablished with reduced strength as UNOSOM II. Things began to go sour for this mission rather quickly. In large measure this was due to a series of mistakes made by the UN, the U.S. government, and other governments. The reduced strength of UNOSOM II meant that it simply did not have the resources (or the image of overwhelming power) that UNITAF had been able to rely on. It was given the mission of disarming the Somali militias, which was a job far beyond its capabilities. Finally, after an ambush of Pakistani peacekeeping troops in June 1993 by the forces of Mohamed Farrah Aideed, the UN publicly declared him a criminal, and orders were issued for his arrest. To many Somalis this meant that the UN forces no longer were a neutral humanitarian force, but had become active participants in the ongoing armed struggle for control of the country, and were therefore legitimate targets in the fighting.

Things came to a head in September and October 1993. Skirmishing between Somali militiamen—particularly Aideed's supporters—and the UN forces became more commonplace. The United States retained forces, which included elements of the Joint Special Operations Command (JSOC) and the Ranger Regiment, in Somalia or just offshore, specifically for direct-action missions. In one of many problems with operational-level planning in Somalia, these U.S. troops had a separate reporting and command-and-control chain from the main UNOSOM II units, which raised serious issues regarding coordination of the forces. On 3 October, in what became known as the "Blackhawk Down" incident, a raid intended to kill or capture Aideed went very wrong, and 18 JSOC troops and Rangers were killed. During the fighting and associated U.S. air strikes, as many as 1,000 Somalis were also killed or wounded. The political fallout of this abortive operation within the United States was significant; by March 1994, Washington had withdrawn all its forces from Somalia, while the UN pulled out all remaining "peacekeepers" in March 1995.

After the U.S. and UN withdrawals, Somalia returned to the reign of the clans and warlords. No group or leader was sufficiently strong to control the country, and it essentially splintered into local fiefdoms. However, two provinces in the north proved to be exceptions. These were Somaliland and Puntland, each of which has rebuilt at least a semblance of normalcy and relative peace independent of events in the capital. Somaliland has managed to conduct credible elections, with the opponent of the ruling president winning the election in July 2010 by a fifty to thirty-three percent margin.[2] Despite the relative success of these proto-states, however, some of the broader unrest in the region has also spilled over. For example, in May 2010 Ethiopian troops reportedly made a brief foray into Somaliland that involved an exchange of gunfire at a border checkpoint.[3] Both areas also have been hit by suicide bombers. Moreover, Puntland has been one of the principal areas from which piracy is conducted in the Gulf of Aden. In contrast to these two regions, since the UN withdrawal the rest of Somalia has seen almost continual conflict of greater or lesser intensity as clan-based warlords fight to retain or expand their areas of control.

The Rise of the Islamists

Even before the fall of Siad Barre, various Islamist groups began to gain adherents in Somalia.[4] During the period after the 1991 coup, and more quickly after the withdrawal of the foreign forces in 1995, Islamist movements began to grow in strength. The first major group was al Itihaad al Islaami (Islamic Union—not to be confused with the Itihaad al Mahakim al Islamiya, the Islamic Courts Union). Although the exact date of the founding of al Itihaad is unknown, it probably began in the early 1980s.[5] During its peak strength in the 1990s, this group, believed to have some links to Al Qaeda, was estimated to have more than 1,000 militiamen.[6] The two main goals of the organization, after the overthrow of Siad Barre, were to establish an Islamic state within Somalia and to unify surrounding territories with populations of ethnic Somalis into a Greater Somalia. The actual popular support for Itihaad among most Somalis remains questionable, as is probably the case with other ideological groups that have more recently arisen. One analyst notes that Somalis were generally "suspicious of politically active Islam and remained attached to the clan as the sole source of protection."[7]

Al Itihaad reportedly received significant funding from charities in the Gulf States and used a portion of it to establish training camps that welcomed a large number of foreign jihadists. Despite this support, the organization at its height managed to control only a few limited areas in Somalia, including the ports of Kismayo and Merka, for about a year. It also held the town of Luuq, near Somalia's tri-border confluence with Ethiopia and Kenya. From this location al Itihaad tried to stir up unrest within the Ogaden region of Ethiopia and conducted bombings in the Ethiopian capital of Addis Ababa itself. It is notable that, unlike in so much of Somalia, al Itihaad maintained law and order, albeit frequently brutally, for the residents of the towns it controlled and therefore gained some local legitimacy.[8] Following Ethiopian raids on its camps in 1997, the group formally disbanded.

The Islamic Courts Union (ICU) was the second major strand of Islamist movements within Somalia. When the central government fell apart in the mid-1990s, along with the warlords, a number of fundamentalist, largely clan-based militias took over local governance and set up governing courts based on rigidly anti-Western sharia law. In 2000 eleven of these groups united to form the ICU, with the intention of reunifying Somalia as an Islamic state.[9] The Union succeeded in gaining loose control of the southern two-thirds of

Somalia in 2006, including Mogadishu. The ICU implemented its strict interpretation of sharia on the areas it controlled, arresting Somalis who attended movies or watched soccer games, prohibiting live music, and banning coeducation. Nevertheless, the improved security situation in ICU areas garnered widespread appreciation from local citizens.[10] The ICU never was a monolithic movement but remained a coalition of various Islamist groups. It also attracted a number of foreign volunteers, although their presence was never admitted by ICU leaders.[11] Despite the reported ties to Al Qaeda, according to one senior ICU official the group offered to meet and cooperate with U.S. officials to try to pacify Somalia.[12] Because the ICU and its top leaders had been designated terrorists by the UN and the U.S State Department in 2001, however, these overtures came to nothing.

The battle for Somalia coalesced around two main opposition coalitions, although there continued to be a host of unaligned actors such as warlords and criminal organizations adding to the mayhem across the country. Against the ICU, which was believed to be working in concert with an Eritrean insurgent group that was launching bomb attacks on Ethiopian army bases, was an entity calling itself the Transitional Federal Government (TFG), made up of anti-Islamist warlords backed by the Ethiopian government and, allegedly, the CIA.[13] By December 2006 ICU forces began threatening to overrun the major city of Baidoa, some 250 kilometers northwest of Mogadishu. In response, Ethiopian forces launched an offensive into Somalia in support of the TFG. Although these military operations putatively were simply to protect the TFG, Addis Ababa was also almost certainly motivated by the ICU's alliance with Eritrea, a major adversary of Ethiopia, and inflamed by the anti-Ethiopian and anti-Christian rhetoric coming from ICU leaders. Eritrean forces in fact actively participated in ICU offensive operations.[14] The Ethiopian operations—involving some 2,000 troops supported by extensive heavy equipment and aircraft—were initially very successful, driving ICU forces into the southern fringes of Somalia and installing the TFG in Mogadishu. By early 2007 the ICU had lost its last major stronghold in Somalia; importantly for later events, however, the majority of the ICU members and leaders remained free, many abiding across the border in Eritrea.

Over time, however, the Ethiopian troops faced increasing problems as they tried to maintain stability. This probably was virtually inevitable, especially because the TFG itself was reportedly bitterly split over the wisdom of the intervention. A significant number of TFG politicians viewed the intervention as a means for President Abdullahi Yusuf Ahmed to crush opposition within the coalition government.[15] Ethiopian soldiers faced repeated ambushes, bombings, and other forms of attacks, forcing Addis Ababa eventually to pull its forces out in January 2009.

One note should be made about assessments of the ICU period in Somalia. A number of pundits and analysts have argued that the rise of its successor entity al Shabab (which will be discussed below) represents a much more dangerous phenomenon than the ICU ever did. They maintain that the United States and other outside powers should have supported ICU rule rather than permit the emergence of a broader threat due to the instability engendered by the collapse of the ICU. Certainly, al Shabab has proven itself to have broader aspirations than the ICU and also has closer links to transnational terrorist groups. The ICU did succeed in establishing relative, badly needed stability in areas under its control, and it also suppressed piracy to a significant degree. At the same time, however, this stability was at the price of draconian rule. Although never at the level of Taliban brutality in Afghanistan, it would have been very difficult politically and diplomatically for most outside countries, especially with the George W. Bush administration's global war on terror in full swing, to have overtly or tacitly endorsed the ICU's methods.

The Transitional Federal Government

In the face of continued instability following the UN withdrawal in 1995, outside governments under the auspices of the UN convened a series of some fourteen talks intended to bring about peace within Somalia or, at the very least, reduce the level of violence. These peace talks were tried in Ethiopia in 1996, Egypt in 1997, Somalia itself in 1998, and Djibouti in 2000. However, most of the talks were marked by a lack of continuity, caused at least in part by boycotts of one or the other conference by various Somali groups.[16] This series of talks culminated in the formation of a Transitional National Government on 13 August 2000, with Abdulqassim Salad Hassan as president. This development apparently had little practical impact on the situation on the ground, but in October 2002, following talks in Kenya, participants (which again did not include all Somali parties) declared a temporary ceasefire, and in September 2003 a Transitional National Charter was enacted.

The Transitional Federal Government (not to be confused with the Transitional National Government, discussed above) was formed in exile in

October 2004, its members drawn largely from traditional clan leaders and their associated militias. However, there were some efforts made to include at least some former members of the ICU. Abdullahi Yusuf Ahmed was elected to be the new president of Somalia by the Transitional Federal Parliament. Unable to wrest control of Mogadishu from the Islamic Courts and the warlords, the TFG largely remained in neighboring Kenya, maintaining a relatively small presence in Baidoa.

To date, the capacity of the TFG to maintain even minimal stability appears to be virtually nonexistent. It was recently estimated to have about 2,900 soldiers, with plans to expand to 8,000.[17] TFG military forces have received training in neighboring countries, including a rather extensive (and expensive) training program run by the European Union, but the actual results of these efforts might be viewed skeptically.[18] One source claimed that graduates of earlier training deserted at rates as high as 80 percent, with many of the deserters joining al Shabab and taking their weapons with them.[19] In June 2010, according to press reports, soldiers who had not been paid for several months stormed the presidential palace of Sheik Sharif Ahmed to demand their salaries. They withdrew only after some gunfire and a personal promise from the president.[20] Since the beginning of 2010, the TFG has announced or hinted of a major military offensive that is imminent, but thus far there has been little perceptible evidence of this actually happening. Meanwhile, al Shabab's forces have been steadily fighting their way across Mogadishu toward the palace and by August 2010 had reduced the government's area of control to a few city blocks around the president's seat.[21]

The TFG appears to spend more time conducting internal feuds—which is not always just a figure of speech—than it does facing Somalia's myriad problems, including the inconvenient issue of the relatively steady military advance of its opponents. As one recent example, the defense minister has accused the prime minister not only of under-equipping the TFG military but also of selling weapons to al Shabab.[22] The current president, Sheik Sharif Ahmed, has seemed incapable of controlling the various factions within the government. However, there has been one potentially bright spot for the government. A relatively moderate Islamist militia, the Ahlu Sunna wal-Jamea, with potentially several thousand fighters, has allied itself with the TFG, but it has shown signs of falling out with the government over not receiving political plums that it claims were promised.

Al Shabab

Al Shabab (also transliterated as al Shabaab) emerged from the remnants of al Itihaad. The group formed some level of independent identity in 2002 but began gaining prominence in 2005. During the ICU's existence, al Shabab became identified as the most militant wing of the union. After the collapse of the coalition, al Shabab continued its offensive operations as an independent group, refusing to enter the peace process. On 1 February 2010 al Shabab reportedly merged with another militant group, Ras Kamboni, led by Hassan al Turki, to form the al Shabab Mujahidin Movement.[23] Both groups have cooperated previously, and this merger appears to be an effort to further formalize their relationship.

Leadership of al Shabab has been somewhat opaque. Some of the identified key leaders have included Ahmed Abdi Godane (originally from Somaliland, known to have trained in Afghanistan), who is considered the group's supreme leader. Others are Fu'aad Mohamed Kalaf "Shangole," Hussein Ali Fidow, Hassan Yaqub Ali, and Ibrahim Haji Jama, who also reportedly trained in Afghanistan. Its spokesman was Mukhtar Robow, later replaced by Ali Mohamud Raghe Dheere. Although some key leaders can be identified, it would be inaccurate to view them as having complete control of the group. Al Shabab remains a very loosely organized and heterogeneous organization, with no individual or leadership council having true command authority.

Given the amorphous nature of the group, it is difficult to ascribe a coherent unifying ideology to al Shabab. In general, however, the organization's goals as stated by its ideologues include "the establishment of a Somali Caliphate, to wage jihad against the enemies of Islam, including the elimination of other forms of Islam contrary to its own Salafi-Wahhabist strand, and the removal of Western influence."[24] Despite this proclaimed idealism, a significant number of al Shabab's fighters reportedly join the group for financial gain rather than any particular ideological commitment.[25] The group reportedly operates several specialized training bases in Somalia: "The Al Faruq Brigades, who train at Elberde in the Hiraan region, for instance, trains suicide bombers, as does the Salahudeen unit in the Huriwa district of Mogadishu. The Muaskar Faruq base in Ras Kiamboni specializes in automatic weapons and hand-to-hand combat, while the Eel Aarfid base specializes in training kidnapping skills."[26]

Although an inclusive Islamist ideology clearly plays a significant role for al Shabab, as an official UN report notes, Somali clan issues continue to influence events:

> On another level, however, the conflict is a product of the clan dynamics that have shaped the Somali civil war for the past 20 years. Recent fighting in central Somalia, for example, has pitted an ASWJ alliance of Habar Gidir Ayr, Marehaan and Dir clan militias against Al-Shabaab militias drawn heavily from the Murosade and Duduble. In the Hiraan region, the Hawaadle clan east of the Shabelle River tends to support the government, while the members of the Gaalje'el and Gugundhaabe on the western bank serve as foot soldiers for Al-Shabaab. In the Juba Valley, the battle between Al-Shabaab, Raas Kaambooni and Anoole for control of Kismaayo has been in many respects a continuation of the multidimensional struggle between Marehaan, Ogaden and Harti (as well as many smaller communities) that has destabilized the area for two decades.[27]

Estimates of the strength of al Shabab vary widely. One author claims it has about 3,000 mainline fighters, with an additional 3,000 militiamen.[28] Added to this mix of locals are some 200 foreign fighters also present in the country. Other estimates have ranged from 2,500 to about 10,000.[29] As is typical with such groups, one problem with accurately gauging strength is that there are multiple forms of membership in al Shabab, ranging from "professional soldiers" to occasional fighters who have only limited allegiance to the group's overall goals. The group reportedly has two major organizational branches, the Jaish al Usra, intended for military operations, and the Jaish al Hesbah, intended to maintain law and order in areas that it controls.[30]

Many of al Shabab's operations have been very similar to those seen in Iraq and Afghanistan. The group has used assassinations, ambushes, and improvised explosive devices against both government and civilian targets. Al Shabab has also increased the number of suicide bombings, including a failed attempt on the Somali defense minister on 15 February 2010.[31] Significant fighting continued in Mogadishu through the summer of 2010. Accurate assessments of casualties in Mogadishu are virtually impossible, but one estimate says that around 21,000 have been killed and another 1.5 million forced out of their homes.[32] As with earlier fighting, the bulk of the casualties have been civilians.[33] On 1 May 2010 the bombing of a mosque during prayers in the Bakara Market area of Mogadishu killed a number of al Shabab members and civilians. However, it failed in its apparent goal of killing Fu'aad Shangole, one of the top al Shabab leaders. Al Shabab immediately blamed the African Union, which is helping defend the TFG, but there also has been speculation that internal struggles within al Shabab were the motivation.[34]

Al Shabab has attempted to expand its reach beyond Somalia. One analyst, citing a leaked UN report, claimed that 700 Somalis went to Lebanon to help Hezbollah battle Israeli forces in 2006 in exchange for military training.[35] At least one al Shabab suicide bomber was a Somali American. Press reports also have suggested that at least a dozen young Somali Americans from Minneapolis may have been induced to join al Shabab. In June 2010 the FBI announced that it had arrested two suspects at John F. Kennedy International Airport as they were purportedly about to fly from the United States to Somalia to join al Shabab. The July bombings of World Cup watchers in Kampala, Uganda, which killed seventy-six civilians, were undertaken as revenge for Ugandan peacekeeping operations to protect the TFG (al Shabab also threatened to execute similar operations in Burundi). In August 2010 the U.S. government indicted fourteen persons, mostly U.S. citizens, for sending recruits and money to al Shabab.[36]

One other armed Islamist group in Somalia should be mentioned because it has also had an impact on the security situation in Somalia. Hizbul Islam (also transliterated as Hizb al Islam or Hezb-ul Islam) was formed in February 2009, reportedly mostly along clan lines.[37] The reported leader is Sheikh Hassan Dahir Aweys, a former head of al Itihaad al Islaami and the ICU, who was put on the U.S. list of people "linked to terrorism" shortly after 9/11 for his avowed support for Al Qaeda.[38] According to a Stratfor analysis, there are four factions within Hizbul Islam, with predictable tension and lack of coordination among them.[39] Hizbul Islam has cooperated with al Shabab in the Mogadishu fighting, but it has fought against the group elsewhere in southern Somalia. There have also been a number of reports that various factions within the group have been shifting their allegiance to al Shabab.[40] By all indications, Hizbul Islam has a less severe ideology than al Shabab and is more focused on Somalia itself. When Hizbul Islam occupied the coastal town of Harardhere, about 450 kilometers north of Mogadishu, in May 2010, a spokesman for the group announced its intention to end pirate operations conducted from there and impose strict sharia.[41] The group did not announce a time frame for doing so, but some witnesses said a large number of pirates drove out of town in the hours before Hizbul Islam's fighters entered.[42] Although Hizbul Islam has managed to provide some level of security for the very few areas it has controlled, it appears to be in sharp decline after failing to reach an agreement with al Shabab during negotiations that took place over the summer of 2010.

Outside Actors in Somalia

There has reportedly been an influx of Al Qaeda members from Yemen to Somalia to support al Shabab.[43] Although their numbers remain rather small, they can provide a very useful tool for mobilizing and training al Shabab members. At least one senior Al Qaeda leader, Fazul Abdullah Mohammed, reportedly the planner of the 1998 East African embassy bombings, relocated to Somalia in 2009. More recently, reports have surfaced of Al Qaeda in the Arabian Peninsula moving its main base of operations from Yemen to Somalia.[44] However, some of these reports must be viewed with a certain amount of caution. Earlier information emanating from Al Qaeda sources suggested that operatives were finding Somalia inhospitable due to its failed infrastructure, strong clan loyalties, and lack of resources.[45] Nevertheless, there is clear evidence of more movement of Al Qaeda members into Somalia. According to the testimony of a U.S. official, "In 2008, East Africa al Qaeda operative Saleh Al-Nabhan distributed a video showing training camp activity in Somalia and inviting foreigners to travel there for training."[46] Less direct evidence also suggests a continuing, if not necessarily rapidly expanding, foreign terrorist presence in Somalia. But it is far from clear that these foreign fighters have been strategically significant in al Shabab's operations.

However operationally important these foreign fighters are, or are not, for al Shabab, the group's leaders have established increasingly strong rhetorical links to Al Qaeda. In early 2010 the group issued a communiqué stating that "jihad of Horn of Africa must be combined with the international jihad led by the al-Qaeda network."[47] At the end of April 2010, al Shabab announced that it had conducted a suicide attack on African Union peacekeepers in Mogadishu in retaliation for the killing of two Al Qaeda in Iraq leaders by coalition forces.[48]

The UN has tried to remain involved in Somalia, but its practical impact on security there may be subject to considerable question. The most recent round of diplomatic efforts—the Istanbul Conference of 2010—once again called for the international community to provide "all the necessary financial and logistical support" to the TFG.[49] This conference, part of the so-called

Djibouti Peace Process, under way since 2008, involved representatives of fifty-five countries. As part of the somewhat detached international diplomatic efforts to help restore stability to Somalia, in December 2006 the United Nations Security Council adopted Resolution 1725, authorizing an armed force composed of African peacekeepers to protect the TFG. The African Union then established the African Union Mission in Somalia (AMISOM), but the force that was deployed has proven to be a major disappointment to date. AMISOM effectively controls only a small part of Mogadishu and no areas at all outside the capital. However, in fairness, after AMISOM offensives in Mogadishu in the latter months of 2010, al Shabab forces were driven back from some of their key positions in the city. According to one report, al Shabab now controls less than 40 percent of Mogadishu, versus the some 60 percent it previously controlled.[50]

In large measure this has been because of a minimal response by other African countries to the call for participation; only Burundi and Uganda actually have forces in Somalia, with Uganda thus far providing the bulk of them. Of the planned strength of 8,000, fewer than 3,000 have been deployed.[51] According to the AMISOM official Web site, these make up only three of the nine authorized battalions, with another battalion planned from Burundi. Of the remaining "pledged" forces, the site indicates that Nigeria might actually deploy some troops but that Ghana and Malawi are "not likely to deploy."[52] At the end of July 2010 both Guinea and Djibouti pledged that a total of 2,000 additional troops would be made "immediately" available, but when they would actually go into Somalia was left unclear.[53] The 2010 Kampala bombings are unlikely to encourage other African regional countries to provide their troops for AMISOM.

According to press reports, U.S. Air Force Special Operations aircraft attacked sites in southern Somalia on 8 January 2007 in an effort to kill three individuals suspected in the 1998 bombings of the U.S. embassies in Kenya and Tanzania. According to an Oxfam report, about seventy persons were killed in these attacks. Other U.S. counterterrorism operations have reportedly been conducted inside Somalia, but details have been very sketchy. These missions reportedly are under control of Special Operations Task Force 88, created after 9/11 specifically to deal with terrorists. Several reports indicate that the United States has maintained active cooperation with various Somali sources directed against Al Qaeda members and close allies.[54] Clearly, this has not been without risk for the Somalis involved, a number of whom have been killed. Given the near-anarchy of Somalia, these killings cannot be ascribed with certainty to the individuals' intelligence collection efforts, but the number killed would make this a reasonable assumption. Washington almost certainly has also shared intelligence with the Ethiopian forces operating in Somalia.

Prospects

There are few if any reasons to be sanguine about the near-term future of Somalia. The government is clearly besieged, armed groups outside the government's control hold sway over more of the country than does the TFG, and the overall security situation remains catastrophic. Increasing the foreign security presence within Somalia to support the TFG appears to be unlikely. Other African countries have limited resources, not to mention internal-security problems of their own, and other non-African states have shown no desire to reengage militarily in Somalia.

Regarding the issue of terrorism emanating from Somalia, perhaps the key question is the realistic reach and intentions of al Shabab. The group certainly has shown itself capable of hitting regional neighbors, and it is probable that future attacks of the sort will be launched, particularly against countries supporting or participating in AMISOM. Very porous borders and a significantly large population of ethnic Somalis throughout the region can make cross-border attacks operationally feasible. Al Shabab has also intensified its rhetorical ties to transnational groups, particularly Al Qaeda. Whether al Shabab actually has the resources and capabilities to expand its reach beyond the immediate neighborhood may well be questionable, however.

The diaspora Somali population is scattered throughout many Western countries. If even a tiny minority of this population, such as the impressionable teenagers from Minneapolis, supports al Shabab operations, they could provide a base for attacks in the areas where they live. Likewise, the apparent desire of at least some al Shabab leaders to support and probably gain some credence with their emerging ally, Al Qaeda, would provide some impetus for out-of-area attacks. The growing use of suicide bombers and other forms of terrorist operations suggest an increasing capability within al Shabab.

Nevertheless, there are several factors that would militate against out-of-area operations by al Shabab. First, by actual numbers the group is relatively small. Most of its forces are deeply engaged in operations in Somalia, and focusing too much attention and too many resources elsewhere could be difficult to sustain. Second, as already noted, many of al Shabab's troops are probably motivated more by economic factors than by ideology. Although impossible to quantify, the actual number of personnel who would be viewed as reliable enough for broader terrorist operations may be very small. Third, even though there are reportedly foreign trainers assisting al Shabab within Somalia, the group's capabilities for sophisticated terrorist attacks may be low. Finally, even with some al Shabab leaders' increasing rhetorical support for Al Qaeda, it is impossible to know how serious this really is; the talk may provide al Shabab with some useful external support, but it does not necessarily mean that the group's leaders are willing to reciprocate by expanding their own operations.

Overall, al Shabab is most likely to remain a threat primarily to the putative government of Somalia and to neighboring states. The group's activities almost certainly will continue to be a running sore for the region, with very little likelihood that al Shabab will collapse or be eliminated militarily in the foreseeable future. Although al Shabab-directed attacks outside of the Horn or East Africa are much less likely, the group does appear to have some level of support among Somali expatriates, which may make it a useful ally for other groups that are more capable of conducting transnational operations.

Notes

1. For a good insider view of this operation, see John L. Hirsch and Robert B. Oakley, "Somalia and Operation Restore Hope: Reflections on Peacemaking and Peacekeeping," United States Institute of Peace, Washington D.C., 1995.

2. "Opposition Candidate Wins Somaliland's Election," Qatar News Agency, 2 July 2010.

3. "Thirteen Killed in Somali–Ethiopian Border Clashes," Qatar News Agency, 22 May 2010.

4. For a discussion of some of these earlier groups, see "Somalia's Islamists," Africa Report No. 100, International Crisis Group (ICG), 12 December 2005, 1–4.

5. Daveed Gartenstein-Ross, "The Strategic Challenge of Somalia's Al-Shabaab," *Middle East Quarterly* 16, no. 4 (Fall 2009).

6. "Counter-Terrorism in Somalia: Losing Hearts and Minds," Africa Report No. 95, International Crisis Group, 11 July 2005, 1.

7. Gartenstein-Ross, "The Strategic Challenge of Somalia's Al-Shabaab."

8. "Somalia's Islamists," 7.

9. "The Supreme Islamic Courts Union/al-Ittihad Mahakem al-Islamiya (ICU)," *Global Security,* 3 August 2010, http://www.globalsecurity.org/military/world/para/icu.htm.

10. "Profile: Somalia's Islamic Courts," *BBC News,* 6 June 2006, http://news.bbc.co.uk/2/hi/5051588.stm.

11. The presence of foreign "volunteers" was stated in the "Report of the Monitoring Group on Somalia Pursuant to Security Council Resolution 1676," U.N. Security Council Committee, New York, November 2006, 42. For the ICU denial, see Gartenstein-Ross, "The Strategic Challenge of Somalia's Al-Shabaab."

12. Ted Dagne, "Somalia: Prospects for a Lasting Peace," *Mediterranean Quarterly* 20, no. 2 (Spring 2009): 98.

13. "The Supreme Islamic Courts Union."

14. Jonathan Stevenson, "Risks and Opportunities in Somalia," *Survival* 49, no. 2 (Summer 2007): 5.

15. "Counter-Terrorism in Somalia," 3–4.

16. For some details of these talks, see Dagne, "Somalia: Prospects for a Lasting Peace," 96.

17. Claude Heller, "Letter Dated 10 March 2010 from the Chairman of the Security Council Committee Pursuant to Resolutions 751 (1992) and 1907 (2009) Concerning Somalia and Eritrea Addressed to the President of the Security Council," S/2010/91, United Nations Security Council, 10 March 2010, 11.

18. For details of the EU program, see Max Delany, "EU Trains Army to Fight in Somalia," *Christian Science Monitor,* 18 June 2010.

19. Ibid. For one specific claim of mass defections, see "Somalia: Hizbul Islam Officials Say 'More TFG Soldiers Joined in Gedo Region Joined Us,'" *Inside Somalia,* 19 October 2009, http://insidesomalia.org/200910192521/News/Politics/Somalia-Hizbul-Islam-Officials-Say-More-TFG-Soldiers-Joined-in-Gedo-Region-Joined-Us.html.

20. "Furious Soldiers Storm Villa Somalia," allAfrica.com, 20 June 2010, http://allafrica.com/stories/201006200011.html.

21. Abdi Sheikh, "Somalia's Al Shabaab Rebels Push Towards Palace," *Reuters,* 25 August 2010, http://af.reuters.com/article/worldNews/idAFTRE67O3BO20100825.

22. "Somali Islamists Seize More of Capital," UPI, 25 May 2010.

23. John Rollins, *Al Qaeda and Affiliates: Historical Perspective, Global Presence, and Implications for U.S. Policy,* Congressional Research Service, 5 February 2010, 19.

24. Paula Cristina Roque, "Somalia: Understanding Al-Shabaab," *Situation Report,* Institute for Security Studies, 3 June 2009, 3.

25. For example, see Scott Baldauf, "Somalia's Al Shabab Recruits 'Holy Warriors' with $400 Bonus," *Christian Science Monitor,* 15 April 2010.

26. Ibid.

27. Heller, "Letter Dated 10 March 2010," 10.

28. Baldauf, "Somalia's Al Shabab Recruits."

29. Heller, "Letter Dated 10 March 2010," 15.

30. Roque, "Somalia: Understanding Al-Shabaab," 2.

31. "Somalia's Defence Minister Survives Bomb Attack," Qatar News Agency, 15 February 2010; Andre Le Sage, "Militias and Insurgency in Somalia," Policy Watch no. 1593, Washington Institute for Near East Policy, 26 October 2009, 2.

32. "Somali Islamists Seize More of Capital"; "Mogadishu Fighting Kills 20 People," Qatar News Agency, 16 May 2010.

33. For reporting on this round of fighting, see "At Least 21 Killed and 60 Wounded in Mogadishu Battle," Qatar News Agency, 3 June 2010; "Somali Islamists Seize More of Capital."

34. Scott Baldauf, "Somalia Mosque Bomb Targets al Shabab Leaders," *Christian Science Monitor*, 3 May 2010.

35. Stevenson, "Risks and Opportunities in Somalia," 11.

36. Howard LaFranchi, "Terrorism Charges Against 14 Somalis in US Reflect 'Disturbing Trend,'" *Christian Science Monitor*, 5 August 2010.

37. Heller, "Letter Dated 10 March 2010," 16.

38. Joseph Winter, "Profile: Somalia's Islamist leader," *BBC News*, 30 June 2006, http://news.bbc.co.uk/2/hi/africa/5120242.stm. Aweys spent some time in Eritrea after the defeat of the ICU and returned to Somalia in 2009.

39. "Somalia: Hizbul Islam Seeks to End Piracy?" Stratfor, 3 May 2010, http://www.stratfor.com.

40. For example, see Solomon, "Hizbul Islam Faction in Southern Somalia Defects to Shabaab," *Ethiopian Journal*, 17 June 2010; Abdi Hassan Belley, "Hizbul Islam of Hiran Formally Joins to Al-shabab," *Diirad* News in English Online, 21 June 2010, http://www.diirad.com/news-in-english/1550-hizbul-islam-of-hiran-formally-joins-to-al-shabab.html. Internal reporting from Somalia can be very unreliable, but other reporting has suggested a similar trend.

41. "Somalia: Hizbul Islam Seeks to End Piracy?"

42. "Somali Islamist Insurgents Seize Pirate Haven," *BBC News*, 2 May 2010, http://news.bbc.co.uk/2/hi/africa/8657060.stm.

43. "Al-Qaida Vets Beef up Somalia Insurgency," UPI, 13 April 2010.

44. "AQAP Leaves Yemen for Somalia," UPI, 5 April 2010.

45. Cited in Roland Marchal, "Warlordism and Terrorism: How to Obscure an Already Confusing Crisis? The Case of Somalia," *International Affairs* 83, no. 6 (November 2007): 1104.

46. Assistant Secretary of State Johnnie Carson, "Developing a Coordinated and Sustainable United States Strategy Toward Somalia," Testimony Before the Senate Committee on Foreign Relations' Subcommittee on African Affairs Hearing, 20 May 2009, excerpts published in *DISAM Journal of International Security Management* 31, no. 3 (November 2009): 90.

47. "Somali Islamists al-Shabab Join al-Qaeda Fight," *BBC News*, 1 February 2010, http://news.bbc.co.uk/2/hi/8491329.stm.

48. "Al-Shabaab Responds to AQI Killings," UPI, 29 April 2010.

49. "Istanbul Conference Stresses Necessity to Support Somalia's Stability," Qatar News Agency, 22 May 2010.

50. “Sending the Boys Home,” *Economist*, 16 December 2010, http://www.econo mist.com/node/17733667?story_id=17733667.

51. Alexander Nicoll, ed., “Conflict in Somalia: Faint Hope of Resolution,” *Strategic Comments* (International Institute for Strategic Studies) 14, no. 4 (May 2008): 1.

52. “Military Component,” African Union Mission in Somalia, http://www.africa-union.org/root/au/auc/departments/psc/amisom/AMISOM_MILITARY_COMPONENT.htm.

53. “Be Beefier,” *Economist*, 31 July 2010, 36.

54. “Counter-Terrorism in Somalia,” 10–11.

18 The Tokyo Subway Attack

Edward E. Hoffer

PRIOR TO THE DEADLY 1995 ATTACK ON TOKYO'S SUBWAY, domestic terrorism was a concern for other nations, but not for Japan. The Japanese took great comfort in two cultural beliefs that pervaded their concepts of national and international security: *heiwa,* meaning "peace," and *jenkin,* meaning "fundamental human rights." Believing that they were a homogeneous and peaceful society, the necessity to counter terrorism and respond to a terrorist attack was culturally difficult to accept.[1] However, on the morning of 20 March 1995, Tokyo, their nation's capital and one of the largest, wealthiest, and most modern cities in the world, came to a fearful standstill from a deadly chemical weapons attack. By the end of the day the attack had killed 12 people and injured more than 3,800. Nearly 1,000 people required hospitalization, with 300 sustaining serious injuries. Of those seriously injured, some remain on life-support equipment.[2]

Following the attack, the largest criminal investigation in Japanese history proved that the religious organization Aum Shinrikyo, led by Shoko Asahara, was responsible. A study of the Tokyo subway attack contains many valuable lessons for all leaders responsible for countering and responding to terrorism. Three key lessons, and the associated issues they involve, stand out. The first one is to understand how a religious belief can become twisted and then exploited by a charismatic leader to justify terrorism. The reluctance of Japanese local authorities to monitor and then to counter Shoko Asahara's activities had disastrous consequences. The second is how failures in national and international information and intelligence sharing made it possible for Aum Shinrikyo to conduct two deadly attacks. The third important lesson is how poor prior consequence-management planning, training, and interagency cooperation, at all levels of the Japanese government, made the attack more deadly than it should have been. All three of these "failures" are important for us to learn from so that we may avoid repeating them ourselves.

A Profile of Shoko Asahara and Aum Shinrikyo

Shoko Asahara's birth name was Chizo Matsumoto. He was born in 1955, in Kyushu, southern Japan, to a poor family of tatami mat weavers. Blind at birth in his left eye and with only limited vision in his right eye, he was bullied at school until his parents enrolled him in a government-funded school for the blind. There, among children completely blind, his limited vision was an advantage, and he would do tasks for them in return for money. Early in his life the pursuit of money became a lifetime obsession. Throughout high school he achieved good grades and earned a black belt in judo. Upon his graduation from high school, his ambitions continued to increase. He explained to family and friends his intentions of joining Japan's ruling political party, then becoming an elected member of parliament, and eventually becoming the prime minister of Japan. For the first step in this plan he enrolled in a preparatory school to help ready himself for entrance into the elite Tokyo University, from which all of Japan's political leaders have graduated. Despite months of hard study and excellent academic scores he was not accepted by the University of Tokyo. Deeply angered and embittered by this rejection, he devoted himself to gaining a financial fortune that he could then use to achieve his political ambition.[3]

Matsumoto's financial road to success began by opening an acupuncture clinic where he combined acupuncture treatments with yoga and folk herbal remedies of his own design (one of his "miracle cures" was tested and found to be tangerine peel soaked in natural alcohol).[4] His clinic was very successful, and Matsumoto soon opened more of them. After several years he was beginning to achieve his childhood ambitions. His financial success was becoming a reality, and he enjoyed a growing reputation as a successful healer. Despite this success, he still felt that he was missing a real sense of purpose that would give his life greater meaning. Like many Japanese during the 1980s, the rapid transition to a highly modern and technical society with its remarkable economic and material success, coupled with post-world-war religious freedom, created a population of highly educated young people in search of a new spirituality that would give purpose and meaning to their lives.

Matsumoto began to practice deep meditation and strenuous yoga. These led him to believe that he had special psychic powers. Wishing to couple his "gift" with an established religion, he selected a Buddhist religious sect called Agonshu to follow. After completing a year of rigorous monastic training, Matsumoto rejected joining the Agonshu religious community. His reason for not joining was based upon his belief that he had obtained true enlightenment and now knew a better religious path for him and the world to follow.[5] Using modern advertising methods and combining his Agonshu training, herbal medicines, and yoga, he achieved remarkable success in gaining adherents to his newly named "Aum Shinrikyo" organization. The name Aum Shinrikyo was derived from the Buddhist mantra *om* or *aum* followed by the Japanese word for "supreme truth."[6]

Matsumoto soon became widely known as a charismatic and caring leader. Young adults and middle-aged professionals were particularly attracted to Aum and were willing to pay thousands of dollars for Aum retreats, treatments, and so-called mental expansion sessions. Despite Aum's remarkable organizational and financial success, Matsumoto personally continued searching for a spiritual reason for his enlightenment and financial success. Finally, during one of his personal spiritual retreats, he met one of his adherents, who stated that he was a student of world history. This adherent informed him that Armageddon, the end of the world, was approaching and that only a race made up of the purest of spirit would survive. Upon hearing this, Chizo Matsumoto knew what his real purpose was: to create through Aum the pure race that would survive Armageddon.[7]

Changing his name to Shoko Asahara, "the guru," he began preaching that he was the enlightened one whose purpose was to assist all who joined Aum to attain spiritual purity. Using this message of personal enlightenment and salvation from Armageddon, Aum rapidly gained thousands of adherents who were primarily under forty years of age and highly educated, but who felt lost and alienated in an increasingly materialistic, restrictive, and isolated work life.[8]

Many who joined Aum completely accepted Aum's instructions to live in Aum communes, break all ties with their families, and turn over to Aum all of their finances and property. Aum also benefited from increasing sales of its herbal health products, publications, and a highly profitable chain of computer stores. Assisting this increase in wealth was Aum's successful application to be accepted and recognized by the Japanese government as an official religion. This freed Aum from paying taxes on contributions and profits. By 1994, Aum was active internationally, with established branches in six countries. Aum's dedicated membership exceeded 45,000 adherents, and Aum's financial assets were valued at 1.2 billion dollars.[9]

The Motivation to Use Terror

Despite Aum's success and Asahara's apparent caring demeanor, he still possessed a desire to strike out at the world that had originally rejected and ridiculed his political ambitions. This anger was also directed at those followers who changed their minds and wished to leave and sever their connections to Aum. During the late 1980s, rather than tolerating the rejection of himself and Aum, Asahara ordered the secret execution of several of these former followers.[10] Also during this period many parents whose sons and daughters had joined Aum began to vocally oppose Aum's practice of separating them from their families, and they began to insist on being allowed to visit and communicate again with their children. Soon several newspaper publications were running stories of Aum's "twisted doctrines" and "unhealthy influences" upon Japan's young people. Although these complaints against Aum were increasing, the police did nothing. They were reluctant to act upon any allegations about Aum's behavior because they did not want to appear to be oppressing the religious freedom that Japan had struggled so hard to achieve following World War II.[11]

At this time a highly experienced and capable lawyer named Tsutsumi Sakamoto began to respond to the pleas of desperate parents and started legal action against Aum. His skillfully applied legal challenges came to the attention of the Japanese media, and soon he was being interviewed on radio and television programs. During these interviews he convincingly accused Aum of holding members against their will and being guilty of fraud and unethical practices. Asahara responded by trying to discredit Sakamoto; when this failed, he resorted to threatening phone calls to his home and office. Sakamoto's response to threats against him and his family was to increase the legal pressure against Asahara.

Unable to silence Sakamoto, Asahara directed several of his closest followers to murder him. Obeying his command, they went to the attorney's apartment early in the morning and killed Sakamoto, his wife, and his infant son. After they had disposed of the bodies, Asahara assured his followers that they had done holy work and that they should not feel guilty about killing the child. The child, he told them, "will be born again in a higher world."[12] The disappearance of Sakamoto and his family quickly made national news, and the media were soon linking Aum's name to the disappearance. Under media pressure, Japanese police reluctantly began to conduct an investigation, but after a year, the police lost interest in the case and closed the investigation.

Impressed with his ability to overcome anyone who opposed him, as well as to avoid legal prosecution for his crimes, Asahara returned to his youthful goal of becoming the prime minister of Japan. In 1990 he initiated a political campaign to run candidates in the upcoming national parliamentary elections. Asahara's strategy was to have a select group of followers contest twenty-five parliamentary seats in the Japanese Diet, or lower house. During their campaign they preached of impending doom while simultaneously promising all citizens freedom, equality, and benevolence. Aum spent millions of dollars on national advertising, and Aum followers conducted numerous street demonstrations supporting their candidates. Despite their strenuous efforts, all twenty-five Aum candidates, including Asahara himself, were defeated. Most disturbing to Asahara was the fact that the total number of votes that he and Aum received was smaller than the total number of Aum supporters who he believed would automatically cast their votes for Aum candidates. To Asahara's mind this could only mean that the Japanese government, as it had denied him entrance into Tokyo University, was again directly opposing him by cheating him of his votes.[13] Also increasing Asahara's paranoia was the intense scrutiny that Aum received by the media as a result of his decision to enter national politics. The many negative media articles, coupled with requests from a growing number of local municipal authorities responding to parents who were concerned for their children who had become Aum members, finally motivated local police to monitor Aum's activities more closely.

Faced with a major political defeat and its repercussions, Asahara announced to his closest advisors the necessity for "extreme measures being required to educate the world about the power of Aum."[14] He spoke of creating an army to fight all who opposed his teachings. Turning for help to his followers within the scientific community, Asahara ordered them to begin working on the development of devastating weapons for Aum's use against their enemies in the approaching war. Asahara told his followers that their enemies, particularly the existing Japanese government and the United States of America, were dedicated to destroying them. It was therefore essential that Aum be prepared to destroy its enemies first. In Asahara's mind the destruction of his enemies would also precipitate his prophesied Armageddon, which would be a war between Japan and the United States that would kill one out of every ten Japanese citizens.[15]

Developing Weapons of Mass Destruction

Among the many Aum followers highly trained as scientists were Hideo Murai and Seiichi Endo. Both were given the mission to determine the weapons that Aum should develop. They realized that Aum's vast business organization, particularly its herbal medicine production facilities, gave Aum the equipment, materials, and chemicals necessary to build and operate laboratories capable of producing biological and chemical weapons. They first turned their efforts towards producing biological weapons. Within several months the first laboratory was in operation attempting to grow clostridium botulinum—the bacteria needed to extract botulism toxin. Botulism toxin is one of the most poisonous substances that occurs in the natural world and is millions of times more poisonous than strychnine. Early tests of the toxin were disappointing because of the numerous difficulties of producing, extracting, storing, and effectively dispersing it.[16]

By 1992, Endo felt that the toxin was ready for use, and Asahara directed that it be used against the Japanese parliament. Endo equipped a truck with a special sprayer unit and, while the parliament was in session, dispersed the toxin around the government center. Although the dispersal system worked, the toxin did not, sparing the Japanese parliamentarians. Undeterred, Asahara pressed Endo to continue his development of several different types of biological and chemical weapons. Asahara felt that his weapons program would soon be successful because he believed that a new source of weapons-development technology, and possibly the weapons themselves, could soon be obtained from Aum followers and supporters in Russia.

Starting in March of 1992, Aum began a very effective advertising campaign in Russia. Coupled with this campaign was a focused program of donations of medical supplies and computers, and the expenditure of as much as

$12 million in the form of payoffs to well-placed officials. These efforts gained Aum thousands of Russian followers and allowed Asahara to form close ties to many top Russian officials, such as Oleg Ivanovich Lobov, chairman of the Russian Security Council.[17] Through Aum's new official Russian contacts, Asahara and his insiders believed they would gain technical knowledge from the Russian scientific and military community and possibly direct access to Soviet weapons. Within several months Aum representatives in Russia had successfully set up an effective black-market operation in an effort to purchase and move Soviet chemical and biological weapons production information (as well as conventional Soviet military weapons and hardware) to Japan. This activity eventually came to the attention of the U.S. intelligence community, but in an effort to protect the sensitive sources of this information, it was not shared with Japanese authorities or with other U.S. allies.[18]

Endo spent the next year trying to develop another effective biological weapon—this time using anthrax. This effort also ended in failure.[19] Endo and Murai decided, based upon information gained from Russian scientists and available open sources of scientific and industrial literature, to concentrate on developing a chemical weapon using the chemical agent sarin because of its ease of production from commercially available compounds. Sarin, or isopropyl methylphosphonofluoridate, was first developed by German chemists in 1938 as a pesticide. German chemists soon realized that sarin was an extremely lethal and effective nerve agent. It is a colorless and odorless liquid, and a single drop on a person's skin is enough to cause death. Within seconds of being exposed to sarin, either as a liquid or gas, a victim's pupils contract, and the nose begins to run. These symptoms are then followed by tightening of the chest. Within minutes, a victim is seized by violent spasms, vomiting, and loss of bladder and bowel control. Without treatment, a fully exposed individual will suffer convulsions, coma, and death.[20]

In the summer of 1993, Masami Tsuchiya, a gifted chemist and Aum follower, succeeded in producing a highly concentrated liquid sarin. Asahara now had his doomsday weapon to punish those who opposed him. To ensure that this was truly the weapon that he was hoping for, Asahara ordered that a secure place be found to test it thoroughly. Fortunately for Asahara, such a secure place already belonged to Aum. Early that year Aum agents had flown to Australia and carefully looked at several properties in the western region of the country. Sect members had told local Australian authorities that they needed a large, remote area to conduct experiments of benefit to humankind, but they did not disclose what the benefits would be. After viewing several properties, Aum representatives had decided to buy the secluded Banjawarn Station, a large sheep ranch covering nearly 190,000 hectares. The station, located nearly 600 kilometers northwest of Perth, was isolated and difficult to reach by road.

On 9 September 1994, twenty-four Aum members, including Endo and Murai, arrived in Perth, bringing with them special tools, generators, protective chemical clothing, gas masks, and respirators. Australian customs officials searching their baggage found large amounts of hydrochloric and perchloric acids. As a result, Endo and Tomomasa Nakagawa, a medical doctor, were each fined $2,400 for carrying dangerous goods on an aircraft. Undeterred, Aum members continued their trip to Banjawarn Station and stayed there for several weeks before returning to Japan.

Following the Tokyo subway attack, Australian federal police conducted a thorough search and forensic criminal investigation at Banjawarn Station and the surrounding area. Soil samples were taken, and laboratory analysis identified the presence of methylphonic acid, which is a residue of the nerve agent sarin. Near the station living quarters, the skeletal remains of twenty-nine sheep were discovered in a confined circle. Soil samples from this location also contained methylphonic acid. Based upon this and other evidence obtained, the Australian federal police concluded that Aum had successfully tested sarin and confirmed its deadly effectiveness.[21] When informed about the test results at Banjawarn Station, Asahara was pleased; he was eager to try it on his enemies.[22]

Aum's First Chemical WMD Attack

Several months before the test in Australia, Aum attempted to buy a food-processing plant in the town of Matsumoto, 150 kilometers northwest of Tokyo. Alarmed upon learning that the plant would be operated by Aum, the plant owner and the town residents filed a lawsuit to invalidate the sale. Aum's lawyers contested the suit, and a long court case took place. The trial ended, and, as occurs in Japanese cases, the three presiding judges retired to consider their verdict. Aum lawyers believed that they would likely lose the case and advised Asahara of their concern. Asahara called an emergency meeting of his "war" council and directed them to use Aum's sarin to eliminate the three judges.

Aum scientists quickly outfitted a large commercial truck with a sophisticated battery-powered aerosol disperser and mixing device loaded with the chemicals necessary to produce 20 kilograms of sarin. On 27 June 1994, Hideo Murai accompanied the truck and at 10:40 P.M. ordered the truck operators to don gas masks and inject themselves with sarin antidote. Knowing the location of the dormitory where the presiding judges where sleeping, Murai had the truck activate the mixing device and aerosol dispenser and slowly drive past the target area. Fortunately for the judges, the mixing device malfunctioned after just a few minutes of operation, and the wind shifted, blowing the sarin away from the intended target area and enveloping homes located nearby. Soon the home occupants were experiencing blinding headaches and violent stomach spasms. Seven people died, and another 500 required hospitalization.[23]

Although the Matsumoto attack did not kill the three judges, Asahara was impressed with the results. The incident generated a large police investigation. At its conclusion, the police did not implicate Aum despite the fact that they had received a message from an anonymous Aum informer detailing how the attack was another effort by Aum to develop an effective method of using sarin. The Japanese police instead arrested a horticulturalist, Yoshiyuko Kono, after their detection equipment gave them a positive indication for sarin in a storage shed on his property. Unfortunately for Kono, the police did not know that sarin (in a vastly diluted form) is the main active chemical agent contained in many agricultural pesticides.

The Japanese media remained skeptical of the investigation findings, correctly pointing out the improbability of making sarin in such a high concentration by accident. Quietly acknowledging their error, Japanese authorities reopened the investigation, this time focusing intensively on Aum and its leader, Shoko Asahara.[24] Those members of the police who were also adherents of Aum kept Asahara fully informed about the investigation. When it became evident to Asahara that the police where completing their plans for a series of raids against Aum communes and facilities, he decided that the time had arrived to deliver a devastating attack against the police and the Japanese government.

The Tokyo Subway Attack

Aum's attack plan was simple but potentially catastrophic. Sarin would be released in the confined spaces of the Tokyo subway system during the morning commuter rush hour. Hideo Murai was again given the task to plan the attack. In an effort to avoid another equipment malfunction he had Aum's scientists prepare chemically resistant polyethylene bags filled with sarin. These bags were placed into shopping bags such as normal subway commuters might carry. Murai selected five trusted assistants who were assigned the task of placing the bags on the subway. Each attacker was given an umbrella with a specially sharpened tip. On 20 March 1995, between 7:30 and 7:45 A.M., the five attackers boarded five subway cars running on three different subway lines: Hibiya, Chiyoda, and Maronouchi. At 7:48 A.M., as each attacker's subway car neared its planned target, they pierced their bags of sarin and exited the subway cars. At around 8:00 A.M., all five subway cars converged at Kasumegaseki Station. Kasumegaseki is the civic center hub for most of Tokyo's government offices, including the National Police Agency (NPA) headquarters.[25]

The attack left twelve dead, hundreds hospitalized, and hundreds of thousands terrorized. Two factors kept the attack from being more deadly than it could have been: The first was the rudimentary delivery method of using punctured bags of liquid sarin, rather than an aerosol method of delivery. This greatly limited the amount of sarin in droplet form released within the subway cars. The second factor was that the sarin used was only 30-percent pure. In its diluted form, sarin is neither odorless nor colorless. This allowed passengers to smell and see that a foreign chemical was present in the subway cars.[26] Despite these two factors, thousands of passengers were affected. Subway stations evacuated passengers en masse, many choking, vomiting, and blinded by the sarin. Fleeing up the exit escalators and stairways, they collapsed in the streets. Police, fire, and emergency medical responders raced unprotected down into the subway to assist the victims—many of them to become victims themselves. As the effects of the attack ensued, the event was immediately broadcast over television and radio: "The images of confusion and chaos dominated the nine o'clock news and provided Tokyo and the world with its first glimpse of an act of terrorism with a weapon of mass destruction."[27]

The Costs of Consequence-Management Failure

The reluctance of Japanese officials to prepare for (or even to *discuss*) the possibility of a terrorist attack was immediately reflected in the actions of those at the scene. On arrival, first responders were unable to recognize that they were dealing with a toxic chemical agent. This lack of threat awareness kept them from gathering and then exchanging critical information to follow-on responders and response agencies. Next to arrive, subway workers and police were not informed enough to tell transit authorities to halt subway operations. This delay allowed the released sarin to continue spreading throughout the subway system. Almost immediately after the attack, sick commuters were staggering from the five attacked trains at several stations. At 8:10 A.M., transit workers on the Hibiya line knew that something was very wrong and ordered all passengers to evacuate at the next stop, Tsukiji Station, but they then allowed the train to continue on to Kasumigaseki Station, where more commuters were waiting to board the train. On the Chiyoda line, commuters pointed out to transit employees two packages leaking an unknown fluid that was making them sick. The employees quickly began to mop up the fluid with newspapers and their bare hands and sent the train on its way.[28] With no centralized monitoring system to report and disseminate information, response teams at each of the three attacked lines continued to struggle separately, unaware that they all were experiencing the same crisis situation. The Marunouchi line continued to operate until 9:27 A.M. The long delay in halting train operations produced a trail of sarin that continued to spread throughout the subway system, exposing thousands of passengers and employees to its harmful effects.[29]

Metropolitan police began receiving calls almost immediately after the attack, but it was not until 8:44 A.M. that the National Police Agency (NPA) determined that it faced a major emergency and that an unprecedented response effort was needed. By 9:00 A.M., the NPA believed that a chemical agent was responsible for the emergency, and the NPA initiated a request for assistance from chemical-warfare experts from the Japanese Self Defense Force (SDF). Having never practiced working together before, the police found it difficult to communicate their requests for assistance as well as to coordinate linking up with and deploying the SDF chemical-warfare experts. Under these circumstances, police and military authorities were not able to identify the chemical agent as sarin for almost three hours after the attack. Even after the agent was correctly identified as sarin, this critical information was not communicated to other emergency-response agencies for another hour. According to many sources, hospitals were never officially informed about what type of agent they were desperately trying to treat.[30]

The inability to communicate information across different agencies was a direct result of long-established bureaucratic barriers. *Tatewari* is a Japanese word that translates roughly as "compartmentalized bureaucracy" and is descriptive of the stovepiped agencies that made up the Japanese government. Japanese agencies had not practiced working together and, in many instances, felt that they were in competition with one another.[31] This common bureaucratic characteristic is found in almost all modern governments and is the leading cause of poor interagency emergency-response coordination. The lack of agreed-upon interagency relationships and methods of centralized response management created a situation where roles and missions were unclear. Most importantly, no single individual was in charge.

To make matters worse, police, fire, and emergency medical personnel continued to enter the subway stations to rescue victims hours after the attack. Unaware of the chemical threat they faced, responders were not wearing protective equipment, and many also became casualties. Further, sarin casualties were not decontaminated on site at each subway station. Ambulance teams loaded contaminated victims into their vehicles, becoming seriously ill themselves from evaporating sarin: "Of 1,364 EMTs, 135 suffered acute symptoms and required medical treatment."[32]

Compounding the confusion even further, responding agencies did not know they were dealing with a multisite attack. Each subway station believed it was dealing with an isolated attack; emergency resources were dispatched in a separate and often uncoordinated manner. Medical-emergency teams were sent to each affected subway station only to find that they were needed immediately back at their hospitals. There, arriving casualties from other locations were overwhelming hospital staffs. Ambulances were directed to take all casualties to the *nearest* hospital rather than reserving the closest hospitals for only the most seriously injured. St. Luke's Hospital received 150 patients the first hour and a total of 641 throughout the day. In addition to lack of structure and poor procedures, no mass-casualty training had ever been conducted.

Hospital staffs were never notified that incoming patients had experienced chemical poisoning from sarin. According to some reports, a physician who had treated victims of the Matsumoto attack called St. Luke's Hospital after viewing news reports of the attack and suggested that the chemical poisoning was from sarin.[33] At many hospitals, internal communications soon became jammed, and hospital staffs resorted to shouting down halls and up stairwells to pass along critical patient information.[34] Nearly 5,500 people went to 280 medical facilities in the days following the attack. Of these, 1,046 patients were admitted to 98 hospitals.[35]

Making the task of treating such a high number of patients even more difficult in Tokyo was the medical-emergency phenomenon known as the "worried well," individuals who had been minimally (or not at all) exposed to sarin who sought medical attention. Although present at the attack sites, many of those requesting medical care were not physically affected. Joining this category of patients were some who, although not even at the incident site, developed psychosomatic symptoms that led them to believe they were in danger. In some cases these symptoms realistically emulated those of true sarin exposure.[36]

Perhaps the most telling example of failed interagency coordination was finally rectified late in the afternoon of the attack with the arrival of units from the Japanese Self-Defense Force (JSDF). The only government resource trained and equipped to conduct chemical agent surveys and then to decontaminate an area found positive for a chemical agent, the JSDF's Special Biological and Chemical Warfare Task Forces had not been designated as first responders for domestic chemical incidents. Between 4:50 P.M. and 9:20 P.M.—over eight hours following the attack—task-force teams began the hazardous work of decontaminating the subway cars with a bleach-and-water solution.[37]

Aftermath

At dawn on Wednesday, 22 March, Japanese police began conducting the largest law-enforcement operation in Japanese history. More than 1,000 police surrounded and then entered the Mount Fuji compound headquarters of Aum Shinrikyo. Search teams dressed in special chemical warfare suits uncovered literally tons of dangerous chemicals. The sarin production facility was, by this time, fully operational and capable of producing over a ton of sarin every day. Simultaneous raids were also conducted on twenty-five Aum offices and compounds throughout Japan. By the first week in April, police had secured enough evidence to begin formally charging and arresting members of Aum. By mid-1996, more than 400 members were under arrest on charges ranging from kidnapping, illegal weapons possession, illegal drug production, to participation in the sarin attack.[38]

Despite the tremendous efforts of Japanese police, Shoko Asahara managed to elude arrest until 16 May 1995. On that day, with a large contingent of Japanese media watching, police again raided Satian 6, a building at Aum's main headquarters compound that had been searched by police many times before. This time police uncovered Asahara's hiding place deep within a side basement extension of the building. On 30 October 1995 Aum's status as a recognized religious organization was ordered dissolved by the Tokyo District Court, thus removing the legal protections guaranteed to religious groups, including tax-exempt status.[39]

The court trials of Asahara and his inner circle began in April 1996. Asahara himself was charged with 23 counts of murder.[40] Following long delays caused by Asahara's constant mumbling and seeming inability to answer any question coherently, he was sentenced to death on 27 February 2004. His legal appeals continue as of this writing.[41]

Conclusion

This case study has attempted to highlight three key lessons (and the governing issues directly related to them) that remain applicable to today's current and emerging terrorist threats. The first lesson is that governments must reserve the right to know what is happening inside religious institutions that may advocate or incite violence against their populations. The methods used for maintaining this awareness, the degree of intrusiveness, and the criteria for government intervention will depend on each nation's unique political and cultural context. The reluctance of the Japanese government to properly inform itself allowed Aum Shinrikyo the unrestrained freedom to carry out several attacks, one of which came very close to inflicting a catastrophic level of casualties, perhaps in the tens of thousands.

The second key lesson is that government officials must share information, both within and between institutions and countries. We should examine the following questions: What if Japanese authorities had been made aware of U.S. intelligence about Aum's attempts to purchase Soviet weapons and technical information in order to produce weapons of mass destruction? What would Japanese authorities have done had they received from Australian Customs information about its seizure of illegal toxic chemicals upon the arrival of Aum's scientific team? Would this shared intelligence and information have allowed Japanese police to stop Aum before it conducted its attack at Matsumoto? At the very least, this information would have led Japanese authorities to determine Aum's responsibility for the Matsumoto attack, resulting in the arrests of Shoko Asahara and his key leaders before they could execute their attack against the Tokyo subway system.

The final key lesson is that agencies that refuse to train together will inevitably fail together. The lack of prior training and preparedness by Japanese response agencies directly increased the damage that occurred on 20 March 1995. Had they participated in regular coordinated exercises, the agencies would easily have identified the need for a recognized and agreed-upon inter-agency incident-command system.[42] Perhaps even more importantly, regular joint training would have led to the inter-agency trust-based relationships that every institution needs in order to perform at full capacity.

Notes

1. Robyn Pangi, "Consequence Management in the 1995 Sarin Attacks on the Japanese Subway System," BCSIA (Belfer Center for Science and International Affairs) Discussion Paper 2002-4, Executive Session on Domestic Preparedness, Discussion Paper ESDP-2002-01, John F. Kennedy School of Government, Harvard University, February 2002, 5, http://belfercenter.ksg.harvard.edu/files/consequence_management_in_the_1995_sarin_attacks_on_the_japanese_subway_system.pdf.

2. Kyle B. Olson, "Aum Shinrikyo: Once and Future Threat?" *Emerging Infectious Diseases* 5, no. 4 (July–August 1999), 513–16, http://www.cdc.gov/ncidod/EID/vol5no4/pdf/olson.pdf (accessed 20 April 2010), or http://www.cdc.gov/ncidod/eid/vol5no4/olson.htm.

3. Patrick Bellamy, Chapter 1: "Blind Ambition," in *False Prophet: The Aum Cult of Terror,* http://www.trutv.com/library/crime/terrorists_spies/terrorists/prophet/1.html (accessed 3 September 2010).

4. Ibid., Chapter 2: "Metamorphosis."

5. Ibid., Chapter 3: "Birth of a Guru."

6. William J. Broad, "Sowing Death: A Special Report: How Japan Germ Terror Alerted World," *New York Times,* 26 May 1998, http://www.nytimes.com/1998/05/26/world/sowing-death-a-special-report-how-japan-germ-terror-alerted-world.html?ref=aum_shinrikyo (accessed 7 September 2010).

7. Bellamy, Chapter 3.

8. Holly Fletcher, "Backgrounder: Aum Shinrikyo," 28 May 2008, http://www.cfr.org/publication/9238/aum_shinrikyo.html (accessed 8 September 2010).

9. Pangi, "Consequence Management," 2.

10. Bellamy, Chapter 8: "The Challenger."

11. Ibid.

12. Bellamy, Chapter 14: "Lethal Empire."

13. John Sopko and Alan Edelman, "Global Proliferation of Weapons of Mass Destruction: A Case Study on the Aum Shinrikyo," Senate Government Affairs Permanent Subcommittee on Investigations, 31 October 1995 Staff Statement, Part III-A-3, http://www.fas.org/irp/congress/1995_rpt/aum/part03.htm (accessed 8 September 2010).

14. Bellamy, Chapter 15: "Bio-Terror Plans."

15. Sopko and Edelman, "Global Proliferation," Part III-B-2, http://www.fas.org/irp/congress/1995_rpt/aum/part03.htm (accessed 8 September 2010).

16. Bellamy, Chapter 16: "Bio-Terror First Attempts."

17. Olson, "Aum Shinrikyo: Once and Future Threat?"

18. Bellamy, Chapter 17: "Perfect Weapon."

19. Broad, "Sowing Death."

20. Federation of American Scientists, Biological and Chemical Weapons Fact Sheets, http://www.fas.org/programs/bio/factsheets/sarin.html (accessed 8 September 2010).

21. "Police in Australia—Issues and Innovations in Australian Policing (Case Studies)," originally accessed at http://www.aic.gov.au/policing/case-studies/afp.html. Internet version is no longer accessible. Hard copy is on file with the author.

22. Bellamy, Chapter 17.

23. Pangi, "Consequence Management," 6.

24. Bellamy, Chapter 25: "Alive and Well."

25. Pangi, "Consequence Management," 7.

26. Ibid., 7–8.

27. Ibid., 9.

28. David E. Kaplan and Andrew Marshall, *The Cult at the End of the World: The Incredible Story of Aum* (London: Hutchinson, 1996), 248–49.

29. Ibid., 250.

30. Pangi, "Consequence Management," 14.

31. Ibid., 14–15.

32. Amy Smithson and Leslie-Anne Levy, "Ataxia: The Chemical and Biological Terrorism Threat and U.S. Response," Stimson Center Report No. 35 (October 2000), 93.

33. Pangi, "Consequence Management," 14.

34. Smithson and Levy, "Ataxia," 96. See also Pangi, "Consequence Management," 30.

35. Pangi, "Consequence Management," 23.

36. Ibid., 31.

37. Ibid., 28.

38. Mark Mullins, "The Political and Legal Response to Aum-Related Violence in Japan: A Review Article," *Japan Christian Review* 63 (1997): 37–46.

39. Ibid.

40. "Lawyers Seek Japan Cult Guru Death Sentence Appeal," Reuters, 30 March 2006, http://www.cesnur.org/2006/aum_01.htm.

41. Ibid.

42. Please see discussion in Pangi, "Consequence Management," 16.

19 The Madrid Train Bombings[1]

Phil Williams

THE MADRID TRAIN BOMBINGS OF 11 MARCH 2004 ENDED AN impressive run of success by West European law-enforcement and intelligence agencies in thwarting planned attacks by jihadist cells. Attacks in Strasburg, Paris, London, and Rome had all been forestalled as a result of extensive surveillance on suspicious groups and individuals, rapid information sharing among European agencies, U.S. support and assistance, and plain good luck. Against this background of successful prevention, the Madrid bombings came as an enormous shock, whose impact was accentuated by the dramatic political developments that followed: The Spanish government lost national elections three days later, and the new government committed to removing Spanish forces from Iraq. Not only had the jihadists outwitted Spanish authorities, but also they had done so with what appeared to be an impeccable sense of strategic timing that gave the attack maximum political effect. The discovery of a jihadi document on the Internet discussing the forthcoming elections in Spain and describing the country as a weak link in the coalition in Iraq endowed the attack with an added cachet: The jihad movement appeared to be thinking and acting with strategic purpose and political acumen.[2] Yet several years later, in spite of an exhaustive and thorough investigation led by Judge Juan del Olmo, there are still many missing pieces and many questions about the attacks that remain unanswered.

For example, it has become axiomatic that the attack was designed primarily to influence the Spanish elections and that the 11 March bombers explicitly set out to change the government and ensure a Spanish withdrawal from Iraq. However, there is a danger in inferring intentions from consequences. Even though the attack was related, at least in part, to Spain's involvement in the military coalition in Iraq, the terrorists could not have known that the incumbent government would destroy its credibility by insisting that the attacks were the work of Basque separatists even when the evidence pointed to Islamic extremists. Arguably, the election became a referendum not on the government's failure to foresee the attack, but on its inept crisis management and particularly its reflexive efforts to pin the responsibility on the Basque separatist organization Euskadi Ta Askatasuna (ETA). It is also worth emphasizing that the train bombings were not intended as a one-off attack; rather, they were the opening salvo in what was to be a continuing campaign of terror. On 2 April, terrorists placed an explosive device on the high-speed rail line between Madrid and Seville. Fortunately, the bomb failed to detonate and was discovered. However, the Madrid network had plans for attacks on a major Jewish center, a synagogue, and a British children's school. All this suggests that the perpetrators were as intent on punishing Spain for its support of U.S. operations in Iraq as they were on forcing political change and policy shifts.

Some of the uncertainties are not surprising. Reconstructing the planning for a terrorist attack is always problematic. In this instance it was harder than usual because on 3 April, seven of the perpetrators committed suicide by blowing themselves up rather than be captured by police, who had surrounded their apartment in Leganes. Although some critical pieces of evidence were recovered in the debris, other clues were lost forever. Moreover, the investigation was carried out in a bitterly partisan atmosphere surrounded by rumors of conspiracy and cover-up. Claims about linkages between the Muslim terrorists responsible for carrying out the attack and the Basque ETA movement had little factual basis but persisted. And with some of the principals no longer alive, the trial, which began on 15 February 2007 and lasted until 2 July 2007, was inevitably anticlimactic. Even putting aside the absence of some of those who were deeply implicated in planning and executing the attacks, the protracted trial was marred by ambiguous and conflicting eyewitness testimony, continued protestations of innocence from those in the dock, crucial differences between Spanish and Italian translations of Italian surveillance tapes, and occasional scuffles between some of the defendants.[3]

Against this background, this chapter provides a brief overview of the train bombings. It then discusses how the Madrid attacks provided important clues about the nature and evolution of Islamist terrorism in Europe. Three interlinked and overlapping dimensions stand out:

- The Madrid bombings provide a case study of the multifaceted nature of radicalization. Those involved were radicalized at different times and places and in different ways, but as they came together they reinforced and reaffirmed a collective extremism and commitment to violence.
- The Madrid attacks provide a case study of Al Qaeda's organizational dynamics. In particular, the attacks illuminate the extent to which the local network responsible for the operation was linked to the wider organization; it was not simply a local phenomenon that had developed entirely from the bottom up.
- Madrid is a case study of terrorist financing, particularly the decline in centralized funding and, concomitantly, the growth of financial self-reliance and self-funding at the local level.

The Madrid attacks were an example of complex radicalization processes linked to and encouraged by Al Qaeda members: Momentum and financial self-reliance came from the bottom up, encouraged from the top down by help with planning and implementation. In addition, the Madrid bombings can be seen as a major intelligence failure by the Spanish authorities. Although several confidential informants had provided data about the perpetrators and broad details of the plot, a lack of both information sharing and interagency cooperation ensured that the significance of the information was evident only in retrospect. Indeed, Spain suffered from many of the same problems that had bedeviled the U.S. intelligence community and law-enforcement agencies prior to 11 September 2001.

Overview

On 11 March 2004, as trains full of commuters converged on Atocha Station in Madrid during the morning rush hour, four of them were struck by a series of explosions that killed 191 people and injured about 1,600.[4] The investigation would show that terrorists had left bombs on the trains in backpacks and detonated them by remote signals from cell phones. Although official fingers were immediately pointed at ETA, the multiple attacks, well-coordinated and carried out without warning, were much more characteristic of incidents perpetrated by Al Qaeda and its affiliates. As evidence was unearthed, it increasingly pointed in the direction of Islamic extremists—something that the government seemed reluctant to acknowledge.

With evidence from several more devices that failed to detonate, and "numerous errors in tradecraft" made by the bombers, the investigation moved quickly.[5] A white Renault van left in a parking lot yielded important clues, including unused detonators, DNA evidence, and a jihadi cassette tape.[6] However, most significant was an unexploded device found in a sports bag that was disarmed and dismantled by police. The SIM cards in the telephone were traced to Jamal Zougam, a Moroccan in the Lavapies district of the city. Zougam was arrested, and the authorities began the task of reconstructing the network responsible for the attacks.

By tracing cell calls and using information from confidential sources, the police were able to identify key figures in the attacks, as well as a safe house where the bombs had been prepared. Their investigation took on even greater urgency after the discovery on 2 April of an intact bomb on the rail line between Madrid and Seville. The following day, police surrounded an apartment building in Leganes where some of those involved in the 11 March attacks were staying. After a siege of several hours, the seven terrorists in the apartment set off a massive explosion that killed themselves and one policeman. Those who died were subsequently identified as Jamal Ahmidan, Serhane Fakhet, Allekema Lamari, Asir Rifat Anoua (whose DNA was linked to the bomb on the rail line), Mohamed and Rachid Oula Akcha, and Abdennabi Kounjaa. In the ruins of the apartment, police found "vitally important evidence, including . . . 236 detonators, 30 kilograms of Goma-2 ECO, 4 machine pistols, jihadist written and audio materials, plans prepared for the carrying out of future terrorist attacks, and a videotape of three of the cell members transmitting a belligerent message to the Spaniards about their motivations and future plans."[7]

The investigation continued, with much attention given to how the explosives had been acquired. On 11 April 2006, twenty-nine indictments were issued, with charges that included murder, membership in a terrorist organization, collaborating with a terrorist organization, and supplying or trafficking in explosives.[8] The seven terrorists who had blown themselves up in the apartment in Leganes on 3 April were not included in the indictments.

Also absent were several other suspects who were on the run. In spite of the continued uncertainties, it is nevertheless possible from the existing evidence to identify the main contours of a terrorist network in Madrid that consisted primarily of Moroccans, but also included members from Tunisia, Algeria, Egypt, and Lebanon. Before describing this network and the major players, however, it is important to look at the way in which many of those involved in the Madrid train bombings were radicalized.

Case Studies in Radicalization

Terrorists are not born; they are created, a process encapsulated in the term *radicalization.* Radicalization is an intellectual, emotional, and even spiritual evolution during which individuals internalize certain extreme or fundamentalist beliefs and ideas. Islamic extremists tend to adopt a "grievance narrative" in which Islam is portrayed as being under attack globally.[9] The narrative links together politically divergent and geographically separated conflicts such as the Balkans wars of the 1990s, the simmering India–Pakistan fight over Kashmir, and the Israeli–Palestinian struggle, and portrays them as part of a coherent whole in which Muslims are the righteous persecuted. Of course, not all extremists are personally willing to use force in the struggle; some content themselves with providing financial support or logistical assistance—what might be described as "level-three" radicalization. Others go beyond this level and are willing to become directly involved in the use of violence, often inspired by what have been described as "identity entrepreneurs"—charismatic individuals able to define a cause and mobilize support.[10] These terrorists operate at the second, more intense level of radicalization. The top tier of radicalization involves a subset of these militants who are willing to become martyrs for the cause, a willingness that is first elicited by the terrorist organization, then solidified. This is often reinforced by what Michael Echemendia terms *social resonance*—that is, broad support from adherents to the cause.[11] In other words, "suicide terrorists" are at the apex of radicalization.

One way to understand the radicalization process, particularly at the third and second levels, is in epidemiological terms, or what is sometimes described as "social contagion."[12] Charismatic leadership plays a part in this spread of ideas, but such leadership, especially in network-type organizations, is often both distant and highly symbolic, and has to be reinforced by relationships that are close and personal. In this connection the Madrid case provides some rich examples of how individuals became radicalized and moved beyond dogma to violence. Yet even here there is no consensus. For example, Marc Sageman argues that the Madrid bombings were perpetrated by a bunch of guys who played together, prayed together, and eventually plotted together.[13] In this view, those involved were not particularly sophisticated, had no direct links to Al Qaeda, and succeeded in carrying out the attack almost in spite of themselves and their ineptitude. However, Jeffrey Bale is somewhat more persuasive in his argument that the transformation of some of the key figures in the Madrid bombings "was facilitated *personally and directly,* at various stages, by key individuals" linked to Al Qaeda.[14] In particular, Al Qaeda members cultivated the "*religious, political, and ideological indoctrination and radicalization*" of Serhane Fakhet, who was to become the driving force behind the attack. Consequently, Bale rejects arguments that the Madrid bombers were self-starters without meaningful connections to Al Qaeda.[15]

However, radicalization is in part an internal, highly individual process that in Fakhet's case was precipitated by some kind of personal crisis. Fakhet had come to Spain in 1994 to study economics at the Autonomous University of Madrid. He subsequently became a successful real estate salesman, although his job performance then declined precipitously, and he eventually stopped working. When he emerged from this crisis, he had become extremist in his views. Because of the internal dimension of radicalization, it is sometimes difficult to determine whether it comes from association with others already committed to an extremist cause or whether such associations are the result of a newly radicalized person seeking out those with similar beliefs and levels of commitment. Whatever the case, by the late 1990s Fakhet had close relationships with members of the Madrid cell, which was an important part of the Al Qaeda infrastructure in Europe.[16] Key figures included Abu Dahdah, a Syrian who had been a member of the Muslim Brotherhood; Abu Musab al Suri, who was to become one of the leading theorists of global jihad; and Amer Azizi, who certainly encouraged, if he did not direct, the Madrid train bombings. The Dahdah cell offered a one-stop shop, "indoctrinating and radicalizing alienated Muslims in Spain, recruiting and training suitable candidates to go abroad and wage jihad on various fronts, and providing medical care and refuge for returning jihadist veterans."[17] Fakhet was one of their products, but he was to wage jihad in Spain, not abroad.

Even after the arrest of Abu Dahdah in November 2001, Fakhet remained in close contact with other extremists. His Moroccan brother-in-law, Mustapha el-Mimouni—who had been recruited by Azizi—was a militant proponent of jihad against the West and was reportedly in Madrid in early 2002, where he met with some of the individuals subsequently involved in the train bombings. Some of these meetings occurred at the home of Mouhannad Almallah Dabas, who, along with his brother, helped to indoctrinate some members of the group. Although el-Mimouni left Spain for a few months, he returned in September 2002 and probably encouraged Fakhet and some of his associates to go beyond the rhetoric and carry out terrorist acts. When el-Mimouni was arrested in the aftermath of the Casablanca bombings of May 2003, Fakhet took over his leadership role, at which he proved very effective.[18] It has also been reported that Fakhet and Rabei Osman became "inseparable friends" and were "seen everywhere together."[19]

If Fakhet has a distinct trajectory of radicalization that linked him to important Al Qaeda figures, others moved along somewhat different paths. In fact, Spanish scholar Fernando Reinares has emphasized that "the individuals responsible for the March 2004 Madrid bombings did not become prone to terrorism at the same place, the same time or through the same processes."[20] Moreover, "four of the 27 individuals" in the Madrid bombing network "clearly internalized an extremist ideology outside of Spain" and therefore could not be regarded as homegrown terrorists.[21] Hassan el-Haski was a leading member of the Moroccan Islamic Combatant Group, while Youssef Belhadj joined this group after becoming radicalized in Belgium. For Rabei Osman, radicalization occurred in Egypt, while Allekema Lamari was involved in the Armed Islamic group in Algeria (GIA) before moving to Spain.[22]

For the most part, the longer that individuals had been radicalized, the more important the roles they played in spreading extremism. Much of the proselytizing took place at the Abu-Bakr and M-30 mosques in Madrid and was reinforced in informal countryside gatherings that seem to have been a mix of social activities and revivalist meetings. For example, the Belhadj brothers helped to radicalize Abdelmajid Bouchar, while Rabei Osman radicalized Fouad el-Morabit Amghar outside one of the mosques.[23] For the most part, extremist ideas were spread and internalized through interpersonal contacts or social contagion.

Prison also played a part in radicalizing some members of the network, including Mohamed Bouharrat. Allekema Lamari was already an extremist before leaving Algeria, but his incarceration in Spain made him particularly angry and intent on some kind of revenge. Jamal Ahmidan, a Moroccan drug trafficker who, along with Fakhet, became a main driver of the bombing plot, had also been partially radicalized in prison. Some observers trace this back to prisons in Spain in the mid-1990s, while others focus on the period between mid-2000 and July 2003, when Ahmidan was incarcerated in Morocco for a murder he had committed some years earlier. Ahmidan's wife claims that it was during this latter imprisonment when she first detected changes in her husband, even though he lived relatively well and had the protection of four or five other prisoners.[24] He told her that when released, he intended to go to Iraq to fight. Another participant in the Madrid network described Ahmidan as "very radical," claiming that he had sent a large "amount of money to Chechnya and Afghanistan," and observed that it "was in the jail in Morocco, where he made contacts, where he was transformed. Now, he came to Spain to roll."[25] After his release from prison, Ahmidan returned home to Madrid, arriving on 29 July 2003. According to his wife, in most respects he was his old self and not particularly extreme. After meeting Fakhet in the summer of 2003, however, Ahmidan wanted to transfer his son from Catholic school to a madrassa at the M-30 mosque, and spent time on the Internet looking at jihad sites.[26] Clearly, Fakhet had a significant impact on Ahmidan if only by crystallizing a process of radicalization already under way.

One factor that does not loom as large in the radicalization process as might have been expected is the Internet. According to Fernando Reinares, "the internet was not a radicalization factor for individuals who adopted a *jihadist* ideology" before 11 September 2001. It was a "limited factor" among those who became jihadis after September 11 but before the invasion of Iraq, and was a "greater factor" for those who "radicalized into violence after the invasion of Iraq."[27] Even among those who became radicalized after Iraq, the Internet more often reinforced an existing process rather than acting as an independent catalyst.

The Madrid Network

Those who analyze criminal or terrorist networks often find it difficult to delineate the boundaries of a particular network—to determine where it begins and ends. This is inescapable: Relationships tend to be highly fluid; they are also multifaceted. Sometimes relatives and friends are simply that; in other instances they are coconspirators. Sometimes the network members are rooted in common experience; at other times separate groups and individuals overlap and intersect in unexpected ways. To further complicate matters, it is important to determine whether or not certain ties are strong or weak, the importance of degrees of separation, and the balance between authority and autonomy in different parts of the network. Such problems notwithstanding, it became clear that the network responsible for the Madrid train bombings emerged from the coalescence of a group in the Lavapies district of Madrid led by Jamal Zougam, a group of religious extremists led by Serhane Fakhet, and a group of Moroccan drug traffickers led by Jamal Ahmidan.[28] In addition, there were links to petty criminals and to lazy and corrupt security guards at a mine from where stored explosives were diverted. In this sense the Madrid network was "emergent," or formed from the bottom up, rather than the top down. At the same time, Fakhet and Zougam were linked back to the Dahdah cell and "maintained extensive ongoing interactions" with the Al Qaeda hierarchy and affiliated networks elsewhere in Europe and beyond.[29] The Madrid network can be divided into four main categories of participants:

- The major players, who took a leading role of one kind or another in the planning, preparation, and implementation of the attacks.
- The costars, who were important in certain respects but generally had a less demanding or critical role.
- The supporting cast members, who played some role in the implementation of the attack or subsequently assisted those who had been more directly involved as they tried to elude capture.
- The "acquisition" players, who were on the margins of the group but helped with the acquisition of explosives and other matériel. This category extends to the mine security guards, who were sloppy, careless, and/or corrupt, but had little importance beyond the failure to do their job.

What remains uncertain is the role of Amer Azizi. He could well have been the instigator of the attacks and, even if not directly involved in the planning, may have provided Al Qaeda's blessing for the operation. Reinares emphasizes that Azizi was linked to the Al Qaeda leadership and was eventually killed in November 2005 in North Waziristan, along with Hamza Rabia, one of the top five Al Qaeda leaders.[30] This is not conclusive evidence of collaboration, but it does suggest a stronger and more direct link to Al Qaeda than some skeptics acknowledge. Uncertainty also surrounds Rabei Osman, known as "Mohammed the Egyptian," who subsequently claimed in telephone calls, monitored by Italian police, that he had been the leader of the group. Such claims seem exaggerated, and most accounts suggest that he was less important than either Fakhet or Ahmidan. The Madrid trial verdict that acquitted Osman remains highly controversial, although he was not found guilty of being a member of a terrorist group only because he had already been sentenced for this in Italy and was protected by the legal safeguard of double jeopardy.

The Leaders

In an arrest warrant issued on 1 April 2004, Serhane Fakhet was described as the "leader and coordinator" of those involved in the Madrid attacks.[31] The trajectory of Fakhet's radicalization is described above; the accompanying anger was intensified by the imprisonment of Abu Dahda (whose real name was Barakat Yarkas) after 11 September 2001 and by Spain's involvement in Iraq, something that reportedly "made him furious."[32] During the trial in 2007, Mouhannad Almallah Dabas, who had met Fakhet at a mosque in 1996 and was accused of recruiting and handling logistics for the cell, claimed that "Fakhet was deeply affected by the war in Iraq and started trying to persuade people to go there to wage jihad."[33] Indeed, even before then, Fakhet's resentment at Spain was so intense that in 2002 he met with Amer Azizi in Turkey to discuss his assistance with some kind of direct action. Most accounts suggest that Azizi would not provide the men requested—perhaps because they were under surveillance. Nevertheless, it is likely that Azizi encouraged Fakhet to go ahead, to use the mantle of Al Qaeda, and to get in touch with Jamal Zougam. In the event, it was another Jamal, however, who was the decisive figure to enable what had hitherto been a group of people long on jihadi rhetoric but short on concrete action to develop the capacity to carry out a well-orchestrated and highly lethal terrorist attack. This individual was a Moroccan drug trafficker named Jamal Ahmidan.

Although Jamal Ahmidan has often been described as the military planner for the Madrid bombings, this description fails to do justice to his role. He was probably the single most important individual in the execution of the Madrid attacks, and without him the attacks would not have occurred. Ahmidan was the successful leader of a small but effective drug-trafficking group that smuggled into Spain hashish from Morocco and ecstasy from Holland.

He had a reputation for violence and a flashy lifestyle. He drove a sleek BMW 530 sedan that "was armor-plated, possibly with lead plates, had 2.5 cm-thick bullet-proof windows, leather seats, a television in the middle of the dashboard, a very expensive sound system, and a television camera at the rear of the vehicle, which could be seen on the screen."[34] The car—discovered in the Spanish enclave city of Cueta in October 2007 thanks to the efforts of a lawyer for one of the defendants—was a symbol of the very success in the drug business that allowed Ahmidan to fund the attacks.

Ahmidan, along with other members of his drug-trafficking group, had grown up in Tetuan, a Moroccan town that subsequently earned a reputation for sending volunteers to Iraq. Yet Ahmidan came from a prosperous family and as a young man was not particularly religious. After migrating illegally to Spain, he appeared to be far more interested in running a criminal business based on drug imports than in Islam. His trafficking business employed primarily family members and friends, hardly surprising given the importance of trust and bonding among the operators in illicit operations. The implicit trust created by close personal ties between members of the trafficking organization, along with the leadership and organizational skills of Ahmidan, also seem to have been critical in the transformation of the group from criminals to terrorists, as well as their subsequent integration into the broader Al Qaeda-linked terrorist network led by Fakhet.

The relationship between Fakhet and Ahmidan was critical in leading to an outcome that neither would have brought about without the other. Fakhet had an infectious zealotry and commitment to violence that would probably have come to nothing without Ahmidan's capacity to organize and implement. Without Ahmidan, Fakhet would have remained a "wannabe" terrorist, full of anger and resentment but lacking the ability to turn his aspirations into reality. And without Fakhet, it seems unlikely that Ahmidan would have channeled his drive, energy, and organizational skills into the train bombings. In the event, Ahmidan's charisma and leadership brought along the other members of his drug-trafficking organization, he played a critical role in obtaining explosives, and he provided "money, weapons, phones, cars, safe houses and other infrastructure."[35] Ahmidan acted as the financier of the attacks, using money, a stolen car, and hashish to pay for the explosives, and also covering the rentals for the safe house, the apartment in Leganes, and the cell phones use to detonate the bombs. The Madrid network was self-sufficient only because of Ahmidan and the use of proceeds from drug trafficking.[36]

The combination of Fakhet and Ahmidan was very formidable, a reality that has largely been ignored by commentators who have looked elsewhere for the "mastermind" of the attack. Together the two men were motivated and capable of planning and implementing the Madrid bombings. If Al Qaeda command and control was neither necessary nor evident, however, this does not imply that Al Qaeda was absent. The Azizi link was critically important. In addition, several people involved in the Madrid bombings were connected to the broader network of global jihad in Britain, Belgium, Morocco, and elsewhere.

The Costars

The three men who perhaps most clearly embodied these broader linkages were Jamal Zougam, Rabei Osman, and Allekema Lamari. They were less important than Fakhet and Ahmidan but still played major roles: Zougam was an important connector to jihadi networks in Norway, Britain, and Morocco; Osman was a jihadi drifter who was good at recruitment and even better at cheerleading; and Lamari brought status, reputation, and legitimacy because of his membership in the GIA and time in prison.

Jamal Zougam had moved to Spain from Morocco and settled in Madrid as a boy. To all outward appearances he was well integrated into Spanish society, and he ran a small mobile telephone sales and repair shop in the Lavapies district of Madrid.[37] In 2001, however, Spanish authorities briefly investigated Zougam after French antiterrorist judges had linked him with David Courtailler, a French citizen who had converted to Islam and become radicalized. When police searched Zougam's home, they found a jihadi video and Amer Azizi's SIM card number, but this was not enough to arrest him. Zougam's extremism and the dangers he posed were not fully appreciated, even though he was linked to the Benyaich brothers and others involved in the Casablanca bombings, to the Kurdish fundamentalist cleric Mullah Krekar in Norway, and, directly or indirectly, to Abu Qatada, the Jordanian cleric who played a central role in recruiting jihadis in London.[38]

Rabei Osman is perhaps the most enigmatic figure among those connected with the bombings. He almost certainly helped the network to coalesce, and he was linked to radicals Basel Ghalyoun and Fouad el-Morabit Amghar, as well as Fakhet. In his role as cheerleader, he became very close to Fakhet and is likely to have taken the opportunity to stoke Fakhet's anger at events in Iraq. Conceivably, Osman could have proposed using explosives detonated by telephone, as he had served as an explosives expert in the Egyptian army.[39] Although he was later to claim authorship of the Madrid attacks, he reportedly left Madrid for France in February 2003, over a year before the attacks occurred. Some reports suggest, though, that he visited Spain several times thereafter, including once in the weeks before the attacks. However, Spanish judicial authorities rejected the argument that he was one of the intellectual authors of the train attacks.

Allekema Lamari is often described as the "emir" of the Madrid network, who provided legitimacy and status. He was imprisoned in 1997 but released in 2002 as a result of a judicial or administrative error. The National Intelligence Centre warned the government that he might become the leader of an Islamic attack in Spain.[40] Clearly, he was very angry at his imprisonment and intent on revenge against Spain. Moreover, his background gave him a certain standing with the group. Nevertheless, there is little solid evidence that he played a key leadership role comparable with that played by Fakhet and Ahmidan.

The Supporting Cast

As suggested above, identifying network boundaries is not always possible. Nevertheless, it is clear that the following individuals were part of the Madrid terrorist network:

- Youssef Belhadj was a member of the Moroccan Islamic Combatant Group (GICM), had SIM mobile phone cards with the dates of both the Madrid and Casablanca bombings, and was reportedly in Spain meeting with Fakhet and others until just over a week before the Madrid bombings.[41]
- Hasan el Aski was another member of the GICM and was involved in the Casablanca attacks. He received prison sentences in both Spain and Morocco. At one time he was suspected of being the architect of the Madrid bombings, but this assessment of his role gradually receded.
- Othman el-Gnaoui helped bring the explosives to Madrid.
- Abdelmajid Bouchar had been at the apartment in Leganes on 3 April 2004, but when he saw the police outside, called out warnings to the other men and fled. He was subsequently arrested in Belgrade.
- Rachid Aglif had helped to bring the various groups together and was important in putting Ahmidan in touch with Rafa Zouhier, who in turn linked him to people with access to explosives.

- Mohamed Bouharrat assisted with recruitment.
- Mouhannad Almallah Dabas, a Syrian, played a role in recruitment but, somewhat inexplicably, had his conviction and twelve-year sentence for being a member of a terrorist group overturned by the Spanish Supreme Court in July 2008.
- Basel Ghalyoun, a Syrian linked to Rabei Osman and Fakhet, was believed to have been on one of the trains, but a witness statement to this effect was retracted. He was deported to Syria in 2008.
- Mahmoud Slimane Aoun, a Lebanese national, helped Ahmidan forge documents. He was given a three-year sentence rather than the thirteen years requested by prosecutors.

This is not an exhaustive list, but it does give some sense of the diversity of those involved. The fourth group of individuals, noted below, played no direct part in the attack but did help to acquire the explosives.[42]

The Acquisition Players

Most of those involved in supplying the explosives stolen from a mine in Asturias had no extremist agenda and were little more than opportunistic petty criminals, albeit criminals with little concern about what they were involved with. This was certainly the case with Rafa Zouhier, a small-time drug trafficker who played a pivotal role in linking Ahmidan with people willing to sell him explosives with no questions asked. Zouhier had been in prison with Antonio Toro Castro, whose brother-in-law, José Emilio Suárez Trashorras, became the main supplier of the explosives used in the attack. The dynamite was easily pilfered because of lazy and corrupt security guards. In the fall of 2003 several meetings were held at various McDonald's restaurants in Madrid to arrange the transaction. In January and February 2004 the explosives were gradually transported from Asturias to Madrid, often in ways that were very amateurish. For example, some of the explosive material was taken to Madrid on a bus by a sixteen-year-old. Ahmidan also took some explosives in his car, and he was stopped by the police for speeding.

The Financial Dimension[43]

Terrorists are notoriously eclectic in their fund-raising efforts; different sources of support tend to vary in their relative importance over time. Before the post-9/11 clampdown on terrorist financial transactions, the main source of Al Qaeda's funding was donations from wealthy individuals, businesses, and charities in Saudi Arabia and the Persian Gulf region. Crime and drugs played a part at the cell level and for some affiliated groups. With the tightening of regulations on charities and the financial sector that followed 9/11, however, cells could no longer rely on funding from the core leadership and increasingly turned to self-financing. The Madrid train attacks were completely self-financed as a result of the involvement of Jamal Ahmidan and his radicalized drug-trafficking group. Indeed, a police report sent to Judge Juan del Olmo noted that Ahmidan was "the central figure in relation to the funding of the attacks." The Madrid attackers accumulated "1.6m Euros in money and drugs but did not receive any funds from abroad. The financial cost of the massacre was between 41,000 and 54,000 Euros." (At the time of the attacks, €1 was worth about U.S. $1.23.)

Spanish police investigated the "financial and property situations" of 55 individuals and examined 185 bank accounts, mostly characterized by low balances and the "constant presence of overdrafts." There were no transfers between accounts and no evidence of "transnational transfers or financial transactions that might have contributed to the funding of the attacks." The conclusion was that most of the defendants were "of low social and financial status." Abdenabi Kounjaa, who committed suicide in Leganes, had sold an apartment in 2003 with a profit of €18,000, while Mouhannad Almallah Dabas had a house with a €152,807 mortgage, but these were exceptions. Yet in addition to what they spent, the bombers had a reserve of €52,295 in cash to continue operating: €25,635 was stashed in Leganes, €7,650 was at the home of Jamal Zougam, and €19,010 was left with Ahmidan's relatives. In addition, Ahmidan had stored 59.2 kilos of hashish and 125,800 ecstasy tablets, valued at between €1,353,677 and €1,537,663. In short, the terrorists had a war chest for a campaign going well beyond the attacks of March 11.

They also had plenty of explosives, having obtained 210 kilos of Goma 2 explosive and 260 detonators from Suárez Trashorras and Toro Castro. Because "no income that could correspond to the sale" was found, investigators concluded that payment was made "in cash, in kind or by means of the exchange of explosives for hashish." Part of the payment was a car, stolen in Madrid on 18 September 2003, which Ahmidan (also known as El Chino) handed to Suárez Trashorras. With the price of hashish between €1,275 and €1,500 per kilo, "the value of the drug handed over by Jamal Ahmidan would amount to a minimum of 31,875 Euros and a maximum of 45,000 Euros."

The other major expenses for the Madrid network were the three bases they rented. The safe house in Chinchon was rented by Ahmidan, who not only paid €2,520 in rent but also—and somewhat inexplicably—spent almost €3,000 for work done by his cousin Hamid Ahmidan, Othman el-Gnaoui, and one other man. The apartment in Leganes was rented by one of the Belhadj brothers, who paid a total of €1,800 for it. A third house was not used, even though Kounjaa and Rachid Oulad paid €800 in advance from the €3,700 that Oulad had withdrawn from Banco Popular on 5 March. In comparison with the explosives and the safe houses, the telephones and SIM cards cost only €1,250, a relatively modest expense.

Conclusions

Although it is tempting to see the Madrid attacks purely in terms of Al Qaeda's transformation from a largely top-down organization prior to 11 September 2001 to a largely bottom-up phenomenon by 11 March 2004, the reality is both messier and more complex. Al Qaeda has always operated with elements of both central direction and local autonomy, and the balance has been different at different times and in different countries and regions. Consequently, the analysis here suggests that although a lot of the impetus for the Madrid bombings was local, key players in the Madrid network were clearly linked to Al Qaeda and in some cases had been radicalized by Al Qaeda figures. The debate over Al Qaeda's evolution is sometimes described in terms of a centrally directed, if not controlled, organization that was forced to morph into a loose social movement by the attacks of its opponents. However, the reality is not an either-or trajectory. Al Qaeda has always had elements of both core networks and social movements, and the Madrid attacks were a very potent example of how deadly such a combination can be.

Notes

1. The author is grateful to Marc Sageman, Jeffrey Bale, and Luke Gerdes for several helpful discussions, although he is solely responsible for the contents of this chapter. He would also like to thank Tomas Malina, a University of Pittsburgh graduate student working at the Ridgway Center for International Security Studies, for his help in identifying the roles played by various individuals.

2. See Brynjar Lia and Thomas Hegghammer, "Jihadi Strategic Studies: The Alleged Al Qaida Policy Study Preceding the Madrid Bombings," *Studies in Conflict and Terrorism* 27, no. 5 (September–October 2004): 355–75.

3. Even the FBI contributed to the chaos of the early investigation when it detained a U.S. convert to Islam, Brandon Mayfield, in Portland, Oregon, based on a fingerprint, after Spanish police had warned them it was a bad match. Mayfield, who claimed he was mistreated in custody, eventually received $2 million and a formal apology from the federal government. Dan Eggan, "U.S. Settles Suit Filed by Ore. Lawyer," *Washington Post,* 30 November 2006.

4. For a good account, see Lawrence Wright, "The Terror Web," *New Yorker,* 2 August 2004.

5. Jeffrey M. Bale, "Jihadist Cells and I.E.D. Capabilities in Europe: Assessing the Present and Future Threat," unpublished draft, Monterey, California, 32. Available from the author.

6. Ibid., 32.

7. Ibid., 37.

8. Pamela Rolfe, "29 Indicted for Roles In Madrid Bombings: Judge Says Al-Qaeda Inspired Local Cell," *Washington Post,* 12 April 2006.

9. The term *grievance narrative* is used frequently by Jack Cashill in *Sucker Punch* (Nashville: Nelson, 2006).

10. Troy Thomas and Stephen Kiser, "Lords of the Silk Route," Institute for National Security Studies (INSS) Occasional Paper no. 43, U.S. Air Force Academy, Colorado, May 2002, 43.

11. Michael Echemendia, "Deliberate Death: How Suicide Attacks Function at the Organizational, Individual and Societal Levels of Analysis," Graduate School of Public and International Affairs, University of Pittsburgh, 2010, 4.

12. On the notion of social contagion generally, see Malcolm Gladwell, *The Tipping Point: How Little Things Can Make a Big Difference* (Boston: Little, Brown, 2000). On the epidemiological model of terrorism, see Paul Stares and Monica Yacoubian, "Rethinking the War on Terror: A Counter-Epidemic Approach," paper presented at the annual meeting of the International Studies Association, San Diego, California, 25 May 2009, http://www.allacademic.com/meta/p99626_index.html.

13. Marc Sageman, "Leaderless Jihad: Radicalization in the West," presentation to the New America Foundation, 20 February 2008, www.newamerica.net. See also, for example, Marc Sageman, "The Next Generation of Terror," *Foreign Policy* (19 February 2008); and Jason Burke, "What Role Did Al Qaeda Play?" *Guardian,* 31 October 2007, http://www.guardian.co.uk/commentisfree/2007/oct/31/whatroledidalqaidaplay.

14. Bale, "Jihadist Cells and I.E.D. Capabilities," 45. Italics in original.

15. Ibid., 46.

16. Ibid., 40.

17. Ibid., 41.

18. The Casablanca attack referred to here involved twelve suicide bombers in five locations and killed a total of forty-five people including the bombers. Five suspected jihadis were arrested in connection with the attack, described as follows: "Salaheddine Benyaich alias Abou Mouhgen and Moustafa Maymouni—both arrested in Morocco; Abdelatif Mourafik alias Malek the Andalusian or Malek the North

African—arrested in Turkey; and Abdelaziz Benyaich (Abou Mouhgen's brother) and Driss Chebli, both arrested in Spain." "5 Suspects in Morocco Attacks Have Al-Qaeda Links," *Middle East Online*, 22 September 2003, http://www.middle-east-online.com/english/?id=7092.

19. *El Pais*, 22 January 2005 and 1 August 2004, quoted in "Media Analysis: Spanish Officials, Media Question Role of Rabi Uthman Al-Sayyid in Madrid Bombings," Open Source Center, FEA20050427002852—OSC Feature—1054 GMT, 29 April 2005.

20. Fernando Reinares, "Jihadist Radicalization and the 2004 Madrid Bombing Network," *CTC Sentinel* 2, no. 11 (November 2009): 16.

21. Ibid., 17.

22. Ibid.

23. Ibid., 18.

24. "Wife Details Husband's Transformation into Spanish Train Bomber," *El Pais*, 7 March 2008, in Open Source Center EUP20070309950010 (Internet Version—WWW), in Spanish, 8 March 2007.

25. See Luisa Barrenechea, "Lost in Translation," *Open Democracy*, 7 June 2007, http://www.opendemocracy.net/lost_in_translation.

26. "Wife Details Husband's Transformation."

27. Reinares, "Jihadist Radicalization," 18.

28. "Spanish Judge Links Madrid Bombings to Al-Qa'idah Global Strategy," Open Source Center, EUP20050211000348, *Madrid El Pais* (Internet Version—WWW), in Spanish, 11 February 2005.

29. Bale, "Jihadist Cells and I.E.D. Capabilities," 41.

30. Fernando Reinares, "Al Qaeda Is Back," *National Interest*, 8 January 2010.

31. Elaine Sciolino, "Complex Web of Madrid Plot Still Entangled," *New York Times*, 12 April 2004.

32. See Laila Bokhari et al., "Paths to Global Jihad: Radicalisation and Recruitment to Terror Networks," proceedings from a Norwegian Defence Research Institute (FFI) Seminar, Oslo, 15 March 2006, 17, http://rapporter.ffi.no/rapporter/2006/00935.pdf.

33. Daniel Woolls, "Alleged Madrid Bombing Cell Recruiter Says He Rejected Offer to Wage Jihad," *Associated Press Worldstream*, 20 February 2007.

34. "Car Used by Suspected Spanish Train Bomber Found in North African Enclave," Open Source Center, EUP20071010950013, *Madrid El Mundo* (Internet Version—WWW), in Spanish, 0000 GMT, 9 October 2007.

35. Sebastian Rotella, "Spain: Jihad's Unlikely Alliance" *Los Angeles Times*, 23 May 2004.

36. For more detailed information on terrorist financing, see Chapter 4.

37. See Frederic Chambon, "The Double Life of Jamal Zougam," *World*, 19 April 2004.

38. For more on the intricacies of these relationships, see "5 Suspects in Morocco Attacks." The most horrifying part of all this, of course, is how obvious the links and dangers appear in the clear light of hindsight.

39. The idea can also be traced back to Najib Chaib, who was close to Dahdah and arrested in January 2002. He reportedly had sketches of bombs similar to those used on 11 March 2004. See "Spanish Daily Charts Build-up to Madrid Bombings," Open Source Center, EUP20040421000279, *Madrid El Mundo* (Internet Version—WWW), 20 April 2004.

40. Concerns in the Spanish intelligence community about Lamari after his inadvertent release from prison are discussed in Fernando Reinares, "The Madrid Bombings and Global Jihadism," *Survival* 52, no. 2 (2010): 89.

41. Reinares, "The Madrid Bombings."

42. For a more detailed list of the defendants and their outcomes, see "Madrid Bombings: Defendants," *BBC News*, 17 July 2008, http://news.bbc.co.uk/2/hi/europe/4899544.stm.

43. All of the information and quotations in this section come from "Spanish Police Identify Financial Mastermind of Madrid Bombings," *El Pais*, 17 May 2005.

20 The Mumbai Attacks

Thomas R. Mockaitis

FROM 26 TO 29 NOVEMBER 2008, A MILITANT ISLAMIC GROUP with ties to Al Qaeda and with at least tacit support from elements of the Pakistani security forces carried out a devastating attack on the Indian port city of Mumbai. The ten-man team went on a rampage that left 173 dead and 301 wounded. Indian security forces killed nine of the terrorists; the tenth was captured and has been sentenced to death by an Indian court. The terrorists launched their well-planned and well-executed operation from the sea, demonstrating the vulnerability of ports to amphibious assault. The poorly coordinated response by the Indian security forces made a bad situation much worse and contributed unnecessarily to the loss of life. The incident thus provides an invaluable case study illustrating the importance of port security and effective emergency response.

Lashkar-e-Taiba

Lashkar-e-Taiba (LeT), "Army of the Righteous/Pure," is a Pakistan-based terrorist organization committed to liberating Indian Kashmir, a border area that it claims should be part of Pakistan. The group originally developed as the militant wing of Markaz-ud Dawa-wal-Irshad (Institute for Preaching), founded by Islamic fundamentalist Hafiz Mohammad Saeed in Lahore in the late 1980s.[1] By the early 1990s, LeT was operating on its own, but other Kashmiri separatist organizations considered it a fringe group of little importance.

During the 1990s, LeT conducted attacks against security forces in Indian Kashmir. Although its exact size is unknown, experts believe the group now has several thousand members.[2]

Although the organization has its headquarters, training camps, and safe houses in Pakistan, it has developed a global network. LeT has cells in Europe, the Persian Gulf states, and the United States. It also operates in Nepal and Bangladesh. The foreign-based cells raise funds and support operations in Kashmir and India.[3] Unlike other Kashmiri terrorist groups, LeT embraced the *fedayeen* fighter methodology of carrying out daring raids deep into India.[4] In 2000 it attacked the famous Red Fort in Old Delhi, killing three people. The Indian government has accused LeT of numerous attacks on its soil, including a December 2001 attack by gunmen on the Indian Parliament (in cooperation with another terrorist group), a 2003 bomb attack against a Hindu temple in Katra, and the 2005 multiple bombings in Delhi that killed sixty people. However, LeT has not accepted responsibility for these attacks.[5] The Indians also accused LeT of the 2006 bombing of trains in Mumbai.

Considerable evidence suggests that LeT has also operated in Afghanistan. In July 2008 a Pakistani national drove a car loaded with 100 kilograms of explosives into the Indian Mission in Kabul. The devastating blast killed fifty-four people, including four Indians. Although LeT did not claim responsibility for the attack, expert analysis suggests that the suicide bomber was an LeT operative.[6]

LeT and Pakistan

The relationship between the government of Pakistan and LeT is complex and has changed over the past decade. Pakistan has been engaged in a near-continuous struggle with neighboring India since the two states were carved out of the British Raj in 1947. They have fought three major wars and several skirmishes over the disputed territory of Kashmir. In the 1971 war, Pakistan, which originally was divided into two widely separated parts, East and West Pakistan, lost its eastern territory, which became the independent country of Bangladesh. Because the disparities of population and resources favor India, the Pakistani government and its semiautonomous security forces have made use of Islamic militants to further the country's security goals.[7] The Pakistani military has employed jihadist "proxies," terrorist groups based in Pakistan, for operations in both Afghanistan and India.[8] Proxies allow Pakistan to pursue strategic objectives while presenting some degree of plausible deniability to the United States, which supplies it with billions of dollars in military aid for the fight against terrorists. Throughout the 1990s and well into the first decade of the twenty-first century, Pakistan was at the very least a state supporter, if not a state sponsor, of terrorism.[9]

LeT has enjoyed both tacit and direct support from the government of Pakistan. In 1988 the group established a training center near Lahore with funds provided by Saudi Arabia to spread its conservative Wahhabi brand of Islam.[10] Like many such groups, LeT engaged in education and charity as well as terrorism to win local support. After Al Qaeda's attacks on 11 September 2001 against the United States, the U.S. government pressured President Pervez Musharraf to outlaw the organization. Rather than disband, however, LeT renamed itself Jamaat-Ud-Dawa (JD), which continued to operate in Pakistan.[11] In 2005 the Pakistani government further empowered JD by channeling funds to it for earthquake relief in Pakistani Kashmir, allowing the group to expand its operating space, gain further local legitimacy, and deflect criticism of its connections to terrorism.[12] The Mumbai train bombings on 11 July 2006, which injured and killed hundreds of commuters, eventually compelled the UN to designate JD a terrorist group in December 2008. In January 2009 Pakistan's Punjab provincial government took over the JD complex in Lahore and the administration of its charities. Since then, JD has changed its name yet again, to Idara Khidmat-e-Khalq. Despite JD's insistence that it is a charitable organization distinct from LeT, most analysts consider it a front organization or an arm of the terrorist group. Nonetheless, it does extensive charitable work, albeit with an ideological and political agenda, running "about 200 mainstream Dawa schools, 11 madrassas, two science colleges, mobile clinics, blood banks, and an ambulance service."[13]

However, LeT has never ceased to exist, no matter how it has sought to disguise its identity with aliases. A report published by the Combating Terrorism Center at West Point demonstrated that one year after the Mumbai attacks, LeT continued to operate more publicly than most jihadist groups in Pakistan: "In exchange for retaining a primary focus on attacking India, being relatively inactive in Pakistan and keeping a historically lower-profile in al-Qa'ida's global *jihad,* LeT has been allowed to operate more openly than other militant groups."[14] Although the Pakistani government has periodically cracked down on LeT, it has done so "as a means of controlling the group, not dismantling it."[15]

International Connections and Strategy

Although it focuses on liberating Kashmir, LeT belongs to a global network of jihadist organizations as one of the signatories of the infamous 1998 "Fatwa Against Jews and Crusaders."[16] Following the 2001 U.S. invasion of Afghanistan, LeT provided shelter and support for Al Qaeda members fleeing across the Pakistan border.[17] LeT also belongs to an association of Kashmiri separatist groups known as *askari tanzeems,* which sometimes cooperate with one another.[18] For example, in 2006 LeT worked with Jaish-e-Mohammed to attack the Indian Parliament. Besides carrying out operations in Indian Kashmir and India proper, LeT has contributed fighters to the anti-Western jihads in Afghanistan and Iraq. The group has also been willing to support operations against the West, but not to carry them out directly.[19] At least one, and perhaps two, of the men who bombed the London Underground (subway) on 7 July 2005 had been to an LeT training camp.[20] David Headley, a U.S. citizen who was arrested in Chicago for plotting attacks in Denmark, had done much of the reconnaissance work for the 2008 Mumbai attack.[21]

However much it might support the cause of global jihad, LeT remains focused on Kashmir. What its leaders fear most of all is a negotiated settlement between India and Pakistan that falls short of securing all of Kashmir for the Islamic Republic, thus removing LeT's reason for being.[22] That peace process began to develop in 2008. In February a new civilian government in Islamabad sought rapprochement with New Delhi. India and Pakistan agreed to "deepen economic relations; launch trade across the Line of Control in Kashmir after a gap of 61 years; and prepare a joint strategy against regional terrorism."[23] LeT launched the Mumbai attacks to disrupt this rapprochement and did succeed in derailing the peace process, at least temporarily.[24] The terrorist operation also revealed a deep rift in the Pakistani establishment. The new civilian government remains committed to improved relations with India, but the army and the Inter-Services Intelligence Directorate (ISI), both of which wield considerable power in policy making, are less enthusiastic about this approach.

The Operation

By all accounts and available evidence, the Mumbai attacks were carefully planned and brilliantly executed. Ten terrorists armed with automatic weapons, grenades, and improvised explosive devices held a city of 20 million hostage for over 60 hours, killing 173, wounding 301, and doing extensive economic damage before an international television audience. They revealed the ineptness of the Indian security forces and derailed the Indo–Pakistani peace process. Seldom has a single terrorist attack by so few accomplished so much.

Preparation for the Mumbai operations began twelve to eighteen months prior to the attack. The one surviving terrorist captured during the raid confessed that he and his nine comrades had been recruited in Pakistan and trained in an LeT camp, where they received intensive instruction in weapons, explosives, and assault tactics.[25] According to one source, an ISI instructor took part in the training, but this has not been confirmed.[26] The suspect said he began his reconnaissance of Mumbai in late 2007.[27] However, new evidence suggests that reconnaissance may have begun even earlier. In 2009 the FBI arrested David Coleman Headley in Chicago on charges of plotting terrorist attacks in Denmark in retaliation for cartoons printed in a Danish newspaper that satirized Islam. Subsequent investigation revealed that Headley visited Mumbai several times between 2006 and 2008 to reconnoiter targets for LeT.[28] However the terrorists obtained their information, by the time they landed, they had a thorough knowledge of the target area, carrying CDs and Blackberries with street maps and diagrams of the targeted hotels.[29] Some accounts maintain that the terrorists had a local support cell in place, but this claim remains unsubstantiated.

LeT's operational objective was to kill as many foreigners and Indian nationals as possible (the "Crusader–Zionist–Hindu Alliance") while inflicting maximum economic damage on the city and disrupting its lucrative tourism industry. Target selection reflected this objective. The central train station at rush hour would be packed with commuters, while the Taj Mahal Palace Hotel and the Trident–Oberoi Hotel, along with the trendy Leopold Café, would be filled with foreigners and well-to-do Indians. The nearby Nariman House outreach center provided Jewish victims. The hospital, cinema, gas station, and crowds along the street that came under attack were probably targets of opportunity. Near-simultaneous attacks against multiple targets served to confuse the security forces, hamper emergency response, and disguise the terrorists' numbers.

The terrorists were well armed and equipped for the operation. They each had a type-56 (Chinese manufactured) AK-47 automatic rifle with seven 30-round magazines, a 9mm pistol with two 12-round clips, and eight to ten grenades. They carried bombs made with the explosive RDX, rigged with digital timer detonators powered by 9-volt batteries.[30] Authorities found five of these devices after the attack. According to some reports, the terrorists also used Heckler and Koch MP5 machine guns, perhaps captured from the security forces. They had a global positioning system tracking device, a satellite phone, and cell phones with multiple SIM cards (to confound efforts to track them), as well as the Blackberries.[31]

From start to finish, the operation went off according to plan. The ten terrorists left the Pakistani port of Karachi in a small boat and boarded a freighter, whose captain was presumably in on the plot to some degree. Forty kilometers off the coast of India, the group captured a fishing boat, murdered four of its five crew members, and made the fifth take them to the port of Mumbai. They then beheaded him and embarked on two inflatable rafts. They landed at a fishing village in the evening of 26 November and divided into four teams, three teams of two and one team of four. This multiple-team strategy confused the authorities and made it very difficult to contain the attacks.

The first two-man team headed for the Chhatrapati Shivaji Railway station, which serves 3.5 million people a day. There, at about 9:20 P.M. local time, they opened fire with their assault rifles and lobbed grenades into the crowd, engaging in an almost unimpeded 90-minute shooting spree that left 58 dead and 104 wounded.[32] When police finally responded in number, the gunmen left the station and headed toward Cama and Albless Hospital via a footbridge over a highway. They entered the hospital firing, and killed six more people. Outside the hospital, the pair encountered a police unit as they crossed a road, and they engaged the officers in a gun battle. During this exchange, a police van carrying two officers and three senior officials, including the head of the counterterrorism unit and his chief assistant, approached. The terrorists hijacked the van, killing four of the five officers and dumping three of the bodies into the street. (The fifth officer survived and served as a witness to the events.) The pair opened fire on a cinema as they drove past. The van broke down, and they hijacked a car. They eventually encountered a roadblock. During the ensuing gun battle, the police killed one terrorist and captured the other.[33] At the end of their rampage, this two-person team alone had accounted for one-third of all the eventual casualties.[34]

As the first attack unfolded, the second two-man terrorist team headed by taxi to Nariman House, renamed Chabad House when it became an orthodox Jewish community center two years before. They lobbed grenades at a gas station across the street from the center, opened fire on the building, and then entered its lobby while continuing to fire. These two men took thirteen hostages and held them for the next two days, murdering in all eight people, including five of the hostages, before the security forces were able to kill them.[35]

The third terrorist team deployed by taxi to the twin Trident–Oberoi Hotel. They entered the Trident hotel first, firing at guests, crossed to the Oberoi, and fired into a restaurant. They then moved to the guest floors, killing people they encountered until they ended up on the sixteenth and eighteenth floors, where they took hostages.[36] The terrorists then called the local media, claiming that there were seven of them and that they would exchange their hostages for "mujahedeen" held by India.[37] This deception may have delayed efforts to retake the hotel. The siege of the Trident–Oberoi lasted forty-two hours and left thirty-three dead.[38]

The single four-man team reached the landmark Taj Mahal Palace Hotel also by taxi. Before entering the hotel, they split into two groups of two. The first pair stopped at the Leopold Café, a popular restaurant frequented by tourists, and opened fire, killing ten people. They then entered the hotel itself via its rear entrance, some 100 meters from the café, and linked up with the other two terrorists.[39] The four worked their way through the hotel methodically, moving from floor to floor, killing as they went. They set fires and kept on the move to confuse the security forces.[40] The siege ended sixty hours later, long after the other teams had been neutralized, and left thirty-one people dead.

In addition to murdering victims with grenades and automatic-weapons fire, the terrorists also set several improvised explosive devices in order to sow further confusion among security forces. Two were left in cabs the terrorists used, where they exploded. One blast killed the driver and his passenger; the other killed three pedestrians and wounded fifteen others.[41] Others were detonated at some of the targets, where the blasts also started fires.

The Indian Response

In retrospect, it is difficult to understand how so few terrorists could have done so much damage. Their success stemmed from excellent training and preparation, combined with a stunningly poor response on the part of the Indian security forces and emergency responders. Despite having suffered seven previous attacks, including the 2006 train bombings that left more than 200 dead, the Mumbai authorities still had woefully inadequate security forces and equally poor emergency-response planning. In fact, previous attacks may have led the Indian government to focus too narrowly on a single threat: truck and car bombs.[42] Mumbai, the largest city in India and its financial and cultural capital, had only 120 police per 10,000 citizens, just over half the number recommended by the UN for an urban center.[43]

In addition to being few in number, Mumbai police lacked proper training and equipment. At every venue, the terrorists outgunned the police. Some officers had only sticks. Others had essentially useless 1950s-era bolt-action .303 rifles and bulletproof vests that could not stop AK-47 rounds.[44] Adequate in dealing with ordinary crimes, the police lacked training in counterterrorism. They failed to establish a wide cordon to contain the terrorists, and many officers remained passive as events unfolded, perhaps because of being outgunned.[45] They also violated a cardinal rule of crisis response and the proven experience of companies operating around the world: Never send more than one of your top people anywhere in the same vehicle. The police antiterrorism squad leader, encounter specialist, and commissioner died when terrorists hijacked their van.

In addition to having too few and poorly trained police, the Indian authorities had failed to harden any of the targets attacked by LeT. The central railway station illustrates this weakness. Following the 2006 train bombings, the Mumbai authorities did install some metal detectors at the station. However, eyewitness accounts revealed that security guards enforced screening very laxly.[46] As a result, the two terrorists, festooned with bombs and automatic weapons, easily got into the station, where they went on a ninety-minute rampage largely unopposed. All of the other targets had equally weak security, with the same tragic results.

Police and other units were remarkably slow to respond to the attacks. Although the terrorists entered the Taj Mahal Hotel at 11:00 P.M. on November 26 and immediately began setting fires, firefighters did not arrive until 3:00 the next morning. They evacuated guests but, because of the security situation, could not completely put out all fires until November 28. Furthermore, even though it was clear from the outset that the terrorists had explosives, a bomb squad did not arrive at the hotel until 5:00 A.M. on November 27. Comparable delays also occurred at the Oberoi–Trident Hotel and Nariman House.

The delay in deploying Special Forces units to Mumbai was particularly egregious. Local marine commandos arrived on the scene fairly promptly, but they lacked the training and equipment to deal with the terrorists and were withdrawn. India has an elite counterterrorism unit, the National Security Guard (also known as the "Black Cat Commandos"), modeled on the British Special Air Service, which is stationed south of Delhi. But because they had no dedicated aircraft, the 200 commandos had to wait until a plane could be found to transport them to Mumbai, which means they did not arrive in the city until 8:50 A.M. on November 27, ten hours after the attacks had begun.[47] Once they had deployed, the NSG were hampered by lack of equipment and poor intelligence regarding the terrorists' numbers, intentions, and precise whereabouts. Inexplicably, they had no diagrams of the Taj Mahal Palace Hotel. They also lacked stun grenades, gas masks, and night-vision goggles.

The Mumbai police compounded these problems. In the van attack carried out by the first terrorist team, which struck the train station and the hospital, the police lost three vital officers.[48] This fortuitous decapitation strike contributed to the lack of organization that plagued the crisis response throughout the three days of the attack. Even without the loss of three top officials, however, the emergency responders would have been hampered by the lack of a coordinated response system.[49] Israeli security experts who have worked with them have commented on the need for a change in the "basic mindset" of the Indian security forces.[50]

Effective emergency response requires not only good special weapons and tactics but also good information management. Here too the Indians proved wanting. Reporters wandered the streets freely, broadcasting as they went and presenting the impression of widespread chaos in Mumbai to the world. The Indian government aided the terrorists by providing details on NSG deployment to reporters, which the terrorists also received and acted upon.[51] Given that terrorists rely on the media to give them a platform and get their message out, managing information flow in a crisis is crucial.

Maritime Security

Crisis-management failures notwithstanding, the terrorist attacks on Mumbai need not have occurred at all. Better maritime-domain awareness could have prevented the terrorists from deploying, or at least resulted in their neutralization upon landing. India divides responsibility for maritime security among three entities: its deep-water navy, the coast guard, and state police maritime units. Poor coordination among these entities hampers their effectiveness. The navy understands its role as war fighting and has little or no counterterrorism capability. The coast guard and state maritime units lack the resources to patrol India's territorial waters.[52] At the time of the Mumbai attack, fewer than a hundred boats were expected to cover 5,000 miles of coast.[53]

Intelligence Failure

Behind most terrorist attacks lies an intelligence failure; Mumbai was no exception. Despite receiving credible intelligence from the United States of an imminent attack on the city, the security forces were still caught by surprise.[54] In addition to information from the Americans, the Indians had intelligence of their own pointing to an imminent attack. In May and September 2008, two different agencies issued reports that LeT was planning a major operation. One week before the attack, Indian intelligence intercepted a phone call indicating that a ship carrying terrorists had left Karachi and was in position fifty miles south of Mumbai.[55] No one assembled these discrete bits of information into a coherent picture and passed it on to maritime- and land-security forces.

A New Terrorist Threat

The apparent novelty of the terrorists' tactics and their stunning success have prompted considerable discussion of the implications of the Mumbai operation for the global struggle against terrorism. Neither an assault from the sea nor an urban commando raid was new to terrorism. The Liberation Tigers of Tamil and Elam deployed terrorists by sea during their long struggle against the government of Sri Lanka. Near-simultaneous attacks by commando teams had also occurred before. On 27 December 1985, two terrorist teams from the Abu Nidal Organization carried out such attacks on the Rome and Vienna airports using assault rifles and grenades. The attacks left 19 civilians dead (along with the 4 terrorists) and 138 wounded. These earlier precedents notwithstanding, however, never before the 2008 Mumbai operation had a terrorist organization so effectively combined a maritime assault with urban-commando tactics.

The effectiveness of the Mumbai attack has raised the question of whether the event was an isolated incident or a harbinger of things to come.

Modern cities are target-rich environments, especially for terrorist groups with no regard for innocent life. Most states harden high-profile targets such as government buildings, museums, and financial centers. Hotels, restaurants, and retail establishments are simply too numerous and, by function, too open to protect. Mass transit, used by millions of people each day, presents special security problems, as do large public gatherings such as sporting events and concerts. Despite years of experience with the IRA and perhaps the densest network of cameras in any urban environment, Britain could not prevent the London Underground attacks of 7 July 2005. Two weeks later, another team of terrorists deployed additional bombs on the same transit system. Only the failure of the charges to detonate saved London from a second tragedy. The vulnerability of cities, the hardening of other targets, and Al Qaeda's fatwa to kill any and all Americans whenever and wherever possible all point to the likelihood of future Mumbai-style attacks. Terrorists have proven themselves innovative and adaptable, often more so than the states they fight.

In addition to a new operational/tactical approach, Mumbai revealed another disturbing terrorist trend. There is a growing synergy between locally focused terrorist groups and global terrorist networks. Although LeT still concentrates on Kashmir, it has shown a willingness to receive aid from and provide assistance to other groups outside its immediate areas of operation. It has expanded its list of enemies from India to the amorphous alliance of "Hindus, Jews, and Crusaders." Target selection during the Mumbai attacks reflected this agenda. While striking India's financial center, the jihadis also aimed to kill as many Westerners as possible, targeting the Jewish center along with prominent Indian targets.

Lessons

The Mumbai attack illustrates virtually all the lessons identified in this volume. The initial intelligence failure resulted from a larger problem endemic to modern bureaucratic states: lack of interagency cooperation. The attacks went forward thanks to an inability to "connect the dots," to form a comprehensive picture from information provided by different intelligence agencies.[56] Most bureaucratic agencies find working together difficult, but intelligence organizations, for which information is power, are particularly reluctant to cooperate.

The truism that good consequence management can snatch victory from the jaws of defeat, while poor consequence management makes a bad situation worse, was amply borne out by the Indian response to the Mumbai attacks. The security forces and emergency responders made virtually every possible mistake that can be made during a crisis. Despite numerous previous terrorist attacks on the city, the police were poorly prepared. Many lacked guns altogether, and others had obsolete weapons. They might have overcome this disadvantage with sheer numbers had they had better tactical training. However, all accounts agree that the police were reluctant to engage the heavily armed terrorists. Inadequate planning and equipment also hampered the national-level responders. India's elite NSG arrived without basic night-vision equipment, which impeded their ability to secure the Taj Mahal Palace Hotel.

As much as good equipment helps, it nevertheless is no substitute for organization and planning. Local police lacked an incident-command system to organize and clarify responsibilities. No one seemed to be in charge of the response, which was uncoordinated and chaotic throughout the attacks. Police cordoned individual sites, but not the entire affected area. Reporters were free to roam and film whatever they saw, conveying an impression of confusion to the world and, in so doing, helping the terrorists spread their message of official helplessness and fear. Worse, officials gave reporters information on their tactical movements, which were duly reported in the mass media and thus directly to the terrorists themselves, who did not hesitate to take advantage.[57]

In contrast with this picture, British authorities during the 2005 London bombings always conveyed an impression of calm and control. Although they made mistakes, their successes more than compensated. The London police secured the affected area rapidly. Knowing they could see little on the streets, reporters went to the police briefing center, where they received a steady but controlled and appropriate flow of information. The Special Air Service rapidly deployed units to London in case they were needed (which fortunately they were not), but the chief constable of the London Metropolitan Police remained in charge throughout. Whereas Mumbai presented itself as paralyzed by the terrorists, London proudly proclaimed that it was "open for business."

The aftermath of the Mumbai attacks witnessed several key developments. The Indian government presented the government of Pakistan with a dossier on the incident that documented that the attacks originated in Pakistan, and demanded action against LeT. Pakistan demurred but eventually made some arrests. Neither country wished the crisis to escalate, but the attacks derailed the peace process, at least temporarily, just as the terrorists had hoped.

India gained a wealth of information from the one terrorist it captured. After being thoroughly interrogated, twenty-two-year-old Ajmal Amir Kasab was tried and condemned to death.[58] He currently awaits execution. The bodies of the nine terrorists killed in the attack lay in the Mumbai morgue for over a year. Muslim authorities refused to bury them, maintaining that those who carry out such heinous acts are not true Muslims worthy of a religious burial.[59] The decision of India's Muslim community to make such a dramatic statement rejecting terrorism may be the one bright spot in the dismal case of Mumbai.

Notes

1. According to reports, the group changed its name to Jamaat-Ud-Dawa, allegedly as a means to get around sanctions imposed on it by the international community. See Victor Comras, "Pakistan Charity Jamaat-Ud-Dawa Added to Global Terrorist List, But Not Its Leaders," Global Terrorism Blog, 30 April 2006, http://counterterrorismblog.org/2006/04/pakistan_charity_jamaatuddawa.php.

2. "Lashkar-e-Tayyiba," *Global Security,* 12 March 2008, http://www.globalsecurity.org/military/world/para/lt.htm.

3. Information on the LeT global network comes from Bruce Riedel, "The Mumbai Massacre and Its Implications for America and South Asia," *Journal of International Affairs* 63, no. 1 (Fall/Winter 2009): 118.

4. "Profile: Lashkar-e-Taiba," *BBC News,* 3 May 2010, http://news.bbc.co.uk/2/hi/3181925.stm.

5. Ibid.

6. "Lashkar-e-Taiba."

7. Jacob N. Shapiro and C. Christine Fair, "Understanding Support for Islamist Militancy in Pakistan," *International Security* 34, no. 3 (Winter 2009/2010): 79.

8. "Pakistan: The Militant Jihadi Challenge," Asia Report no. 164, International Crisis Group, Washington, D.C., 13 March 2009, i.

9. A state supporter of terrorism does not typically plan and render operational assistance to terrorists, but limits its support to providing resources. These can be vital, including financing, equipment, moral and rhetorical support, and sanctuary. "State sponsorship" can also take the form of toleration, where governments do not oppose terrorist organizations in exchange for immunity from their attacks, and state inaction, where weak governments are simply unable to do anything against terrorists operating from their ungoverned space.

10. "Pakistan: The Militant Jihadi Challenge," 8.

11. Ibid.

12. Ibid.

13. Arabinda Acharya, "Terrorist Attacks in Mumbai: Picking up the Pieces," International Centre for Political Violence and Terrorism Research, Singapore, 2009, 16.

14. Stephen Tankel, "Lashkar-i-Tayyiba: One Year After Mumbai," *CTC Sentinel* 2, no. 11 (November 2009): 3.

15. Ibid., 4.

16. "Pakistan: The Militant Jihadi Challenge," 8. See also Shaykh Usamah Bin-Muhammad Bin-Ladin, Ayman al-Zawahiri, Abu-Yasir Rifa'i Ahmad Taha, Shaykh Mir Hamzah, and Fazlur Rahman, "Jihad Against Jews and Crusaders: World Islamic Front Statement," 23 February 1998, an English translation of which is available at the Federation of American Scientists Web site: http://www.fas.org/irp/world/para/docs/980223-fatwa.htm.

17. Riedel, "The Mumbai Massacre and Its Implications," 118.

18. Shapiro and Fair, "Understanding Support for Islamic Militancy in Pakistan," 88.

19. Tankel, "Lashkar-i-Tayyiba: One Year After Mumbai," 5.

20. Riedel, "The Mumbai Massacre and Its Implications," 118–19.

21. Ibid., 5.

22. Ibid., 1.

23. "Pakistan: The Militant Jihadi Challenge," 1.

24. Ibid., 1.

25. Riedel, "The Mumbai Massacre and Its Implications," 112.

26. "Mumbai Attack Analysis," New York Police Department Intelligence Division, New York, 2008, 6. India's home secretary, G. K. Pillai, recently announced that ISI's involvement in the attacks "was not just a peripheral role." Krittivas Mukherjee, "Pakistan ISI Behind Mumbai Attacks: India Official," Reuters, 14 July 2010, http://www.reuters.com/article/idUSTRE66D11720100714. The information came from convicted LeT operative David Headley, who told investigators that "the ISI was engaged" closely with the LeT leaders who planned the attack. R. Vasudevan, "David Headley Says Lashkar Was Guided by ISI for Mumbai Attack," *Asian Tribune*, 11 June 2010.

27. Angel Rabasa, Robert D. Blackwill, Peter Chalk, Kim Cragin, C. Christine Fair, Brian A. Jackson, Brian Michael Jenkins, Seth G. Jones, Nathaniel Shestak, and Ashley J. Tellis, "The Lessons of Mumbai," Occasional Paper 249, RAND Corporation, Santa Monica, California, 2009, 13.

28. Bobby Ghosh, "The Chicago Suspect: Are Pakistani Jihadis Going Global?" *Time*, 8 December 2009, http://www.time.com/time/nation/article/0,8599,1946118,00.html.

29. Rabasa et al., "Lessons of Mumbai," 13.

30. Ibid., 14.

31. "Mumbai Case Dossier: Evidence 1," presented to Pakistan, 5 January 2009, scanned English version available from *The Hindu* (online edition), 3, http://www.hindu.com/nic/dossier.htm.

32. Closed-circuit footage shows two Indian constables with one carbine between them trying to keep the gunmen from advancing from the train platform into the

main part of the station. See "CCTV from Night of Mumbai Attacks," *BBC News*, 2 December 2008: http://news.bbc.co.uk/2/hi/south_asia/7760690.stm.

33. The preceding account of the first teams is based on "Mumbai Case Dossier," 5–6; Rabasa et al., "Lessons of Mumbai," 14–15; "Mumbai Attack Analysis," 25–30; and Acharya, "Terrorist Attacks in Mumbai," 14–16. The accounts differ on some details. The dossier has the van being hijacked following a gun battle on the road and makes no mention of shootings at either the hospital or the cinema.

34. Rabasa et al., "Lessons of Mumbai," 15.

35. Ibid., 15–16.

36. "Mumbai Case Dossier," 8.

37. Rabasa et al., "Lessons of Mumbai," 16.

38. "Mumbai Case Dossier," 8.

39. Because the terrorists split up and entered the hotel in this way, some accounts refer to five teams of two terrorists each, instead of three teams of two and one of four. Acharya, "Terrorist Attacks in Mumbai," 16. "Mumbai Case Dossier" also refers to five teams.

40. Rabasa et al., "Lessons of Mumbai," 16.

41. Acharya, "Terrorist Attacks in Mumbai," 20.

42. Ibid., 37.

43. Acharya, "Terrorist Attacks in Mumbai," 31.

44. Rabasa et al., "Lessons of Mumbai," 20.

45. Ibid., 20.

46. Ibid., 32.

47. Ibid., 10.

48. "Mumbai Attack Analysis," 29.

49. Acharya, "Terrorist Attacks in Mumbai," 32.

50. Ibid., 32.

51. Rabasa et al., "Lessons of Mumbai," 8.

52. The preceding discussion of Indian maritime-security issues is based on Premvir Das, "New Naval Concerns for India," *U.S. Naval Institute Proceedings* 136, no. 3 (March 2010): 60–65.

53. Rabasa et al., "Lessons of Mumbai," 9.

54. Acharya, "Terrorist Attacks in Mumbai," 31.

55. Das, "New Naval Concerns for India," 60–65.

56. Ibid., 60–65.

57. Rabasa et al., "Lessons of Mumbai," 11.

58. Rama Lakshmi, "India Gives Death Penalty to Gunman in Mumbai Terrorist Attack," *Washington Post*, 6 May 2010.

59. "A Year Later Muslims Refuse to Bury Terrorists' Bodies," *National Catholic Reporter*, 11 December 2009, 4.

21 The Irish Republican Army

Thomas R. Mockaitis

CASE STUDIES ARE VALUABLE TOOLS FOR UNDERSTANDING terrorism. They put flesh on the bones of theory, allowing students and researchers to examine how principles have been applied, misapplied, and adapted to actual, dynamic situations. Like most tools, case studies can also be misused, with disastrous results. Academics and practitioners will sometimes fixate on a successful example, turning it into a template and then applying it slavishly to future campaigns. The strategic-hamlet program used in the Vietnam War illustrates this point. Encouraged by the example of the Malayan Emergency (1948–c. 1960), U.S. forces relocated South Vietnamese from their villages to protected compounds. They failed to consider that the Malayan Chinese squatters had no attachment to the land from which they were removed, while the Vietnamese peasants bitterly resented removal from their ancestral villages.[1] Thus, the result was the opposite of the intent. However, properly analyzed case studies may yield broad lessons applicable to future conflicts.

Northern Ireland provides a particularly poignant example. The conflict known colloquially as "the Troubles," which raged for thirty-eight years, involved an armed insurgency, terrorism, and organized criminal activity. During its counterinsurgency campaign, the British government made every mistake a threatened state can make until it developed a winning strategy, based on half a century of experience in colonial wars adapted to new circumstances.

Background: The Roots of the Troubles

The conflict that broke out in the summer of 1969 had its roots in the division of Ireland in 1923. The treaty ending the Anglo–Irish War (1919–1921) gave the twenty-six counties of the South independence as the Irish Free State. "Northern Ireland," consisting of six counties of the historic province of Ulster, remained part of the United Kingdom. Partition protected the Protestant majority of the North from inclusion in a Catholic state, but it trapped a large number of Catholics in a Protestant-dominated province, where institutionalized discrimination relegated them to the status of a permanent underclass. By 1966, Londonderry had a population of 20,102 Catholics and 10,724 Protestants, but because of gerrymandering the city had twelve Protestant and eight Catholic councilors.[2] The same disparity existed in public services. Between 1945 and 1967, Protestants received 82 percent of the 1,048 council (publicly funded) houses in County Fermangh, considerably more than their share based on demographics.[3] In 1971, Catholic male unemployment exceeded that of Protestants by 2.62 to 1.[4] Catholics also remained seriously underrepresented in the skilled trades, the professions, and the civil service.

To enforce Protestant domination, the Northern Ireland Parliament passed the Civil Authorities (Special Powers) Act in 1922. The act granted the police extraordinary powers of arrest, detention without trial, and other draconian measures normally reserved for a state of emergency. The Constabulary Act passed the same year transformed the old Royal Irish Constabulary into the Royal Ulster Constabulary (RUC) and created three new reserve units. Of these units, the B-Specials, created specifically to deal with Irish Republican Army incursions in rural areas, would become infamous for their excesses during the riots in 1969.[5]

In 1949 the Free State refashioned itself as the Republic of Eire with a constitution committing the nation to incorporation of the North. However, neither the Republic nor an insurgency had the means to unite the island by force. What precipitated the crisis of 1969 thus was not nationalism but official, systematic discrimination.

The Catholic Response

For forty years, resistance came not from Northern Ireland's oppressed Catholic minority but from across the border. The newly independent country of Ireland never accepted the legitimacy of partition but could do nothing about it. However, one group did pursue the goal of a united Ireland. The Irish Republican Army (IRA) had waged a successful insurgency against the British during the 1919–1921 Anglo–Irish War. Following that conflict, the newly independent Irish Free State suppressed the IRA, which did not accept the peace terms offered by London. The clandestine organization remained underground, and it revived enough in the 1950s to conduct cross-border raids into Northern Ireland. The British Army in cooperation with the B-Specials easily suppressed the campaign, and the IRA became largely moribund in the 1960s.

Northern Irish Catholics then took up their own cause. Inspired by the civil rights movement in the United States, Bernadette Devlin and other university students formed the Northern Ireland Civil Rights Association to protest institutionalized discrimination. During the spring and summer of 1969 their nonviolent demonstrations often faced attacks from angry Protestants. Violence escalated during the Protestant "marching season," public commemorations of various battles from the age of religious wars. Members of Protestant Orange lodges tossed pennies from the walls of Derry into the Catholic neighborhood (a traditional gesture of contempt) and received rocks and bottles in return.[6] Rioting ensued, and the RUC mobilized the B-Specials, who made things worse. Trained for operations in rural areas and unaccustomed to urban riots, they fired indiscriminately at crowds. As the situation deteriorated, the Northern Ireland government called in the British Army. Asked by a representative of the cabinet whether he could deploy two battalions to the province, a general in the Ministry of Defense replied, "Yes, but you'll never get them out."[7] His observation proved prophetic: It would take almost forty years before British troops could be withdrawn from Northern Ireland.

The Troubles

The Troubles, which spanned almost a quarter of a century, may be divided roughly into three phases. The first phase, from 1969 to 1972, saw the British Army drawn into an escalating conflict that it little understood and for which it was ill-prepared. Standing to the fore as the police were rebuilt and the newly commissioned Ulster Defense Regiment raised and trained, the army labored under divided political control from the Northern Ireland government in Stormont and the British government in Westminster. This period witnessed the application of repressive measures against Catholic protestors, such as internment, which proved both ineffective and politically unacceptable. However, the army also learned valuable lessons and began to apply them to the campaign. During the second phase, from 1972 to 1990, the security forces settled into a long counterinsurgency campaign and by 1990 had fought the insurgents to a standstill, encouraging them to negotiate. This stalemate, along with waning Catholic support for the war, led to the third phase, during which both sides moved towards a negotiated settlement of the conflict. Negotiations produced the 1994 ceasefire, the 1998 Good Friday Accords, the 2005 decommissioning of weapons, and the creation in 2007 of a power-sharing government.

Phase 1: Escalating Violence

The beleaguered Catholics initially welcomed the British troops, who stopped the hated B-Specials from brutalizing them. Cheers went up as the soldiers marched into Derry, causing Republican leader Bernadette Devlin to yell, "Don't make them welcome. They have not come here to help us."[8] Despite her admonition, Catholics often served refreshments to the soldiers. "We could have drowned in tea," one officer observed.[9] The Hunt Report, commissioned by the British Parliament in 1969, recommended disbanding the B-Specials and disarming the RUC as a first step in de-escalation.[10] The report predictably produced a violent reaction among Unionists, which led to the shooting of Constable Arbuckle by a Protestant during a protest march in Belfast; Arbuckle was the first member of the RUC to die in the conflict. The King's Own Yorkshire Light Infantry then entered the Protestant Shankill neighborhood of Belfast and forcibly suppressed the riots.

At this point, nationalism played little role in what was still a civil rights movement. "What we must at all times make clear," wrote Devlin in 1969, "is that we are fighting for the economic rights of an underprivileged people, not to win back the Six Counties for Ireland."[11] By the end of the year, violence had temporarily subsided, and a more enlightened policy might have kept it from recurring. The 6,000 soldiers sent into Ulster by September had proven themselves willing to face down Protestant as well as Catholic crowds. The hated B-Specials were to be disbanded, and civil rights legislation was in the offing, while the new Ulster Defense Regiment showed signs of becoming a truly nonsectarian force.[12] However, a series of major mistakes prevented the security forces from ending the conflict. To begin with, they failed to establish a strong presence in Catholic areas. Realizing that the RUC had victimized the Catholics, the British government instructed the troops to stay out of Catholic neighborhoods, which came to be called "no-go" areas, thus essentially ceding control of them to Irish Republican militants.

It was in this period that the nationalists displaced the civil rights movement in Catholic neighborhoods. The traditional IRA had eschewed violence, so a splinter group calling itself the "Provisional" IRA (PIRA) took up the cause in December 1969, claiming—with some truth—that it alone could protect Catholics from Protestants. PIRA increased its membership from 100 in January 1970 to 800 by December and now felt confident enough to take the offensive against the army and the RUC with sniping and bomb attacks.[13]

Unfortunately, the government in Stormont and the security forces played into the hands of the insurgents. Civil rights legislation addressing most of the demands of 1969 offered too little too late. Disbanding the B-Specials and disarming the RUC did not appease the Catholics, but it did hurt military–police cooperation. The government also failed to restrict Protestant demonstrations and marches, thereby managing to alienate both communities. As a result, it faced riots in Belfast and Londonderry, and suffered attacks from both PIRA and Protestant paramilitaries such as the Ulster Volunteer Force (UVF).

British security operations further exacerbated the situation. In July 1970 the army imposed a tight curfew and conducted extensive house searches, after saturating the area with CS gas, in the largely Catholic and nationalist Lower Falls Road area of Belfast. The sweep produced "52 pistols, 35 rifles, 6 automatic weapons, 14 shotguns, 100 home-made bombs, a grenade, 250 lbs. of explosives, some 21,000 rounds of ammunition and 8 two-way radio sets." Five people were killed, 75 injured, and more than 300 detained.[14] For this very small return in seized contraband, the operation "changed a sullen Catholic population into a downright hostile one."[15] "It can be argued," one army officer observed, "that the failure to ban the 1970 Orange parades, and the massive arms searches and curfew in the Lower Falls area which followed, was the last chance to avoid the catastrophe that has since engulfed Ulster."[16] The PIRA gained thousands of supporters among previously uncommitted Catholics.

Dusting off a tactic used in their colonial campaigns, in the following year the security forces incarcerated large numbers of suspects without trial, often in very harsh conditions, a move virtually guaranteed to further alienate Catholics. Operating frequently on outdated and inaccurate RUC information, they arrested many innocent people along with a few guilty ones.[17] Detention centers thus became insurgent recruiting grounds as committed nationalists radicalized fellow detainees. The soldiers themselves saw, and felt, the deleterious effects of the operation. "Breaking into a bedroom in the middle of the night to see a child sit up in fright and scream for his mummy makes it hard to sustain one's morale and the morale of one's troop, no matter what the child's father may have done," concluded one Royal Marine officer.[18] Sweeping arrests also led to an upsurge in PIRA violence.

This internment policy lasted until 1975 and produced widespread allegations of prisoner abuse. The Compton Commission, which was created to investigate these allegations, concluded that in apprehending detainees the security forces generally exercised "commendable restraint and discipline" under difficult circumstances. However, it also raised serious concerns about interrogation "in depth," a process learned from the Chinese during the Korean War. "We consider," the Commission concluded, "that the following actions constitute physical ill treatment: posture on the wall, hooding, noise, deprivation of sleep, diet of bread and water."[19] In some instances interrogators forced detainees to stand with their hands against a wall for four to six hours at a time and flooded their cells with piercing noise. There were widespread allegations as well of strippings and beatings by guards and interrogators.[20]

Despite the warnings of the Compton Report, interrogation-in-depth nevertheless continued, as did the controversy surrounding it. A new commission reexamined these methods in 1972. Although the majority found them acceptable, Lord Gardiner, commission member and former High Chancellor of England, submitted a minority report noting their deleterious effect on prisoners and also noting that "the society which employed them was morally on a slippery slope. . . ."[21] Gardiner concluded with an indictment of those who had implemented the practice:

> The blame . . . must lie with those who, many years ago, decided that in emergency conditions in Colonial-type situations we should abandon our legal well-tried and highly successful wartime interrogation methods and replace them by procedures which were secret, illegal, not morally justifiable and alien to the tradition of what I still believe to be the greatest democracy in the world.[22]

Prime Minister Edward Heath wisely accepted the minority report, ending interrogation in depth. If there was more damage to be done, however, the ugly episode further hurt relations between the government and the Catholic community. By 1971, optimistic estimates for the duration of the conflict were four years; pessimistic ones were ten to fifteen years.[23]

If arms searches, internment, and interrogation-in-depth were not enough, the events of 30 January 1972 cemented the enmity of the Irish Catholic population against the British government. On what became infamous as "Bloody Sunday," members of the security forces shot dead thirteen Catholic demonstrators during a civil rights march in Londonderry. The Widgery Tribunal, convened to investigate the matter, generally exonerated the troops but noted that "at one end of the scale some soldiers showed a high degree of responsibility; at the other . . . firing bordered on the reckless."[24] In 1998 the British government opened yet a new inquiry, the Saville Commission, which spent the ensuing twelve years reexamining the incident. It submitted its findings to the government in March 2010, and they were finally made public in June of that year. The army, declared the report, fired the first shots and was unequivocally to blame for what were termed unjustifiable killings.[25]

Bloody Sunday began the deadliest year of the Troubles. In 1972, 322 civilians and 146 police and soldiers died in the fighting. On 21 July of that year, "Bloody Friday," the PIRA detonated more than a dozen bombs (estimates range from 15 to 22) across Belfast, killing 9 and injuring 130. While the insurgents inflicted many casualties on the security forces, the insurgents suffered 95 killed, more than in any other year of the Troubles. Operating in traditional "brigade formations," they could not match the army's strength or training, and, in the words of one junior officer, "Their security was worthless."[26] At this point, the British settled down for a long conflict.

Phase 2: An Acceptable Level of Violence

In 1971 Home Secretary Reginald Maudling had landed in Belfast and declared the security forces were "achieving an acceptable level of violence."[27] In addition to inflicting casualties on the PIRA, the security forces made significant changes in the organization of the campaign. On 24 March 1971 the British government, finally recognizing that the Protestant-dominated provincial government had systematically oppressed the Catholic minority, took over full control of security and created the Northern Ireland Office. Among other effects, this decision made the British Army the major target of insurgent violence. When the government at Stormont resigned in protest at London's decision, Heath eliminated Northern Ireland's autonomy altogether and imposed "direct rule."[28]

The security forces also eliminated the no-go areas. On 31 July 1972 operation "Motorman" removed the barricades surrounding the Catholic neighborhoods in Londonderry and Belfast. Army strength in the province peaked at almost 22,000, the highest level it was to reach during the campaign. A new intelligence-gathering effort accompanied Motorman: "The army carried out a virtual door-to-door census and compiled detailed data on every household, right down to the number of bottles of milk they received each morning." The data could then be compiled with the aid of computers.[29] This "Doomsday Book" allowed the security forces to keep track of activity within troubled areas. They also installed a computer system to track automobiles traveling from the border to Belfast or Londonderry.

At the same time, the army further improved its counterinsurgency tactics. Four-man patrols, called "bricks," replaced platoon and company sweeps. These bricks traversed an area in systematic grid fashion, updating information on households, setting up vehicle checkpoints, and occasionally rousting out an insurgent. Long-term surveillance by small stakeout units, placed in hiding for days at a time, further restricted PIRA activity.[30]

The British also improved military–police cooperation. Operations in Northern Ireland were coordinated by a series of security committees. A Security Coordinator in the Northern Ireland Office oversaw the committees and directed the intelligence-gathering effort. A Security Policy Meeting attended by the Permanent Under Secretary for Northern Ireland, the RUC Chief Constable, and the General Officer Commanding, Northern Ireland, met once a month to provide strategic oversight of the campaign, assisted by two other province-wide committees, the Security Coordinating Meeting (SCM) and the Operations Coordinating Group. The SCM consisted of the Assistant Under Secretary for Northern Ireland, the Head of the Law and Order Division, the Deputy Chief Constable, the Commander of the Land Forces, and the Chief of Staff, Headquarters Northern Ireland. The Operations Coordinating Group included the Deputy Chief Constable, the Commander of the Land Forces, the Chief of Staff, and various senior staff officers. Both groups met monthly. Beneath these Provincial Committees were the Regional, Divisional, and Sub-divisional Action Committees, joint RUC/army bodies attended by the senior military, RUC, and Special Branch officers, which met biweekly or weekly.

A primary purpose of any such committee system is the gathering and dissemination of intelligence in a timely manner. In Northern Ireland the system worked well at the higher levels but less so at lower levels. Difficulties in collecting and disseminating information, historical distrust, and misconceptions concerning the nature of the campaign and their respective roles in it hampered cooperation. Army patrols gathered information for their unit intelligence cells, which entered it into computers and made it widely available on a need-to-know basis. By contrast, the RUC collated intelligence by hand at each station, slowing the process of dissemination. Special Branch (the unit tasked with investigating politically motivated crime) also collected information but passed it along to its own regional headquarters for use by Tasking and Coordinating groups responsible for covert operations. Only in 1990 were Special Branch, RUC, and military jurisdictional boundaries made to conform.

The British also reformed the legal framework for combating insurgency. The first adjustment to Northern Ireland's security legislation came in 1973 on the recommendation of the Diplock Commission. The 1973 Emergency Powers Act gave soldiers the right to make arrests, and it created special "Diplock Courts" in which offenses could be tried before a magistrate instead of a jury subject to sectarian loyalties or intimidation.[31] It also empowered the army to conduct searches of individuals, vehicles, and premises; detain suspects for up to four hours; establish vehicle checkpoints; and disperse crowds. The act provided for the careful documentation of arrests and reasonable safeguards for suspects. The subsequent Prevention of Terrorism Act (1984), applicable to the whole of the United Kingdom, allowed initial detention of suspects for forty-eight hours and for an additional five days by order of the Secretary of State. The Northern Ireland (Emergency Provisions) Acts of 1978 and 1987 augmented the 1973 measure. These acts empowered soldiers to arrest suspects and detain them for up to four hours without warrant, and to search premises, vehicles, and persons. The Northern Ireland (Emergency Provisions) Act of 1991 renewed the regulations of the earlier statutes but required "reasonable suspicion" for security personnel to search, detain, and arrest. The acts also proscribed most of the Catholic and Protestant paramilitaries and made it an offense to conduct military training, wear disguises in public, or collect information on the security forces. The Criminal Evidence (Northern Ireland) Order of 1988 abridged freedom from self-incrimination by stipulating that refusal to answer questions could be held against suspects in terrorism cases.

However, the insurgents proved equally as good at adaptation as the government. In 1977 PIRA's leaders reorganized on the hub-and-spoke model. They grouped operatives into units of four or five that were constituted for a specific mission and disbanded afterwards. Because each member knew only those in his or her cell and one point of contact to the hub, he or she would compromise few others if captured. An upper echelon of commanders (chief of staff, quartermaster, etc.) and a seven-member army council provided strategic direction but "remarkably little overt command and control of operations, of the selection of targets, of the daily course of the armed struggle."[32]

Insurgent tactics also changed. PIRA continued to attack members of the security forces and the Protestant community in Northern Ireland, but it also began bombing on the British mainland and assassinating off-duty soldiers stationed in Germany. The first attack on the British mainland occurred in Birmingham in 1974 and was followed by a full-scale bombing campaign in 1981. The insurgents intended to bring the war home to average Britons and thus encourage them to pressure their government to withdraw from Northern Ireland. In addition, as the security forces tightened control of the province, "soft targets" became increasingly hard to find in Ulster.[33] Bombings in Britain had the added advantage of attracting international attention, although this did not always favor the insurgents. Attacks included the bombing of a Birmingham pub that killed nineteen in 1974; twin bombings of the Royal Green Jackets band and the Horse Guards in Hyde Park in 1982; bombing of Harrods department store in 1983; bombing of the Grand Hotel, Brighton, which killed five people and narrowly missed Prime Minister Margaret Thatcher in 1984; bombing of a Warrington shopping mall that killed two children in early 1993; and two bombings in London's financial district in 1993.

A renewed cross-border campaign accompanied the rise in urban terrorism. The mid-1970s witnessed a dramatic increase in rural violence, particularly in South Armagh, a Northern Ireland cul-de-sac jutting into the Irish Republic. In addition to smuggling arms into the north, the insurgents sniped at British security forces from the safety of the Republic, planted bombs that could be detonated from across the border, and sent units across for hit-and-run operations. The 123-mile frontier could not be sealed, for political as well as practical reasons, even with cooperation from the Republic of Eire's army and its police force, the Gardai. In 1975 alone, Irish security forces conducted 800 patrols, set 5,500 checkpoints, responded to 44 bomb-disposal calls, and conducted 64 searches—all for a yield of 24 rockets and 3 rocket launchers.[34]

Phase two of the conflict also saw increased violence among insurgent groups. PIRA and the Protestant Ulster Volunteer Force murdered members of each other's communities in what came to be called the "tit-for-tat" war. In July 1977 PIRA feuded with the official IRA, and in 1987 the Irish National Liberation Army, a smaller Republican insurgent group, destroyed itself in a bloody internal feud.[35] These struggles accomplished nothing but added to the rising death toll.

Efforts to reduce the role of the army and hand more responsibility to the police met with limited success. The classified 1976 report "The Way Ahead" called for greater RUC participation in the fight against terrorism and a higher profile for the Ulster Defense Regiment (UDR) (since renamed the Royal Irish Regiment).[36] Because Protestants dominated both units, however, the regiment enjoyed little credibility among Catholics and sometimes failed to act impartially. By 1993, only 3 percent of the UDR's 6,000 members were Roman Catholic.[37] Catholics made up approximately 11 percent of the RUC throughout the crisis.[38] Between 1985 and 1989, twenty-nine members of the UDR were convicted of crimes related to the insurgency as compared to six members of the RUC and eight British soldiers from other units.[39] The government received 4,663 complaints of wrongdoing by the RUC in 1992 alone.[40] Enough claims that RUC members leaked information on IRA members to Protestant paramilitaries who then murdered them have been made to suggest that at least some of them are credible. A policy of "Ulsterization," the handover of security to local forces, also remained limited by the need to deploy army units in "hard" areas. Beginning in 1986, PIRA received more-lethal types of arms, including the highly effective plastic explosive Semtex, from Libya, where PIRA members trained.[41]

By the end of the 1980s, both the insurgents and the security forces could do little more than maintain the status quo. PIRA had been "reduced to a concentration on tactics."[42] The insurgents began to behave more and more like a criminal syndicate than a liberation movement, ruling Catholic neighborhoods with an iron fist and funding themselves through extortion and racketeering.[43]

During this period of stalemate, however, the British government did make considerable progress in improving the quality of life for Catholics. It spent millions of pounds on housing and economic development, to the point where residents of some neighborhoods in Belfast and Londonderry enjoyed better housing than many people in London, Liverpool, or Leeds. From 1971 to 1994 the Northern Ireland Housing Authority built 17,000 new dwellings and spent £130 million renovating another 8,000 in Belfast alone. It built 1,800 houses in Londonderry and redressed the problem of unfair housing allocation throughout the province.[44] The 1976 Fair Employment (Northern Ireland) Act, strengthened by subsequent legislation in 1989, outlawed discrimination on the basis of political affiliation or religion. In the public sector, which accounts for 40 percent of all jobs, Catholics now constituted 42 percent of the workforce, more than their proportion of the population.[45] Antidiscrimination laws remained harder to enforce in the private sector.

Despite these improvements, "relative deprivation" remained a problem.[46] A 1991 Labor Force survey revealed a Catholic unemployment rate of 18 percent, more than double that of the Protestant population. Ten percent of Catholics lived in overcrowded households as opposed to only 4 percent of Protestants, and Catholics were still underrepresented in the skilled trades and the professions.[47]

As these social changes were being implemented, the army worked to improve its relations with the Catholic community. Soldiers became more sensitive in carrying out their difficult duties. In 1980, 605 of Catholics interviewed said they joined PIRA because of some personal grievance: "their brother being shot, their house ransacked."[48] The troops understood how heavy-handedness had aided insurgent recruitment. As one brigadier explained, soldiers went from asking "How much force will the law allow?" to asking "How will my actions contribute to resolving the conflict?" "A smile," observed another officer, "is your best weapon in Northern Ireland."[49] Such restraint, coupled with a sense that the quality of one's life mattered to the troops, softened the attitude of many Catholics. They would not inform on insurgents, but they might provide the occasional tip that saved the life of a solider or policeman: "Best not to go down that alley tonight, sir."

Phase 3: Political Resolution

Improved counterinsurgency tactics and economic development could not resolve a conflict that was at its core political. Majority rule would not work in an ethnically divided society. The goals of all parties seemed irreconcilable. PIRA wanted to unite the six counties of Ulster with the twenty-six of the South. Articles II and III of its constitution committed the Republic to annexing the North. Britain insisted that Northern Ireland could not be detached from the United Kingdom without the consent of the majority of Northern Irish men and women.

However, military stalemate can sometimes open the door for compromise. War weariness may impel even the most intransigent adversaries to accept the proverbial half a loaf. Over time, Catholics and Protestants tired of bloodshed and social stagnation, and the Irish Republic realized that it could not afford—and really did not want—to incorporate the North. Progress toward peace would depend on a two-fold approach: gaining the cooperation of the Republic and implementing a complex system of government known as power sharing in Northern Ireland. In March 1973 the people of the province elected an assembly based on proportional representation and an executive with offices divided between the majority and minority blocks. In December of that year the British and Irish governments signed what was known as the Sunningdale Agreement. The agreement required the Republic to publish a declaration that Northern Ireland would remain part of the United Kingdom as long a majority of its people so desired, and created a Council of Ireland with representatives from North and South. A May 1974 general strike by Protestant loyalists of the Ulster Workers Council (UWC) scuttled the power-sharing agreement, and a Unionist bomb attack on May 17 that killed thirty-two—the worst single act of violence in the Troubles—threatened to reignite full-scale violence. The British prime minister's failure to confront the UWC left Northern Ireland virtually ungovernable, so direct rule was reinstated. But a precedent had been set.

Cooperation with the Republic eventually proved to be more successful. In December 1980 the Irish Taoseach (prime minister) reaffirmed the Sunningdale Agreement. The following year, Britain and the Republic created an Inter-Governmental Council of Ministers to further dialogue. These efforts led to the 1985 Anglo–Irish Accord, also known as the Hillsborough Agreement. The accord pledged the two governments to mutual cooperation on a variety of judicial, security, and cultural issues. Perhaps a measure of its value was the fact that the IRA and its political arm Sinn Féin, on the one side, and the Unionists, on the other side, were equally disdainful of the agreement, for entirely opposite reasons. In by-elections held soon after, both political parties lost ground, an encouraging sign of change.[50] Further progress toward peace depended on changes in attitude among the belligerents themselves, which by the early 1990s had begun to occur. A 1991 survey revealed that 35 percent of Catholics, along with 92 percent of their Protestant counterparts, favored remaining a part of the United Kingdom, while only 53 percent of Catholics favored a United Ireland.[51] An improved standard of living for Catholics and war weariness in both communities were weakening PIRA's hand, while the ascendancy of Sinn Féin's Gerry Adams as spokesperson for the Republican side helped legitimize the Republican position.[52]

As Anglo–Irish cooperation and concessions to the Catholic community progressed, however, Protestant intransigence hardened. Terrorism by Protestant paramilitaries increased dramatically after the Hillsborough Agreement and has remained a concern ever since, despite the Good Friday Agreement. The principal Loyalist paramilitary organizations were the Ulster Defense Association, with a membership of 1,500–2,000, and the Ulster Volunteer Force, numbering from 750 to 1,000 members.[53] Protestants accounted for only 20 percent of the political murders in the 1980s, but they perpetrated 52 percent of such homicides in 1992.[54]

This backlash notwithstanding, the government engaged in proximity talks with PIRA, which resulted in a ceasefire in 1994. Unfortunately, for domestic political reasons the Conservative government of Prime Minister John Major could make no further progress toward a resolution of the conflict. As their majority in the House of Commons dwindled, the Tories depended on the twelve Protestant Unionists from Ulster to stay in power. Insurgent patience wore thin, and in February 1996, PIRA ended the ceasefire. However, violence never returned to pre-1994 levels, and the new bombing and assassination campaign looked more and more like mere terrorism than insurgency. Fortunately, the people of Northern Ireland did not have long to wait for further progress toward peace. In May 1997 a revived Labour Party led by Tony Blair won a landslide victory. The new prime minister made resolving the conflict a top priority. Close engagement in the peace process by the administration of U.S. President Bill Clinton helped the talks along. In July, PIRA declared another ceasefire, and direct negotiations began in September. These talks resulted in the historic Good Friday Agreement of 10 April 1998. This complex accord created a North–South ministerial council and a British–Irish council, assuring both Catholics and Protestants of support from the larger entity with which they identified. The agreement committed the government to police reform and provided a framework for the accelerated release of PIRA prisoners.[55]

Two further obstacles to lasting peace remained, however: the decommissioning of PIRA weapons and a power-sharing agreement. Although the insurgents were loath to give up their arms, the 11 September 2001 attack on the United States and the 2005 London bombings so discredited terrorism that they had little choice. Just weeks after the July 2005 attack, Sinn Féin leader Gerry Adams announced decommissioning.[56] On 7 May 2007 the Northern Ireland Office surrendered its authority to a power-sharing executive. London withdrew all but the small contingent of troops regularly stationed in the province. The thirty-eight-year insurgency had ended.

Conclusion

The Northern Ireland conflict offers several valuable lessons. The first thing that becomes painfully clear is that complex, chronic insurgencies of this type cannot be won with just a modicum of economic improvements and suppression of the insurgent organization. The British government's initial unwillingness to consider the validity of Catholic claims of injustice led London to treat the violence as a security rather than a political matter. However, winning hearts and minds requires not only improving the general quality of life but also finding a workable political settlement that respects majority rule while protecting minority rights.

In a civil conflict such as Northern Ireland's, properly trained security forces can play a positive role with a strategy to contain the violence and perhaps stalemate the insurgents, thus creating circumstances favorable for compromise. However, they must be careful to avoid the kinds of tactical mistakes—most notably the use of excessive force—that will make a bad situation worse by further alienating a wavering populace. Excesses such as the internment policy that did so much damage to civil–military relations in Northern Ireland are more likely to occur when the army, which is generally not trained for civil operations, is forced to take the lead because the police are unable or unwilling to do so. The creation of "no-go" zones in Belfast and other cities, reinforced by physical barriers on the streets, only served to magnify the perception, on both sides, of Catholics as a besieged population. Worse, it left the army blind with regard to what was going on behind those walls and reliant on whatever intelligence, good or bad, it could get from informers. What is more, with the army kept out, the PIRA operated with a relatively free hand to control and radicalize the population.

As the security situation improves, soldiers should fall back and allow police to step forward. Maintaining, or reinstating, the rule of law and respect for human rights is essential to gaining legitimacy and resolving insurgent conflicts. Only when the parties involved are seen to be legitimate—by one another and by the populations they claim to represent—will a political resolution be able to take hold. Only when Gerry Adams managed to convince the British government, and eventually the American intermediaries, that he could speak for the Republicans and was an honest partner in the peace process did they in turn pressure the Unionist leadership to accept Adams and allow talks to go forward.

Finally, the longer such a conflict lasts, the more likely it is that the insurgents will resort to criminality and mere terrorism to perpetuate themselves, especially as they begin to lose the population's support. Insurgency has a shelf life. Either it succeeds in replacing the government, or it devolves into something worse. Using a wise strategic mix of incentives and disincentives, governments can avoid the former and prevent the latter.

Notes

1. Thomas R. Mockaitis, *British Counterinsurgency, 1919–1960* (London: Macmillan, 1990).

2. J. Bowyer Bell, *The Irish Troubles: A Generation of Violence* (New York: St. Martin's, 1993), 43.

3. Ibid., 49.

4. Tom Wilson, *Ulster: Conflict and Consent* (London: Blackwell, 1989), 107.

5. Details on the two acts are from Bowyer Bell, *Irish Troubles*, 44–46.

6. The Orange Order originated in the late seventeenth century among followers of the Protestant Dutch Prince William of Orange, who deposed Catholic King James II in battle and thus assured Protestant dominance of the United Kingdom. Factions of the Orange Order in Northern Ireland became known during the Troubles for their willingness to incite violence against Catholics.

7. Thomas R. Mockaitis, *British Counterinsurgency in the Post-Imperial Era* (Manchester: Manchester University Press, 1995).

8. Cited in Desmond Hamill, *Pig in the Middle: The Army in Northern Ireland 1969–1984* (London: Methuen, 1985), 13.

9. Mockaitis, *British Counterinsurgency in the Post-Imperial Era*, 99.

10. "Report of the Advisory Committee on Police in Northern Ireland" (Hunt Report), Cmd. 535, Her Majesty's Stationery Office (HMSO), Belfast, 1969.

11. Bernadette Devlin, *Price of My Soul* (New York: Knopf, 1969), 167.

12. By March 1970, Catholics numbered 946 of 2,440 new recruits. Chris Ryder, *The Ulster Defence Regiment: An Instrument of Peace?* (London: Mandarin, 1992), 38–39.

13. Lt. Col. Michael Dewer, *The British Army in Northern Ireland* (London: Arms and Armour, 1985), 47.

14. Hamill, *Pig in the Middle*, 35–36.

15. Dewar, *British Army in Northern Ireland*, 47.

16. Ibid., 39.

17. Ibid., 65.

18. Mockaitis, *British Counterinsurgency in the Post-Imperial Era*, 102.

19. "Report of Enquiry into Allegations Against the Security Forces of Physical Brutality in Northern Ireland Arising out of Events on 9th August 1971" (Compton Report), Cmnd. 4823, HMSO, London, 1972), v, 71.

20. See "Report on Allegations of Ill-Treatment Made by Persons Arrested Under the Special Powers Act After 8 August, 1971," Amnesty International, 30 October 1971, http://cain.ulst.ac.uk/events/intern/docs/amnesty71.htm.

21. "Report of the Committee of Privy Counsellors Appointed to Consider Authorised Procedures for the Interrogation of Persons Suspected of Terrorism" (Parker Report), Cmnd. 4901, London, HMSO, 1972: 18, 21, 22.

22. Ibid.

23. Alan Chalfont, "The Army and IRA," *Survival* (June 1971): 208.

24. *Report of the Tribunal Appointed to Enquire into the Events on Sunday, 30th January 1972, Which Led to Loss of Life in Connection with the Procession in Londonderry on That Day* (Widgery Report), HMSO, London, 1972, 38–39. Thirteen people died on the spot, while a fourteenth died later in hospital.

25. In an unprecedented apology, newly elected Tory Prime Minister David Cameron said he was "deeply sorry" for the incident. "Bloody Sunday Report Published," *BBC News*, 15 June 2010, http://www.bbc.co.uk/news/10320609. Also see the Bloody Sunday Inquiry Web site, http://www.bloody-sunday-inquiry.org, accessed 22 May 2010.

26. Member of the British security forces, conversation with the author, quoted in Mockaitis, *British Counterinsurgency in the Post-Imperial Era*, 106.

27. Hamill, *Pig in the Middle*, 84.

28. The BBC offers a history of Ireland's mostly violent relations with Britain. See *Northern Ireland: The Troubles, 1963 to 1985*, BBC History Online, 1 February 2007, Part 5, "Direct Rule," http://www.bbc.co.uk/history/recent/troubles.

29. Ryder, *Ulster Defence Regiment*, 53.

30. Dewar, *British Army in Northern Ireland*, 177–205.

31. The act was based on the recommendations of *Report of the Commission to Consider Legal Procedures to Deal with Terrorist Activities in Northern Ireland* (Diplock Report), Cmnd. 5185, HMSO, London, 1972.

32. J. Bowyer Bell, "An Irish War," *Small Wars and Insurgencies* I, no. 3 (Winter 1988): 257.

33. Ibid., 258.

34. Hamill, *Pig in the Middle*, 187.

35. Bowyer Bell, *Irish Troubles*, 736–37.

36. Ryder, *Ulster Defence Regiment*, 84–117.

37. "The Royal Irish Regiment," Northern Ireland Brief, Northern Ireland Office, Belfast, 1992, 2.

38. Paul Arthur and Keith Jeffrey, *Northern Ireland Since 1968* (London: Blackwell, 1988), 70.

39. Ryder, *Ulster Defence Regiment,* 184. Ryder's excellent chapter "Bad Apples" details UDR abuses: 150–85.

40. "Chief Constable's Annual Report 1992," HMSO, London, 1993, 71.

41. Margaret Thatcher, *The Downing Street Years* (New York: HarperCollins, 1993), 411.

42. Bowyer Bell, "An Irish War," 260.

43. See Paul Clare, "Subcultural Obstacles to the Control of Racketeering in Northern Ireland," *Conflict Quarterly* 10, no. 4 (Fall 1990): 25–50.

44. "Building on Success: The Story of Northern Ireland Housing Since the 1970s," Background Brief, Foreign & Commonwealth Office, London, 1992, 1.

45. "Fair Employment in Northern Ireland," Northern Ireland Brief, Northern Ireland Office, Belfast, 1993, 5.

46. Caryl Philips, *The European Tribe* (London: Faber, 1987), 127.

47. *Key Facts, Figures and Themes* (Belfast: Northern Ireland Office, 1992), 50.

48. David Clark, "IRA: Long Wait," *Time Out* (25–31 July 1980), 13.

49. Mockaitis, *British Counterinsurgency in the Post-Imperial Era,* 113.

50. BBC, *Northern Ireland: The Troubles,* Part 8, "The Anglo–Irish Agreement."

51. Cited in *Northern Ireland, The Background and the Facts* (London: Foreign and Commonwealth Office, 1993), 7.

52. Sinn Féin, the political voice of the IRA, sought to distance the political process from the sectarian violence after the 1975 ceasefire. Gerry Adams became the chief representative and negotiator for the Republican side in the talks that led up to the Good Friday Agreement.

53. "Loyalist Paramilitary Organizations in Northern Ireland," Northern Ireland Brief, Northern Ireland Office, Belfast, 1992, 1–3.

54. "Chief Constable's Annual Report 1992," 31.

55. Richard English, *Armed Struggle: The History of the IRA* (New York: Oxford University Press, 2003), 297–98.

56. The Unionist paramilitaries resisted decommissioning far longer but are generally believed to have completed the process in early 2010.

22 Al Qaeda in the Arabian Peninsula

Lawrence E. Cline

AL QAEDA IN THE ARABIAN PENINSULA (AQAP) REPRESENTS one of the newer "franchises" associated with Al Qaeda. Although it has coalesced as a unified group only relatively recently, it draws on separate existing *takfiri* terrorist movements in Saudi Arabia and Yemen. Both countries have faced significant terrorist threats in the past, and the emergence of AQAP will likely exacerbate both the internal threats and the prospects for transnational terrorist operations. In particular, Yemen, with its already significant internal stresses and security problems, will likely find its stability significantly at risk from AQAP, especially with popular unrest now convulsing the major cities.

This chapter begins with a look at these two strands, starting with Saudi Arabia, the birthplace of Osama bin Laden, Al Qaeda, and Wahhabism, the particularly fundamentalist form of Islam that has inspired the most violent Muslim terrorists. The Saudi government, which had ignored the problem of indigenous Islamic terrorism for decades, has recently taken some steps to intervene and "rehabilitate" terrorists, but it is apparent that Saudi militants have been infiltrating Yemen and other Gulf countries for some time.

The chapter next details the spread of terrorist ideology and behavior in Yemen. Since the attack on the *USS Cole* in 2000, Yemen has seen considerable violence, mostly car and suicide bombings against both government and Western targets. In 2009 Saudi Al Qaeda cells joined forces with those in Yemen to form Al Qaeda in the Arabian Peninsula. Ethnic divisions, weak democracy, endemic official corruption, and a mismanaged economy have contributed to overall instability, making Yemen a useful base for operations and its young people ripe targets for recruitment by terrorists.

The Saudi Strand

The Saudi government historically tended to minimize the potential threat it faced from Al Qaeda's activities within Saudi Arabia. This began changing in 2003, when terrorists launched a series of attacks within the kingdom itself. On 12 May 2003 simultaneous vehicle bombs struck three compounds housing Westerners in the capital city of Riyadh, killing nine Americans. In response, the Saudi government cracked down on known militants, and by November 2003 the foreign affairs advisor announced that more than 600 suspected terrorists had been arrested. These detentions did not stop the attacks, however. On 8 November 2003 an attack against a predominantly Arab housing compound (which may have been mistaken for a Western compound) killed seventeen. The year 2004 was an especially bloody one in Saudi Arabia. A car bombing on 21 April at the Directorate of Traffic in Riyadh killed five and wounded 150. This was followed a month later by attacks in Yanbu against Western energy workers and in al Khobar against multiple targets. In June terrorists also abducted and later killed an American working for Lockheed Martin in Saudi Arabia. That same year Saudi security forces killed the leader of Al Qaeda in Saudi Arabia, Khaled Ali Hajj, a Yemeni and former bodyguard of Al Qaeda leader Osama bin Laden. Finally, in December 2004 gunmen stormed the U.S. consulate in Jeddah, killing five employees and four members of the Saudi National Guard.

Much of the internal unrest in Saudi Arabia has subsided since then, in large measure because of both increased government attention and improved internal-security operations. The Saudi government has also developed some innovative techniques for dealing with internal terrorism, such as its rehabilitation program for detained terrorism suspects.

According to Saudi government sources, some 2,000 detainees have participated in the rehabilitation program, around 700 of whom actually renounced their jihadist beliefs and were subsequently released. Some 1,400 prisoners have refused to participate.[1] Based on somewhat earlier figures, the same author states that of a total of 1,400 participating detainees who have been released, only thirty-five have been rearrested for security violations, which amounts to about a 2-percent recidivism rate. Concerning a similar program set up to reintegrate Saudis released from the Guantanamo Bay prison camp, an earlier Saudi report stated that 117 were repatriated, none of whom re-offended.[2] There have been some serious setbacks for the rehabilitation program, however. Last year, the Saudi Interior Ministry released a "wanted" list of eighty-five alleged terrorists, many of them suspected of joining foreign jihadist groups. According to certain Saudi officials, eleven men on the list were former detainees at Guantanamo Bay who had gone through the counseling program. The seeming contradiction in these reports may be due to a reluctance on the part of some Saudi officials to tarnish the success of their program.

The Saudi claims of rather spectacular success in their rehabilitation program should probably be viewed with some level of skepticism. First, although some of the detainees are caught by good intelligence and security operations, others—perhaps the majority—are simply careless or stupid enough to be caught; these are unlikely to be the key players in any terrorist network. Even among this population, it is probable that the major rehabilitation success stories are likely to be wannabes and newer recruits. The significant numbers of detainees who either have refused to participate in the program or who are deemed ineligible also suggests a large number of irreconcilables.

The second potential problem is how permanent individuals' renunciation of terrorism may actually be. The program has been in existence for only a few years, so this question is still open. At least one "successful" former radical has noted that his current life is simply not as emotionally fulfilling as was his time as a jihadist; this may certainly be a broader trend.[3] Trying to settle into a conventional middle-class life may be difficult for a number of jihadists, most of whom come from middle-class to lower-middle-class families. On a more practical level, any detainee who has been released has a vested interest in keeping a low profile, knowing that he is under observation by Saudi security. As time passes and the level of surveillance likely decreases, it seems probable that some of the "rehabilitated" jihadists will reemerge as security threats.

Finally, the Saudi government seems to be focused almost exclusively on this counseling program as its way of countering internal terrorism, while ignoring the fact that the displacement of Saudi terrorists to other countries may pose an increasing regional threat. Supposedly rehabilitated graduates of the program have been spotted operating in Yemen. Given the fairly cavalier attitudes of Saudi officials in the past, these movements of Saudi terrorists are probably not viewed with special concern by the kingdom's government. From the Saudi standpoint, minimizing or ignoring the exodus of the program's failures to other countries probably is preferable to grappling directly with the indigenous jihadi problem. From the larger regional and international standpoint, of course, it is becoming disastrous.

With the formation of AQAP, Riyadh may well be forced to take the "leakage" of Saudi terrorists more seriously. The problem for Saudi Arabia, Yemen, and the region in general is that it is likely still relatively easy for terrorists to move from Saudi Arabia to Yemen, compared to other countries in the Gulf that have tighter entry controls. There are many reasons why Yemen is a good place to base terrorist cells and from which to conduct operations.

The Yemen Strand

Al Qaeda has had a long-standing presence in Yemen, but sympathizers for jihad predate the actual formation of Al Qaeda under bin Laden. Yemenis were second in number only to Saudis as members of the anti-Soviet international brigade in Afghanistan. The number of Yemeni mujahedeen who maintained their allegiance to Al Qaeda after 1989 is unknown, but probably is substantial. Some 40 percent of detainees in Guantanamo have been from Yemen, several of whom are known to have returned to Al Qaeda once they got back home. These are in addition to the number released from Saudi rehabilitation programs who, as mentioned above, have entered Yemen and also rejoined Al Qaeda there. It is known that Al Qaeda maintained training camps in Yemen until the late 1990s. Although several of these have been targeted by the Yemen government, it would be overly optimistic to conclude that all such sites have been completely eliminated.

Yemen has been the scene of numerous Al Qaeda-associated operations since the turn of the century. Specific claims of responsibility have been episodic, but evidence points to at least some level of Al Qaeda involvement. These operations have included the following:

- October 2000: A suicide-bomb attack targets the destroyer *USS Cole* in the port of Aden.
- June 2001: Eight are arrested for a plot to blow up the U.S. embassy in Sana'a.

- June 2002: An accidental explosion kills two Al Qaeda members; 650 pounds of explosives are recovered.
- October 2002: A suicide-bomb attack targets the French oil tanker *Limburg*.
- December 2002: Three American missionaries are killed by a gunman; Al Qaeda's involvement is uncertain.
- July 2007: A car-bomb attack on tourists kills eight Spaniards and two Yemenis.
- January 2008: Two Belgian tourists and their Yemeni drivers are shot to death.
- March 2008: A mortar attack on the U.S. embassy kills a child and a school guard in an adjacent building.
- March 2008: AQAP takes credit for several attacks on Yemen's energy sector.
- July 2008: Successive attacks on police headquarters in Sayoun kill one policeman and wound seventeen others. A group calling itself the Islamic Jihad Organization claims responsibility.
- August/September 2008: A combined double car bomb, small arms, and rocket attack on the U.S. embassy leaves ten Yemeni troops and six jihadis dead. No Americans are hurt.
- March 2009: Four South Korean tourists and a Yemeni are killed by a roadside bomb; the investigating delegation is also subsequently attacked.
- August 2009: An AQAP suicide bomber with a bomb apparently hidden in his rectum tries and fails to assassinate Prince Mohammed bin Nayef, the Saudi security chief, in Riyadh.
- December 2009: On Christmas Day a Nigerian claiming connections to AQAP attempts to bomb a Delta flight coming into Detroit, but the bomb fails.

Following some of the earlier terrorist attacks, Yemeni security forces conducted security sweeps and detained a number of suspects. However, the Yemen government's response to Al Qaeda has been inconsistent over time. It has been common for terrorist suspects to remain in detention without trial, but it is far from clear in this case that the most significant figures were kept in prison even if they were caught. Furthermore, even with detentions or convictions, the government was not particularly successful at actually holding prisoners, a topic that will be discussed in more detail below. Besides some high-profile escapes, the government also released a number of suspected or convicted jihadis for "good behavior."[4]

Despite these prosecutorial weaknesses, Al Qaeda has come under pressure from both the U.S. and Yemen governments. In 2002 a CIA drone attack killed Abu Ali al Harthi, leader of Al Qaeda in Yemen and believed to be a planner of the *Cole* bombing.[5] In late 2003 his replacement, Mohammed Hamdi al-Ahdal, a Saudi citizen implicated in the *Limburg* bombing, was arrested by the Yemen government; he was tried in 2006 and reportedly received a three-year sentence.[6] More recently, in July 2009 a Yemen court sentenced sixteen militants for the attacks on the U.S. embassy and on the Belgian tourists; six were sentenced to death and the others given prison sentences. The Yemenis also have begun a terrorist-rehabilitation program akin to the ongoing Saudi program. An earlier variant was not well-resourced and had rather poor results, but it is too early to judge this new program.[7]

In February 2006, twenty-three prisoners—including Jamal al Badawi, the alleged mastermind of the *USS Cole* bombing, and Jaber al Banna, on the FBI's most wanted list—tunneled their way from prison and escaped. Although it was never proven, there has been widespread speculation that they received some inside help. All except two eventually were recaptured or killed. Al Badawi eventually turned himself in to the Yemen government in 2007 and promised to cooperate with authorities, but his case became a running sore between Sana'a and Washington. Claiming that the Yemen constitution does not permit extradition, Sana'a essentially allowed al Badawi free rein. One of the two escapees still at large, Nassar al Wahishi, a former aide to Osama bin Laden, became the chief of Al Qaeda in Yemen, while the other, Qasim al Raimi, has also remained active.

The formation of Al Qaeda in the Arabian Peninsula, which was announced in a press release by the group itself in January 2009, represented a merger of the Yemen and Saudi Al Qaeda strands, with Nassar al Wahishi at its head.[8] In its propaganda video AQAP also named two Saudi leaders of the group, Said Ali al Shihri and Abu Hareth Muhammed al Awfi, both former Guantanamo detainees and "graduates" of the Saudi rehabilitation program. Al Awfi surrendered to the Saudi government shortly afterwards and, ironically, was again remanded to the rehab program, but al Shihri remains a leader of the group. Al Wahishi's Yemeni second-in-command is Qasim al Raimi, who reportedly was a principal target of a December 2009 raid against his cell, but who escaped. The Yemen government has suggested that al Wahishi and perhaps al Raimi were killed in a second raid, but as of this writing, this has not been confirmed.[9]

Current estimates of the strength of AQAP vary from 50 to 300.[10] According to Ali al-Ahmed, Director of the Institute for Gulf Affairs, Yemen has become the third-largest haven for Al Qaeda, and the group there is perhaps the most stable when compared to units operating in Iraq, North Africa, and South Asia: "The one in Yemen now is really the most comfortable . . . it's probably the best funded. . . . It's not the best trained [, and] it doesn't have the best talent—that's why it hasn't been able to mount successful attacks. But it will come around in the coming years, and it will become a major threat."[11]

According to one expert, AQAP has "an administrative structure, a deputy, a consultative council, a media department, a legislative committee and a military committee."[12] It also has a Sharia Council for ideological and religious guidance. The primary religious figures in the Sharia Council are Ibrahim al-Rubaish, Khaled Batarfi (aka Abu Miqdad al-Kindi), and Adel al-Abbab (aka Abu al-Zubair). Al-Abbab, the most public figure of the three, has declared that AQAP is religiously justified to label all Gulf State rulers as infidels and also justified to attack foreign embassies in the region.[13]

AQAP runs a sophisticated propaganda campaign that includes a glossy, high-quality magazine, *Salah al Malahim* (*The Echo of Battle*). Beyond the typical *takfiri* articles, the magazine also includes advice columns and very professional graphics.[14] It also is one of the few terrorist propaganda conduits that is published on a fairly consistent schedule.[15] In addition to the magazine and press releases, AQAP has produced a number of audiotapes and videos aimed at recruitment.

In its propaganda organs and public statements, AQAP has announced several goals. It has called for the Saudi royal family to be overthrown as the first step toward establishing a true Islamic "caliphate," the utopian paradise on Earth that is supposed to be the ultimate goal of jihad. Deputy leader al Shihri said the group also wants to gain control of the strategically important strait of Bab al-Mandab, which connects the Gulf of Aden to the Red Sea. By doing so, they could "close the door and tighten the noose on the Jews, because through [the strait], America brings support to them by the Red Sea."[16] Of course, AQAP also promulgates the general Al Qaeda strategy of attacking Jewish and Western interests around the world, with the goal to drive them out of the Middle East and thence usher in the caliphate, presumably with one of themselves as caliph.

The Broader Strategic Context for Yemen

From Sana'a's perspective, there are three critical ongoing threats to internal security. Al Qaeda is certainly one, but the other two—the Houthi uprising in the North along the Saudi border and political unrest in the South around the port of Aden—are probably viewed with considerably more concern by the Yemen government. Although each threat is significant in its own right, the possibility of overlap among them in the future is even more worrisome. These specific problems are even further exacerbated by a long list of broader social, economic, and political stressors, all of which undermine Yemen's ability to respond adequately to any of them.

The Houthi (also transliterated as Huthi) uprising reportedly began in 2003–2004, in response to a quasi-police operation to arrest a former parliament member, Husein al-Houthi. Although al Houthi was killed early in the fighting, the struggle against the government continued under the leadership of his relatives. From the rebellion's inception, the Houthi claimed to be defending *Zaidi* Islam (a sect of the Shi'a school of Islam) from a hostile Yemen government, claiming that Sana'a was increasingly falling under the influence of *salafis,* Sunni fundamentalists (Yemen is primarily Sunni, except for its northern region). Also (and perhaps more importantly), it likely represents a clan/tribal attempt to preserve traditional power structures in the area. The fighting has centered in Saada Province in northwestern Yemen, but some operations have expanded beyond this area.[17]

Ideologically, the Houthi movement is very difficult to nail down. In large measure this is deliberate: "In a July 2008 interview, al-Houthi explained that he and his supporters refused to articulate any kind of political agenda because doing so would cause people to start fighting to see such demands satisfied—contradicting what he sees as the reactive dimension of the war."[18] Although some of the rhetoric among some members of the rebellion is very militant—death to the United States, death to Israel, condemnation of U.S. activities in Yemen, etc.—there have been few, if any, indications thus far that the rebels have any particular ties to or sympathy for Al Qaeda. This, of course, has not stopped the Yemen or Saudi governments from insisting that the Houthi are aligned with Al Qaeda and AQAP.

The fighting has been marked by a series of battles, ceasefires, and negotiations, followed by more fighting. It has also divided the tribes of the region and reignited some old tribal feuds; for example, the Hashid tribal federation is fighting on the side of the government, while the Bakil confederation supports the Houthi rebels. Some areas have remained under consistent rebel control, while in others the fighting has left considerable destruction in its wake. At least 150,000 people have been displaced.[19]

The situation with the Houthi rebellion became even more complicated on 5 November 2009. A reported Houthi attack on a Saudi border post, in which a border guard was killed, led Riyadh to send a bombing raid against alleged Houthi positions on both sides of the border in response. Since then, the Houthi claim that the Saudis have launched over 160 missiles against northern areas. Although specific operations are difficult to corroborate conclusively, independent reporters in the area confirmed significant Saudi air and ground operations following that initial air raid. The Saudi government has acknowledged that seventy-three of its nationals have been killed, with twenty-six missing in the fighting.[20] The Houthi claimed to have captured at least nine Saudi troops.

A major ongoing controversy in the open-source media is whether the Houthi are receiving practical support from Iran. Middle East media have claimed that the Houthi have received training and some equipment from the Iranian Revolutionary Guard Corps, and there have been allegations of Iranian shipments of weapons to the group via Iranian ships.[21] Yemeni Foreign Minister Abu Bakr al-Qirbi recently stated that there are "indications" the rebels are getting support from religious groups in Iran and Shiite organizations in Arab countries and Europe. He continued: "Once the evidence mounts and it is made public, then I am sure Iran will rethink its position because they know the implications of it. Everybody will understand the danger of such a role."[22]

If there is debate about whether Iran is covertly sending supplies to the Houthi, Tehran has been very vocal in diplomatic and propaganda channels to signal its interest in the situation. Iranian Foreign Minister Manouchehr Mottaki warned that certain regional states seek to foment discord between the Yemen government and its people by fueling violence, while the Iranian government itself has offered to "mediate" the dispute. The Iranian official press has broadcast a steady stream of opinion in support of the Houthi and has sought to tie the United States directly to attacks against the rebels. Given the Saudi use of U.S.-made aircraft in their air strikes, this particular theme may resonate well in the Houthi area.[23]

As mentioned earlier, fighting between the government and the Houthi has been interspersed with negotiations. A number of approaches have been tried, including indigenous mediation committees based on traditional models of governance, and the use of religious and local mediators. One recurring issue has been the apparent lack of coordination between the Yemen military and government mediators; in some cases, mediators have had to postpone talks due to fresh military offensives.[24] The government has paid "compensation" to tribal leaders associated with the Houthi, and offered a series of amnesties to try to win local cooperation. Although most such efforts have been internal, the neighboring state of Qatar has also made significant efforts in pushing negotiations.

Despite the various missteps in the negotiations, a fresh ceasefire was successfully implemented in February 2010. Parties to the negotiations agreed to concrete terms for each side to withdraw from forward positions, and the return of displaced populations. Given a new uptick in violence in the summer of 2010, however, the prospects of long-term peace and stability have dimmed again.[25] Sana'a has refused to consider any increased autonomy for the Houthi areas and insists that the rebels "join a recognized political party and 'operate within the framework of the constitution,'" while Houthi leader Abdel Malik al-Houthi vows rather vaguely to keep fighting "for more rights for his own people."[26] The Yemen government, already extremely weak, desperately needs peace in the North so it can turn its attention to its many other problems.

Southern Unrest

Another area of internal unrest is around Aden, the former capital of South Yemen, where antigovernment demonstrations and riots erupted in May 2007. Both internal-security forces and army troops have tried to quell the unrest, killing a number of demonstrators in the process. Southern Yemenis complain that since independence, the North has raided the South for its natural and human resources without any return investment in the southern economy.[27] Local grievances have included job discrimination, lack of equal rights, and in one case, the purported punitive discharge of former South Yemen military officers who were supposed to be covered by earlier amnesties. As the unrest has continued, there have been increasing calls for the "liberation of the South." Many southerners rue the country's 1990 unification and suggest that the South should be free to change its mind, as it tried to do in 1994, a move that led to civil war and even stronger subjugation of the South to northern rule.[28]

The first organized opposition movement in the South was the Society of Retired Military Officers, formed in 2007. The relatively peaceful marches and sit-ins that this group organized were met with violence by security forces and widespread arrests.[29] As a result, the protests quickly broadened to incorporate many elements of southern society who felt marginalized by the North. The Yemeni Socialist Party, the main political party representing southern interests, was a significant mobilization agent in spreading the secessionist movement, which has become known as the Southern Movement or Movement of the South. Although there is a putative "Council for the Leadership of the Peaceful Revolution of the South," this council reportedly has little direct control over the large number of groups involved.[30] As the protests have escalated, so have the demands, with many southerners now calling openly for independence.

Most violence involving the protesters thus far has been on the part of government security forces, with predictably counterproductive results, but there has been scattered violence attributed to supporters of the Southern Movement. In most cases this has consisted of isolated rock throwing, Molotov cocktails, and the like, but there have been a few murders and attacks attributed to movement supporters. The comments by one retired colonel in the Southern Movement may be representative of sentiment in the South: "There will be war when the money runs out. President [Ali Abdullah] Saleh is a clever man—he knows how to play the tribes off one another, but this takes money. . . . The people here will wait until he is weak enough and then they will strike."[31]

The strong presence of Al Qaeda in the South complicates matters and obscures the various actors' motivations. According to one area expert, AQAP has certainly tried to turn local anger over air strikes into anti-Western jihadism by tying Sana'a's actions to U.S. policy.[32] One concern expressed by a number of analysts has been whether or not AQAP can use the northern and southern unrest to develop links with other antigovernment movements. Some of these linkages might in fact be developing. According to reporting by *al Jazeera*, suspected Al Qaeda commanders addressed a rally in southern Yemen, condemning the December bombing raids; members of the Southern

Movement reportedly participated in the rally.[33] In addition, on 13 May 2009 AQAP released an audio statement titled "To Our People in the South," in support of southern Yemeni secession efforts.[34] AQAP has also supported the Houthi movement, but with no apparent reciprocation.[35] However, it should be stressed that in both rebellious areas there have been no indications that AQAP has thus far managed to form firm alliances.

Although not directly involved in unrest, another area of concern is potential AQAP links with those Yemeni tribes not involved in the rebellions. Yemen remains very tribal, particularly in the eastern part of the country. Probably not coincidentally, this is where a significant number of Yemen's former mujahedeen fighters, who joined the war in Afghanistan against Soviet occupation in the 1980s, returned and settled, often marrying into local tribes. The East is also where Sana'a's power is weakest. AQAP propaganda has specifically targeted tribal groups, fanning anger over civilian casualties that have resulted from governmental operations against AQAP.[36] Although AQAP's increasingly internationalist goals probably do not resonate particularly well with most tribes' essentially local interests and desire for patronage, tribal perceptions of a lack of governmental support and counterterrorist operations that result in significant tribal casualties could provide inroads for further AQAP expansion in the outlying areas.[37]

The Religious Component

Yemen's people are divided into two major religious branches: the smaller Shi'a *Zaidi* sect, which is followed primarily in the North and Northwest, and the dominant *Shafa'i* school of Sunni Islam, which is mostly in the South and Southeast. The *Zaidi,* which include the rebellious Houtha regions, historically followed a theocratic form of local governance. Both schools of Islam historically have been fairly moderate. As Ali al-Anissi, head of the Yemeni Bureau of National Security, stated with some justification, "Zaidism is a Shiite strain within Sunni Islam, and Shafaism is a Sunni strain within Shiite Islam."[38] In keeping with the complications involved with this religious divide, President Ali Abdullah Saleh himself is a *Zaidi* in a predominantly Sunni government.

One potentially important change to this balance in recent years has been the inroads made by fundamentalist *Salafi* Islam, particularly in southern and eastern Yemen.[39] Wahhabis from Saudi Arabia have been increasingly active within Yemen, and local *Salafi ulema* (religious leaders) have become more vocal about their conservative views. A key question for Western observers has been the role of al Iman University in Sana'a in the spread of *Salafi.* It has been portrayed (primarily by locals) as solely an institution of Islamic higher learning, but a number of outside observers have charged that al Iman is akin to an ideological training camp for terrorists. This view has been supported by the behavior of some of its alumni, such as John Walker Lindh, Umar Farouk Abdulmutallab, and several other foreign students who were subsequently arrested.[40] The university has also been very reluctant to open itself to outside observers. President Saleh has publicly defended the school, and he has spoken there. As area expert Gregory D. Johnsen has observed, the reality probably lies somewhere between the two positions, and al Iman will continue "to straddle this divide as a legitimate religious institution and as a fundamentalist pipeline."[41]

Al Iman University is headed by Sheik Abdulmajid al Zindani, who is designated as a terrorist financier by the UN's 1267 Committee, and as a spiritual advisor to bin Laden by the U.S. Treasury Department. He also is head of the Islah Party, a political party in sporadic opposition to the regime.[42] In the convoluted world of Yemen politics, however, al Zindani reportedly is an ally of President Saleh and focuses his main opposition at secular and socialist movements. Exactly how much influence he actually exerts on the regime is debated, but it is cause for concern.

Social and Economic Issues

Beyond the purely security issues, Yemen faces a host of broader problems. Perhaps the most salient is tribalism, which still exerts tremendous influence throughout much of Yemen. The country is marked by significant poverty, with a per capita income of about $723. The literacy rate is very low. Large areas are sparsely inhabited, potentially providing safe haven for bad actors. Both oil and water resources are dwindling, further threatening the country's economic viability.[43] Interspersed with all these other issues is the virtually endemic use of qat, a mildly narcotic drug. Trying to assess the direct impact of qat use on other social and economic problems is virtually impossible, but any visitor to Sana'a would note how much of the male population essentially shuts everything down in the afternoon to enjoy their chew.

Regionally, Yemen has also faced a problem with human trafficking from Somalia, and—perhaps a case of desperation overtaking forethought—

significant refugee flows from there as well. According to the UN High Commissioner for Refugees, as of September 2009 there were more than 153,000 registered Somali refugees in Yemen, and the rate of inflow has been increasing in recent months as fighting in Somalia heats up again.[44] According to some reports in early 2010, AQAP recently moved some of its leadership structure to Somalia.[45] Yemen has also traditionally been a gateway for arms and drug smuggling, and this is unlikely to change. One analyst has claimed that Yemen has 60 million weapons for a population of 22 million people.[46] Piracy in the Gulf has also affected trade in and out of Yemen.

Better Governance Is the Cure

President Saleh, who was first elected in 1978, continues regularly to be elected president by lopsided margins, together with his General People's Congress. The stagnated political system suggests a sham democracy such as is common in the Middle East, but official outside election observers have held that the elections generally have been "open and genuine."[47] It is unlikely that Saleh's repeated victories have been the result of any particular popularity; it is much more likely that they have been the result of his adroitness in maneuvering between Yemeni power centers, at least until the recent period. President Saleh is required constitutionally to step down in 2013; even if he wanted to change the constitution to allow him run again, his age (he was born in 1946) virtually ensures succession in the relatively near future. These considerations further complicate the regime's political stability because of stresses that are already emerging over the leadership succession and whether Saleh's son will continue the family business or whether other key players in the regime will manage to replace him. The ongoing political turmoil within Yemen—much of which is based on the traditional fault lines of tribalism and southern unrest, but to which has been added a critical mass of traditionally more quiescent Yemenis—has further clouded the picture. Most significantly, traditional allies of Saleh, including some key members of the security apparatus, have either turned against him publicly or have shown signs of sitting on the fence until they can determine the political winds.

The increasing political uncertainties in Yemen offer potential inroads for a variety of violent opposition groups, including AQAP. This weakness has been realized by at least some senior officials in the regime. Yemen's foreign affairs minister, Abu Bakr al Qirbi, argues reasonably enough that the best counterweight to AQAP is better governance in Yemen:

> Yemen cannot really build a modern state unless we re-define the role of government. If one spends a fraction of the money that is spent on combating terrorism, on how to rehabilitate and how to address some of the issues that lead to extremism—education and poverty—maybe we would have achieved a greater success in fighting terrorism.[48]

With the exception of the failed December 2009 aircraft bombing (and, arguably, inspiration for the Fort Hood shootings a month earlier), AQAP operations thus far have been focused locally. Taking its public statements at face value, however, the group's leaders clearly have much broader aspirations. Given the myriad stresses within Yemen and its strategic geographical position on major shipping routes between Africa, Europe, and the Middle East, the country offers a good base from which to rebuild the movement. Other countries—most notably the United States and Britain—have significantly increased both their attention to Yemen and more practical support in the form of aid. Yemen's government has also stepped up its internal operations to try to quell rebellion, but Sana'a's attention must be split among multiple sources of unrest. It also faces broader economic and social problems, some of which are likely intractable. Until and unless Yemen reaches a much more stable footing, AQAP almost certainly will remain a very viable—and dangerous—member of the global Al Qaeda movement.

Notes

1. Christopher Boucek, "Extremist Reeducation and Rehabilitation in Saudi Arabia," *Terrorism Monitor* (Jamestown Foundation) 5, no. 16 (16 August 2007).

2. Christopher Boucek, "Counter-Terrorism from Within: Saudi Arabia's Religious Rehabilitation and Disengagement Programme," *RUSI Journal* 152, no. 6 (December 2008): 61. Similar figures, with a claim of about 3,000 detainees participating, are cited by Susan Mohammed, "To Deprogram a Jihadist," *Maclean's,* 2 February 2009, http://www2.macleans.ca.

3. Katherine Zoepf, "Deprogramming Jihadists," *New York Times,* 9 November 2008.

4. Even the Yemen foreign minister acknowledged that the government of Yemen has "not sufficiently focused" on Al Qaeda. "Yemeni Official: Other Conflicts Diverted Focus from Al Qaeda," CNN, 6 January 2010, http://edition.cnn.com/2010/WORLD/meast/01/06/yemen.al.qaeda/index.html. See also Steven Erlanger, "Yemen's

President Says Government Is Willing to Talk to Disarmed Qaeda Fighters," *New York Times,* 10 January 2010, http://www.nytimes.com/2010/01/11/world/asia/11yemen.html.

5. "U.S. Missile Strike Kills Al Qaeda Chief," CNN, 5 November 2002, http://archives.cnn.com/2002/WORLD/meast/11/05/yemen.blast.

6. "Al-Qaeda Deputy Tried in Yemen," *BBC News,* 13 February 2006, http://news.bbc.co.uk/2/hi/middle_east/4708640.stm.

7. Gregory Johnsen and Christopher Boucek, "The Dilemma of the Yemeni Detainees," *CTC Monitor* 1, no. 12 (November 2008): 1–4.

8. Fred Burton and Scott Stewart, "Al Qaeda in the Arabian Peninsula: Desperation or New Life?" *Stratfor Global Intelligence,* 28 January 2009, http://www.stratfor.com/weekly/20090128_al_qaeda_arabian_peninsula_desperation_or_new_lie.

9. See Mohamed Sudam, "Yemen Says Fort Hood-Linked Imam May Be Dead," Reuters, 24 December 2009, http://www.reuters.com/article/idUSTRE5BN0S220091224.

10. Jeremy M. Sharp uses the figure of 100 to 400, but there is wide divergence on estimates elsewhere. Jeremy M. Sharp, *Yemen: Background and U.S. Relations,* Congressional Research Service Report 7-5700, Washington D.C., 13 January 2010, 14.

11. Ali al-Ahmed, quoted in "Al Qaeda in the Arabian Peninsula," *Al Jazeera,* 29 December 2009, http://english.aljazeera.net/news/middleeast/2009/12/2009122935812371810.html.

12. Abdel Ilah Haidar Shae'e, "Extracts from a Paper Delivered at the Afif Cultural Foundation," published in "Al-Qaeda in the Arabian Peninsula (Part 1/3)," *Yemen Times,* 20 March 2010.

13. Murad Batal al-Shishani, "Adel Al-Abbab: Al Qaeda in the Arabian Peninsula's Religious Ideologue," *Militant Leadership Monitor* (Jamestown Foundation) 1, no. 3 (31 March 2010): 10–11.

14. *Takfir* is a complicated term actually meaning "apostate" or "excommunicant," applied to violent, extremist Muslims.

15. Brian Palmer, "It's Like *Slate* for Terrorists: What's in Al-Qaeda's Web Magazine?" *Slate,* 28 December 2009, www.slate.com.

16. "Al Qaeda Offshoot Calls for Jihad," *BBC News,* 8 February 2010.

17. For details on the origins of the conflict, see "Yemen: Defusing the Saada Time Bomb," Middle East Report Number 86, International Crisis Group (ICG), 27 May 2009: 2–5.

18. Joost R. Hiltermann, "Disorder on the Border: Saudi Arabia's War Inside Yemen," *Foreign Affairs,* 16 December 2009, http://www.foreignaffairs.com/articles/65730/joost-r-hiltermann/disorder-on-the-border.

19. "Yemen—Sa'ada," Emergency Situation Report No. 4, United Nations Office for the Coordination of Humanitarian Affairs, 8 September 2009.

20. "Weeks of Fighting Yemen Rebels Killed 73 Saudis," Associated Press, 22 December 2009.

21. For example, see Paul Salem, "Avoid the Trap of Escalation in Yemen," *Al Hayat,* 26 November 2009.

22. Tony Czuczka and Henry Meyer, "Yemen Sees 'Mounting Evidence' Iran Is Arming Rebels," Bloomberg, 25 November 2009.

23. For Iranian reports of the fighting, see http://www.presstv.ir.

24. For details, see "Yemen: Defusing the Saada Time Bomb," 19–25.

25. Robert F. Worth, "Yemen Clashes Reflect North–South Tensions," *New York Times*, 23 July 2010, A6.

26. Hashem Ahelbarra, "Yemen: Ceasefire Imminent?" *Aljazeera* Blogs, 11 February 2010, http://blogs.aljazeera.net/2010/02/11/yemens-imminent-ceasefire.

27. Worth, "Yemen Clashes."

28. Heather Murdock, "Yemen's Separatists Call for Southern Uprising," *Voice of America News*, 28 July 2010, http://www1.voanews.com/english/news/middle-east/Talk-of-Succession-in-Yemeni-South-99477069.html. For more background on North–South grievances, see "Yemeni Civil War—1994," *Global Security*, 1 February 2010, http://www.globalsecurity.org/military/world/war/yemen1.htm.

29. "In the Name of Unity: The Yemeni Government's Brutal Response to Southern Movement Protests," Human Rights Watch, New York, 15 December 2009, http://www.hrw.org/en/reports/2009/12/15/name-unity.

30. Ibid., 16.

31. Michael Horton, "Why Southern Yemen Is Pushing for Secession," *Christian Science Monitor*, 15 December 2009.

32. Glenn Greenwald, "Salon Radio Transcript: Gregory Johnsen," 24 December 2009, http://www.salon.com/news/opinion/glenn_greenwald/radio/2009/12/24/gjohnsen_transcript/index.html.

33. "Al-Qaeda Leaders Make Yemen Speech," *Al Jazeera*, 22 December 2009, http://english.aljazeera.net/news/middleeast/2009/12/2009122273913988616.html.

34. Abdul Hameed Bakier, "Al-Qaeda in Yemen Supports Southern Secession," *Terrorism Monitor* (Jamestown Foundation) 7, no. 16 (12 June 2009), http://www.jamestown.org/single/?no_cache=1&tx_ttnews%5Btt_news%5D=35108.

35. "Al Qaeda Offshoot Calls for Jihad," *BBC News*, 8 February 2010.

36. For example, see Sarah Phillips, "What Comes Next in Yemen? Al-Qaeda, the Tribes, and State-Building," Middle East Program no. 107, Carnegie Center, Washington D.C., March 2010, 4–5.

37. For a further expansion of this point, see ibid.

38. "Yemen: Defusing the Saada Time Bomb," 8.

39. For an explanation of *Salafi* Islam and its offshoot Wahhabism, see "Salafi Islam," *Global Security*, 1 January 2010, http://www.globalsecurity.org/military/intro/islam-salafi.htm.

40. See "Profile: Anwar Al-Awlaki," *BBC News*, 3 January 2010, http://news.bbc.co.uk/2/hi/middle_east/8438635.stm.

41. Gregory D. Johnsen, "Yemen's Al-Iman University: A Pipeline for Fundamentalists?" *Terrorism Monitor* 4, no. 22 (16 November 2006).

42. For a detailed examination of Islah's relations with the government, see Amr Hamzawy, *Between Government and Opposition: The Case of the Yemeni Congregation*

for Reform, Carnegie Papers, Carnegie Endowment for International Peace, Washington, D.C., November 2009.

43. For a good overview of the major issues facing Yemen, see Christopher Boucek, "Yemen: Avoiding a Downward Spiral," Carnegie Papers, Carnegie Endowment for International Peace, Washington, D.C., September 2009.

44. http://www.irinnews.org/Report.aspx?ReportId=86830.

45. "Qaeda Transfers Its Positions to Somalia-Based Al-Yemen," *Yemen Post,* 10 April 2010; Sudarsan Raghavan, "Somalis Fleeing to Yemen Prompt New Worries in Fight Against Al-Qaeda," *Washington Post,* 12 January 2010.

46. Shari Villarosa, "Al-Qaeda in Yemen," remarks at the conference sponsored by the Carnegie Endowment for International Peace, 7 July 2009.

47. "Yemen: Final Report. Presidential and Local Council Elections," European Union Election Observation Mission, September 2006, www.eueom-ye.org. Despite this overall positive finding, the EU observers noted that there was unfair use of state resources, together with bias by the state media, detention of opposition supporters, and problems in the ballot-counting process.

48. Micelle Shephard, "Al Qaeda in the Arabian Peninsula: A Primer," *New Republic,* 1 January 2010, http://www.tnr.com.

23 Conclusion

Paul Shemella

WE HAVE TRIED TO SHOW IN THIS VOLUME THAT TERRORISM exists within a larger field of transnational threats to which governments must be ready to respond collectively. Insecurity at the individual level anywhere can now reduce security at the national level everywhere. Political dissent can be expressed in a range of ways, but insurgency and terrorism are all-too-common paths for dissatisfied citizens to follow. National leaders provide incentives and disincentives to encourage nonviolent behavior among their own citizens, but once individuals and small groups take up the path of violence, governments' options (and prospects for success) are reduced considerably.

Insurgency starts with the shared belief by a group of disaffected citizens that changing the government through violence is the only way to address their grievances. Insurgents in much of the world enjoy some legitimacy, especially if they limit their use of terror and focus it on government security forces. But, as Thomas Mockaitis has observed here, insurgency has a shelf life. If it does not succeed quickly (and if the government does not destroy it completely), insurgency devolves into terrorism or organized crime. However, terrorist groups born from insurgency may still be amenable to having the government co-opt them into the political system, and these groups may respond favorably to soft-power approaches. The Irish Republican Army is of course the best-known example of this shift to legitimacy.

But some terrorist groups begin with terrorism (the systematic use of terror). What is more, groups that start with terror generally stay with terror (although most of them would like to claim the relative political legitimacy of insurgents). Governments must then distinguish between terrorist groups that use terror as a means to an end and those that use terror as an end in itself. Conflating the two types of terrorism diminishes the chances that a government will apply the right remedies to either; both kinds of terrorist group practice terrorism, but responses to the latter type may require more hard power.

Audrey Kirth Cronin writes that terrorism has six pathways to some kind of end: decapitation, negotiations, success, failure, repression, and reorientation.[1] We have introduced here a set of approaches that can be used to produce four of the six outcomes (government repression is often linked to terrorist success). If governments adopt core, offensive, and defensive strategies simultaneously, and execute them with due interagency and international coordination, terrorists will never find strategic success. Individual by individual and group by group, governments can use good strategy to remove the cancer from their own societies before it can spread to others. Acting together, governments should seek an end state that reflects the transformation of terrorism from a global security threat to a national law-enforcement problem.

The biggest obstacle to such a scenario is that no government has the capacity to develop and execute successful strategies on its own; generating them will require allies, regional partners, and friends to assist one another in building the robust institutions needed to pursue long-term campaigns against terrorism in all its forms. Two of the recurring themes in all the contributions to this volume have been the requirement for unity of effort *within* governments and then unity of effort *among* governments. The focus of this book is national, but national-level approaches will not be enough. *We believe that regional strategies for combating terrorism are the key to global success.*

Multinational cooperation and coordination are vital, but there are many constraints to factor into the process. First among these are differences in how governments define and understand terrorism. Threat perceptions vary widely, and it is probably fair to say that most countries do not consider terrorism a major policy issue until they fall victim to it. Legal and judicial differences, as well as public opinion, can have a strong impact on the degree to which governments are willing to cooperate. At a more practical level, governments have varying levels of resources and capabilities that can be deployed against terrorism. Beyond that, multinational efforts require increased levels of planning complexity.

We have said that terrorism will never be defeated completely, and history provides ample justification for that. Nor do we think that terrorism is the new Communism and that this long conflict will end in the collapse of the opponent like the Cold War did. However, there are three possible outcomes that we *should* consider. The first two foresee that terrorism as a global threat will gradually become either better or worse, depending not only on whether terrorists can sustain their mutually supporting networks but also on the collective efforts of governments to disrupt them. The third possible outcome borders on the unthinkable: the use of nuclear weapons by terrorists to destroy the structure of modern society. We have justifiably argued that such an outcome is unlikely, but we have also warned that unlikely outcomes must nevertheless be planned for.[2]

In the end, success against terrorism will be measured in terms of how effectively governments can reduce violence and promote a climate of security within which all their citizens can feel safe. That means helping society tolerate uncertainty without surrendering to fear, through good planning, good infrastructure, and good governance. Take the fear away, and terrorism loses its effectiveness.

Extremist ideology isolates terrorists and their constituents from the rest of society, forcing them to rely on the shared delusion that they are right and everyone else is wrong. Success in fighting terrorism hinges on discrediting these ideas, not on killing or jailing more and more terrorists. Combating terrorism is in fact a war of ideas that can only be won with better ideas, which means the battlefield we are contesting here is not physical; it is psychological and intellectual. Governments, private enterprise, and civil society, especially if they work together, have the resources to win this fight.

The Strategic Precepts of Combating Terrorism

In closing, we offer a list of precepts that best sum up what governments must do to eliminate root causes, disrupt dark networks, defeat existing terrorist groups, and reduce the likelihood of terrorism in the future:

1. Develop a comprehensive set of strategies. Define where you want to go and how to get there, measuring results and making adjustments along the

way. Use all the tools you have, and think critically about using them in new ways, starting with intelligence. It takes entire governments, along with the diverse resources of their societies, to master the challenges of terrorism.

2. Keep the use of force limited and appropriate, but be *prepared* to use coercive force. Kinetic operations are a holding action until soft-power approaches can take effect. There will always be a need for coercive force in combating terrorism, but the art of applying it requires thoughtful decision making and a clear assessment of consequences at the strategic level.

3. Build consensus all around. No single institution within one government can bring strategic success, nor can a single government eliminate transnational threats. The path to a national consensus against terrorism winds through each government's polity. Open societies divide opinion but forge consensus for great causes. Beyond borders, solidarity among governments is an ordinary citizen's best hope and a terrorist organization's biggest fear.

4. Hold the moral high ground. The rule of law should guide all activities that suppress terrorism, but long-term success takes more than that. States cannot stop the spread of terrorist ideology without *moral* supremacy. There is no other basis on which to challenge those who work to enlist ordinary citizens in a campaign against the values that should bind them together. Legitimacy is the key to winning this fight, and harnessing moral power is the way to accumulate it.

5. Strengthen social cohesion. All human beings wish to belong to something larger than themselves, be that civil society, youth gangs, tribes, sports teams, terrorist organizations, or the nation itself. Political leaders should recognize this truth as an opportunity to strengthen national identity. A cohesive society insulates individual citizens from those trying to take it apart, and inoculates the population against the virus of extremist ideology.

6. Build institutional capacity. Avoid letting smart, dedicated individuals populate corrupt and dysfunctional institutions. What all states need is lean but high-capacity security institutions that can work together for the only institution that really counts, the government itself. Leaders are critical to building such institutions, but long-term institutional strength requires dedicated professionals at all levels. Individuals pass through institutions, improving them as much as they can, but it is the *institution* that sustains capacity.

7. Improve border security. Terrorism and its associated transnational threats not only ignore borders; they also use them to avoid the institutions

that pursue them. Regional cooperation is therefore critical. Often murky and complicated, modern borders can only be truly secured when governments take care of the people who live on the fringe. Ungoverned spaces, including the maritime domain, must be governed, or terrorists and other nonstate actors will impose criminal and violent alternatives. It is tempting to try and "fix" porous borders with technologies and manpower, but human factors are far more important.

8. Educate everyone. Open societies encourage learning. Government officials need to learn the art of good governance and the value of strong institutions; law-abiding citizens must be instructed in what the government is doing for them and what they can do to strengthen government; terrorists have to be taught that governments, assisted by ordinary people, cannot be intimidated. Everyone must learn enough to see terrorism for what it is: the manipulation of human fear. In the long term, education at all levels and for all audiences is the single most effective remedy for the complex problem of terrorism.

9. Control the narrative. Authorities must learn to use information to deny terrorists the mouthpiece of the media to further their ends. This requires these authorities to craft well-conceived messages to two audiences that can steal the narrative: terrorists and other societies. At the same time, governments must explain clearly to their own publics what they are doing and why. Transparency is, after all, the fuel that makes democratic machinery run. In a fight for legitimacy, information is more than a tool; it is a weapon.

10. Govern well. Weak, oppressive, and/or corrupt governance is one of the most significant root causes of terrorism anywhere. Conversely, good governance goes a long way toward solving the problem, and governing well is what most leaders want to do anyway. All governments must balance security and liberty according to the laws and traditions of the nation. Terrorism throws that balance into question by tempting leaders to compromise civil liberties, and even human rights, for the sake of keeping their people safe. Traditional national security now requires effective human security, and good governance is the key to delivering both.[3]

Notes

1. Audrey Kirth Cronin, "No Silver Bullets: Explaining Research on How Terrorism Ends," *CTC Sentinel* 3, no. 4 (April 2010): 16–18.

2. This characterization of the future reflects the thinking of Phil Williams, a contributor to this volume.

3. It is too soon to predict precisely how the wave of revolutions spreading in the Middle East will transform the region, but we *can* see that these changes are driven by the desire of human beings everywhere to be governed well. Terrorists, at least so far, are watching from the sidelines.

About the Authors

EDITOR

Paul Shemella retired from the U.S. Navy at the rank of captain in 1996 after a career in special operations. During his military service he planned and executed operations in Latin America, Europe, and other regions. He earned a master's degree in national security affairs at the Naval Postgraduate School and attended the Kennedy School of Government at Harvard University as a senior fellow in national security. Captain Shemella has been with the Center for Civil–Military Relations (CCMR) since 1998. He is currently the CCMR Program Manager for the "Combating Terrorism Fellowship" program (CTFP), focusing on civil–military responses to terrorism of all kinds. In that capacity he develops and teaches seminars and workshops worldwide. Captain Shemella is assisted in these efforts by a network of civilian and retired-military faculty members drawn from the Naval Postgraduate School, civilian universities, government organizations, and the private sector.

AUTHORS

Peter Chalk is a senior policy analyst with the RAND Corporation, Santa Monica, California. He has worked on a range of projects, including studies examining low-intensity conflict threats in the Philippines, Thailand, Indonesia, India (Kashmir), Pakistan, and Sri Lanka. Prior to joining RAND, Dr. Chalk was an assistant professor of politics at the University of Queensland, Brisbane, and a postdoctoral fellow in the Strategic and Defense Studies Centre of the Australian National University, Canberra. He is a specialist correspondent for *Jane's Intelligence Review* and associate editor of *Studies in Conflict Terrorism*—one of the foremost journals in the international-security field. Dr. Chalk has regularly testified before the U.S. Senate on issues pertaining to national and international terrorism and is the author of numerous books, book chapters, monographs, and journal articles dealing with various aspects of low-intensity conflict in the contemporary world. Dr. Chalk has taught regularly for CCMR since 2005.

Lawrence E. Cline completed a career as an intelligence officer and Middle East foreign area officer in the U.S. Army. His military service featured tours of duty in Egypt, Lebanon, El Salvador, and Somalia, as well as Joint Staff and Special Forces assignments. He holds an M.A. in international relations from Boston University. Dr. Cline earned a Ph.D. in political science from the State University of New York at Buffalo, writing a dissertation on Islamic insurgent movements. He has published a number of articles on international-security and internal-security affairs in various academic journals, and has given numerous conference presentations and lectures on aspects of low-intensity conflicts. He has been a regular faculty member for the CCMR academic program "Civil–Military Responses to Terrorism" since 2002. In 2006 Dr. Cline volunteered for recall to active duty and served as an intelligence advisor in Iraq.

Timothy J. Doorey served as an intelligence officer in the U.S. Navy until 2009. Captain Doorey's last military assignment was as a faculty member senior intelligence officer at the Naval Postgraduate School. While there, he became an adjunct for CCMR, specializing in intelligence support for counterterrorism, including cyber terrorism, strategic communications, information operations, and force protection. During his career, Captain Doorey provided direct tactical, operational, and strategic intelligence support for U.S. and coalition forces involved in operations in Lebanon, Grenada, El Salvador, Panama, Afghanistan, Iraq, and the global war on terrorism. Captain Doorey earned master's degrees from the Naval War College (national security and strategic studies) and the Naval Postgraduate School (national security affairs). He attended Harvard University's John M. Olin Institute for Strategic Studies as a Navy federal executive fellow. Captain Doorey is now a regular faculty member for CCMR, leading mobile education teams in all regions of the world.

Edward E. Hoffer completed a thirty-year career in the U.S. Army in 2002. From 2002 to 2005 he was the project leader for training United States Army Chemical, Biological, Radiological, Nuclear, and Explosive (CBRNE) Response Teams throughout the Pacific theater. Since 2005 he has been a regular faculty member for CCMR, specializing in strategy development, risk assessment, and consequence management. Mr. Hoffer has extensive experience in strategy against terrorism. Following the 11 September 2001 attacks, he was selected by Admiral Dennis Blair to lead the command-planning effort that produced the PACOM Combating Terrorism Plan, which was used by the Secretary of Defense as a model plan for interagency coordination in the war against terrorism. Mr. Hoffer holds a master's degree in history from James Madison University and is a graduate of the U.S. Army School for Advanced Military

Studies (SAMS). He is an expert in game design and takes a leading role in uploading CCMR's academic content on the Internet.

Thomas R. Mockaitis is professor of history at DePaul University. He earned his B.A. in European history from Allegheny College and his M.A. and Ph.D. in modern British and Irish history from the University of Wisconsin–Madison. Professor Mockaitis is the author of numerous books on terrorism and insurgency, the most recent of which is *Osama bin Laden: A Biography*. He coedits the journal *Small Wars and Insurgencies* and frequently provides commentary regarding terrorism issues on a variety of radio and television networks. Professor Mockaitis is a renowned expert on government responses to irregular security threats. He has lectured at military educational institutions all over the world, including the Royal Military Academy Sandhurst (UK). In 2004 Dr. Mockaitis held the Eisenhower Chair at the Royal Military Academy of the Netherlands. He has been a regular faculty member of CCMR since 2003.

James Petroni retired in 2002 from a long career in public safety. He is currently an active consultant in the field of international and homeland security, addressing the threat potentials of both human and natural catastrophes. Beginning in the fire service, Mr. Petroni acquired experience in a wide variety of emergency-management disciplines, often serving in significant roles during California's major emergencies. A long-time faculty member at the California Specialized Training Institute, Mr. Petroni pioneered emergency-management procedures that have been adopted around the world. He has served as a consultant and lecturer to various federal agencies, including the Department of Defense, the Federal Emergency Management Agency, the Federal Bureau of Investigation, the Central Intelligence Agency, the Department of State, and the Congress. Mr. Petroni has worked closely with a number of foreign governments on disaster and terrorism-training programs. He has been a regular CCMR faculty member since 2006.

Robert Schoultz entered the Navy after graduating from Stanford University with a B.A. in philosophy. During a thirty-year career in special operations, Captain Schoultz served in operational and staff assignments in Germany, the United Kingdom, and Panama. He earned a master's degree in national security and strategic studies from the Naval War College. Captain Schoultz was a fellow at the U.S. Naval Academy's Center for Military Ethics and went on to become the director of officer development at the academy. He is currently the director of a master's degree program in global leadership at the University of San Diego. He has continued his study of military ethics and leader development as a frequent guest speaker for officer-education programs at the Naval Special Warfare Command. Captain Schoultz has been associated with CCMR since 2003.

Phil Williams is professor of international security in the Graduate School of Public and International Affairs at the University of Pittsburgh and a former director of the university's Matthew B. Ridgway Center for International Security Studies. During the last ten years his research has focused primarily on transnational organized crime, networks, and terrorism. Dr. Williams has published extensively on a wide range of related topics. He has been a consultant to the United Nations, the OSCE, and U.S. government agencies on organized crime and has also given congressional testimony on the subject. Dr. Williams has done extensive work on alliances among criminal organizations, global and national efforts to combat money laundering, and trends and development in cyber crime. While a fellow at the U.S. Army War College in 2008, he published an influential monograph titled *The New Dark Ages.* Dr. Williams has been a regular faculty member for CCMR since 2003.

Index